MALEDICTA

THE INTERNATIONAL JOURNAL OF VERBAL AGGRESSION

Volume V · Numbers 1 + 2   Summer + Winter 1981

REINHOLD AMAN

EDITOR

MALEDICTA PRESS

WAUKESHA

COPYRIGHT © 1981 BY MALEDICTA PRESS

All Rights Reserved. Except for brief quotations embodied
in critical articles or reviews, no part of this publication
may be reproduced, stored, transmitted, translated,
or used in any form or by any means—graphic,
electronic, or mechanical, now known or hereafter
invented, and including photocopying, recording, taping,
or any information storage & retrieval system—without
the prior written permission of the Publisher.

Library of Congress Catalog
Card Number 77-649633

ISSN 0363-3659

ISBN 0-916500-25-X

First Edition

NIHIL + OBSTAT

R 26 November 1981 A

Printed in the United States of America

CONTENTS
VOL. V, NOS. 1+2 · 1981

ELIAS PETROPOULOS FESTSCHRIFT

*Pseudonym

LAUDATIONES *MALEDICTÆ*

C. M. Crist

If you collect Obiter Dicta
Write Aman, care of Maledicta.

Nostradamus did predict a
Huge success for Maledicta.

Professors swear, "There's nothing wick'der
Than insults found in Maledicta."

Jack took his dick and quickly nicked 'er;
Jill fenced him off with Maledicta.

The farmer had a mule and kicked 'er,
Muttering oaths from Maledicta.

For V.D. ills that now afflict 'er,
She finds the words in Maledicta.

His odd sex quirks did not constrict 'er,
For she'd been raised on Maledicta.

While her husband nightly pricked 'er,
She just kept reading Maledicta.

As he gulped and hotly licked 'er,
He kept one finger in Maledicta.

She said (let no oaf contradict 'er),
"It tops them all! Vive Maledicta!"

The nun knew by the way he tricked 'er
The Pope subscribed to Maledicta.

In Germany lives an obscene Dichter
Who often dichts *for Maledicta.*

It reads nine on the scale by Richter,
This latest volume of Maledicta.

DEDICATION

Twenty-eight years ago, I had my first contact with a Greek. He was Takis, a student from Kavalla, who was studying Chemical Engineering with me in Augsburg, Germany. I didn't speak Greek; he didn't speak German. None of the other students bothered with poor Takis who could not even pronounce *Schwefelsäure* (H_2SO_4); but always interested in other cultures, I became his German *Kulturführer* and translator, while murdering French, the language in which we communicated. (Well, perhaps I just *assaulted* French, but Takis definitely *murdered* it.) Within a week I had picked up more Greek than Takis knew French, and soon I was able to help him and his sister to a good start.

About four years ago, I made the acquaintance of another Greek, Elias Petropoulos. We have not yet met in person, but from the moment I learned of him and his selfless work to preserve the folklore of Greece, I knew that we would be friends. We correspond as much as our heavy workloads permit — again in French. (Elias's wife, Mary, knows English, but I prefer practicing my French, regardless of how many irregular past participles I have to check up while writing.)

Elias and I have much in common: we are both foreigners in our adopted countries, respectable outcasts, strong advocates of freedom, individuality and independence, students of languages, cultures and folklore, and poor. But we also differ.

Like our other honored friends G. Legman and E. Borneman, E. Petropoulos is on the "wrong" side of the political fence. As a fiercely anti-political person — and I base my op-

7

position to all politics on the fact that politicians, left and right, have brought more misery upon mankind than all diseases and natural disasters combined — I am dismayed when friends waste their time on political *engagement*. But then, unlike these three friends, I was never thrown in prison by The State.

Elias, the Socialist, practices what he preaches by spreading the little he has among his friends. That's redeeming and very unusual for a Socialist. The run-of-the-mouth (rich) Socialists and their sick brethren, the hard-line Marxists, are greedier than the Capitalists they attack, never ever sharing one *red* penny with their fellowmen.

But Elias, a true Socialist, is liberal with his pink pennies and rose-colored *francs*. He is one of the finest people I have met in my 45 years. Knowing that a Greek writing Greek books in France is not showered with royalties, I am embarrassed at Elias's generosity. The books he has sent fill a shelf. In the earlier, black years of *Maledicta*, when I didn't have twenty dollars to buy food for my wife and daughter (because the anal-retentive cacademic cretins and the ignorant masses did not buy *Maledicta*), Elias sent me money to keep us going. Whenever he received a bigger payment from his books or lectures at European universities, he thought of me and ordered gift subscriptions for his friends in France, Greece and Turkey. His American collaborator in Athens, Katharine Butterworth (who directs the Study in Greece Program there), also was instructed to send books and money to me, to keep *Maledicta* alive.

Now, thanks to Zeus and *The Wall Street Journal* (March 25, 1981), we are in good shape financially and can start reciprocating the favors. I won't forget that poor Greek writer in France who provided financial and moral support when I needed it most.

Even if Mr. Petropoulos had not become a friend through his help, he deserves to be honored. He ranks high among the handful of untiring *private* scholars who collect, analyze and produce incredible amounts of research — all without one single penny of support by the government, cacademia or private foundations. Elias Petropoulos, Ernest Borneman, Gershon Legman, Vance Randolph and a few others (like Jonathan Lighter) really are heroes, models, inspirations, benefactors of humanity whose intellectual and tangible output could never be matched by a horde of cacademics with cushy jobs, bunches of helpers and a financial teat.

At 53, Elias is still young and can produce and preserve much more. That is, if he doesn't get killed by fellow-Greeks. Last June, Elias was walking along Rue Mouffetard in Paris and spotted a Greek restaurant owner painting over exposed beams that had been classified by the French Government as a historical monument. Naturally, Elias, the Folklorist, told the restauranteur that the paint would ruin the wooden beams. He had not finished his sentence when the other called him "a dirty Communist" and "a lover of Turks" and violently attacked him. When Elias woke up in the hospital, he had a swollen black eye, a swollen nose and a concussion. When Mary took him home in the afternoon, the painter-restauranteur and his gang of fifteen Greek geeks waited outside Elias's house in Coye-la-Forêt, ready to finish him off. Luckily, Mary saw them in time and called the police who drove the thugs away. And next day, Elias was working again on his *Wooden Doors in Greece.*

As said, we have much in common; we say what must be said, even if we have to pay for our thrills. But let's hope that there won't be a parallel to that event. I have been attacked verbally by an Austrian hillbilly whom I had queried about terms of abuse, and I nearly was killed by a drunken Ojibwa Indian who claimed that there were no insults in his language but who did jump me when I tried *animosh* ("yellow dog") on him. So far, so good. But I have a feeling that some day a bunch of Born-again Assholes and scatophagous Moron Minority Meatheads will curse me for studying cursing in the Bible and then beat the living bejesus out of me.

— *Reinhold Aman*

Mary Koukoules · 6 August 1980

ELIAS PETROPOULOS

ELIAS PETROPOULOS, THE *MOUNÓPSIRA*

John Taylor

As the furor grows in Greece and elsewhere concerning his latest conviction (23 October 1980) to eighteen months of prison and a $1,500 fine for *The Good Thief's Manual* (*Enkheirídhion toú Kaloú Kléfti*), perhaps Elias Petropoulos will finally begin to receive the fame, respect and notoriety he has so long deserved in the international literary and academic community. One problem has been, of course, that few of his works are available in either a French or English translation. There are, for example, three albums in French (*Le Kiosque Grec*, *Cages à Oiseaux en Grèce*, *La Voiture Grecque*), three albums in English (*Ironwork in Greece*, *The Graves of Greece*, *Old Salonica*) and an article ("Fist-Phallus") which appeared in *Maledicta* (1979). His poem *Body* has appeared in both French and English, and even German. At this writing, my translation of *The Good Thief's Manual* is in press, as well as a selection of 150 rebetic songs (*Rebetika*; also my translation) from his anthology *Rebetic Songs* (*Rebétika traghoúdhia*). And over the next year we can expect a series of albums about Salonica, in both French and English. Despite these, however, and despite a few non-Greek book reviews (the earliest going back to Kimon Friar's favorable appreciation of *Rebétika traghoúdhia* in *Books Abroad* [Spring, 1969]), it must be noted that Petropoulos, who has written numerous articles and nearly forty books, has remained a relatively unnoticed modern Greek author, many of whose most important books are as yet inaccessible to the reader not familiar with Greek.

I would like to add, however, that the true reason for his relative obscurity on an international level (in Greece, of course, he is extremely well known), is less due to a problem of translation than it is to the originality of Petropoulos's work itself. If Socrates was the gadfly of Athens, and suffered for it, then Petropoulos is the *mounópsira*, the woman's crotch louse, which in Greek also means a person who digs down into the finest details to uncover startling aspects of reality. As with many authors whose work constitutes in itself a fundamental inquiry into its chosen subject and is not simply a regurgitation of past inquiries (what minor authors have merely read elsewhere), Petropoulos, from the very novelty of his approach to numerous manifestations of Greek folklore, for example, has suffered undue, yet perhaps inevitable, misunderstanding neglect. As Friar noted in a second review in *Books Abroad* (October, 1972), this time writing about *Kaliardá*, the first dictionary of homosexual slang to be published anywhere, "...he has courageously undertaken what professional linguists and folklorists have avoided, that as a devil he has barged in where academicians have feared to tread." This keynotes the work Petropoulos has done in fields as disparate as music, architecture, art, literature, history, sociology, folklore, and linguistics.

If Petropoulos has suffered some neglect on the international level, he by no means has been neglected by the Greek government. Indeed, certain ministers, judges and police chiefs have been among his most avid readers. Petropoulos has been one of the most persecuted writers in the West, having been sent to prison three different times (five months for *Rebétika traghoúdhia* in 1969; five months for *Kaliardá* in 1972; and seven months for *Body* in 1972), convicted a fourth time (in 1980; but Petropoulos will not serve this sentence as he is now living in France), and trailed and arrested on countless occasions as he was taking photographs and making sketches for his albums to the extent that Amnesty International has become interested in his case: see Britt Arenander's Swedish article in *Amnesty Bulletin*, October, 1980.

In his work, Petropoulos has unceasingly and courageously pursued his vision of Greek culture, going to whatever extremes

were necessary to collect, document and describe diverse manifestations of Greek folklore before it was too late—before the
onslaught of industrialization, the apathy of the general population, and the police and governmental oppression caused
them to perish forever. We will see how Petropoulos's vision
has led him into subjects as diverse as birdcages, kiosks, automobile decoration, wrought ironwork, graves and cemeteries,
coffee, brothels, lice, homosexual and underworld slang, underworld songs and art, shadow theater, criminals, prisoners,
prisons and imprisonment, poetry, translation, modern art
and literary criticism, and history. This is the vision and the
task which has been anathematic to the Greek government,
both during and "after" the dictatorship.

At the core of the originality of Petropoulos's work lie a
number of seeming paradoxes. A reading excursion through a
book by Petropoulos is to experience an astonishing scientific
rigor and candor, yet at the same time a humor and irony found
only in the wisest novelists. Petropoulos can spend a page examining the recondite etymology of a commonly-used word
not found in any Greek dictionary because it is of Turkish
origin, and he can also spend a page recounting a comical anecdote about a pickpocket he once met. Petropoulos loves to
tell us precisely how people do and say things, especially about
techniques which are likely to disappear and be forgotten or
words and expressions destined for oblivion. *The Good Thief's
Manual* is just what its title claims it is: a handbook for the
would-be thief. In *Turkish Coffee in Greece* (*O toúrkikos kafés
en Elládhi*), the reader not only learns how to make and serve
a good Turkish coffee, but also 46 different ways to order it,
and dozens of ways to insult the coffee-maker if it isn't up to
his standards. Petropoulos is also capable of telling fortunes
from the dregs left in an empty coffee cup, and the technique
for performing this stunt is included as well in the book. The
notes to the songs in *Rebétika traghoúdhia* contain anecdotes,
legends and stories about famous, infamous, and not-so-famous
underworld figures, hash dens, coffee houses, prisons, and
other hangouts and hideouts; plus explanations on how hash-
ish was smoked, bullies were stabbed, dances danced, and much

more. What is remarkable about the personality of Petropoulos is that after all the persecution levied against him he has not become bitter, as the poet Oswald Wiener noted in his recent article in *Die Zeit* (Hamburg, 28 November 1980). He is often sarcastic, of course, but never for sarcasm's sake. In his introduction to *Old Salonica*, for example, he grills two Greek professors who had openly plagiarized him. Plagiarism, incidentally, is often practiced against Petropoulos; there have been unsigned articles in well-respected foreign newspapers concerning subjects Petropoulos (and only Petropoulos) has treated, containing only a vague reference to him amidst information which had been copied practically word-for-word from his Greek edition.

Petropoulos's basic subject is modern urban folklore in Greece. From his albums to his slang dictionaries, from his books about criminality and prisons to his anthologies of underworld art forms, up to and including his upcoming albums about Salonica, the term "urban folklore," if not understood merely in its narrow academic sense, comprises most of the work Petropoulos has published to date. In fact, one important facet of Petropoulos's vision has been his attempt to reorient the Greek folklorists' typical concentration on obsolete or virtually nonexistent pastoral aspects of Greek folklore towards the city and town. As he states in his introduction to *Cages à Oiseaux en Grèce*:

> Greek popular culture today is a set of habits and simple things— for example, underworld songs, plastic toys, flower pots on the balconies, the curses you can hear everywhere, decorated automobiles, expressive gestures, words tossed to passing women by guys hanging out in the street—also birdcages with their gaudy singing birds—but Greek folklorists don't seem to care very much about the significance of reality.

Petropoulos's strategy has been to go out into the streets and document just that significance. Often he has been the only one interested, despite the fact that, as he remarks in the introduction to *La Voiture Grecque*, "In Greece, as in all underdeveloped countries, Western Civilization brusquely arrived during the period 1945-1975, destroying every manifestation of local folklore."

In the early part of his career, Petropoulos—both carless and cameraless—would take advantage of any friend's excursion out of town to borrow a camera and roam about the streets of towns and villages all over Greece looking for birdcages, decorated automobiles, wrought ironwork, kiosks, and graves. While his friends were lying out on the beach or seeing more typical tourist sights, Petropoulos began compiling his extensive archives (some of which [for *Rebétika traghoúdhia*] have been donated to the American Library in Athens, others to the Bibliothèque Nationale in France). As a result, Petropoulos has now published five albums (with more to come) which are each the first of their kind.

Four of these albums (*Le Kiosque Grec*, *Cages à Oiseaux en Grèce*, *La Voiture Grecque*, *Ironwork in Greece*) consist of collections of photographs of, respectively, kiosks, birdcages, decorated automobiles, and wrought ironwork as they are found in Greece. By no means are these albums mere anthologies of the strangest or the most elaborate or the most beautiful kiosks, birdcages, decorated automobiles, and ironwork Petropoulos managed to run across; although, naturally, quite unusual examples are to be discovered in each of them. Were this the case, then it could be said that the albums had merely been designed for tourists searching for something "cute" to take home with them from Greece. There are, of course, many such books around. Petropoulos's objective, however, has been to present examples of all the kinds of birdcages or kiosks or automobile decorations or ironwork as may be observed in contemporary Greece. In each album there is an attempt to categorize the objects found and, what is perhaps more important, to determine the evolution of the styles. In this manner, Petropoulos has been able to find (create) new touchstones (birdcages and kiosks, for example) by which the growth and evolution of Greek culture may be measured. At the same time he has documented manifestations of Greek folklore which all other folklorists had either ignored or discounted as being trivial and which are rapidly disappearing, leaving no other trace than what has been preserved in these albums. All the introductions to these albums contain the typical Petropoulos humor, which at times may be no more than his mirror, or ear, held up to reality. He tells us, for example, how a kiosk owner will secretly slip a condom into his customer's hand or fold a leftist newspaper in two so the police won't see its name; or how a depressed canary can be cheered back into singing; or how Greek drivers swear at each other.

Since his exile to France, Petropoulos has been gathering photos of weathervanes, sundials and public clocks in France. One day, while visiting him at his home in Coye-la-Forêt, I had a chance to see him at work. We had decided to take a walk in the forest near his home. Elias had brought along a camera, supposedly so that we could take a few pictures of each other in the woods. As we were walking out of the village, Elias suddenly stopped in front of the half-opened iron gate of a mansion and began adjusting his camera for a picture. He stealthily pushed the gate open, informing me that such undertakings in wealthy neighborhoods were often dangerous because of the watchdog that would attack if one stepped past the gate's threshold.

"But you don't want your picture taken here, do you?" I asked, still unable to understand why we had stopped so soon.

Elias chuckled and began focusing his camera towards the roof of the mansion. "I just saw this the other day." On the gabled roof I saw the simple black weathervane which apparently had attracted his attention. I was perplexed.

"You aren't going to take a picture of that, are you?"

"Sure. Why not?" he replied. "People put up all sorts of weathervanes. Why should I eliminate certain weathervanes from my collection for personal aesthetic reasons? A conscientious folklorist doesn't have personal preferences."

The fifth album, *The Graves of Greece*, is not a collection of photographs but rather a collection of drawings made by Petropoulos in cemeteries all over Greece. The drawings are of gravestones, grave slabs, crosses, and grave decorations. In this album, which was rejected by all the Greek publishers because of its supposed morbidity and cost, and which the author eventually published at his own expense, Petropoulos reveals himself not only as a master folklorist but as an artist as well. Both the format of the book and the presentation of the drawings are striking. In this album, more than in the other four, Petropoulos fuses the scientific and poetic aspects of his work in such a complementary manner that the result is in a class by itself.

The Graves of Greece will eventually be complemented by *The Cemeteries of Greece*, which will contain the photographs made at the same time as the drawings, as well as a long essay by Petropoulos on the Greek way of dying, death, and burial. It will be as large and comprehensive a book as *Rebétika traghoúdhia*, and will undoubtedly be equally a masterpiece.

Petropoulos has written a series of three books (*The Bordello* [*Tó bourdhélo*], *Turkish Coffee in Greece*, and *Lousology: The Book of Lice* [*Psirologhía*]) which also treat aspects of urban folklore, but not in the same manner as the albums. Although all three books contain drawings and extensive photographic documentation, they are books, not albums. In *Lousology*, for example, Petropoulos—who on the title page informs us that he is a Professor in the Parasitology Department of the Sorbonne—discusses such diverse insects as lice, fleas, bedbugs, flies, mosquitos, gnats, cockroaches, centipedes, ticks, scorpions, spiders, butterflies, ants, glowworms, crickets, bees, wasps, and grasshoppers. In this book, as well as in *The Bordello* and *Turkish Coffee in Greece*, one of the "scientific" goals is to pursue the tortuous etymologies of such words, to dig out all the popular synonyms and derivatives, and to list and explain the countless expressions and proverbs containing them. "Lice and bedbugs have their own folklore," the author tells us on the first page, "the hour has come for the louse to get its book." All three books are rich in the anecdotes and information that Petropoulos gathered from his research and from his numerous contacts both within prison and without. In *The Bordello*, dedicated to Reinhold Aman (who has never been in a Greek whorehouse), Petropoulos delves into such subjects as the different types of brothels, madams, pimps, slave-traders, clients entering the brothel for the first time, experienced clients, sodomy, syphylis, gonorrhea, male prostitution, and much more.

Equally important is Petropoulos's demonstration that in

fact we know very little (if anything) about the true nature
of prostitution:

> We cannot formulate a definition of prostitution because we are
> not able to perceive clearly what happens, exactly, between the
> prostitute and her client during sexual intercourse. The prostitute
> delivers her body for a price, but we don't know if this is, legally, a
> rented thing or transient selfsale or the simple use of an animated
> good. We don't know, legally, if the relationship between the pros-
> titute and the client consists of a one-sided or two-sided agreement.
> We don't know if the paid coition is the same thing for the prosti-
> tute as for the client. Finally, we don't know if the paid coition is a
> legal fact or simply a practical condition.

The same argumentation is then used to demonstrate our ignorance as to the nature of a house of prostitution. Amidst
the humor and sarcasm, amidst the learnèd discussions of etymologies and evanescing techniques, it must never be overlooked that one of the most original and enduring aspects of
Petropoulos's writing is simply his attempt to delineate, in
nearly all the subjects he treats, what we don't know or, even
more simply, *that* we don't know.

I would even go so far as to suggest that it is precisely this
which lies behind Petropoulos's recent conviction for *The
Good Thief's Manual*, and not his more blatant attacks on
judges, the Justice Ministry, the Government, and the Police.
For nowhere else is his attempt to honestly perceive what we
know and what we don't (or can't) know, what we understand and what we don't (or can't) understand, pushed to
more extremes of rigor and devastating clarity than in *The
Good Thief's Manual*. The questions posed at the beginning
of "Lesson 26" (Who Designates Crime?) remain unanswered:

> I doubt if the notion of Crime exists for Minerals, Plants, or Ani-
> mals. According to our legislative wisemen, only Man commits a
> Crime. The instructive academic definition speaks of Crime as "an
> act (or omission of an act) which is unjust, charged against its per-
> petrator, and punished by the Law." The chilling schematization of
> this definition imposes the following questions:
>
> > *Who defines the type of Crime?*
> > *Who is represented by the Legislator?*
> > *Who is protected by the Penal Code?*
> > *What is a Human Act?*
> > *What is Injustice?*

Who is the Perpetrator and why does he act?
Why is the Perpetrator punished?
Who punishes the Perpetrator?
What does Punishment mean?
How much does Punishment hurt?
Why is there a Punishment for every Crime?
Why is the Perpetrator identified with the Punishment?
Is the Perpetrator born a Perpetrator?
Why does the Judge hate the Perpetrator?
Does the Perpetrator govern himself?

I suspect that the powers-that-be in Greece reacted so violent-ly to this book principally for the reason that it shows up so well the myths, falsehoods, lies, misunderstandings and down-right ignorance which comprise their justification of power.

As we have already seen in *The Bordello*, *Turkish Coffee in Greece*, and *Lousology*, urban folklore comprises linguistics. Nowhere is Petropoulos's work in this domain more spectacu-larly carried out than in *Kaliardá*, the dictionary of Greek ho-mosexual slang. To the latest edition of *Kaliardá* (1980) an appendix has been added, containing not only new words and expressions for the dictionary, but also the "Story of a Book" which recounts how Petropoulos first became acquainted with homosexual slang (he himself is not a homosexual) and how he eventually managed to put this dictionary together. I would like to translate a passage from the "Story," for I feel it sums up well the kind of experiences which go into a book by Petropoulos:

> In October, 1944, my father died. I was forced to quit school and go to work. I found a job as a road construction worker.... During the first part of the year 1946 I was a guard in the big park of Salo-nica, where I worked until September, 1949, going to night school at the same time. In September, 1949, I accepted a transfer to Sa-lonica's Public Library, but was fired a few days later for being a Communist. How well I understand today that that big park in Sa-lonica (and its perimeter) was a Great University for me. It was there that I first became acquainted with whores, junkies, bullies, fags and thieves. It was there that I first smelled the sweet smell of hashish (I have unfortunately never smoked hash). It was there that I learned the Rebetic Songs, even if I had begun to hear them in our home. And it was there that I was first impressed with *kaliardá*....

Petropoulos's books are all based on his personal experiences. From nowhere else has he made better use of his experiences than of those from his three stretches in prison. His prison experiences, especially his conversations with the underworld figures he was able to meet and befriend there (such friendships are extremely rare for the non-initiated, which speaks for the sincerity of Petropoulos), have created to date two books directly about the prison (*On the Prison* [*Tís filakís*], *The Good Thief's Manual*), a third book dealing with the underworld and the Greek Shadow Theater (*Hypokosmos and Shadow Theater in Greece* [*Hypokósmos kaí karagiózis*]), much of the information contained in the extensive introduction and notes to *Rebétika traghoúdhia*, as well as countless references in *Turkish Coffee in Greece*, *The Bordello*, and even *Lousology*. Petropoulos is also in the process of preparing a dictionary of Greek underworld slang.

On the Prison is a collection of ten essays on such subjects as prison graffiti, tatoos, and prisoner embroidery work and handicrafts. Most of the items displayed in the book were sketched (since cameras were prohibited) while Petropoulos was in prison. It is this book which contains the tatoo that is often mentioned in reviews of Petropoulos's work: that of the prisoner who had had *A. P.* (the Greek initials for "City Police") tatooed on his penis. The same prisoner had also had a fish tatooed on his tongue to show he could keep quiet.

The Good Thief's Manual is at once a parody of professorial discourse, guised as a handbook of forty-one lessons for the would-be thief, and a severe yet truthful accounting of the Greek judiciary system. Detail by detail, Petropoulos shows how pickpockets, burglars, picklocks, safecrackers, and many more such underworld figures live, work, are arrested, tortured, tried, and sent to prison. I have already mentioned that one of the most devastating aspects of this book is its revelation of how little we in fact know about the phenomena of thievery, arrest, torture, trial, and imprisonment. Another original contribution of this book is its evidence on how the architecture of the prison tortures the prisoner. Petropoulos is no Foucault, whom he parodies by misspelling his name "Fouceaut," compiling pages of indecipherable historical data and

construing lofty ratiocinations. In Petropoulos we descend into the inferno of the prisoner's everyday life: the toilets without stools, the narrow cells, the concrete beds, the solitary-
confinement cells, the absence of heaters, the prohibition of
forks, knives, matches and mirrors. One day Petropoulos told
me about the humiliation of having to defecate in front of the
other prisoners (this is also in the book). For in some Greek
prisons there are not only no stools, but no stall doors either.
So the prisoner defecates out in the open while his fellow prisoners are washing their faces and hands just a few feet away.
"I know this is not particularly interesting," he told me on
that occasion, "but for the prisoner it is his everyday reality,
and a torture."

An equally important contribution of *The Good Thief's
Manual* is its examination of how thieves, burglars, pickpockets, etc., are treated by the judges, lawyers, wardens, guards,
police, and common citizens in a society based on the sacredness of private property. "Theft is the crime against property
par excellence," he declares, weaving in and out of his parody
statements often so ludicrous that we don't realize for a moment how true they are: "I consider the Thief to be more revolutionary than the Communist." And whereas in the communist and socialist countries it is the crime against ideology
(dissident writing, for example) which is the most severely punished, Petropoulos reveals all too well how the crime against
property (theft) is punished in the West.

Hypokosmos and Shadow Theater in Greece is Petropoulos's attempt to study Greek Shadow Theater (*karagiózis*) in
the light of his knowledge of the underworld, an approach
which had previously been completely ignored by all other
historians, critics and sociologists of this theater. He brings
his knowledge of highway robbers and bandits, *manges* (the
Greek underworld tough guys), Turkey and Turkish theater,
coffee houses and hash dens, clothing, and language to bear
on what one actually sees in a shadow-theater production.
The book is accompanied by many photos, drawings and diagrams of the shadow puppets, and photos of the people who
made and manipulated them.

It is perhaps *Rebétika traghoúdhia*, however, which must be considered Petropoulos's masterpiece to date. Through this anthology, Petropoulos has become to the rich culture of the modern Greek underworld what Meleager was to the ancient Greek poets—a master anthologist, collecting and preserving for posterity an exceptionally interesting literature (many of the songs, taken individually, are poetic masterpieces, not to mention their interest for historians, sociologists and musicians) which otherwise would have been lost forever. Petropoulos also put to work here certain tools Meleager didn't possess. In this monumental anthology of over 700 pages and 1400 song lyrics, Petropoulos has also included an extensive introduction (unfortunately untranslated; but an introduction by Petropoulos is contained in our recently published translation of 150 of these songs, *Rebetika*); a "Photo-History" section, containing such memorabilia as autographs, notes, manuscripts, identity cards, passports, and instruments, plus drawings, photos, and engravings of the *manges*, the hash dens and taverns, the singers, dancers, composers and musicians; and a third section, comprised of articles by other writers on rebetic music, as well as sketches, stories, memoirs, and even a movie scenario. The entire book is beautifully illustrated by Alexander Fasianos, who has also illustrated many other books by Petropoulos. *Rebétika traghoúdhia* is an encyclopedia, a prime example of both Petropoulos's humanist concern for the downtrodden and his command of knowledge and fact from countless domains, both so rare among the intellectuals of our time.

No introduction to Elias Petropoulos and his work would be complete without one further anecdote, which I will insert here before passing on to his poetry, translations, art criticism, and upcoming books on Salonica. For it was Elias Petropoulos who in the midst of the last dictatorship challenged in Greece's highest court the Greek law stating that only marriages consecrated in Greek Orthodox churches are valid. The case was eventually dismissed on some ridiculous technicality involving fiscal stamps, but nonetheless stands as one further example of the author's courage and daring.

Petropoulos has also published three poems (*Body, Suicide, Five Erotic Poems*) which just this year were united in one volume, *Poems*. As mentioned before, one of the poems, *Body*, was potent enough to earn Petropoulos five months of prison. The judge objected to the line: "I forget even the motherland when I see a young naked female body." The line in question is typical of most of the other parts of this long poem, which evokes the labyrinth of thoughts one experiences in perceiving a nude female body (the last line: "All this, and much more that frightens me and which cannot be written down, passes through my mind when I see the bodies of naked women"). Despite a few outpourings of less intellectual emotion ("O sacred slit eternal. / O snakemother and snakehole and snakenest. / O unlovely slit, propylaea of boredom. / O my sweet chastisement"), the tone of the poem is *très sage* (sensible, wise, well-behaved), as the journalist in *Liberation* (25 October 1980) put it in a recent article about Petropoulos.

Elias Petropoulos has also translated *The Apocalypse of John* (*Ioánnou Apokálypsis*) and a selection of twelve poems from the Palatine Anthology (*Dhódheka traghoudhákia apó tín Palatiní Antbologhía*) from ancient Greek into modern Greek. As for the latter, he expresses the wish at the end of the volume that some composer will put them to music. As for the former, his interest in translating *The Apocalypse* seems to have stemmed from his interest in the Greek language which, as we have witnessed before, is one of the principal concerns of his work in all domains. One day Petropoulos declared that Odysseus Elytis, the Nobel poet laureate, was one of the five people in Greece who know Greek. I often wonder if Petropoulos himself isn't the other four! In the course of the five translations I have done for Petropoulos over the last year, I have had frequent recourse to him for words and expressions on which I suspect he is the sole authority anywhere. For slang terms from the underworld the actor in him comes out. One day I asked him about a strange word in a rebetic song. He hopped up, held a ballpoint pen out to me and with a gesture showed me it was a knife. Opening his mouth, he passed the pen slowly back and forth across his tongue. "The tough guy has just stabbed someone," he related. "Now, according to the old underworld custom, he's going to lick the blood off his knife. That's what your word means."

His interest in contemporary Greek literature and art led Petropoulos to begin his career with six monographs, *Nikos Gabriel Pentzikis* (1958), *Paulos Mosxidis* (1959), *Yiorgos Paralis* (1959), *Karolos Tsizek* (1959), *Kharaktiti / P. Tetsis* (1960), *Georgios Derpapas* (1965), which are not really "criticisms" as such but rather what might be called "appreciations." A quite remarkable book, which has been reedited, is *Elytis Moralis Tsaroukhis,* which was the first book (first published in 1964) to be written about Elytis anywhere. Reproductions of Elytis's collages are contained in the second half of this book, as well as reproductions of the art of the other two artists.

Recently, Petropoulos has been working on a new series of albums that actually began with the 1959 album *Thessaloniki / 1865*. In passing, I should also mention *Album Turc*, the reprinting of a series of drawings Petropoulos found in the Paris flea market and published in France in 1976. The drawings in *Album Turc* (with commentary by Petropoulos) give a good indication of the modes of dress during the Ottoman Empire. In this new series of albums, Petropoulos will be offering equally original evidence on the history of Salonica. In these albums, he will be publishing his archives of old postcards and photos in an attempt to provide a type of historical documentation which until now had been ignored by professional historians. One of them, *Old Salonica*, has just been published in English, while the others (*La présence ottomane à Salonique*, *Salonique: L'incendie de 1917*, *Les églises de Salonique*) will be in French. The thrust of these albums will be to offset the typically chauvinistic approach of the Greek historians towards the history of Salonica. This, of course, is vintage Petropolous, who loves to point out something typically Greek which is in fact Turkish, Albanian or Armenian. "The Greeks don't like to admit they're Greek," he says in the introduction to *Cages à Oiseaux en Grèce*. As it turns out, this Greek, the *mounópsira*, master of his language and culture, who in fact loves more than all the Greeks that Greece his persecutors would destroy, is one of the most original, refreshing and enduring writers to emerge from Greece since the last war.

THE REBETIC SONGS

John Taylor

The rebetic songs, which were anthologized by Elias Petropoulos in *Rebétika traghoúdhia*, originated in the lowest socioeconomic class in the urban parts of Greece in the late 19th and early 20th centuries. This class comprised a group of people called *rebetes* (plural) or *manges* (plural) who were generally thieves, pimps, hash-den owners, casino owners, and tough guys in certain districts of Salonica, Athens and Piraeus. These songs are not only rich sources of information for the historian, sociologist and linguist (they were written in the often esoteric slang of the Greek underworld), but are also in themselves poetic masterpieces, expressing a truly remarkable pathos through a slang and manner of speaking which was thoroughly despised by the upper and middle class during the first half of this century. In this and other respects, the rebetic songs (presented here in my translation) may be compared to the blues, Negro spirituals and country music in America. The fact that over 1400 song lyrics are contained in Petropoulos's *Rebétika traghoúdhia* is a tribute to the diligence and courage of the anthologist (he was imprisoned 5 months for publishing this anthology), who wrote many of them down while in prison, literally right from the prisoners' mouths, an oral literature which otherwise would have perished.

WITH THE STILETTO

Stab me with that stiletto, prick,
And all the blood that flows you can lick.

Old bully song. After stabbing his victim, the *mangas* (the Greek underworld tough guy; I usually translate *mangas* by "ace") licks off his knife.

IF YOU'RE REALLY AN ACE

If you're really an ace
Where's your blade?
Where's your red sash?
Where're your suedes?
You see this crowbar behind the bar!

An old bully song mentioned in Petros Pikros's *Toubeki* (1927). Sometimes an ace's sash, worn like a belt around his waist, would be as long as 10 yards. Petropoulos gave me a demonstration: one ace would hold the sash's end while the other would wind himself up in it. The sash's ends would then be dragged along behind the ace like a wedding train. If you happened to step on one of them, you were asking for big trouble. As for the *suedes*, they were a sort of loafer with the backs broken down— the ace would wear them like clogs. In this song, the tavern owner recognizes a "false" ace.

I'M A JUNKIE

What can I do? I'm a junkie, see,
An' wherever I go they shit on me.

Nothin' but holes, my clothes in tatters,
Junk my whole life done really battered.

Home I don't remember, in a freight car I creep
An' on a burlap sack lay me down to sleep.

They take one look an' puke, I don't give a fuck—
Junk's all I live for, I don't live for luck.

And, friend, the cops gonna come along when I die—
Not in a hearse but in a garbage can I'll lie.

But get me up, friend, an' all Athens belongs to me.
What else can I do? I'm a junkie, see.

Khasapiko (a dance for two or three people) by Tsaousis, with lyrics by an unknown writer. Sung in the 1930s.

NEW HASH-HEADS

I learned ya shoot craps, that you're a hash bum,
That you're an ace, chic dude, a night owl.
Gonna come, gonna come, gonna come, gonna come?
Come on, hey, ace of mine, let's go an' howl!

I learned ya shoot craps, pick fights with the best,
Know your way around games, a real rowdy.
Come on, hey, ace of mine, say yes
An' don't be afraid of little ol' me.

Zeybekiko composed under the pseudonym of Paul. Recorded in 1925.
An old song from Smyrna.

HEROIN

As soon as you've tried
Aunt Heroin,
You ain't gonna open your trap
To criticize her no more.

An old junkie song. Other verses exist. Today, this verse has become a
proverb.

I GONNA SNORT

I gonna snort from a hare's shin
To get the gram in my nose an' spin.

I gonna snort from a hare's toes
To get all that shit up my nose.

Old jail song. Greek junkies used the shin and toe bones of a hare to snort.

THEY MET KHAROS

Five or six hash heads met up with Kharos
An' asked him how life-lovers made out in Hades:
"Hey, Kharos, tell us, an' may you enjoy your black darkness,
Do they have bread? Do they have *raki* to drink in Hades?
Tell us if they have *bouzoukis* and a *baglamas* to play.
Can they hustle? Do they have joints to hang out in till day?
Tell us if they have ladies, sweet mamas to woo
An' hash cigarets to roll in a good mood.
Hey, Kharos, tell us, an' may you have joy, what do the bums do?
Do they sit around talkin' in the Lower World, can they get their booze?
An' if out of heartbreak someone goes to Hades, tell us,
Does he get cured down there or waste in the darkness?
Take two drams of this Bursa hash an' five of this scented stuff
An' give 'em to our brothers down below to puff.

Kharos is a modern version of the ancient Greek *Kharon*, the Styx boat-man, and the Christian Archangel *Michael*. He is dressed in black and comes with drawn sword to kill men and take away their souls. He hears no pleas for mercy, and only the cleverest man is able to trick him, but this is very rare. The *bouzouki* and *baglamas* are two stringed instruments used in accompanying the rebetic songs.

THE DERBEDERISSY

Run, big shot, an' ask those guys about me.
I'm a fine ol' chick, a derbederissy,
An' I've shot men like craps.

Love don't turn me round, I just want a thrill,
To get my drinks lined up an' have my fill
While he-men fight over me.

Yeah, I'll be yours, but shut up about it—
I don't dig sweet talk, ya got it?
Born as I was in the bars an' cabarets.

Zeybekiko by Tsitsanis. First recorded in 1949. Derbederissy (in Greek, *derbederissa*) is an underworld slang word for a very special type of woman admired by the *rebetes*. This song brings out a number of aspects of her personality: independence, toughness, a love of life, a disdain for all permanent attachments, and yet a very conscious femininity.

THE HANDSOME STUD

Ya make me hurt real bad, baby, don't think I forget it.
But even screwin' round as ya do, ya fuckin' stud,
I can forgive ya, you're an ace an' a handsome stud.

Ask for it an' you'll get it, believe me, you're loved by a fool.
Even gobble down all the dough, ya crazy stud,
An' I'll forgive ya, you're an ace an' a handsome stud.

I don't even regret it. Bitterness? I can get over it.
An' even if I'm a-dyin' right now for you, ya fuckin' stud,
I can forgive ya, you're an ace an' a handsome stud.

Zeybekiko (a dance for one person) by Tsitsanis. First recorded in 1948.

I CARESSED IT JUST A LITTLE

I caressed it just a little
Your darlin' little pup,
But then you said stop! stop!
Not to caress it so far up!

They all want to caress it,
They all just dream of it,
They've all caressed it, even me —
I wouldn't stop anyone from doin' it!

I saw you had it washed,
Its hair is all tufted up.
I think I should caress it,
Play with your little pup.

But you ask: "Hey, what d'ya doin'?
Enough! Don't take too much of it.
I want to be caressed
By him who first procured it."

Khasapiko by Khrysaphakis. This is a good example of a particular kind of rebetic song filled with double meanings and puns. In the last line, for example, the pun refers not only to the person who procured the pup, but to the pimp, the procurer.

WOW, TONIGHT YOU'RE WHAM-DAMN!

Tonight you're wham-damn! Tonight you're wham-damn!
They get one look at you, jam on the brakes, stop the tram.
You're flashed up fit to kill an' you know it — wow!
Here's to the dude who decked you out, an' how!
Tonight you're really wham-damn!

Lean back in the car, lean back in the car.
Let's go live it up in a high-class bar.
If you get up to dance, dame, wow! you'll be the best.
In that taverna there ain't gonna be one glass left
For tonight you're really wham-damn!

Wow! You look great! Wow! You look great!
Because of you men stop short an' do a doubletake.
We're gonna bust the world wide open, tonight's on me.
They're gonna tear their hair out from jealousy
For tonight you're really wham-damn!

Zeybekiko by Tsitsanis, with lyrics by Tsitsanis and Routsos. First recorded in 1952.

MAKE THE BED FOR ME TO SLEEP

I hit the road but I'm a-comin' back
In the rain an' I'm soaked.
Hearin' your steps I whistled.
Don't toss me back to the heap:
Make the bed for me to sleep!

Dry me off with kisses
In the heat of your embrace
An' don't lemme out again to chase.
I'm here for you to keep:
Make the bed for me to sleep!

What eye's gonna see
If as before ya turn the little key? —
Ya got my word, sweetie,
No way now I'll make ya weep:
So make the bed for me to sleep!

Zeybekiko by Tsitsanis. First recorded in 1950, and then again in 1961.

NOW TURN OFF THE LIGHT

Don't get started on the naggin'.
Leave me alone, my blues run deep.
Let's don't drag it out, your tongue's a-waggin'.
Now turn off the light so we can sleep!

Ya got my head a-spinnin'.
Can't ya cut out this nit-pickin'?
Tomorrow, I know, gonna get my lickin'.
Now turn off the light so we can sleep!

Come on over now an' give me a kiss.
Turn off the light an' hold me to your tits.
By fightin' we ain't gonna find no end to this.
Now turn off the light so we can sleep!

Khasapiko by Papaioannou. First recorded in 1948.

WHEN A MAN GETS OLD

When a man gets old
His voice goes stout,
His balls hang cold
An' his prick starts to pout.

A song sung by the composer Batis as an old man. During the evenings he used to hang out in the tavernas of Piraeus and play his *baglamas*.

TOM, DICK AND HAIRY

NOTES ON GENITAL PET NAMES

Martha Cornog

I am sitting in a room with about thirty women. We are all attending a session on "vaginal consciousness raising" at a conference entitled "A View Through the Speculum." [1] The session leader, a beautiful, vibrant woman of a "certain age," asks us each to give the word(s) we use for our own genitals.

"Vagina." — "Pussy." — "Pussy. Vagina." — "Cunt." — "Mama's box." — "Henrietta."

Some people, like the last two women, use pet names to refer to their genitals. In *Lady Chatterley's Lover*,[2] the fictional Mellors calls his penis "John Thomas"[3] and Constance Chatterley's vulva "Lady Jane." Names like these (*Mama's Box, Henrietta, John Thomas*) I call genital pet names. They function as proper names[4] and refer to an *individual's* genitals only. In this way, they differ from general slang terms for genitals (e.g., *pussy, bearded clam, box*; *dick, cock, hog, one-eyed wonder worm*)[5] because they are personal, proper names.

Not only fictional characters like Mellors use pet names: real people name their genitals, too. To date, I have collected over thirty such pet names.[6]

The information given with each pet name follows this pattern (where supplied): significance or meaning of name; circumstances of naming or "christening"; the age of the owner of the genital at the time the name was used; and location.

PET NAMES FOR THE PENIS

Alice: "Put Alice in Wonderland." From Lewis Carroll's book. *See* **Wonderland.** Private language between lovers.

Baby: "Does Baby want to go Home?" *See* **Home.** Private language between lovers. Age 20. Indiana.

Broom: Couple undergoing marriage counseling (*see* text, below). Indiana.

Casey: After Casey Jones, the brave engineer, who took a trip "into the promised land." Private language between lovers. Named by the woman. Age 20. Rhode Island.

Chuck: Middle name of owner. Private language between lovers. Named by the woman during sex play. Age 33. Ohio.

Dipstick: Couple undergoing marriage counseling. Indiana.

Driveshaft: Couple undergoing marriage counseling. Indiana.

Four on the Floor: A car's gearshift. Couple undergoing marriage counseling. Indiana.

Gearstick: Couple undergoing marriage counseling. Indiana.

George: "Let George do it." Age 24. Pennsylvania.

Gnarled Tree Trunk (G.T.T. for short): Shape of penis (heavily veined). Private language between lovers. Named by the woman during sex play. Age 50. Pennsylvania.

Hank: Named by owner at male drinking party (*see* text, below). Age 60. Pennsylvania.

Jason: London, England.[7]

Jawillbemy: Possibly a shortening of "Jane will be my. . ." Private language of flirtation (couple were not lovers). Age 18. Oklahoma.

Lazarus: "He rises from the dead." Age 33. Washington, D.C.

Little Weese: "Weese" is a Midwestern mispronunciation of owner's surname. Private language within intimate network of three couples. Age 20. Ohio.

Little Willy: Owner named Bill. "Little" is ironic, as "Little Willy" is nine inches long, according to Bill's ex-wife.

Mortimer: Private language between lovers. Named by the woman during sex play. Age 28. Ohio. *See* **Eunice,** below.

Periwinkle: Private language between lovers. May have been used previously by the man.

Peter J. Firestone: "Peter" from common slang for penis,[8] "J. Firestone" from middle initial and last name of owner. Private language between lovers. Age 18. Ohio.

Putz: Yiddish for "penis." Private language within intimate network of three couples. Age 20. Ohio.

Sniffles: Man had slight genital discharge; doctor suggested that maybe he had "caught a cold." Private language between lovers. Age 20. Toronto, Canada. Man (informant) is originally from the U.K.

Winston: "Tastes good, like a cigarette should." Private language between lovers. Age 30. Pennsylvania.

Zeke: Private language within intimate network of three couples. Age 20. Ohio.

▼ ▼ ▼

PET NAMES FOR THE VULVA[9]

Eunice: Old-fashioned name, corresponding to **Mortimer** (*see* above). Private language between lovers. Named by the man during sex play. Ohio.

Henrietta: Pennsylvania.

Home: "Does Baby want to go Home?" *See* **Baby**. Private language between lovers. Age 20. Indiana.

Honeypot: Couple undergoing marriage counseling. Indiana.

Little Monkey: "Can I pet the Little Monkey?" Couple undergoing marriage couseling. Indiana.

Mama's Box: Age 35. Pennsylvania.

Rochester: From the city where she lost her virginity. Private language within intimate network of three couples. Age 20. Ohio.

Virginia Vagina: Alliteration. Private language within intimate network of three couples. Age 20. Ohio.

Wonderland: "Put Alice in Wonderland." *See* **Alice**. Private language between lovers.

Although this list of names is not long, we can discern some patterns of naming, particularly for the penis. Most names of penises fall into one of the following categories:

1. A variation of the owner's name (*Little Willy, Chuck, Peter J. Firestone*).

2. A name suggesting a joke or catchy phrase, usually alluding to erection or sex acts (*Lazarus, Winston*).

3. What Sanders and Robinson call "power slang" [10] (*Driveshaft, Four on the Floor*).

4. Human first names that appealed or occurred to the namer for no reason that could be recalled by the informant. "The Saturday night of Opening Day [of trout season] I can remember vividly. [My father] he was drunker than a warthog. . . . We get out on the porch [to urinate] and he's. . .singing 'I took my organ to the party,'. . .he gets his fly open. . . and he starts to relieve himself—a fairly steady stream—and he starts talking to his organ and, by God, he calls the thing 'Hank.' He says, 'Aw, look at old Hank here, poor, poor old guy.' And he says, 'You and I, we've been in a couple of tight places together and we've had our ups and downs, but I want you to know, you old sonofabitch'—and this is where he starts shaking it off—'that I outlived you!'. . . That was the first time I had heard him allude to 'Hank' [and] I think it was just a spur-of-the-moment thing."

Some of the same patterns occur among the names for vulvas (*Wonderland*, for example). However, I have collected too few names for vulvas to be able to generalize at this point.

Who names genitals? In those cases where I was told the full story by the informant of the "christening" (16 cases out of 33), it was most often a group or couple interaction, or the other partner who produced the name. (For the remaining cases, this information was not available.) Penises seem to be named more often than vulvas.

Why do some people give proper names to genitals? After all, no one names feet, hands or elbows. Genital proper or pet names serve one or more functions.

First, the name(s) can serve as a private language between lovers or other groups of people who know each other well. Such a language permits discussion of sexual matters in front of unknowing friends and parents. The woman who told me about *Peter J. Firestone* said, "We would be sitting at dinner [with his parents] and he would toss off this comment, 'Well, maybe we could double-date with Peter tonight,' and then we'd go, 'Ha, ha, ha,' and hope that his mother didn't see me turn red!" Similarly, the owner of *Winston* and his girlfriend took great pleasure in discussing "Winston's good taste" in front of friends and relatives. One sex manual advises genital naming for this purpose:

> Pat your man's penis during nonsexual moments. Give it a pet name such as "John Thomas," used by Lawrence's Lady Chatterley; or name it after its owner, calling it "Junior" — "David, Junior," "Mark, Junior," etc. A girl I know has long hilarious conversations with someone named Penis Desmond — P.D., for short — who answers her in a high-pitched falsetto voice. This little act is a fun way to humanize a woman's relationship to a man's penis.[11] [Note that here the woman partner is advised to do the naming, and to pick a variation of the owner's name.]

When Sanders and Robinson solicited genital terms from college students, they found that the spouse/lover context elicited the greatest number of idiosyncratic responses, including pet names. To explain this, they quote Mark L. Knapp (*Social Intercourse*, Boston: Allyn and Bacon, 1978, p. 15): "The process of constructing a more intimate relationship eventually reaches the point where we are interacting with the other person as a unique individual rather than as a member of a particular society. Uniqueness in communication simply suggests the adoption of a more idiosyncratic communication system adapted to the peculiar nature of the interacting parties.[12]

In a broader sense, the pet name can also serve as a method of facilitating communication about sex. Many people, particularly women, are uncomfortable with the common generic terms for genitals.[13] One of my informants was a marriage counselor for several years:

> One of the things we frequently encountered were persons who were having a great deal of difficulty verbally communicating

about sex, and the reason was that they were extremely...uncom-
fortable with what they considered to be profane words, and they
were uncomfortable with the official Latin terminology. And what
was typically going on, then, was just nothing. With lack of a label,
people weren't talking. So...after playing around with it for a
while, I thought about the possibility of using made-up words. So
we started doing that in therapy [having the couples make up names
for body parts and sex acts] and we found it to be very successful.
A lot of couples who had had trouble before really got into it,
found it very enjoyable and developed a whole new vocabulary for
sex organs and sexual acts.... From a therapeutic point of view, it
was a very good idea, because, in addition to giving them a label
that they could use to communicate and increase the effectiveness
of what they were doing,...it [also] created a very nice thing for
them to do together. The process of thinking up names and developing this new vocabulary was a very enjoyable process of sharing
for most of the couples that tried it.[14]

Finally, the pet name bestows an identity upon the genitals: they have a personality which *is distinct* from the identity of the owner:

The experience of genital excitation parallels the experience of the
I in that it has a somewhat detached quality.... In men the penis is
often given a name to indicate that it has a degree of independence
from the self. It may be called "John," or *le petit homme* [the little
man], or "Peter," to denote this independence from the self.[15]

Much current popular literature on sex and psychology
describes the alienation and the love/hate relationship men
often have with their penises: "...He curses his penis for not
performing, as he sweats and strains and informs his partner
that *he* really wants to, even though something is wrong with
it."[16] And Jerry Rubin gives the dialog:

My penis: I don't want to get turned on here. This bed is not safe
for me.
My mind: Shut up! Perform! Don't let me down!...You're humili-
ating me in front of Rosalie![17]

A man having some of these feelings who gives a pet name to
his penis can thereby both wash his hands of what "it" does

and also diffuse his anxiety through humor. Lawrence's Mellors illustrates this process:

> The man [Mellors] looked down in silence at the tense phallos, that did not change. — "Ay!" he said at last, in a little voice, "Ay ma lad! tha'art thee right enough. Yi, the mun rear thy head! Theer on thy own, eh? an' ta'es no count o' nob'dy! Tha ma'es nowt o' me, John Thomas. Art boss? of me? Eh well, tha'rt more cocky than me, an' that says less. John Thomas! Dost want *her*? Dost want my lady Jane?... Tell Lady Jane tha wants cunt, John Thomas....[18]

Thus, we have the theme of genitals-as-personality. We can also call this "genitomorphism." It goes much further than the practice of giving proper names to genitals. It reaches into psychology, folklore, literature, art and religion. Included in this theme of genitomorphism are the subthemes of talking genitals (Thompson Motif D1610.6), genitals *talked to* and genitals acting on their own volition. Finally, of course, we have Genital Gods, i.e., phallic worship. Above, I have noted some of the psychological correlates of naming genitals. Gershon Legman discusses the folklore of genitomorphism. In his *Rationale of the Dirty Joke* (First and Second Series), he provides nearly twenty jokes or tales dealing with genitals named, speaking, spoken to, or acting on their own. Several examples, condensed here:

1. Groom on honeymoon to bride: "Honey, would you like to see *Oliver Twist*?"
   Bride: "Why not? I've seen it do everything else!"

2. Prostitute sees reflection of her vulva in a puddle: "There you is, you l'il ol' money-maker!"

3. Man amputates penis accidentally while shaving. Severed penis: "I know we've had lots of fist fights in our time, but I never thought you'd pull a knife on me!"[19]

And a wonderful cartoon was described to me, reportedly published in *The Realist*, of a man holding his penis, *which is saying* (via a cartoon "balloon"), "Not tonight, dear, I have a headache!"[20]

In literature, I have already mentioned *Lady Chatterley's*

Lover. I have found other interesting examples. In *Portnoy's Complaint*, Portnoy has a long dialog with "the maniac who speaks into the microphone of my jockey shorts."[21] Henry Miller, in *Tropic of Capricorn*, gives a long and detailed typology of "cunt personalities."[22] The hero of Petronius's *Satyricon*, Encolpius, has a violent argument with "a part of me which no serious man thinks worthy of his thoughts."[23] Legman cites several additional references from literature.[24]

In the graphic arts, genitals have been depicted as self-contained beings, or as the heads of otherwise human bodies. Fourteen plates in *The Complete Book of Erotic Art* depict this theme,[25] including a delightful series of Japanese prints of a Sumo wrestling match between a penis and a vulva, which ends (not surprisingly) with the penis being engulfed by the vulva/vagina.

Finally, a substantial literature concerns phallic worship. Edwardes gives one example in *The Jewel in the Lotus*, where he describes "the evil *jinee El-A'awer* (one-eyed penis genie), patron spirit of the ravisher."[26]

As Vance Randolph and Gershon Legman point out, "a fascinating monograph could be written on these themes of the speaking privates of both sexes...."[27] Genitals *named*, genitals *spoken to*, genitals *acting independently*, and genitals *deified* are related themes. All are subsumed under the broader concept of "genitals-as-personality." But we have yet to understand fully why genitals are personified, the cultural conditions under which personification happens and, finally, what it means to people who say *Henrietta* or *Winston* to genitals.

FOOTNOTES

1. A View Through the Speculum: A Workshop on Vaginal Health and Politics. Sponsored by the Elizabeth Blackwell Health Center for Women. Philadelphia, Pa., May 17, 1980.

2. David Herbert Lawrence. *Lady Chatterley's Lover* (New York: New American Library, 1959), pp. 196-97, 212-14, 283.

3. "John Thomas" is also generalized slang for the penis, as quoted from *The Pearl* by Tim Healey in "A New Erotic

Vocabulary," *Maledicta* 4(2):191, Winter 1980. Mellors, how-ever, uses it as a personal pet name.

4. "Proper names" are explained by David Schwarz as "semantic atoms. They cannot be constructed by a speaker out of pre-existing material; they must be learned individual-ly." (*Naming and Referring: The Semantics and Pragmatics of Singular Terms* [New York: De Gruyter, 1979], p. 51.)

5. For additional terms for genitals, *see* Tim Healey's won-derful compendium [*op. cit.*, pp. 181-201] and "Naming the Vulvar Part" by Clyde Hankey [*Maledicta* 4 (2): 220-22, Winter 1980].

6. All owners and informants, with the exception of *Jason*'s and *Sniffles*'s owners, were U.S. citizens. None was self-identified as homosexual. I do not know if the patterns of genital naming by homosexuals are different in any way from heterosexual patterns.

7. *Jason* was the name a male stripper gave his penis, re-ported in "A Big Gland for the Little Ladies." [*Oui* 4(3): 13, March 1975.] Was *Jason* looking for the Golden Fleece?

8. *Firestone* is a pseudonym for the surname of the owner.

9. I was going to call this section "Pet Names for the Va-gina" until I read Mildred Ash's "The Vulva: A Psycholinguistic Problem" [*Maledicta* 4(2): 213-19, Winter, 1980, with accom-panying mnemonic].

10. Janet Sanders and William Robinson. "Talking and Not Talking About Sex." *Journal of Communication* 29(2): 22-30, Spring, 1979, p. 28.

11. Xaviera Hollander. *Xaviera's Supersex: Her Personal Techniques for Total Lovemaking* (New York: New American Library, 1976), p. 134.

12. Sanders and Robinson. *Op. cit.*, p. 29.

13. Sanders and Robinson's data suggest that women have fewer terms for sexual parts and acts than men, and verbalize less about sex, particularly about their own genitals. (*Op. cit.*, pp. 27-28.)

14. David Weis. Personal communication. Dec. 12, 1980.

15. Alexander Lowen. *Fear of Life* (New York: Macmillan, 1980), p. 87.

16. Herb Goldberg. *The New Male: From Self-Destruction to Self-Care* (New York: William Morrow, 1979), p. 120.

17. Jerry Rubin and Mimi Leonard. *The War Between the Sheets* (New York: Richard Marek Publishers, 1980), p. 68.

18. Lawrence. *Op. cit.*, pp. 196-97.

19. Gershon Legman. *Rationale of the Dirty Joke: An Analysis of Sexual Humor.* First Series (New York: Grove Press, 1968), pp. 285-86, 301, 371, 490, 750-51. Second Series *No Laughing Matter* (New York: Breaking Point, 1975), pp. 169, 229, 236-37, 589, 597, 604-05, 629, 874-76, 878-89. One of these tales is treated at greater length in Vance Randolph and Gershon Legman, "The Magic Walking Stick," *Maledicta* 3(2): 175-76, Winter, 1979. The three jokes given come from First Series, p. 490 and Second Series, pp. 229, 605.

20. Arno Karlen. Personal communication. April 10, 1981.

21. Philip Roth. *Portnoy's Complaint* (New York: Random House, 1969), pp. 126-28. (Cited by Legman, *op. cit.*, Second Series, pp. 586-87.)

22. Henry Miller. *Tropic of Capricorn* (New York: Grove Press, 1961), pp. 194-95. (Cited by Legman, *op. cit.*, First Series, p. 371.)

23. Quoted by Robert S. De Ropp in *Sex Energy* (New York: Delacorte Press, 1969), p. 125.

24. Legman. *Op. cit.*, First Series, pp. 750-51; Second Series, p. 237.

25. Phyllis and Eberhard Kronhausen. *The Complete Book of Erotic Art*, Volumes 1 and 2 (New York: Bell Publishing, 1978); plates 146, 326 in Vol. 1; plates 23, 123, 130, 335, 337-46 in Vol. 2.

26. Allen Edwardes. *The Jewel in the Lotus* (New York: Julian Press, 1959), p. 109.

27. Randolph and Legman. *Op. cit.*, p. 175.

WHAT IS THIS THING CALLED, LOVE?
MORE GENITAL PET NAMES

Reinhold Aman & Friends

I

After Martha Cornog turned my attention to her genital pet name research (*see* preceding article), I asked myself what pet name I use for my own appendage. But, having been accused and accursed of "letting it all hang out" in this journal, I shall restrain myself for a change and not reveal the pet name I used to use in my early days of marriage (1960s). It was the name of a minor character in the "Yogi Bear" cartoons.

An endearing name puts one in better standing with one's necessary evil than speaking of him as "the old pecker." In jest, I have used the pet names below for the penis, as well as these three names that can be used for the vulva and the penis, depending on how one feels about certain acts: **Problem** and **Enemy** (they should be licked) and **S.A.L.**, short for **Self-Adhesive Label** (stick it — don't lick it!).

The punsters amongst you surely will be able to come up with similar genital pet names based on word plays. Here are a few pet names one can call a penis, together with the reasons for it: the Middle English **Sumer** (it's *icumen in*), the **Lord** (he's come), the **Savior** (he came upon a midnight clear), the **Kingdom of Heaven** (close at hand, and soon to come), **My Prince** (some day he'll come), **Seven Up** (from Hebrew *záyin* "7" and "penis"), **Cornucopia** (the Horn of Plenty), the **Sun** (rises every day), the **Moon** (rises in the evening), the **Law** (don't take it into your own hands), and my favorite, the **South** (will rise again).

Several actual pet names have been reported to me which will be published once we have more than a handful, as it were. Meanwhile, three friends who have to remain anonymous have informed me of genital pet names they or their friends have used.

II

First, from the American linguist Karin (East Coast), four penile pet names:

Haupttorschlüssel: Used by an Austrian man and an American woman. Both mid-twenties. Austria. *Haupttorschlüssel* is German for "main gate key." In Austria, Germany and many other countries, the key to the main door or gate of private homes and apartment buildings is an enormous, heavy, five-inch instrument, quite unlike the typical American two-inch key. Thus, it is appropriate for a lady to ask, "Is that your *Haupttorschlüssel* in your pocket, or are you just happy to see me?"

Left-Hand: The penis leaned toward the left. Used by an Austrian man and an American woman. Both mid-twenties. Austria and U.S. East Coast.

Moishe: Hebrew for *Moses.* "Moishe" is a very common first name in Israel. Used by an Israeli man and an American woman. Both mid-twenties. U.S. East Coast.

Old Faithful: "Because you can always count on him when you need him," and the name of a famous U.S. geyser. Used by an American man and woman. U.S. East Coast.

III

Then there is Wanda (Southern California), another American linguist, who has gathered many pet names in her bumpy life. In addition, she has given her vibrator the pet name *Vladimir* (*-mir* means "peace"). First vulvar pet names, all used by men in Southern California:

Famfulja and **Famfuljica:** Serbo-Croatian for "ass" and "whore." Assimilated from *fànfulja.* -*ica* is the endearing, diminutive suffix. Used by man. Age 47. Yugoslav.

Òpanak: The Serbo-Croatian word for the pointed-toe leather shoe worn by peasants. (In northern Serbia, the tip of the shoe curls all the way around.) Also used as a derogatory term meaning 'peasant.' In this case, the user implied derogatorily that the woman's vulva and vagina are old, big, worn out, leathery. Used by man. Age 47. Yugoslav.

Pičić and **Pičkica:** Serbo-Croatian for "cute little pussy." Terms of endearment. Used by man. Age 47. Yugoslav.

Pizdenjak and **Pizdurina:** Serbo-Croatian for "big cunt." Terms of derision. Used by man. Age 47. Yugoslav.

Fustukh: Arabic for "pistachio nut." Term of endearment, as the pussy "resembles a nut and is delicious." Used by man. Age 30. Lebanese.

And some penile pet names:

My Pee-Pee: Children's language. Used by man. Age 35. Israeli.

Hank Junior: Owner's name is Hank. Comical, endearing. Used by man. Age 42. American.

Happy Fella: "His penis enjoys sex." Comical, endearing. Used by owner's wife. Age 40. American.

Draganović: Serbo-Croatian for "Little Dragan." Owner's first name is Dragan. Used by man. Age 26. Yugoslav.

My Charlie: No reason known. Comical, endearing. Used by owner. Age 35. Bulgarian.

Ya'irello: Hebrew-Italian for "Little Ya'ir." Owner's name is Ya'ir (Hebrew), with Italian diminutive-endearing suffix -*ello* added. Used by man. Age 25. Israeli.

The following four Serbo-Croatian names are used by the owner, a 47-year-old Yugoslav: **Belègija** ("whetstone, grindstone"; also, "a long strip of (dried) meat"; and in southern Serbia also "lazy, negligent woman; slattern"), **Čuskia** or **Čuskija** ("crowbar"; also, "stupid"), **Oklàgija** ("rolling pin"), and **Vàgīr** ("beam scale" and "wooden part of a yoke").

(I wish to thank Dr. Victor Friedman for supplying information on these Serbo-Croatian terms.)

IV

Finally, Chris, a Canadian-American scientist in Georgia, submitted his collection of genital pet names:

Virginia: From the state's advertisement "Virginia is for lovers." Pet name for her vulva/vagina, used by a 19-year-old American female.

Miss Muff: Used by a 20-year-old Canadian female for her vulva.

Winston: "Winston Tastes Good." Used by a 17-year-old American male for his penis.

Hamlet: Reason unknown. Used by a 16-year-old American male for his penis.

Longfellow: The poet. Used by a 16-year-old American male for his penis. He also called his testicles **John & Henry**.

Sequoia: Named for the gigantic tree; given to the "monster-cock" of an 18-year-old American male by another boy.

Victory: Reason unknown. Used for his penis by a 26-year-old Chinese male living in the USA.

Most interestingly, in the course of growing up, Chris has called his own penis various names:

Excalibur: "Slew everyone." Age 12-15.

Vivekanada: "This name had such an ejaculate sound, like 'Geronimo!'" Age 15-18.

Ozymandias: A tyrant; named after the figure in Shelley's sonnet: "Look on my works, ye mighty, and despair." 18-19 yrs.

Agamemnon: Named after the ancient Greek king, "a real butch dude." Age 19-27. His wife especially liked this name but was not inspired to correspondingly name her v/v "Clytemnestra."

Vivitar: Named after his Vivitar camera lens which goes from a modest 90 mm (3.54") to three times that length at the 1:1 reproduction ratio; he says he experiences a great emotional release when the shutter clicks and his twin flashes go off. Age 27-31 (present).

PETER METRE

*Donald Charles

Hours after New York writer Pete Hamill had heard of Beatle John Lennon's death, he wrote a lengthy article in *New York* (22 December 1980, pp. 38-50), glorifying Lennon and reminiscing about his own finer qualities. (Pete and John were quite alike, you see.) Hamill's "sick-making" article so infuriated the New York literati that one "Donald Charles" dashed off his anti-Hamill diatribe, which was circulated widely in photocopy form among the New York City intelligentsia. To preserve it for posterity, we are publishing it here, as an example of scurrilous attacks by writers on other writers, a genre of literary abuse that has its origins in antiquity. (*Editor*)

Peter Hamill meretricious
Vainglorious and ambitious
Dirty, evil, credit-seeking
Whose work is mewling machoid squeaking
Pete back-of-taxi-cab disrober
Pete hateful drunk, more hateful sober
Windbag Hamill, sulfurous dog fart
Failed scripter of Amelia Earhart
Hamill balding, warty, meaty
Brother out-law of Warren Beatty
Hamill of the yellow eye
Hamill who deserves to die
Hamill tedious, Hamill grating
Hamill half-blind from masturbating
Hamill rapturous at pennin'
Eulogies for poor John Lennon.

Hamill sneaking and obsequious
Hamill sly and proud and devious
Hamill wrongheaded, Hamill boring

Hamill crass who makes for snoring
Pete fired by the *Daily News*
Pete ardent swain of jet/set cooze
Hamill pushy, Hamill rude
Hamill disgusting clothed or nude
Hamill far above his station
An unsuitable presence at any occasion
Title defender on his knees
Bootlicker to celebrities
Hamill facile, Hamill banal
Hamill flotsam *du canal*
Hamill gate-crashing at Elaines
Name-dropping on Long Island trains
Hamill presumptuous, Hamill spiteful
Pseudo-tactful, pseudo-insightful
Phony kind and ersatz tough
Heart full of green and runny stuff
Hamill noisy, vulgar, coarse
Hamill's breath would stun a horse
Hamill inflated, Hamill droopy
Hamill, the press-card-flashing groupie
Pete supercilious, arch, superior
Hamill palpably inferior
Hamill pretentious pompous ass
Aspiring to the working class
Pete made-for-television man
Pete cocaine dealer to Duran
Pete ugly, greedy, graspy, grabby
Stage-Irish Hamill, Hamill flabby
Pete impotent, Pete kiss and tell
Pete of the damp and cheesy smell. . .

Enough! Why beat my broadsword blunt
Belaboring this stupid cunt?
But bear in mind I'll start again
If Hamill ever lifts his pen
To violate the taste of men in
More drool about poor dead John Lennon.

TRADE NAMES OF AMERICAN CONDOMS

*Sir Maurice Sedley

For the past three years, thanks to some entrepreneur who sold my name and address to the Carrboro, N.C., mail-order firm of "Adam & Eve" which specializes in the sale of what in the United States is euphemistically called "marital aids," I have been receiving the firm's annual catalog.

One recent afternoon, while idly perusing the firm's 1979 and 1980 catalogs, the large variety (N=52) of condom trade names caught my attention, and after classifying them, I found that all fifty-two names could be subsumed under five general categories: (1) AGGRESSION: N=6, 11.5%; (2) HEDONISM: N=29, 55.5%; (3) MORPHOLOGY or SHAPE: N=6, 11.5%; (4) NEUTRALITY: N=7, 13.5%; (5) PROTECTION or SECURITY: N=4, 8%.

Considering the rampant egocentric male-chauvinist piggery and hostility-aggressiveness which has long characterized typical American masculine sexual attitudes and behavior — the former exemplified by the classic "4F" joke, *viz.* First American Male: "In my sexual relationships, I always follow the 4F Rule." Second A.M.: "What's that?" First A.M.: "Find 'em, feel 'em, fuck 'em, forget 'em." — the latter exemplified by the snide question-and-answer puzzle, *viz.* Q: "Describe the typical American male's sexual behavior in five words." A: "Slam! Bam! Thank you, Ma'am."— it was surprising to find such a small percentage of obviously aggressive condom trade names in the observed set.

An analysis of the six identified aggressive condom trade

names indicates that all of them imply a potential violent physical assault on the female body.

Bold 45: The 45 refers to a .45 caliber handgun which a behatted, jean-clad female is playfully pointing, thus setting herself up as a "target" to be "hit" or "scored upon" by the male's "gun."

Conquerer: A robust, horn-helmeted Viking with a murderous-pointed spear in hand just waiting for the opportunity to go into action.

Musketeer: Shades of Cyrano de Bergerac, Athos, Porthos, Aramis and D'Artagnan which transfer military aggressiveness into sexual aggressiveness tacitly directing it against the female body as a fortress to be taken by assault.

Olé: A lover as a matador out to overpower or vanquish female sexuality by means of a skillful but deadly assault.

Rough Rider: A triple entendre indicating various types of assault, *viz.* (1) studs on the condom to increase its roughness when in use; (2) the female body as enemy to be vanquished by a saber-waving, war-whooping cavalryman charging up the "San Juan Hill" of Venus; (3) rider of a spirited but not totally manageable mount determined to tame the mount.

Superstud: A female as breeding-stock assaulted for hire.

Categorized List of Fifty-Two Condom Trade Names

AGGRESSION
Bold 45
Conquerer
Musketeer
Olé
Rough Rider
Superstud

MORPHOLOGY or SHAPE
Conture
Hugger
Nu-Form
Pointex
Slims
Trojan-Enz

NEUTRALITY
Fourex
Jellia
Naturals
Plus
Prime
Sta-Tex
Wrinkle Zero-0

PROTECTION or SECURITY
Convoys
Guardian
Shields
Trojan Guardian

HEDONISM
- Adam's Rib
- Apollo
- Black Cat
- Cavalier
- Embrace Her
- Eros
- Excita
- Fiesta´ (colored)
- Fetherlite
- Geisha Thins
- Gold Circle Coins
- Hotline
- Jade (green, blue, gold, red)
- Longtime
- Nuda
- Patrician
- Peacock
- Pleaser
- Ramses
- Saxon
- Scentuals (musk, banana, strawberry, lime)
- Score
- Sheik
- Skinless Skin
- Stimula
- Sultan
- Tahiti
- Texture Plus
- Tingla

Little Dickie Cavity, the "intellectual" television host, likes to make fun of Germans and their language — something Mark Twain did long ago, and far better. On the "Tonight Show" of 28 October 1981, Dick Cavett told Johnny Carson that the German word for "condom" is *Geschlechtsgliedbeschützer.* Balls! This contrived word literally means "sex-member-protector" which no German-speaking person ever uses.

The four most common terms are *Gummi* "rubber," *Pariser* "Parisian" (cf. English 'French letter'), *Fromms* (a brand named after its producer and ironically meaning "pious, religious"), and *Überzieher* "overcoat," lit. "over-puller," something one pulls over one's penis. Other common terms are *Präservativ* "preservative," i.e., something that protects one from getting VD, and the learnèd *Kondóm.*

In his *Sex im Volksmund* (1971), Ernest Borneman lists about 50 more or less humorous euphemisms for condom, among them *Gummihandschuh* "rubber-glove," *Gummimantel* "rubber-overcoat," *Luftballon* "balloon," *Nahkampfsocke* "close-combat sock," *Pfeifenpullover* "pipe-pullover" (pipe = penis), *Schwanzfutteral* "tail-sheath," *Tropfenfänger* "drop-catcher," and *zweite Haut* "second skin." Most of the remaining terms listed are used rarely, or are regional. (*Editor*)

ON TRANSLATING CHOMSKY

J. Peter Maher

TEXT*	TRANSFORMATION [- Bullshit]
In these lectures I would like to discuss certain topics in an area of convergence of linguistics, logic, and psychology.	*Linguistics, logic, and psychology converge.*
I will not try to relate this subject matter directly to current interests in the field of automata, but I think that certain connections will be fairly obvious, not only with such problems as Mechanical Translation and Information Retrieval, but also with more theoretical studies of learning and cognition.	*I pretend here not to claim what I am claiming, i.e.* *Machine translation, Information Retrieval and the human brain obviously work the same way. The computer is a model of the brain, I say.*
Going beyond the available evidence, however, I would hazard the guess that the general properties of this description of English (e.g. the use of transformations of the type defined below, though not, of course, the same transformations) will carry over to a wide range of natural languages, perhaps all.	*I haven't done my homework on languages* *but* *my transformational grammar explains all human languages; and I hope you think I'm being modest with that "perhaps."*
Recent work at M.I.T. on other Indo-European languages, Turkish, and certain American Indian languages gives some empirical support to this guess.	*If M. Halle, R. B. Lees, P. Postal, e.g., have done their homework,* *their work supports my guess.*

---

*Noam Chomsky, "Linguistics, Logic, Psychology, and Computers," in John W. Carr, III (ed.), *Computer Programming and Artificial Intelligence* (Ann Arbor: Univ. of Michigan College of Engineering, 1958), 429-56.

RUDE WORDS

INSULTS AND NARRATION IN PREADOLESCENT OBSCENE TALK

Gary Alan Fine

An interesting irony implicated by the behavior of those who wish to protect us from ourselves is the belief that children must be shielded from obscenities, which, it is believed, could warp their moral development. The irony of this belief is that children, particularly boys, are well-versed in obscene talk. By not permitting preadolescents to hear or read the words which they already know, we do not protect the innocence of our children, but protect our own innocence regarding them. It has been reported that collectors of children's lore (e.g., Opie and Opie, 1959) deliberately omitted content which they considered improper (*see* Heyer, 1979:4). As Ian Turner has remarked, "If we cannot publish the literary creations of pre-adolescent children, what can we publish?" (1972:2)

My goal in this article is to examine how preadolescents employ obscenity in their talk, and how this use of vernacular language allows them to demonstrate and learn skills considered by peers to be a mark of maturity. This concern with obscene talk is particularly startling in light of the belief by many adults that their own children are unaware of obscenities. This lack of knowledge by adults indicates the considerable skills that children have in impression management (*see* Goffman, 1959; Fine, forthcoming). Boys trading dirty jokes will tell each other to "shut up" when one spies an adult coming within earshot. This parental ignorance was made dramatically evident to me when I discovered that one of my preadolescent contacts had been grounded for a week for remarking in front of a traitorous babysitter that "my cock has teeth," a phrase a Freudian analyst would find deliciously symptomatic. The mother was shocked by this report, having no idea that her little boy *ever* spoke like that.[1] For their own protection, children learn in which contexts certain language must not be used and where they are an appropriate indicator of sociability.

RESEARCH SETTINGS

In order to learn what preadolescents really did and what they really talked about, I conducted participant observation research for three years in four communities in New England and Minnesota; a fifth community in Minnesota was studied by a research assistant. Originally, the focus of the research was to be on the development of culture in the context of the small group (Fine, 1979), and for this reason Little League baseball teams were chosen for study. However, in the course of observation it became apparent that preadolescent male culture could only be understood in the context of other leisure activities. During the spring and summer, I spent considerable time with these boys (304 days in total), attending most of their Little League games, and hanging around with them before and after games. Over the course of the season, I established bonds of trust with the boys, and as the spring progressed they let me listen to their private conversations, although there were always certain settings to which I was never invited — when they were "mooning"[2] or held boy-girl parties at which "making out" was planned.

The five communities examined were: 1) Beanville,[3] an upper-middle class professional suburb of Boston, Mass., 2) Hopewell, an exurban township outside of the Providence, R.I. metropolitan area, comprised of a collection of small towns, beach-front land, farms, and a campus of the state university, 3) Bolton Park, an upper-middle class professional suburb of St. Paul, Minn., similar to Beanville, except for geographical location, 4) Sanford Heights, a middle-to-lower-middle class suburb of Minneapolis, comprised largely of developers' tract homes, and 5) Maple Bluff, an urban, upper-middle class area of St. Paul (examined by my research assistant, Harold Pontiff). Although these sites are not a representative sample of American communities, they do cover a moderately wide range of environments, and the data can serve as an indicator of preadolescent behavior in other locations as well.

OBSCENE TALK

All those who have studied children closely have recognized that aggression, sex, and excrement are important components of preadolescent talk. Heyer (1979), studying children's playground rhymes, found that 22% referred to violence, sorrow, cruelty, or death; 19% were taunts; and 16% made reference to "bathrooms, bare behinds, or underwear." Unfortunately, Heyer did not classify sexual taunts separately, but presumably those remarks are included as violent or taunting.

Yet, such an approach does not sufficiently recognize that the meaning of obscenity is derived from the context in which it is used and that the use of obscenity is a speech achievement of the child. Collecting rude words or nasty stories outside of their natural context is perhaps akin to butterfly collecting: if one wishes to learn how butterflies fly, one cannot be satisfied with mounting them.

One way in which obscenity can be classified is in terms of *how it is used in the course of talk.* On some occasions, a boy will employ obscenity as part of an on-going conversation, often in the form of an insult. On other occasions, a boy uses obscenity as part of a lengthier narrative, such as when telling a joke or explaining the "facts of life." While there is not always a clear line between talk as *interaction* (insults) and talk as *narration* (jokes or "facts"), this distinction has some analytic utility for differentiating types of talk. In the case of obscenity as interaction, the speaker is talking at the expense of another, attempting to put that other—temporarily or permanently, jocularly or seriously—in a less desirable social position. In the case of narration, the speaker is showcasing him- or herself, making him-/herself the center of attention. Although all interaction involves some narrative skills and all narration is part of an interaction sequence, this distinction does allow us to classify types of preadolescent talk in such a way as to permit a better understanding of how and when children use obscenity.

INTERACTIVE INSULTS

All insults are not created equal. Calling a boy a "faggot" when he is not present may have quite different implications from describing him in the same way when he is present. Even face-to-face insults carry different implications depending upon the relationship of the parties and the paraverbal cues given off by the insulter (*see* Leary, 1980). Calling a friend a "faggot" can even be a non-sexual term of comradeship if spoken correctly.

In order to indicate how insults serve as interactive achievements for preadolescents, I shall examine three uses of insults. First, and perhaps most frequently, obscenity may be spoken within a context of peer sociability to promote a consensual view of a situation or person. Although the obscenity may be quite cruel, it often is expressed "joyously" because of the *communitas* among participants in the interaction. Second, preadolescents use obscenity as playful banter, where the obscenity jocularly challenges its target, present in the situation, but has and is seen as having no malicious intent. The third class of talk is, despite its relative infrequency, seen as the insult prototype—when one person is angry at another and expresses this rage through talk. In all three types of talk, the insult is grounded in the on-going interaction and is responsive to the rules of social talk.

DENIGRATING OTHERS:
CONSENSUS THROUGH OBSCENITY

Frequently, obscenity is used as a means of altering the reputation of another (*see* Weinstein and Deutschberger, 1963) and of promoting consensus among the interactants. Despite the intensity of the insults, they are expressed with a feeling of good fellowhip. Scapegoating seems to bring the participants closer together, as in this example, spoken into a tape recorder:

Rich: *Malkis sucks, yeah, yeah, yeah.*

Jerry: *He licks my ass.*

Many: *Yeah, yeah, yeah.*

Rich: *Go play with Zit-face.* [Denny Malkis's girl friend]

Tom: *Go screw Zit-face.*

Rich: *Yeah, go screw Zit-face, and Malkis, I wish you'd stop hanging around me, because you look so ugly, and I wish you'd go to hell. Hey, Malkis, Malkis, I saw you fucking the hell out of your sister last night. How come you hang around with your sister? Tell me, huh? How come you like that ninth-grader who beat the fucking hell out of a teacher, and how come she's a zit-face?*

Tom: *A fucking whore.*

Rich: *You're so fat and you're so slutty, and you stink.*
  (Taped transcript)

Particularly notable about this short transcript is how insults build upon each other, increasing in a crescendo of abuse. The later abuse can only be said because of what has gone before, and thus is an interactive achievement created jointly by the participants. All speakers in this interaction are orienting their talk in the same direction—to besmirch the moral credibility of this boy, not present to defend himself. Denny's reputation is well-known and so the participants can simply use their shared knowledge to create an artistic speech act. In other cases the consensus is created through the interaction:

Author (to Rod): *I thought your girl friend was Sara.*

Rod: *Sara went the same day I told you.*

Vicki (to Pam): *You like Sara?*

Pam: *She's got a big mouth.*

Vicki: *She lies so much.*

Pam: *She flirts with all the boys.*

Rod: *Why do you think I dropped her? She doesn't know what's going on.* (Taped transcript)

It is clear that the participants have achieved a consensual view of Sara, a view which seemed not to be present at the

beginning of this segment of conversation. Note in both examples, although the talk has hostile implications, it is not
used in a hostile fashion within the context of talk; the talkers
are not themselves angry. Although some of the content may
be similar to hostile face-to-face insults, as talk the two types
of denigration are markedly different.

TEASING OTHERS:
OBSCENITY AS BANTER

If one listened to preadolescent talk, only comprehending the
denotative meanings of their talk (i.e., the slang denotations),
one might conclude that preadolescents don't like each other
very much. At this age children do not admit easily that they
"like" each other, and most evaluations of others seem on
their surface to be critical. However, this interpretation would
miss the connotations of preadolescent talk. Boys call each
other "scum", "womaneater", "hairsnatch", "fag", or "queer."
These insults are accepted in the spirit in which they are intended, as friendly ragging, and often receive a response in
kind. The fact that these insults are on other occasions considered "fighting words" indicates that children have the ability to recognize intent.

Friends are allowed, and even expected, to insult each
other, as a show of camaraderie. The nature of the insult is
signalled by a smile or grin, permitting the target to "accept"
the insult or even playfully to act in accord with it. For example, when a boy is teased by being called a "faggot" or "fem",
he may plant a kiss on his insulter or behave in a stereotypi-
cally effeminate manner. In one instance, a boy said to a friend:
"Go suck a cow" and a third friend went "moo." These occasions are instances of fraternal sociability. While we should not
ignore the "deeper" anxieties implicated by these insults and
their responses (a fear of homosexuality, for example), these
statements are insults in form, not in function.

Participants in these interactions recognize that the overt
meaning of the remarks is not what they really mean. However,
this does not indicate that the location of such statements in

conversation is random. Often they involve social control, in that such a remark may follow an inappropriate behavior. For example, a boy who does something which is considered "childish" is accused of being gay. The remark does not usually imply that the boy is disliked, but that his *action* is deemed improper or immature. An insult can warn the boy of the normative boundaries of preadolescent action. The difficulty for the individual preadolescent who wishes to avoid these teasing insults is that the standards of behavior are nowhere made explicit and are continually changing. As a result, the process of behavioral adjustment is a continuing issue, given direction by the cultural leaders of the preadolescent group.

Although insults may be used as direct responses to particular actions, they may also constitute an on-going interaction in which participants playfully insult each other. This type of interaction is similar to the ritualized insult contests found in numerous cultures (Elliott, 1960), such as the *dozens* in the black adolescent subsociety (e.g., Dollard, 1939; Abrahams, 1970). While it would be misleading to suggest that the insults traded by these middle-class white preadolescents are as formalized or ritualized as those in black culture, the similar use of insults for sociability is clear. The following examples of male-female interaction show this process of jocular obscenity:

Barb: *You're worth shit, Jordan.*
Tom: *You're fucking right.*
Jerry (to Barb): *You got your cork* [tampon] *in?*
Barb: *Shut up.*
Tom: *Hey, Barb, you got your cork in?*
Barb: *Rich lost his balls. They were all eaten up by, they had real teeth marks in them from Tom Jordan.*
Tom: *Hey, fuck you.* (Tape transcript)

Or the following interchange between other boys and girls, who are standing by my car:

Gordy: Pam wasn't even born. She was hatched. . . . Hey, some bird crapped on your [car] *hood. Probably Pam.*
Pam (to Vicki): *Them guys are big bloopas.* [To Gordy, who is holding my camera] *I make a beautiful picture.*

Gordy: Get out of there, turkey. You'll probably break the lenses. (Tape transcript)

* * *

Gordy: I take after Dan Gregory.
Rod: They're both fems.
Gordy: Faggot.
Vicki: Suck on Rod's balls.
Gordy: Big cunt-fuck.
Vicki (to Gordy): *You and Rod are faggots.* (Tape transcript)

Although the insults in these selections seem overtly harsh and derogatory, they are not taken as such and the participants do not become seriously angry at each other. This talk is seen as linguistic art with each participant attempting to outdo the others in vividness of imagery. Because of the friendship context in which it is embedded, the talk is not defined as serious, although clearly it transmits messages about proper sexual behavior.

ATTACKING OTHERS:
INSULTS WHICH INSULT

Sometimes insults are spoken to hurt and are expressed from anger, rather than sociability. As noted above, the content of these remarks is similar to teasing insults, but their implications as pieces of interaction are quite different. Thus, a boy can kiddingly call a close friend a "fag", and scorn an immature teammate by hissing, "you're a fag, you know it", mincingly imitating his "effeminate" behavior. I found insults as the following intended hostilely: "You're a fucking ass", "I'll push your face in, Brandon, you little maggot", or "Roncalio, you're a wimp."

In contrast to other forms of insult, angry insults have less art and less complexity. They represent images from the heated heart rather than witty put-downs. Insults, like other verbal forms, seem more successfully created in tranquil (or at least pleasant) surroundings. Typically these angry insults are used singly, not building upon each other, as a single insult can express the full anger of a boy.

Although the angry exchange of abuse may be perceived as the prototypical form of insult behavior, it actually occurs fairly infrequently. Such abuse occurs either when the insulter has just experienced some major frustration or when the target has acted outside the legitimate boundary of preadolescent behavior—particularly when that individual is a low-status member of the group. Thus, the location of the insults is sharply limited by the social conventions of the group. Angry insults do not just happen, they happen in a particular interactional context and are influenced by participants' norms and expectations.

OBSCENE NARRATIONS: SHOWCASING ONE'S SELF

Because of their pointedness and brevity, insults tend to focus the attention of listeners on the target of the insult rather than on its speaker. However, even when considering insults it is apparent that the competent insulter receives social credit for linguistic sophistication and skill. The boy able at put-downs becomes feared and respected by his peers. There are other modes of obscene talk in which the focus is much more clearly on the speaker, and we now turn to two of these: joking and sexual instruction. In the former, the goal of the speaker is entertainment, which he produces by a subtle mastery of the sexual vernacular. The goal of the latter is enlightenment, which requires actual experience or at least the ability to present talk so as to convince others that one has this experience. In that both of these modes of talk require the speaker to present material in a logically sequenced and extended fashion, we speak of them as *narration.*

JOKES AS ENTERTAINMENT

Through their jokes, preadolescents are able to display their knowledge about sexual matters in an indirect fashion, incidentally permitting others to learn about sexual topics without direct questioning. The boy who can tell dirty jokes well and who has a large supply of these jokes is highly esteemed, and preadolescents compete with one another in their joking sessions:

Wiley: *See there was this guy, he really wanted to get,* [he giggles] *so he went up to this place and he went, "Can I get* (PAUSE)*." And he goes, "Go upstairs."*

Tim: *Get what? C'mon.*

Wiley: *Get laid.* [they giggle] *So he goes upstairs and waits there, and he saw a bag of potatoes, uh, tomatoes, so he started eating. So he goes, "Where's my girl?", so he goes, "Go back and wait", and so he eats the bag of tomatoes, and he goes back down, "Where's my girl!?", and he goes, "Go back upstairs and wait", and so he goes back up, finishes, see another bag of tomatoes, finishes them, and then he comes back down, "Where's my girl!! I'm sick of eatin' those tomatoes." "Those weren't tomatoes. These were last week's abortions."*

Steve: *Mine's about an abortion. There was this girl who really loved tomatoes. She went to a hospital —*

Tim: *Where does tomatoes come into abortion?*

Steve: *It's red.... She went to the hospital, she saw, oh, she was looking out the window, she saw some really red things: "Oh, they must be tomatoes." So she eats them. And the nurse says, "You know that thing you were eating you thought was a tomato?" She goes, "Tell me, tell me, tell me." "It was an abortion."*

Wiley: *This guy and this girl didn't know how to fuck, so they,* [loud giggling] *so they asked their doctor, and he goes, "Try, try running at each other." And it didn't work. "Try closing your eyes." So they run, run at each other, and the guy goes out the window,* [Laughter] *and he lands on his back* [Laughter] *and he goes, "Uhhhhh!", and he's dead practically, and so he goes, "You think you're bad, we're still trying to get your wife off the doorknob."* [Loud Laughter]

* * *

Tim: *There was a guy with a really high voice and wanted to, he wanted to have a low voice —*

Wiley: Oh, there's Mrs. Tataglia. Shut up! Shut up! Hi, Mrs. Tataglia. [She passes by us]

Tim: And everybody made fun of him because he had a really high voice. So he said, [in a very high, squeaky voice] "I want to get my voice lowered. I want to get my voice lowered." He said, "The only way you can get your voice lowered is to cut off your prick." And he said, "No, no. [High voice] No, no, no, no." So he goes away.

Steve: Lower or higher?

Tim: Lower. So he keeps on going to all the doctors that he can think of. So one day he's trying to get over this, and he goes to the beach, and he's swimming, and he sees a shark and says, [High voice] "Help. Help. A shark. [Low voice] He caught me." [Laughter]

Lewis: Now listen to this! Listen to this! There was this princess who everyone wanted to marry, and she loved ping-pong, and so she said the person with the ping-pong balls she liked best she would marry, and so one guy came in, and they were, and they were dented and cracked and everything. She said, "No good. Not you." The next guy came in and he had this gigantic, um, ping-pong balls and they're all gushy, and she said, "Wait a minute! These aren't ping-pong balls." And he said, "Oh! I thought you said King Kong balls." [No Laughter] Get it? (Taped transcript)

This transcript raises several issues about obscene joking among preadolescents. First, it is apparent that the jokes which are told in natural contexts are not carefully polished productions, such as we read in jokebooks. Oral narrative is considerably different in length, content, and style from written accounts (*see* Danielson, 1979). Yet, despite the linguistic ambiguity (particularly in regard to pronominal references), the audience is able to understand the content of the humor. This roughness is not only characteristic of preadolescent talk, but of all natural interaction, which when transcribed verbatim displays this rough-hewn quality. These texts, although from preadolescents still mastering their joke-telling skills, have the characteristics of adult informal talk in their grammatical carelessness and vivid imagery.

Second, it is clear that the performers are competing with each other to determine who can tell the best jokes, as measured by the laughter of the audience. Among preadolescents, it seemed that those jokes which relied upon sexual knowledge rather than linguistic competence, appeared to be the most successful. Lewis's joke which was based on the aural similarity of "ping-pong" and "King Kong" was the least successful of those in this joking session, whereas Wiley's joke about the couple who didn't know how to have intercourse received the most laughter. In this case the laughter served not only as a humor rating, but also as an indication by the members of the audience that they comprehended the physiology on which the joke was predicated. To laugh at such remarks indicates that one has understood it, and the laugh also serves as a release from the tension the listeners have while listening (would they understand the joke, or would they be shown to be immature?). The audience congratulates both the speaker and themselves on getting through the joke by their laughter. This dynamic is less important when the joke is "only" a pun.

Third, despite the possibilities for entertainment through the joke narrative, we should not ignore the possibilities for indirect learning. Tim's joke is particularly striking in this regard in that Tim has apparently confused the relationship between voice pitch and castration; his joke suggests that one can gain a lower voice through castration. Steve attempts to correct Tim, but when Tim rebuffs him, Steve remains quiet. Although in this case it is not clear whether Steve or the other members of the audience knew that Tim was wrong or whether they learned incorrect information, these jokes do suggest that sexual joking can be a source for preadolescent sexual knowledge. Through jokes one can acquire sexual facts from presumably knowledgeable peers without having to confront directly these delicate and sometimes embarrassing topics.

SEXUAL INSTRUCTION AS ENLIGHTENMENT

The learning that occurs in obscene jokes is typically indirect. However, more direct sexual communication also occurs, as when preadolescents pass along stories or accounts of sexual activity. As with joking, the narrator takes center stage and reaps the reward of the attention of his peers, as he tells his friends "the facts of life." While these accounts may have little basis in fact, they are listened to eagerly and in most cases are believed. For example, one preadolescent account told of a sexual education teacher whose method of instruction was rather progressive. As one boy recounted the story: "He'd have the boys go out. He'd have girls and he'd pull down his pants and he'd have girls come under his desk and suck his dick." This account instructs boys in the sexual state of the world and serves as a narrative device by which a particular boy can gain status in his peer group.

The contribution of talk to presentation of self can also be seen in the account of one preadolescent leader of how to "French" ("French kiss"), which he eagerly explains to two friends who listen avidly as I am driving them home:

Author (to Hardy): *How did you and Lindy* [his girl friend] *meet?*

Tom (laughing): *Frenching.... They first met in a telephone booth when she was frenching with the telephone.* [Tom giggles] *And then Hardy goes, "It ain't good for you to do it to a telephone." She goes, "Oh!" And Hardy didn't know how and he goes, "How do you french?" She goes, "Well, it's very confidential. But I could tell you. All you do is stick your tongue out, put some barbecue twang on it, lick your fingers, stick it in your butt, and lick the finger. That's good for it."* [Hardy giggles] *Remember, you have to stick it in the butt or it doesn't...the frenching doesn't twang. First of all you take your finger and you lick it, and you stick it in your butt and you lick it again.* [All giggle] *You stick it on the end of your tongue, make sure you get all the particles. And you go into a kissing mood.*

Hardy: *Ahhh! Ahhh! Ahhh!* [All laugh]

Tom: *That's good for a kissing mood.*

Hardy: *Ahhhh! Oh! Ah!*

Tom: *Now that's very good. That's very good there, Hardy. Hardy, that was excellent. Can you do that once more?*

Tom and Hardy (together): *Ahhhhhh!* [All laugh]

Tom: *That's very good, Hardy. I enjoy your act. But that ain't the way you do it.... OK, now you need the temptation. She says, "Ahhhhhh!", and you go, "What is ... THAT?" And then you, first of all, you gotta make sure you don't got no more "Ahhhk!" burps in your mouth.* [Hardy and Frank laugh] *It would be very crude to burp. I mean you make sure you don't have a cold, 'cause greenies going through there,* [Tom laughs] *going through her mouth would taste awful horseshit.* [All laugh]

Frank: *And one thing, don't spit while frenching.*

Tom: *And make sure...make sure you don't breathe out of your mouth* [All laugh] *unless you're doing mouth-to-mouth resuscitation. After all that frenching you just gotta do mouth-to-mouth to keep your air up. OK, now you take a squirt of your favorite after-shave. You rub it on your hair, and you rub it all around you. And you* [Tom giggles hysterically] *and you rub it all around. It sure feels good.* [More giggling] *Frank's choking under pressure. Listen,* [More hysterical laughter] *he's got a boner* [erection] *and he'd like to suck it off.*

Hardy: *Listen, listen, his lips are on it.*

Tom: *He's sucking.* [All laugh]

Frank: *Nuhhh. Nuhhh. Nuhhh.* [Joking, making almost mooing sounds, seemingly simulating a sexually excited woman]

* * *

Tom: *This is my second lesson of frenching. My second lesson to french. My first lesson was pretty rotten. My first lesson, that's only for juniors, but when you get up to Frank's age, you know about eight or ten,* [All laugh; Frank is twelve] *you get a boner when you start frenching. Like Frank. Talking about all that stuff gives him a boner. Oh, and now he's giving me the tongue action we all know.* [Frank laughs] *Frank, could I hear some of that tongue action, please?*

Frank: *Uh. Uh. Uh. Uh. Uh.*

Tom: *That is very good, Frank. Hardy, do you like to put anything in my act?*

Hardy: *No.*

Tom: *Only that he's got a, Ahhh!, stiff boner.* [Hardy giggles] *Frank. Frank ain't got stiff, uh-uh. Since we're talking about Hardy's girl friend, he's sorta, you know what I mean, doncha?*

Hardy: *No!* [Frank laughs]

Tom: *He sorta hit the jack, uh, hit the jack. Hit the jack-off, you know.*

Hardy: *No, I don't know.*

Tom: *I do.* [Tom and Hardy both laugh] *Well, anyway, I get to my second lesson. First, you walk in, you see a sexy girl in the telephone booth. You don't know what she is, just see the back of her. Gotta make sure she doesn't have a big butt, you know.... You just walk into the telephone booth, put your arm around her and say, "Hi." And she goes, "Uhhh! Ohhh, Hi."* [Tone is at first "surprised", then "feminine" and "willing"] *With her tongue around, wrapped around, wrapped around the microphone, her teeth, her teeth are chattering from so much shock. You just take your pants ...no...well.*

Hardy: *You take her pants.*

Tom: *Well, you just stick out your tongue, and you say* [Tom sings in a mock romantic fashion]: *"Want to, oh baby, you mean it, you let me under your skin."* (Taped transcript)

This is just a small portion of a much longer conversation among these three friends—just one of numerous conversations among one set of close friends in this community. It must be emphasized that there is nothing particularly unique about the dynamics of this snippet of talk, although Tom is a more accomplished narrator than many of his peers. Note how Tom manages to control the conversation, keeping himself in its center by providing sexual enlightenment to his friends, and he is accepted in this role as sexual talker.

Through conversations like this, boys learn traditional sex role attitudes and what is expected of them in theri social roles. It is not necessary to assume that they are acquiring sophisticated techniques of french kissing (although some of this specific learning does occur); more significantly, they are acquiring the means to present themselves as males in inforperative for preadolescents. In order to be considered a "normal" member of one's age cohort, a boy must learn to discuss sexual issues publically and without embarrassment. Boys acquire the rhetoric of sexuality and obscenity from friends slightly more advanced, who are themselves trying out their linguistic skills. Thus, it is in the interest of both parties not to embarrass the other. The teller is mastering skills of talk, while the listeners are learning the content and context of talk. A potential difficulty arises when a boy who is less advanced attempts sexual talk with those more skilled. For example, when Rod mentions that he has been going with his girl friend for eleven months, Hardy remarks, "That's almost enough time to have a baby," causing everyone to laugh at Hardy's error. Hardy, realizing his mistake, lamely attempts to recoup by adding, "Rod works slowly." The fact that Hardy was among friends meant that he could get away with a certain amount of ignorance without losing face or being condemned. Preadolescent friendships are thus particularly important in that they permit greater evaluative leeway than do other social relationships.

CONCLUSION

I have attempted to examine obscenity as talk, recognizing that this talk may take several forms. I divided obscene talk into talk which is directly responsive to interaction, as are insults, and obscene talk which stands alone—narrative. In the case of insults, the obscene talk is directed at an audience, and typically the spotlight on the speaker is less significant; narrative, on the other hand, does focus attention on the speaker who assumes the "performer" role. Further, within each of the categories there are several types of talk which differ in intent, tone, and permissible setting. Although the arguments presented in this article are speculative, they do, I think, point in valuable directions for future research. We must go beyond the notion that obscenity is merely words on a page, to be classified and listed in glossaries, to see how obscenity is used *in situ* both by our children and by ourselves.

FOOTNOTES

1. To indicate this phenomenon, fourteen twelve-year-olds and their parents from Sanford Heights were asked if they had heard several words which I had heard children in the community use. Parents typically were not aware of the slang of their offspring. Ten children reported having heard the expression "bite me," whereas only one parent knew of it or had heard his son use it. Twelve preadolescents knew what a "snuggie" was (a prank in which one sneaks up behind another child, and yanks at his underwear), but only two parents were aware of the prank. Nine children and one parent had heard of the prank "Ding Dong Ditch," in which a child will ring a stranger's doorbell and run away.

2. "Mooning" refers to the act of showing one's naked backside in public. In Beanville, it usually involved a group of boys pulling down their trousers and underwear in unison, while facing away from a major street. The "moon" takes no more than several seconds to complete.

3. All names used in this article are fictitious.

REFERENCES

Abrahams, Roger. 1970. *Deep Down in the Jungle.* Revised Edition. Chicago: Aldine.

Danielson, Larry. 1979. "Toward the Analysis of Vernacular Texts: The Supernatural Narrative in Oral and Popular Print Sources," *Journal of the Folklore Institute* 16:130-54.

Dollard, John. 1939. "The Dozens: Dialectic of Insult," *American Imago* 1:3-25.

Elliott, Robert C. 1960. *The Power of Satire.* Princeton, N.J.: Princeton University Press.

Fine, Gary Alan. 1979. "Small Groups and Culture Creation: The Idioculture of Little League Baseball Teams," *American Sociological Review* 44:733-45.

———. "Friends, Impression Management and Preadolescent Behavior," in S. R. Asher and J. M. Gottman (eds.), *The Development of Children's Friendships.* New York: Cambridge University Press, 1981. Pp. 29-52.

Goffman, Erving. 1959. *Presentation of Self in Everyday Life.* New York: Anchor.

Heyer, Diana. 1979. "Eeny Meeny Miney Mo: Violence and Other Elements in Children's Rhymes." Paper presented at the American Folklore Society Annual Meeting, Los Angeles.

Leary, James P. 1980. "White Ritual Insults," in H. B. Schwartzman (ed.), *Play and Culture.* Corning, N. Y.: Leisure Press.

Opie, Iona and Peter Opie. 1959. *The Lore and Language of Schoolchildren.* London: Oxford University Press.

Turner, Ian. 1972. *Cinderella Dressed in Yella.* New York: Taplinger.

Weinstein, Eugene and Paul Deutschberger. 1963. "Some Dimensions of Altercasting," *Sociometry* 26:454-66.

"I WANNA HOT DOG FOR MY ROLL"
SUGGESTIVE SONG TITLES

Laurence Urdang

In "You Know What," Allen Walker Read treated the subject of "veiled language" and discussed the substitution formulas *You know what*, *You know who*, *You know where*, etc.[1] Although language can be explicit, its suggestive nature yields some interesting observations; we must continually deal with metaphor and allusion. *You know what* and its variants are broad examples of this genre; a more subtle example is *it*, which serves as a suggestive substitute for sexual intercourse and for various parts of the male and female anatomy. As a corpus for examination, I have selected song titles chosen from a major (but not exhaustive) reference work on the subject.[2] Song titles and song lyrics are before us a good deal of the time. Some titles, e.g., *Indian Love Call*, *Song of India*, etc., have little to do with their lyrics; in fact, some have no lyrics at all. But a great number of popular songs composed in the period 1892-1942 have titles derived from the lyrics. In this study, however, I have ignored the lyrics entirely to concentrate on the titles. Thus, it may be found that in many cases the titles are suggestive but the lyrics are relatively straightforward. Also, I have not resorted to any tampering with the titles as one might be tempted to do, for example, by inserting a comma in *What Is This Thing Called, Love?*

I

It, being a pronoun, can scarcely be termed a "substitution formula"; yet it does serve the same function as *You know what* —often more explicitly— depending on the imagination of the listener (or reader). Thus, it may stand for 'sexual intercourse' in titles like these:

> *Can I Get It Now?* *
> *Do It Again*
> *Do It A Long Time, Papa*
> *Do It, Baby*
> *Do It If You Wanna*
> *Do It, Mr. So-and-So*
> *Everybody Does It In Hawaii*
> *Everybody Does It Now*
> *Get It Southern Style* *
> *He Wouldn't Stop Doing It*
> *How Do They/You Do It That Way?*
> *I Ain't Gonna Do It No More*
> *I Am Going To Have It Now* *
> *I Don't Want It Now* *
> *If It's Good Enough For The Birds and Bees*
> *If You Don't Do It Like I Want It Done*
>   *(I'll Get Somebody Else)*
> *If You Don't Give Me What I Want*
>   *(I'm Gonna Get It Somewhere Else)* *
> *I Got To Have It, Daddy* *
> *I Know How To Do It*
> *I Like The Way He Does It*
> *I Like What I Like Like I Like It* *
> *I Must Have It* *
> *I Wanna Get It* *
> *Mama Like To Do It*
> *That's The Way She Likes It* *
> *When I Can Get It* *
> *Why Can't You Do It Now?*
> *Woncha Do It For Me?*
> *You Can't Do It*
> *You Can't Get It Now* *
> *You Can't Guess How Good It Is* *
> *You Don't Like It—Not Much* *

---

*Items so marked appear in Sections I and II, for they can be ambiguously interpreted as a sexual organ.

*You Make Me Like It, Baby**
You've Got To Learn To Do It
*You've Got To Sell It**

II

Titles in which *it* substitutes for a sexual organ are:

Bring It Back, Daddy
Bring It On Down To My House
Bring It On Home
Bring It On Home To Grandma
Bring It With You When You Come
*Can I Get It Now?**
Daddy, Let Me Lay It On You
Don't Give It Away
Don't Lose It [virginity?]
Don't Name It
Don't Wear It Out[3]
Ease It To Me
Give It To Him
Give It To Me Good
Give It To Me Right Away
Givin' It Away
He Took It Away From Me [virginity?]
How Can I Get It (When You Keep
Snatching It Back)?
How Do I Know It's Real?
*I Am Going To Have It Now**
*I Don't Want It Now**
If That's What You Want, Here It Is
If You Don't Give Me What I Want
*(I'm Gonna Get It Somewhere Else)**
I Got It, You'll Get It
*I Got To Have It, Daddy**
*I Like What I LikeLike I Like It**
I'll Keep Sittin' On It (If I Can't Sell It)
I'm Sorry I Ain't Got It You Could Have
Had It If I Had It Blues
*I Must Have It**

It Must Be Hard
It Must Be Jelly
It's Right Here For You (If You Don't
    Get It— 'Tain't No Fault Of Mine)
It's The Talk Of The Town
It's Tight Like That
It Won't Be Long
I've Got What It Takes (But It Breaks
    My Heart To Give It Away)
I Wanna Get It*
I Want Every Bit Of It (I Don't Like It
    Second Hand)
Nobody's Using It Now
Put It Right Here (Or Keep It
    Right Out Of There)
Put It Where I Can Get It
Take It, 'Cause It's All Yours
Take It, Daddy, It's All Yours
Take It Right Back ('Cause I Don't
    Want It In Here)
Take Your Finger(s) Off It
Take Your Hands Off It
That's The Way She Likes It*
Throw It In The Creek (Don't Want
    Your Lovin' No More)
When I Can Get It*
Who'll Get It When I'm Gone?
Who Said, "It's Tight Like That"?
Wobble It A Little, Daddy
Won't You Get Off It, Please?
You Can't Get It Now*
You Can't Guess How Good It Is*
You Can't Have It All
You Can't Have It Unless I Give It To You
You Don't Like It—Not Much*
You Got To Wet It
You Make Me Like It, Baby*
You've Got To Sell It*

III

There are other suggestive terms which, in the present context, look quite explicit:

Blow, Gabriel, Blow
Blow, Katy, Blow
Blow My Blues Away
Blow That Horn
Climax Rag
Come, Josephine, In My Flying Machine
Comin' Thro' The Rye
Everybody Wants To See My Black Bottom
Fast-Fadin' Papa
Feeling My Way
For Sale (Hannah Johnson's Big Jackass)
Get Me Out Of That Crack
Holding My Own
Hot and Ready
Hot Nuts (Get 'Em From The Peanut Man)
I Ain't Givin' Nobody None
I Ain't Givin' Nothin' Away
I Ain't Gonna Sell You None
I Ain't Gonna Give Nobody None
   O' This Jelly-roll
I Ain't Gonna Let You See My Santa Claus
I Ain't Got Much, But What I Got, Oh, My!
I Can't Do That
I Go For That
I Just Want Your Stingaree
I'm Going To Show You My Black Bottom
I Needs A Plenty Of Grease In My Frying Pan
I Wanna Hot Dog For My Roll
Someone's Been Ridin' My Black Gal
Take Your Black Bottom Outside
Who'll Chop Your Suey When I'm Gone?
Who Played Poker [Poke 'er?] With Pocahontas?
Yes Flo (The Girl Who Never Says No)
You Ain't Gonna Feed In My Pasture Now

> *You Can Dip Your Bread In My Gravy,*
> *   But You Can't Have None Of My Chops*
> *You Can't Get To Heaven That Way*
> *You Done Tore Your Pants With Me*
> *You Go To My Head*
> *You'll Never Miss Your Jelly Till*
> *   Your Jelly Roller's Gone*

IV

Thing serves almost as broad a purpose as *it*:

> *Daddy, Don't Put That Thing On Me Blues*
> *Daddy, You've Done Put That Thing On Me*
> *Do That Thing*
> *I Can't Use That Thing*
> *I Kept On Rubbing That Thing*
> *I Like That Thing*
> *I Love That Thing*
> *What Is This Thing Called, Love?* [with liberties]
> *You've Got That Thing*
> *You've Got To Save That Thing*
> *You Wonderful Thing*

V

Finally, there are the somewhat more obscure canting ambiguities:

> *Back Water Blues* [also known as
> "Retromingent Blues"?]
> *Ballin' The Jack*
> *Daddy, You've Been A Mother To Me*
> *Everybody Wants My Tootelum*
> *My Old Daddy's Got A Brand New Way To Love*

Of course, there are many others, particularly those that employ the words *jazz* and *jive*, which have (or once had) entirely different referents in Black English from those in White English.

Suggestive songs (like *She Said No*, in which the coyly risqué banter between a man and a woman is finally revealed as relating entirely to his attempts at selling her a subscription to *Liberty* magazine) and suggestive popular records (like *John and Marsha*, in which a man and woman utter one another's names in tones of increasingly feverish passion) depend on the fertility (and lubricity) of the listener's imagination. It may be interesting to explore whether such records have ever been banned from record shops or radio the way current censors ban books and magazines whose offensiveness rests in the minds of their readers. Such explicit (or assumed as explicit) recordings as one rendition of *The Old Oaken Bucket*, rumored to have contained specific obscenities, are rare.

FOOTNOTES

1. Originally presented at the Ninth Annual Conference of Linguistics, sponsored by the Linguistic Circle of New York, on March 14, 1964. First published in *Language*, April 1964; reprinted in *ETC.*, September 1964; reprinted, in a slightly modified version, in *VERBATIM*, Volume II, Number 3, December 1975, and in *VERBATIM: Volumes I & II*, Essex, Conn., 1978.

2. Brian Rust. *Jazz Records.* New Rochelle: Arlington House, 1978; 2 volumes, xic + 1966 pp.

3. This may be in the same category as, "It looked so nice out this morning that I decided to leave it out all day."

Editor's Notes

• As for *Hot Nuts*, above, for the past 26 years, Doug Clark's "Hot Nuts" band has enchanted fraternity parties throughout the U.S.A. Described by David Zucchino (in the Detroit *Free Press* magazine, 22 July 1979, pp. 19-25) as "titillating, vile, insipid, lascivious, juvenile, vulgar, trashy and foul," the "Hot Nuts" have been charming their college audiences with suggestive songs like "The Gay Caballero," "Milk the Cow," "My Ding-A-Ling," and lyrics such as "Roses are red and ready for plucking, girls out of high school are ready for . . . college." (Information supplied by Marie Helfrich.)

● Found in G. Legman's *The Limerick*, p. 456:

Girl (to music-store clerk): "Have you got 'Hot Lips' on a 10-inch Decca?"

Clerk: "No, but I've got hot nuts on a 9-inch pecker."

Girl: "Is that a record?"

Clerk: "Well, it's better than average."

● Also, related to *thing*, above: in a sketch of the "Benny Hill Show," there hangs a poster on the wall announcing a science fiction movie: **THE THING WITHOUT A THING.**

A RECIPE FOR THE FESTIVE SEASON
TURKEY WITH POPCORN DRESSING
(Serves 12)

One 15-lb. Turkey	*2 Cups Bread Crumbs*
Seasonings	*2 Diced Onions*
1 Can Bouillon	*3 Cups Popcorn*
½ Cup Diced Celery	

Method: Stuff turkey and bake at 325° about five hours, or until the popcorn blows the turkey's ass clear across the room.

A RECIPE FOR ALL SEASONS
BANANA BREAD
(Serves 2)

4 Laughing Eyes	*2 Milk Containers*
4 Loving Arms	*1 Fur-lined Mixing Bowl*
2 Well-shaped Legs	*1 Banana and 2 Nuts*

Method: Looking into laughing eyes, spread well-shaped legs slowly. Squeeze and massage milk containers very gently, until fur-lined mixing bowl is well greased. Check frequently with middle finger. Add banana and gently work in and out until well creamed. Cover with nuts and sigh with relief. Bread is done when banana becomes soft. Be sure to wash mixing utensils, and don't lick the bowl.

Note: If bread rises, leave town.

POTENTIATION OF A SPANISH INSULT

Mario E. Teruggi

Hijo de puta, "son of a whore," is undoubtedly the most common personal insult in Spanish, and it is found in the classical literature of Spain as the contracted form *hideputa*. Of course, the formula is found in other languages, either straight or edulcorated, like *son of a bitch*, *son of a gun* and similar expressions in English.

In *hijo de puta* the emphasis is placed on the person whose mother is accused of having been a harlot; but, very often, the interest is displaced towards the mother herself, and the insulting formula is changed to *la puta que te parió*, "the whore that bore you." The English translation is very weak because there is no satisfactory equivalent of *parir*, since "to bear, to give birth, to foal" or "to calve" all lack the force and feeling of rudeness of the Spanish verb.

La puta que te parió, at least in Argentina, is now more frequently heard than *hijo de puta.* With the minor change of the dative pronoun *te* for the neuter *lo* (*la puta que lo parió*), it has an everyday use to discharge one's wrath, annoyance or ill humor against all sorts of inanimate objects, minor accidents or difficulties that stand in our way. The sentence is often reduced to a mere *¡Que lo parió!* which is also employed to denote surprise or astonishment.

The frequent use of *la puta que lo parió* has, pebble-like, reduced much of its aggressiveness by the rounding off of its cutting edges and corners. That is the reason why, when we are really mad at somebody, we resort to two insults in order to give full vent to our indignation, saying in the same breath *¡Hijo de puta y la puta que te parió!* It is to be observed that the equivalents of *motherfucker* and *motherfucking* are not used in Spanish, although they would be perfectly understood and can be heard in Mexico (*¡Chinga tu madre!*, etc.).*

Luckily for the people who want or need to utter their verbal aggressions with superlative strength, the Spanish language offers the possibility of raising the insult to a higher power, so to speak. In Argentina the maximum reinforcement is found in the utterance *¡La reputísima madre que te recontra mil parió!* which requires some explaining.

The prefix *re-*, as in English and many other languages, is used in Spanish to imply repetition or duplication. *Putísima* is the superlative of *puta*, here used as an adjective to be translated as "most whorish." *La reputísima madre* then means "twice the (your) most whorish mother." As to *recontra*, it means "twice against" (*you* is implied) and is commonly used as a reply to an insult by simply muttering *que te recontra*, connoting "the same to you but twice." In the insult we are here considering, as a final reinforcement, the noun *mil*, "one thousand," is added to *recontra*.

Thus, the whole sentence can be translated: "The twice most whorish mother that bore you again and again one thousand times!"

In a mathematical approximation, if **W** stands for "whorish" and **B** for "bore," the insult formula would be:

$$\text{Insult} = 2 \times W^2 \text{ mother} \ldots B\,(1+1) \times (1000)$$

Actually, $(1+1) \times (1000)$ is not understood in the sense that the mother gave birth 2000 times to the same child but as a definite reinforcement of the mother's whorishness.

In a nutshell: the mother that bore you was twice 2000 times squared a whore.

One wonders if other tongues have this possibility of numerically increasing common insults. Of course, one could simply say, "Your mother was a billion times a whore," but it is the multiplying, doubling and squaring that, in a long crescendo, fills the utterer's mouth with a resounding and cathartic sonority.

---

*Larry M. Grimes. 1971. El Tabú Lingüístico: Su Naturaleza y Función en el Español Popular de México. Cuernavaca, CIDOC Cuaderno Nº 64.

SIGMA EPSILON XI
SEX IN THE TYPICAL UNIVERSITY CLASSROOM

Don L. F. Nilsen

If you are wondering where to find sex in the typical American university, you need only look as far as the classroom desks. There you will find it in all its lurid detail, carved neatly into the woodwork. For the past three years now my university students and I have been reading our desks as well as our texts. And we have collected an amazingly large and diverse sample of creative graffiti. We were expecting sex to be one of the important preoccupations, but we did not realize the extent of its significance until we counted and found that approximately one out of every five pieces of graffiti related in some way to sex.

Most of what we have collected is going into a textbook showing how creativity works in language, but that which is sex-related is so entertaining that we were afraid people would concentrate on the content instead of the language processes. Besides with censors being what they are, a textbook containing such choice tidbits would probably never make it into the classroom. But believing in what the National Council of Teachers of English calls, "The student's right to his own language," we did not want to see all of this creativity disappear as the new formica-top desks replace the old wood ones. Therefore all the sex-related graffiti are being brought together in this article and what follows are uncensored samples of classroom graffiti, written but not signed, by various university students. The collection is a testament not only to college students' interest in sex but also to their ingenuity and their creativity.

To illustrate the innovative aspect of university graffiti, consider those sex-related graffiti where a word is broken in the wrong place, as in **It is better to have loved a short man, than never to have loved a tall** or **I like ass bestus**, where in the first case the *t* which belongs to the first word (*at all*) is placed on the second word instead (*a tall*), and in the second case the single word (*asbestos*) is divided in an unexpected way (*ass bestus*), which does not reflect the true make-up of the word.

Not only is there creativity at the word (or morphemic) level, but there is also great creativity at the sentence (or syntactic) level, as in **Use erogenous zone numbers**, where an expression is expanded by the addition of another word (*erogenous*), or as in **Have fun kids; it's later on you'll think**, where the expression "It's later than you think" is altered to give the new expression an entirely different effect. A graffiti dialogue goes:

> HE: *How do you like Kipling?*
> SHE: *I don't know, you naughty boy, I've never kippled!*

In this example the play on words is based on the *-ing* of Kipling's name. This has the same form as the *-ing* which marks a present participle, and therein lies the punning potential of Kipling's name. It is also possible to change the part of speech of a word without adding an ending at all. Everybody knows that in *meat loaf* the first word, *meat*, is a modifier of the noun *loaf*, but by changing the sentence, it is possible to make *meat* into a noun subject with *loaf* being the verb, as in **Don't let your meat loaf!**

Good graffiti writers are very careful in their word choices, with these choices more often than not being made on the basis of shock value. In such graffiti as **One man's queen is another man's sweathog** and **I did it in the privacy of my own crysalis while in metastasis**, the graffiti writer begins with set expressions and makes lexical substitutions into these expressions to change the tone, but in this case not the subject, of the expressions. This jarring relationship between particular words and the rest of the sentence can also be seen in **Let's be lewd** and in **Lassie is a bitch**.

One of the most common techniques of graffiti writers is the word play, or pun. Sometimes the word play is based on words which sound the same but are spelled differently, as in **Masseurs are people who knead people, Report obscene male — to obscene female** or **Go Hawaiian: Give your guy a lai,** where the play is based on the *need/knead*, *male/mail*, and *lay/lai* relationship. At other times the pun is based on a word which has two senses even though it has only a single spelling, as in **To go together is blessed; to come together is divine, It's all right to love a nun sometimes; just don't get into the habit, Coed dorms promote campus unrest** or **Raise the wages of sin.** One of the most common puns among graffiti writers is based on the multiple meanings of *screw* and related ideas as the following examples illustrate: **Alimony: The screwing you get for the screwing you got.** — **If Nixon would do to his wife what he's doing to the country, she'd be a lot happier.** — **Life is like a dick; when it's soft you can't beat it, and when it's hard you're getting fucked.** — **The earth is a whore and the human race is fornicating on her.** — **If you want a good screw, go to the local hardware store.** — **There are no virgins left; society has screwed us all.**

Sometimes the graffiti writer tries to force the reader into an indiscretion rather than writing the indiscretion himself. No one can read **Smuck fog** without being aware of the impending danger. There is even more potential for misreading something like **I am not the fig plucker but the fig plucker's son, and I can pluck figs until the fig plucker comes.** And the choice of the last word in **Nixon is a Cox sacker** was certainly as much on phonological as on semantic grounds. I am beginning to wonder if even such a harmless term as **Huck Finn** when written on a desk might have been written there in the hope that someone would mispronounce it.

University graffiti are not only full of lexical and phonological innovations, but logical innovations as well. Especially in the area of sex-related graffiti implication is common. What does the *it* refer to in **Motorcycles do it in the dirt?** Why would anyone want a person to **Vote for horizontal phone booths?** Just what kind of experience is being referred to in **I'm just an inexperienced little thing—looking for experience?** How would the graffiti reader know that the answer to the question **What goes in hard and comes out soft and sticky?** is "Bubble-gum"? What high-frequency word has been omitted from **Yuck rhymes with: muck, duck, luck, buck, cluck, stuck, truck, tuck, etc.**? It is interesting that this same high-frequency word has also been omitted from *Webster's Third New International (Unabridged) Dictionary*. And exactly what is implied by the very slight alteration of the last word in **A jug of wine, a waterbed, and WOW!**? What is meant by the *something* of the following formula?

$$\text{♂} = 0$$
$$\text{♂} - \text{♀} = 0$$
$$\text{♀} - \text{♂} = 0$$
$$\text{♀} + \text{♀} = 0$$
$$\text{♂} + \text{♂} = 0$$
$$\text{♀} + \text{♂} = something$$

And finally, consider the implications of the following three-fourths of a poem:

I told him how to do it, how to hold his lips just so.
I told him to be ready when I gave the signal go.
He tried his best to please me, and he did as he was told.

The graffiti reader at this point is not sure exactly what is being implied, but he certainly assumes that it has something to do with sex, and is therefore surprised to read the last line:

But it's hard to learn to whistle, when you're
only three years old.

What impressed us most about university sex-related graffiti was the number of subjects treated. They run the gamut from the perfectly acceptable topics of marriage, family life, dirty old men, and beauty through the controversial issues like birth control, overpopulation, and women's lib, and even extend into taboo areas like fetishes, sex-related diseases, homosexuality, incest, masturbation, prostitution, swinging, rape, and oral sex. These subjects will be treated in pretty much this same climactic order so that the reader can adjust gradually to the tone and wording, which in some cases may be shocking.

Marriage is a fairly frequent subject and puns are a frequent device, as in **Women without horse sense become nags** and **Statistics show great increases in marriages. Life seems to be just a marry chase.** Other statements are based on unusual logic that ranges from tautology, as in **Marriage is the prime cause of divorce**, to incongruity, as in **Stamp out first marriages.** In between there are all kinds of logical strangenesses like **A wife who can't cook and won't is better than one who can't cook and will, Don't marry for money: you can borrow it cheaper,** or **The marriage ceremony is a knot which is tied by your tongue, but which cannot be untied by your teeth.** Most of the marriage statements have a negative tone to them, as in **Let our priests marry; it will give them a working description of hell.**

To graffiti writers, the family is not an institution above criticism, as can be seen in **He who is henpecked may lend ear to other chicks, Richard Nixon can't stand pat,** or **Night Student, where is your wife now?** But in their usual technique of semantic inversion (putting good words in bad environments and bad words in good environments), writers reverse some of the old stereotypes, as in **I'm not a dirty old man, I'm just a sexy senior citizen** and **Bridge the generation gap. Turn an old man on.** The subject of beauty is also susceptible to semantic inversion, as in **Donna shaves her legs with a chain saw, You were never lovelier—and I think it's a shame!** and **Figures show that the average woman spends 75% of her time sitting down.**

We now come to the controversial issues like birth control. Some of the graffiti are in support of having children, as illustrated by **Support National Motherhood Week: Make one today!** or **May all your hang-ups be drip-dry** and **May all your consequences be little ones.** But most graffiti about having children are about not having them, as the following examples indicate: **Birth control is a high fly. — Make love, not children. — Orange juice for birth control; not before or after, but instead of. — Support planned parenthood now — before Mary has another lamb. — Tiny Tim wears a chastity belt. — Beware of Greeks bearing Trojans. — Nixon, pull out like your father should have. — The trouble with Nixon is that when he** withdraws, he only sticks it in again someplace else. — True planned parenthood is kidnapping. — Pope Paul leads a rhythm band. — Accidents cause people. — Familiarity breeds contempt — and children.

Much of the graffiti supporting birth control make special reference to "that pill," "the pill," or "a pill," which need not be further identified, as in: **Gather ye rosebuds while ye may, but take that little pill each day.** — **Pop the pill for pleasure.** — **Pope Paul pops the pill.** — **The pill: a gadget to be used in any conceivable circumstance.** — **A pill in time saves nine...months.** — **A pill a day keeps the stork away.**

When the unwanted pregnancy occurs, graffiti writers advise **Look homeward pregnant angel.** They ask **Would you be more careful if it were you who got pregnant?** And on the subject of overpopulation they write **Overpopulation begins in the home, Overpopulation is everybody's baby,** and **Children should be seen and not had.** But even though university students seem to be for birth control (or at least planned parenthood), and are against overpopulation, most of them seem also to be against abortion, as shown by **Abortion is hard on little babies.** — **Abortion: Legalized murder.** — **Abortion is murder.** — **Abortion: Pick on somebody your own size!** and **Aren't you glad you weren't aborted?**

College students are as confused as everyone else is about the feminist movement, as shown by the question **Are the women in this country really revolting?** The male chauvinist point of view is apparent in **Women's lib is okay— I just wouldn't want my sister to marry one, There's only two ways to handle women, and no one knows either one of them, Join Male Chauvinism!, Rise up sisters!**—*Rather difficult for a sister, isn't it?*, and **UNI women read books.** One example refers to the movement itself in **Women's Lib is a Msleading organization.** Compare this to the graffito representing the women's viewpoint **Women's Lib is NOW.** Other graffiti representing the female viewpoint include **Pray to God and SHE will help you, A Woman's work is never done—or recognized, or paid for, or honored, or commended...,** **Beware chauvinists! Today's pig is tomorrow's bacon** and **You'll never be the man your mother**

was. Perhaps these last examples were not written by advocates of women's rights because they are rather flippant in tone, and it seems that most feminists are more serious. But at any rate, the male chauvinists and the women's libbers would probably both rally to the single graffito **Ban the bra!** but for entirely different reasons.

The bra is not the only article of clothing that appears in university graffiti. Some clothing goes up, as in **Up with skirts** and **Up the mini.** Other clothing goes down, as in **Down with pants!, Down with fig leaves, Down with zippers,** and **Hemlines are coming down; expect to hear some thighs of relief,** with this last graffito obviously having been written from the female point of view. And there are still other references to clothes, as in **Mickey Mouse loves the Minnie,** and **Sigmund's wife wore Freudian slips.** There are also graffiti that refer to no clothing at all, as in **Shame on the naked truth,** and **Those who sleep in the raw are in for a nude awakening.**

Various types of fetishes are also represented in graffiti. Clothing is mentioned in such graffiti as **George Washington wore ribbons in his wig,** and **Barry Goldwater wears pink underwear.** A shoe fetishist is defined as **A man who looks downward when he hears, "Gee, what a pair!"** There are also graffiti representing fetishes for various parts of the body. For knees there is **I'm in love with your knees!**; for thighs there is **Is the thigh the limit?** and **Able Mable Thunderthighs**; for the lips there is **Pat is a frog, cuz that is how he kisses**; for the derrière there is **Lady Godiva's ride made her cheeks rosy,** and **Anal erotics are behind us all the way.** It will probably surprise no one that the part of the anatomy most referred to, directly or indirectly, is the breasts. The following are representative: **Mother Earth is not flat. — Eva Gabor wears a training bra. — I don't care if your name *is* Napoleon, get your hand out of my blouse. — Raquel Welch wears falsies. — Aunt Jemima is stacked. — Raquel Welch is a stuffed shirt. — Hugh Hefner keeps abreast of the times. —** 👫 **Two men walking abreast.**

Hair is also an important topic for graffiti writers. Referring to the type that grows on the top of the head there is

Brunettes forever, Redheads are for everyone, and The average Blonde has an I.Q. equaling that of a medium-sized radish — from experiments conducted at the University of Michigan. The other type of hair is referred to in Puberty is a hair-raising experience, Richard Nixon is a pubic hair in the teeth of America, and Lower the age of puberty. And since we are in that region of the body, we will add two rather astute observations: It takes leather balls to play rugby and Santa Claus has pop-corn balls.

It is as if Santa had a disease of some sort — and indeed there are sex-related diseases that appear in the writings of graffitists: VD is God's perfect punishment for promiscuity, VD: The gift that keeps on giving, and VD is nothing to clap about. In the graffiti there is also reference to The girl from Emphysema, and it is rumored that Books give you syphilis. But there is a positive side as well, as when you are admonished to Hire the morally handicapped, or when you are told that Mononucleosis can be fun. It is heart-warming to know that Moby Dick and Grape Nuts are not social diseases. Probably the sex-related illness that affects the most university students is menstruation. Kotex is defined as Carpeting in the playroom, and Tampax as Manhole covers.

Men's sexuality received a small amount of desk space, as in Zap! You're sterile, and as when the three stages of man are listed in chronological order as Tri-weekly, Try weekly, and Try weakly! We were surprised to find no graffiti mentioning frigidity. Perhaps it has something to do with the age of the writers that they were more concerned with virginity, as the following illustrate: Chaste makes waste. — Virtue is its own punishment. — Have you heard about Joe and his girl friend? He called her Virge for short, but not for long. — Olive Oil is not a virgin — Sweet Pea is popeye's kid. — To the virgins: Thanks for nothing. — Virginity can be cured. Pledge yourself now. Give until it hurts. — Virginity is like a bubble on the ocean — one prick and it's gone forever. — Virginity is not incurable. — Fighting for peace is like screwing for chastity. — Mrs. Robert Kennedy is a virgin. — Impatient virgins never die. They just lose their cherry pie.

This last example is a play on the expression, "Old soldiers never die, they just fade away," but the graffiti writer has taken so many liberties with the expression that it is difficult to see the relationship to the original. Two graffiti that are superficially quite similar are **James Bond is a virgin** and **Grumpy is a virgin**. These two graffiti seem to be the same except that different names are used in the subject position. There is a further similarity in that these names are both masculine, even though there is an incompatibility between males and the concept of virginity. But logically, these two statements are very different. The people being referred to are not random males. James Bond was chosen because of all males he is probably the least likely to actually be a virgin. Grumpy was chosen because of all males he is probably the most likely to actually be a virgin, and furthermore, this explains why he is Grumpy.

One of the favorite sex topics of graffiti writers is homosexuality. Sometimes the expression *homosexual* or *homo* is written into the graffito, as in **My mother made me a homosexual, bless her heart**, or as in the dialogue *Enke is a homo. — He is not. — I am too*, or as in the misinterpreted syntactic and semantic graffito, **My mother made me a homosexual. — Would she make me one too if I brought her the yarn?** At other times the word *gay* is used, normally as a pun, as in **Ben Gay is hot for your body**, or **The Gay Nineties took place in Greenwich Village**, or **Go gay!** and **Nobody loves you when you're old and gay**. There is even a graffito poem that is based on the ambivalent meaning of *gay* as well as on many other words that have both sexual and nonsexual connotations:

> *I'm so happy, I'm so gay*
> *That's cause I come twice a day.*
> *I'm your mailman.*
> *Knock your knockers,*
> *Ring your bells.*
> *Gee, I bet you think I'm swell.*
> *I can come in any weather*
> *Cause my bags are made of leather.*
> *I don't need no keys or locks,*
> *I just slip it in your box.*
> *I'm your mailman.*

There are other homosexual terms used like the *queer* in **I'm near enuf if you're queer enuf; I'll die laughing while you die trying**, and the *faggot* in **Support Birth Control! Become a faggot**. At other times there is no direct mention, only an implication, as in **My mom dresses me funny**, or **Denny Hoffman loves Tom Chapman; strange but true**. Then there are the homosexual graffiti where there is a certain logical incompatibility, as in **Tiny Tim wears a cross-your-heart bra**, and **My Aunt Harold has a problem**.

Let us now turn to some lesbian graffiti. There is **Have you thanked a lesbian today for not contributing to the world's population explosion?**, **George Wallace is a Jane**, and **All men at Harvard are homosexual except one, and he's a lesbian**. The expression from the lesbian vocabulary that is used most often is *dildo*. There is the **Dildo depth gauge**, the **Dildo floodlight attachment**, and for Christmas we are admonished to give a **Sheaffer pen and dildo set**. But the most mind-boggling reference to this item is the **Goodyear dildo blimp**, and the most homosexual of all is the simple and succinct autosexual statement **I love Me!!!** which brings us to the subject of masturbation.

Graffiti writers may pun in this area: **Do you think masturbation will get out of hand?** They may imply: **If it hangs, fondle it**. They may metaphorize: **An acid trip is mental masturbation followed by spiritual orgasm**. Or they may hypothesize: **I think I've fallen in love with my hand.** — *Thank God you're not ambidextrous*. The reader must supply his own interpretation to this last graffito. If a person were ambidextrous, would this introduce a third party in a love triangle or would it just provide a situation with too much sex (if that's possible) or what?

The most salient quality of incest graffiti is the recurring theme of family togetherness. These graffiti are typically very pleasant and positive in tone: **Incest: A game the whole family can play.** — **Incest and charity are alike; they both start at home.** — **Incest: A family affair.** — **Incest begins at home.** — **Incest is best.** — **Incest is best kept in the family.** — **Incest is like watching TV—the whole family does it.** We found only one exception to this light, airy treatment of incest: **Oedipus was a mother fucker!**

Most of the graffiti relating to prostitution are merely language play with the value system of the writer not reaching the surface. In **Casanova was a pimp**, and **Joe Namath is a pimp for Truman Capote**, there is merely a surprising incompatibility between the subject and the activity being referred to. In **A madam is one who offers vice to the lovelorn** there is a pun on *advice*. Most of the graffiti either take prostitution for granted, as in the above examples, or else are in favor of it, as in **Be ready to serve your country; be a call girl!** and **Support free enterprise; legalize prostitution.** The only statement that put prostitution in a negative light was **Pollution, like prostitution, is any departure from purity.**

There was an occasional reference to swinging, such as **John loves Mary; too bad he's married to Sue**, **Love thy neighbor, but don't get caught**, and **Jane sits home while Tarzan swings**, but judging from the small number of statements that we found on this subject, swinging is not very important to university students. Rape, on the other hand, is fully represented. In a graffito that has something of the same effect as the end of Shakespeare's *King Lear*, a dirty old man is defined as **a person who rapes a deaf-mute, and then cuts off her fingers so she won't tell.** Then there was the simple incongruity, **Rape— I'll vote for that**, the understatement **Rape is inconsiderate**, and the pun **Rape is an unnegotiated peace.** The definition of Russian Rape as **Ivan Toratitov** has syntactic ramifications since the name "Toratitov" can be viewed as either one word or four. Sometimes there is a comparison of rape with seduction, which after all, have certain aspects in common. For example, there's **Patience is the difference between rape and seduction**, and **Rape: Seduction without salesmanship.** One rape graffito which seems to make sense yet doesn't quite is **Fighting for peace is like raping for war!** Perhaps the writer copied it from **Fighting for peace is like raping for love**, but got confused.

Since graffiti are written anonymously, even a subject as taboo as oral sex can be treated. We are told to **Try to be a**

sucksess, and **Milking machines suck.** We are even told that **There is no gravity; the world sucks.** And we are furthermore told that **Nixon had to see** *Deep Throat* **three times before he got it down pat,** and in pseudo-story-telling form we are told, **Meanwhile back at the oasis the Arabs were eating their dates.** We can see the effect of advertising on graffiti writers in **If he kissed you once will he kiss you again? Be sure! Use Vespray Feminine Hygiene Deodorant.**

Commercials have had an important effect on sex-graffiti in general. The *sex* in **A day without sex is like a day without sunshine,** and SEX : **Breakfast of champions** was not there in the original versions, nor was *Spanish Fly* in the original version of **Spanish Fly makes better loving through chemistry.** In some cases the product name remains a part of the graffito, as in **Love is like Jello; there's always room for more,** and **Colonel Sanders' wife is a cock raiser** and **Colonel Sanders says "The only way to get a better piece of chicken is to be a rooster."** What better endorsement could he have for his "fingerlicking" product? Then there are the graffiti which have commercial overtones in a more general way, as in **This chair is rated G(IRLS),** **Sin now—pay later!** and **You may not approve of free love, but you've gotta admit the price is right.**

In comparing graffiti about love and sex, it appears that the love graffiti are typically more tender, as in **Lay down, I think I love you.** − **Love's just not in the making, but in the knowing.** − **Lovers, like bees, enjoy a life of honey.** − **Buy land, but invest in love.** − **Milk-drinkers make better lovers.** − **I never met a nympho I couldn't love.** − **Love 'em all; you might miss a good one,** or the succinct and somewhat poetic **Love is neato peato,** and finally the philosophical,

If you love something, set it free.
If it returns, it's yours.
If not, it never was.

Sometimes the love graffito is a bit more flippant, as when we are told that **Sweden is a nice place to visit, but I would not want to love there,** **If loving is an art, we should all aspire to be Picasso,** and **Remember Girls, the way to a man's heart** is through the left ventricle. Or when we are let in on the following dialogue: **Love is of God.** — *God?* — **Yes, God.** — **Well, I'll be damned!** — **Probably.**

There are some negative love graffiti, as in **It's better to have loved and lost** — much better, **Love is a four-letter word,** and **Love isn't the answer; it's the problem.** But the preponderance of love graffiti is positive and the general philosophy of graffiti writers seems to be **Make love, not war,** or better put, **When the Power of Love overcomes the Love of Power, there will be peace.**

The graffiti related to sex in general have a similarly positive tone to them. Some of it is based on puns like **Of all my relations, I like sex best, Sex isn't good for one; but it's great for two,** or **Into the valley of death rode the sex hungry.** Some have a special phonological ring, as **Sex is emotion in motion.** Some relate to university life like **Preserve wildlife** — throw a party, **Conserve water; shower with your steady, Leda's lover is a quack,** or **My place or yours?** Some graffiti are negative (or fake negative) assertions like **Too much sex affects the vision,** or **Sex is like a snowfall** — You're never sure how many inches you'll get. Some are positive assertions, like **Candy is sweet, but sex doesn't rot your teeth,** and **Sex is good exercise.** Some are in the form of questions, like **Is there sex after death?** or **Remember when the air was clean and sex was dirty?** Indeed, just as there seems to be no end to the variety of sex, there seems to be no end to the variety of sex graffiti. And the exciting thing about it is that it's constantly being created all over so that by the time this is published, there will already be new examples just waiting to be collected.

ACKNOWLEDGMENT

My appreciation goes to Frank J. D'Angelo, one of the greatest graffiti collectors of all time, for his help on this article.

[*Editor's Note*: This article was submitted in March, 1977; thus the many dated anti-Nixon graffiti.]

OH, SCHICK!
A GUIDE FOR THE PERPLEXED

Reinhold Aman

You know how it is. Someone or something gets you angry, and you want to hiss or blast a soul-relieving *Oh, shit!* But the holier-than-thou buggers won't let you, stigmatizing you as "vulgar" if you did say in public what they say in private.

What can you do other than *Shex!* this and *Fex!* that? Well, you can use other words beginning with the *sh*-sound. In addition to draining off your anger verbally, while maintaining a civil tongue, you can play one-upmanship with your critics who never thought you were that cultured. To achieve this, use the name of a famous person that begins with the *sh*-sound. The famous folks below are from a broad spectrum of professions and can be selected to suit the source of your anger. For example, if your Toyota is on the fritz, shout "Oh, Shigemitsu!" If a poet or lawyer annoys you, a heartfelt "Oh, Shapiro!" will do fine. Your FM radio fades while you are listening to Russian music? "Oh, Shostakovich!" Some would-be Tarzan snatched your girl friend? "Oh, Schwarzenegger!" will soothe your soul. You get the drift. Here are some examples:

Oh, Schacht!	Oh, Schweitzer!	Oh, Sholokhov!
Oh, Schick!	Oh, Shakleton!	Oh, Shostakovich!
Oh, Schicklgruber!	Oh, Shaftesbury!	Oh, Shute!
Oh, Schiller!	Oh, Shakespeare!	Oh, Sienkiewicz!
Oh, Schleiermacher!	Oh, Shapiro!	Oh, Staudinger!
Oh, Schliemann!	Oh, Shastri!	Oh, Steinmetz!
Oh, Schmidt!	Oh, Shays!	Oh, Stern!
Oh, Schnitzler!	Oh, Shelley!	Oh, Stieglitz!
Oh, Schopenhauer!	Oh, Shepard!	Oh, Stinnes!
Oh, Schubert!	Oh, Sheraton!	Oh, Strauss!
Oh, Schurz!	Oh, Sherrington!	Oh, Streicher!
Oh, Schuschnigg!	Oh, Shigemitsu!	Oh, Stülpnagel!
Oh, Schwarzenegger!	Oh, Shockley!	Oh, Stursa!

Try it. It's fun. No Schick!

CATULLUS XLII

Joseph Salemi

The following poem is a *flagitatio*, a sustained insult directed against
one person—in this case a prostitute who has taken the poet's *codicillos*
or writing tablets.

> All my verse feet come together, all wherever
> you may be:
> Some filthy harlot's got my notebook, and
> won't give it back to me.
> Can you believe it? Let's pursue her, and de-
> mand she give it up.
> Who, you ask? The one you see there, smirking
> like a Gallic pup,
> Cruising with her hips in motion, up and down
> the public road.
> Surround her and demand the notebook — see
> if stinging words can goad:
> "Rotten whore, return the notebook — give me
> back the thing you stole.
> Stinking whore, I want that notebook — I don't
> have time for games, you hole!"
> No response? "You muck-drenched strumpet,
> sweepings of a brothel floor,
> Or if there could be something else that's viler
> than a dirty whore!"
> Let's not leave it just at that — although it seems
> an uphill race,
> If nothing else we'll force some color in that
> bitch's brazen face.
> Louder still: "You stinking harlot — where's my
> notebook? Now I'm miffed!"
> Still no progress. She's a statue. Our strategy
> will have to shift.
> Maybe with this variation we'd get closer to
> our book:
> "Virgin-pure and modest maiden — give us back
> the thing you took."

Adeste, hendecasyllabi, quot estis
Omnes undique, quotquot estis omnes.
Iocum me putat esse moecha turpis,
Et negat mihi nostra reddituram
Pugillaria, si pati potestis.
Persequamur eam et reflagitemus.
Quae sit, quaeritis? Illa, quam uidetis
Turpe incedere, mimice ac moleste
Ridentem catuli ore Gallicani.
Circumsistite eam, et reflagitate,
"Moecha putida, redde codicillos,
Redde, putida moecha, codicillos!"
Non assis facis? O lutum, lupanar,
Aut si perditius potes quid esse.
Sed non est tamen hoc satis putandum.
Quod si non aliud potest, ruborem
Ferreo canis exprimamus ore.
Conclamate iterum altiore uoce
"Moecha putida, redde codicillos,
Redde, putida moecha, codicillos!"
Sed nil proficimus, nihil mouetur.
Mutanda est ratio modusque uobis,
Siquid proficere amplius potestis:
"Pudica et proba, redde codicillos."

NOTES

Moecha turpis: "Vile adulteress" is the strict sense here, but *moecha* in
this context means "whore."

Turpe incedere: "To strut indecently." If the woman addressed in this
poem is indeed Catullus's Lesbia (Clodia Metelli), then even Cicero
commented on her penchant to carry herself "not only like a whore,
but a shameless and impudent one to boot."

Mimice: "Like a mime," i.e., with a stupid, buffoonish grin.

Catuli ore Gallicani: "With the mouth of a Gallic puppy." The term *puppy* or *whelp* is maledictive in several languages (cf. "Insolent puppy!")

Putida: "Rotten, stinking"

Lutum, lupanar: "Scum, brothel." The woman is not just a whore — she
is an entire whorehouse.

Ferreo canis...ore: "From the iron face of this dog." The Romans said
"iron-faced" where we would say "brazen." The word *canis* brings
us back to the animal image of *catuli* in line 9.

Pudica et proba: "Modest and virtuous." The sarcasm hits us like a club.

[Gaius Valerius Catullus († *ca.* 54 B.C.). Translation & Notes by J. Salemi]

ACRIMONIOUS ACRONYMS
FOR ETHNIC GROUPS

Irving Allen

Many derogatory nicknames for ethnic groups, both minority and majority, are various kinds of word play, such as puns, pig latin, blends, alterations, clippings, reduplications, and other devices. The *acronym* (e.g., **SAM**, for **S**outhern **A**ppalachian **M**igrants in the industrial cities of Ohio) and its cousin, the *initialism* (e.g., **P.R.**, for **P**uerto **R**ican) are perhaps the newest devices for forming nicknames for ethnic groups in the slang of North American English. I found a score of these terms in my research compiling the historical inventory of nicknames for American ethnic groups. About a third appear in *Acronyms, Initialisms, and Abbreviations Dictionary* (Crowley, 1978). The editor, Ellen Crowley, pointed these out to me in scholarly exchange for ones I found independently, which relieved me of the awesome prospect of scanning 178,949 entries.

Acronyms, while an old device, became famous as names of the "alphabet soup" agencies of the New Deal and from military use in the Second World War. Organizations, industrial processes, and many other things are now named so that the acronym spells something pronounceable, preferably with one syllable. At their most inventive, acronyms spell a word that alludes to an attribute of the named thing, such as **WASP** (**W**omen's **A**irforce **S**ervice **P**ilots, World War II; all wasps fly) and, I would like to think, **CREEP** (**C**ommittee for the **Re**-**E**lection of the **P**resident). Long, cumbersome proper names are sometimes given just so the acronym will spell something catchy and mnemonic, such as **MOUSE** (**M**inimal **O**rbital **U**nmanned **S**atellite of **E**arth). Many acronyms have entered the language as words and their acronymic origins are half forgotten, such as **SNAFU** (**S**ituation **N**ormal—**A**ll **F**ucked **U**p; World War II).

Acronyms are especially amenable to use as slang and slurs. An acronym can denote its referent and, in addition, it can be devised to characterize it by the connotation of the word spelled. Some acronyms for ethnic groups also have the pejorative sound connotations that mark derogating words in English (Wescott, 1971).

The earliest acronyms for ethnic groups probably were coined by social workers and social scientists to refer to their "clients" and "subjects" in a way that seemed scientific. **SAM** (**S**outhern **A**ppalachian **M**igrant), **WASP** (**w**hite **A**nglo-**S**axon **P**rotestant), the initialism **P.R.** (**P**uerto **R**ican), and others probably originated in this way. This professional jargon quickly passed into the locutions of pop sociology where it took on epithetical overtones.

The earliest acronym for an ethnic group I have found originated in social studies. **WIN** (apparently, for **w**hite, **I**ndian, **N**egro) was coined by Estabrook and McDougle (1926: 13) for their book, *Mongrel Virginians: The Win Tribe.* This pronounceable acronymic shell was a pseudonym for a rural community of racially mixed persons whom social scientists now call "tri-racial isolates." **WIN** is the only permutation of the three initial letters that spells anything.

It was not until the 1960s and the spate of ethnic consciousness that acronymic nicknames for ethnic groups became popular. **WASP** (**w**hite **A**nglo-**S**axon **P**rotestant) was the first and most influential. It deserves a close look because its success as slang made it the model for others.

John Higham (1975:13), the historian of Protestant America, noted that by the 1960s **WASP** was the only ethnic slur that could be safely used in polite company, for its use was part of a socially just assault on certain bastions of ethnic exclusiveness; the term quickly came to stand for a desiccated, life-denying culture. I have documented elsewhere the life history of **WASP** as an epithet in social science (Allen, 1975). It has since increasingly become clear that the secret of the success of **WASP** as a derogatory nickname for Establishment Protestants lies in its capacity for playful duplicity. Denotatively, it is just a "sociological" descriptive for the racial, national-origin, and religious traits of the historically and culturally dominant ethnic group in North America. Connotatively, partly through the rhetorical redundancy of white *and* Anglo-Saxon, it conjures up a whole laundry-list of things many intellectuals hate. Some guilt-ridden white Protestant liberals turned the label on themselves with self-loathing, while others, through semantic inversion, adopted the term as an ethnically proud self-descriptive.

As a term of pop sociology, **WASP** is the spiritual heir of the epithets *bourgeois* in the 1930s and 1940s and *suburban* in the 1950s and 1960s. **WASP** connotes the coincidence of class privilege, suburban conformity, *and* the smugness of majority ethnicity—all rolled into one word. It is all the rage with literary intellectuals. Writers at the *New York Times* and *Time* magazine use it straight. William Safire is a man who knows exactly what words mean—and how to use them. Safire (1980), describing the fiasco of the UN vote near the end of the Carter administration, wrote: "That was when Cy Vance —white, Wasp and thus expendable—was told that the test of a good lawyer is his willingness to pretend he has been disbarably incompetent." (Note, now, the triple tautology of white on white on Anglo-Saxon, suggesting that the acronymic element *white* in **WASP** is being forgotten; *Wasp* has become a word, even a proper noun with a capitalized initial.)

Wasp is now standard dictionary fare. Stein and Urdang's *Random House Dictionary of the English Language* (1966) was the first to list it and to label the term "often derogatory." The British soon imported **WASP**, with the same meaning but referring to the British counterparts, as another Americanism to describe the seeming Americanization of their own race relations.

A curious little mystery surrounds the origin of the term. Originally, there were two **WASP**s. By the mid-1950s, **WASP** was Chicago slang and Ohio Valley social workers' jargon for white Appalachian Southern Protestants—the poor whites who migrated to the industrial cities of northern Ohio and the Great Lakes. In Cincinnati, the same people were called **SAM**s (Southern Appalachian Migrants). About 1960, the other, more familiar **WASP** (for white Anglo-Saxon Protestant) emerged and the hillbilly **WASP** buzzed off. The middle-class suburban

WASP has swept the field and few know that the acronym perhaps first referred to the poor country cousins of the Establishment. I have never resolved whether the two **WASP**s evolved independently or, like a hermit crab, the latter inhabited the shell of the former.

The first published use of **WASP** (meaning white Anglo-Saxon Protestant) in professional sociology that I have found is by Professor Erdman B. Palmore (1962), then of Yale University, in the *American Journal of Sociology.* The term became widely known after the publication of E. Digby Baltzell's (1964) *The Protestant Establishment;* both sociologists used it as a simple descriptive, not as an epithet. John Higham (1975: 13) pointed out what is perhaps the earliest literary use. Saul Bellow in *Herzog* (1964:377) has Moses Herzog ruminating on his defiance of "the Wasps, who...stopped boiling their own soap circa 1880, took European tours, and began to complain of the Micks and the Spicks and the Sheenies."

Successful slang terms inspire variants. Tony Randall, John V. Lindsay, and other member wags logically suggest that the tautological **WASP** ought to be simply **ASP**. But they miss the point that the redundancy is the key to the pejorative connotation and the rhetorical force of **WASP**. **ASP** just does not have the same sting. Nonetheless, **ASP** had a brief life in the late 1960s and was recorded by Barnhart (1973). **WASP** soon got an initialism, **NN**, tacked on as a kind of tail stinger. Weed (1973) wrote: "The largest minority is the so-called '**WASP-NN**,' that is, White Anglo-Saxon Protestant Native born of Native Parents." But that was stretching a point and it was never heard from again.

WASP, one of the best buzzwords of the 1960s and 1970s, became the model for imitators. **WASC** (white Anglo-Saxon Catholic) has been used for English Catholic communities in Kentucky and Maryland. Joan Cooper (1978), a social worker, coined **WECC** (white English Celtic Catholic) to call attention to another Catholic minority from the British Isles. In Canada, **QWASP** (Québec white Anglo-Saxon Protestant) was hatched from the conflict between the Anglo-Canadians and the Québeckers (Malcolm, 1979). **TOM** is an acronym for a Canadian national elite, predominately Anglophones, who seem to concentrate in Toronto, Ottawa, and Montréal (Colombo, 1979). **TOM** also suggests *tom* and *tommy*, which are old nicknames for the British.

There are yet other spin-offs of **WASP**. In the 1960s, a few blacks scolded other, assimilating blacks as **NASPs** (Negro "Anglo-Saxon" Protestants), which is roughly equivalent to *uncle tom, afro-saxon*, or *oreo*. **BOWP** (black ordinary working people) is listed by Crowley (1978), but she says in a private correspondence that it may be a nonce word. Slang from the world of the physically handicapped gives us **WASPA** (white Anglo-Saxon Protestant ambulatory) as a bitter comment upon what is required to get a job. Ethel Strainchamps (1971:244), a lexicographer, editor, and feminist, by way of fixing blame for epithets for women, coined **WASMs** (white Anglo-Saxon males). The last word is yet another **WASP**, reportedly an ephemeral item of Israeli slang in the early 1970s, for white Ashkenazic Sabra with pull (Crowley, 1978).

Yet the most bizarre acronym prompted by **WASP** is **PIGS** (Poles, Italians, Greeks, and Slavs), which was presented, if not coined, by Michael Novak (1971:46-47) in his book, *The Rise of the Unmeltable Ethnics*. Some in the white ethnic movement apparently felt a need for an acronymic protagonist against the **WASPs**. If the **WASPs** were the "un-ethnics," then who were the real "ethnics," acronymically speaking? Mostly, he says, they are Poles, Italians, Greeks, and Slavs. (The more assimilated Irish were kept out of this acronymic **PIG**-sty, perhaps also because they would ruin the spelling.) The ordering of the group names is not by alphabet, group size, or any other ranking; it merely spells something useful in political rhetoric. Abrahams and Kalčik (1978:233) write that the term **PIGS** "is an insulting self-polluting label, and [is] the claim to belong to the margins of society rather than to be part of the center or establishment [and] also reverses the assimilation process and brings down on the ethnics' heads the charge of being different, non-Anglo." **PIGS** never caught on and apparently died a quiet death, perhaps never leaving the pages of Novak's book.

An ingroup joke, the famous notion of the Jewish Princess, has been acronymized on the campuses as **JAP** for Jewish-

American Princess. The hyphenated -*American* was added, I presume, to give a vowel and make it spell something. **JAP** was quickly taken up by non-Jewish students, who sometimes plug in Prince to make the acronym do double duty. This also suggests that the kids have heard about but not really understood the Princess business.

I have found several initialisms that refer to ethnic persons. While an acronym is usually pronounced as a word, an initialism is pronounced letter by letter. Mencken reported the earliest initialism that I have found. **F.M.C.**, Free man of color, was used for blacks after the Civil War. Dunlap and Weslager (1947) relate that the *G-and-B Indians*, a settlement of "tri-racial isolates," got their name from living near the Grafton and Belington Railroad. **P.R.** for Puerto Rican appeared in the 1950s or 1960s, at a time when migrants to the mainland were settling heavily in the cities and were a concern to social workers, who perhaps originated the initialism. The old epithet *house-nigger* for a black sycophant recently was euphemized and coded to **H.N.** Working in the other direction, *jaybee*, a derogatory nickname for a black person, is a phonetic spelling, ironically modeled on *jaycee*, of the initialism **j.b.** for jet black.

The general awareness of acronyms has spawned a new line of free association in folk etymologies. Nowadays when people don't know the origin of a word, they sometimes imagine that it must be an acronym (Eisiminger, 1978). At least three well-known nicknames for ethnic groups are widely but mistakenly believed to derive from acronyms. A popular story has it that **wop** for an Italian is an acronym for **W**ith-**o**ut **P**apers (or sometimes **P**assport) and was applied to illegal immigrants who were deported in the 1920s. Another story has *wop* as an acronym for the phrase **W**ork(s) **o**n **P**avement, which is probably suggested by the occupational stereotype of Italians as concentrated in masonry and road-building. But etymologists seem in wide agreement that *wop* is a clipped and phonetically spelled version of Neapolitan and Sicilian *guappo*, 'a daring, handsome man': a dude.

A similar belief is that **wog** comes from an acronym for **W**onderful (sometimes **W**ily) **O**riental **G**entleman. No one really knows the origin of *wog*, but Merriam III says it may be a variant of *golliwog*, the name of a grotesque black doll in a children's story. **Pome** and its diminutive form *pommy* are nicknames for Australians. Crowley (1978) relates one possibility that *pome* is an acronym for **P**risoner **o**f **M**other **E**ngland, supposedly a nickname for a convict in a nineteenth-century penal colony in Australia. She also relates a second hypothesis that *pome* is short for *pomegranate*, a red fruit, and alludes to the sunburn that fair-skinned Englishmen often acquired on arrival in Australia. The prisoner story is highly unlikely, though the pomegranate story has some possibility and is similar to one of several possibilities of the origin of *pommy* given by Partridge.

In conclusion, I will relate a curiosity whereby an initialism, in a roundabout way, might have given birth to the nickname **charlie** for the Vietnamese in the recent war. Flexner (1976:371-72) reports that *charlie* is derived from the initialism **V.C.** for **V**iet **C**ong, the short form of the Vietnamese phrase meaning "Vietnamese Communist." They were simply called *the Cong. Viet Cong* was also abbreviated to **V.C.** The military communication code word for **V** is *Victor* and for **C** is *Charlie*. So the *Viet Cong* or the **V.C.** were called *Victor Charlie* or simply *charlie*, corresponding to the short form *Cong*. I will add that this usage may have been reinforced by the coincidence that *charlie* is also a popular slur that is a general term for several Asian groups.

Nicknames for ethnic groups formed on acronyms and initialisms are just the newest wrinkle in the old game of intergroup name-calling. Certainly, others are around in the streets —and in the groves of Academe.

BIBLIOGRAPHY

Abrahams, Roger D., and Susan Kalčik. 1978. "Folklore and Cultural Pluralism." In R. M. Dorson (ed.), *Folklore in the Modern World* (The Hague: Mouton), 223-36.
Allen, Irving. 1975. "WASP—From Sociological Concept to Epithet." *Ethnicity* 2 (June), 153-62.

Baltzell, E. Digby. 1964. *The Protestant Establishment: Aristocracy and Caste in America.* New York: Random House.

Barnhart, Clarence L., Sol Steinmetz, and Robert K. Barnhart. 1973. *The Barnhart Dictionary of New English Since 1963.* New York: Barnhart/Harper & Row.

Bellow, Saul. 1964. *Herzog.* New York: Viking Press.

Colombo, John Robert. 1979. "Canadian Slurs, Ethnic and Others." *Maledicta* 3 (Winter), 182-84.

Cooper, Joan. 1978. "A WECC (White English Celtic Catholic) Tells How It Is." *New York Times* (March 11), Op-Ed page.

Crowley, Ellen T. (ed.). 1978. *Acronyms, Initialisms, and Abbreviations Dictionary.* 6th edition. Detroit: Gale Research.

Dunlap, A. R., and C. A. Weslager. 1947. "Trends in the Naming of Tri-Racial Mixed-Blood Groups in the Eastern United States." *American Speech* 22 (April), 81-87.

Eisiminger, Sterling. 1978. "Acronyms and Folk Etymology." *Journal of American Folklore* 91 (January-March), 582-84.

Estabrook, Arthur H., and I. E. McDougle. 1926. *Mongrel Virginians: The Win Tribe.* Baltimore: Williams and Wilkins.

Flexner, Stuart Berg. 1976. *I Hear America Talking.* New York: Van Nostrand-Reinhold.

Higham, John. 1975. *Send These to Me.* New York: Atheneum.

Malcolm, Andrew H. 1979. "McGill University in Montreal Confronts a Dual Challenge." *New York Times* (September 10).

Novak, Michael. 1971. *The Rise of the Unmeltable Ethnics.* New York: Macmillan.

Palmore, Erdman B. 1962. "Ethnophaulisms and Ethnocentrism." *American Journal of Sociology* 67 (January), 442-45.

Safire, William. 1980. "Breakdown in Morality." *New York Times* (March 6), A-23.

Strainchamps, Ethel. 1971. "Our Sexist Language." In V. Gornick and B. K. Moran (eds.), *Woman in Sexist Society* (New York: Basic Books), 240-50.

Weed, Perry. 1973. *The White Ethnic Movement and Ethnic Politics.* New York: Praeger.

Wescott, Roger W. 1971. "Labio-Velarity and Derogation in English: A Study in Phonosemic Correlation." *American Speech* 46 (Spring-Summer), 123-37.

THE RAB-SHAKEH'S VERBAL AGGRESSION AND RABBINICAL EUPHEMISM

Benjamin Urrutia

Late in the eighth century B.C., Sennacherib, King of Assyria, sent a large army to take Jerusalem. An Assyrian leader, called the Rab-Shakeh, delivered a speech to the defenders of the city with the clear objective of "softening up" their will to resist. This speech, a masterpiece of verbal aggression and psychological warfare, is reported in three different places in the Bible: 2 Kings 18:19-35, Isaiah 36:4-20, 2 Chronicles 32:9-19. The delegation from the King of Judah was so enervated by the Rab-Shakeh's words that they made a request of him with which — as they should have known — he would not comply: "Speak, I pray thee, to thy servants in Aramean which we understand, and don't talk to us in Judean in the ears of the people on the wall." The Assyrian's reply was a vicious classic: "Is it only to thy master and to thee that my master sent me to speak these words? Is it not also to the men who sit on the wall, so they can eat their shit and drink their piss with you?"

The above is my own translation of parts of verses 26 and 27 of chapter 19 of 2 Kings. The King James (or Authorized Version) of this passage is rather unsatisfactory, especially in its choice of "the Syrian language" and "the Jews' language" — a clumsy way to translate *Aramith* and *Yehudith*, which are simply Aramean (Aramaic) and Judean. On the other hand, the words "dung" and "piss" were probably good choices back in 1611 A.D. — neither prissy not vulgar. However, the language has evolved in such a manner that *piss* has become taboo, while *dung* has retained its primeval neutrality. In Modern English, the middle ground has been lost: all words describing body processes seem to be either too coarse or too elegant. But there is no doubt in my mind that the Assyrian Rab-Shakeh, if he were delivering his dyspep-talk today, in English, would say "crap" or "shit"—and would use something even stronger if it were possible. My belief is that a translator should try to faithfully convey the original author's intention.

The rabbinical editors of the Massoretic (traditional) text of the Bible did not share this philosophy. Under *kharayhem* (their crap) they placed the footnote: *tsoatam qre* (read: "their excrement"); and under *shineyhem* (their piss): *mimey ragleyhem qre* (read: "their leg-water").

But this bowdlerizing, to be sure, took place centuries after the speech was first recorded, and so the question remains on whether those tabooed words only became so in rabbinical times, and were neutral in the days of Sennacherib and Hezekiah, or whether they were already impolite things to say back in the eighth century B.C. If the latter, then the Rab-Shakeh's speech could well be one of the earliest recorded usages of taboo words in verbal aggression.

Since all human societies everywhere have verbal taboos, there is no doubt that these have existed for as long as language itself; but the question remains: *when* was the breaking of such taboos first used as a verbal weapon? And was it first used as a weapon against a different group, as the Rab-Shakeh did, or within the group?

———————

[*Editor's Note*: Two German-language Bibles checked show that a Catholic version (1957) uses *Kot essen* ("to eat excrement") and *Harn trinken* ("to drink urine"), whereas a Protestant / Lutheran version (1956) uses *Mist fressen* ("to devour dung/manure") and *Harn saufen* ("to guzzle urine"). The Protestant version thus is closer to the original, as it does not use the elegant *Kot* but *Mist*, a less elegant word. It also shows the speaker's nastiness—without using *Scheiße* and *Pisse*—by not using the neutral *essen* and *trinken* but the coarse *fressen* ("to devour; eat greedily and sloppily like an animal") and *saufen* ("to guzzle; drink greedily and sloppily like an animal").]

CHINESE VALUES AS DEPICTED
IN MANDARIN TERMS OF ABUSE

Shu-min Huang *and* D. M. Warren

A study of verbal abuse in China faces several difficulties. The first is the tremendous language diversity. Besides the approximately fifty ethnic minorities—numbering around fifty million persons—the majority ethnic Chinese group, the Han, is also characterized by language diversity. There are nine major language groups among the majority Han Chinese, each of which is comprised of numerous dialects. In this study, we selected Mandarin, the official language of China, as our subject for analysis. Mandarin is the predominant indigenous language in north-central China; it is also used in official contexts and in school teaching throughout China. The terms of abuse in Mandarin may not be found in other Chinese languages, just as the other major languages of China may contain terms which have no equivalents in Mandarin.

The second difficulty faced in this study is the evasive quality of abusive terms used in Mandarin. Traditional Chinese culture strongly emphasizes literary achievements and appropriate and courteous behavior. Using abusive terms is always discouraged among both children and adults. Given the long historical tradition in China, one finds that many abusive terms are euphemistic, wrapped in historical anecdotes and moral teachings. The user of certain abusive terms may know neither the exact meaning nor the origin of the terms. An analysis of the Mandarin abusive terms can, however, provide insights into the values of Chinese.

One value appears to be the relatively low status of women in traditional China. There are far more terms focusing on the behavior of women than on that of men. Women are considered potentially licentious, talkative, and untrustworthy. This reveals the male as a dominant value of traditional China. Another value reflected in the abuses is a negative nature of certain animals when associated with humans. The analogy between a person and such animals is definitely derogatory given the clear demarcation between humans and animals in traditional Chinese culture. Moving across this demarcation line is a certain means to degrade a person. Other Mandarin terms of abuse indicate a strong emphasis on proper behavioral conduct, particularly in terms of maintaining prescribed social relations. Conformity to existing hierarchical social relations — parent-child, superior-subordinate, emperor-common citizen, learnèd-illiterate — are underlying values found in many of the abusive terms. The deviation from such behavioral codes constitutes serious offenses, the focus of many terms.

The arrangement of entries follows the system used by Warren and Brempong (*Maledicta* I/2:141-166). The three main categories are ***deviations attacked*** (physical, intellectual, social); within these groups they are categorized by ***provenance***; and within these subgroups, ***alphabetically***. For more details on the rationale of this categorization system, *see* R. Aman's "A Taxonomy of the Provenance of Metaphorical Terms of Abuse," *Maledicta* I/2:317-322.

PRONUNCIATION GUIDE

The romanization system used in this article follows the Pinyin system as it is used in current official Chinese literature. Basically, the **j** sounds as in 'jeer'; **q** as in 'cheer'; **x** as in 'ship'; **z** as in 'zeal'; **zh** (sometimes also indicated as **ẑ**) is a voiced *z* with the tip of the tongue rolled back to the temple area; no such sound in English; **c** as in 'rats' or 'train'; **ch** (same as **ĉ**) is a voiced *c*, with the tip of the tongue to the temple area; no equivalent sound in English; **s** as in 'sand'; **sh** (same as **ŝ**) is a voiced *s*, with the tip of the tongue rolled back to the tem-

ple area; no equivalent sound in English; **ü** as in '**yo**uth' or in
German **ü***ber*. Tones: ´rising; `falling; ˇfalling, then rising.

非 非

MANDARIN TERMS OF ABUSE

I. INSULTS ATTACKING PHYSICAL DEVIATIONS AND SHORTCOMINGS

A. Body (size, shape, function)

1. Human Provenance

ǎi-ze (1) 矮子

"short junior": a dwarf; a short man. *Ze* is a diminutive
meaning 'minor, guy, fellow.' Mostly referring to males.

lài-ze (2) 癩子

"blotty person": one who has stain-like spots on the skin
resembling cankers or lesions; a blotty fellow

tū-ze (3) 秃子

"bald junior": a man who has no hair due to a physiological problem; 'baldy'

2. Animal Provenance

dú-yěn-lún (4) 独眼竜

"one-eyed dragon": a man who has lost an eye

tū-lü (5) 秃驴

"bald donkey" : a bald man who resembles a donkey; also, a monk

3. Plant Provenance

cán-hūa bài-lǐu (6) 残花败柳

"faded flowers and withered willows": a fallen woman; a
woman beyond her prime age of beauty

4. Objects Provenance

kāi tīen-chūang (7) 开天窗

"open-sky window": a person who has syphilis which has
resulted in muscle deterioration or scarring on the forehead

5. Body Parts Provenance

bèn-shǒu bèn-jiǎo (8) 笨手笨脚

"clumsy hand and clumsy leg": a person who lacks adroitness

ló-hàn tuěi (9) 罗汉腿

"legs like Arhan": a man who has bandy legs. Arhan was one of Buddha's 500 disciples; they often squatted on the ground while crossing their legs, resulting in bandied legs.

tā-mā-de (10a) 他妈的

mā-de-bī (10b) 妈的尻

"his mother's...", "mother's cunt": common terms expressing disapproval or disappointment; vulgar but not insulting terms; equivalent to "damn it!" in English.

B. Cleanliness

1. Human Provenance

còu-biǎo-ze (11) 臭娠子

"stinky whore": an insult to a woman who is not actually a whore

2. Objects Provenance

lā-tā (12) 遒遒

"slovenly disgusting": a person who appears dirty in dress or physical appearance

3. Body Parts Provenance

còu jī bā (13) 臭雞巴

"stinky vulva": an insult to a woman

II. INSULTS ATTACKING INTELLECTUAL AND MENTAL DEVIATIONS AND SHORTCOMINGS

1. Human Provenance

shǎ-ze (14) 傻子

"stupid junior": a foolish, gullible man

yòu-zè (15) 幼稚

"young child": an immature, unsophisticated person; an ignoramus

2. Animal Provenance

jǐng-dǐ zē wā (16) 井底之蛙

"well-bottom frog": a person who has narrow perceptions or views on anything, like a frog who sits at the bottom of a well; an ignorant and arrogant person

lú-dàn (17) 驴旦

"donkey's balls": a person as stupid as a donkey. *Dàn* literally means "eggs"; cf. German vulgar *Eier* 'balls.'

wú-tóu chāng-yíng (18) 无头苍蝇

"headless fly": a mindless person

3. Body Parts Provenance

bèn dàn (19) 笨旦

"foolish balls": a born fool; an idiot. *See* No. 17.

liù-shéng wú-zhǔ (20) 六神无主

"six souls without a master": an absent-minded person; a mindless person. All living Chinese are considered to have six different souls; a deceased Chinese is considered to have seven spirits.

shē-húen lò-pò (21) 失魂落魄

"lost soul and discarded spirit": a mindless person

xīn-lǐ bièn-tài (22) 心理变態

"distorted mind": a psychotic person

4. Characteristics Provenance

jié-jié bā-bā (23) 结结巴巴

"stammering" : a tongue-tied person; an inarticulate person. Two types of stammering are distinguished in Mandarin.

wú zhē (24) 无知

"no knowledge"; "void of knowledge": an ignorant person who has neither formal education nor common-sense knowledge

5. Plant Provenance

shǎ-gūa (25a) 傻瓜

dāi-gūa (25b) 呆瓜

"stupid melon": a foolish or gullible person

III. INSULTS ATTACKING INDIVIDUAL AND SOCIAL DEVIATIONS AND SHORTCOMINGS

A. Character and Personality

1. Human Provenance

lì-hài (26) 利害
"sharp and damaging" : a shrewd person

ì-qì iòng-shè (27) 意气用多
"emotion dominates events": a person who loses control over himsclf or herself

2. Animal Provenance

cē-lǎo-hǔ (28) 雌老虎
"old female tiger": a derogatory term for a woman who is dominant and short-tempered

3. Body Parts Provenance

hěn-xīn (29) 狠心
"cruel heart": a cruel person

4. Characteristics Provenance

cán-rěn (30) 残忍
"brutal patience": a person who inflicts extraordinary sufferings on others and who enjoys witnessing other persons' sufferings

lǎo wán-kù (31) 老顽固
"old stubborn": a stubborn old man

mí-xìn (32) 迷信
"confused belief": a superstitious person

xü-rúng (33) 虚榮
"unreal glory": a vain person

B. Personal Conduct and Behavioral Patterns

1. Human Provenance

bài-jīa jīng (34) 败家精
"failing family demon": a person who wastes the family fortune, resulting in the downfall of the family

bài-jīa zě (35) 败家子

"failing family junior": a man who wastes the family fortune, resulting in the downfall of the family

chūn-fū yǔ-fù (36) 村夫愚妇

"village husband and stupid wife": ignorant peasants

èr máo-ze (37) 二毛子

"second-class hairy people": Chinese Christians who use their religious prestige to oppress other Chinese. The Chinese converts are called "second-class hairy people" because the missionaries, who are mainly Westerners, are called **da máo-ze**, "the big hairy people."

hàn-jīen (38) 漢奸

"Han Chinese traitor": a Chinese who collaborates with a foreign war-time enemy

jīen-fū yín-fù (39) 奸夫淫妇

"adulterous man and licentious woman": male and female adulterers

jīen-shāng (40) 奸商

"treacherous merchants": dishonest businessmen. Traditional Chinese social values placed merchants at the bottom of the four major social categories of intellectuals, farmers, craftsmen, and merchants. Businessmen are regarded as always being greedy, manipulative and dishonest.

jīen-xì (41) 奸细

"adulterous petty person": a spy or traitor who works for any opposing power

lǎo-bù-sě (42) 老不死

"old, but not yet dead": a useless old man

qǐ-gài (43) 乞丐

"beggar": a poor person who lives by begging

rén jìn kě-fū (44) 人尽可夫

"every man can be the husband": a lascivious woman who takes any man as a lover or husband

sān-gū liù-pó (45) 三姑六婆
"three aunts and six grandmothers": women indulging in gossip

shǒu-cái-nú (46) 守財奴
"Property-guarding slave": a stingy rich man who guards his property so relentlessly that he himself looks like a slave

tān-gūan wū-lì (47) 貪官污吏
"greedy officials and corrupted administrators": government officials who are objectionable to the public. This term has been popular during the revolutionary period.

wáng-gúo nú (48) 亡国奴
"lost country slave": a person whose own country has been conquered by an enemy, the person having become a slave of the conquering power

wáng-mìn zē-tú (49) 亡命之徒
"lost life people": an outlaw or desperado; a villain who does not care about his or her own life

xiàng-gūng (50) 相公
"young gentleman": a catamite; a boy kept for pederastic purposes

xīang-yuèn (51) 鄉愿
"an old country man": a man who tries to please everyone; a "yes man"

xiǎo-zá-zǔng (52) 小什种
"little bastard": a person whose mother is sexually loose; hence one is not certain about his or her real father

yáng-nú mǎi-bàn (53) 洋奴買办
"foreign slave and agent": commercial agents for foreign companies; collaborators of a foreign country who work only for material gains

yào-sě bù-húo (54) 要死不活
"looks dying, not alive": a person who has no strength or tenacity

2. Animal Provenance

chuēi-níu (55) 吹牛

"blowing up the bull": a braggart who blows up a dead bull's hide to make it look bigger

gō-níang yǎng-de (56) 狗娘养的

"raised by a dog's mother": an insult to a person which implies that his/her mother is a dog. Equivalent to 'son of a bitch' in English.

guēi ér-ze (57) 龟兒子

"turtle's son": an insult to a man which implies that his mother was loose enough to have been impregnated by a turtle.

guēi-gōng (58) 龟公

"male turtle": a pimp

guēi sūn-ze (59) 龟孫子

"turtle's grandson": an insult to a man which implies that his grandmother was sexually loose enough to have been impregnated by a turtle

huèn-dàn (60) 混旦

"scoundrel's balls": a rowdy blackguard. *See* No. 17.

lài-há-ma (61) 癞蛤蟆

"a blotty toad": a man who doesn't realize the extent of his own ugly appearance; one who chases after pretty girls despite an ugly appearance; a man who lacks self-estimate

shè-kuěi (62) 色鬼

"lustful ghost": a person, especially a man, who engages in continuous sexual adventures

shè-láng (63) 色狼

"lustful wolf": a person, especially a man, who engages in continuous sexual adventures

shè-mó (64) 色魔

"lustful demon": a person, especially a man, who engages in continuous sexual adventures

sǔ-bèi (65) 鼠輩

"rat's companions": thieves

tù-săi-ze (66) 兔羔子

"rabbit's illegitimate son": a male homosexual

wáng-bā dàn (67) 忘八旦

"forgotten eight virtues' balls": a man who forgets about the eight cardinal virtues of life (filial piety, brotherly submission, loyalty, sincerity, propriety, righteousness, modesty, and a sense of shame); a valueless human being (17)

zhǒu-gǒu (68) 走狗

"running dog": a person who is willingly manipulated by others behind the scenes; collaborators with a foreign power, especially during the war

zhū-ló (69) 家猥

"pig": a man who acts or eats like a pig; a dirty and greedy person

3. Objects Provenance

dǎng-gùn (70) 党棍

"party stick": a party loyalist who lives by promoting party propaganda. The term "stick" refers to inflexibility, something solid and without its own mind.

dì-pí (71) 地痞

"rough earth": a rascal; a person without a stable job

jiào-gùn (72) 教棍

"religious stick": a devout religious follower who lives by selling his or her beliefs

jīen-shuān kè-bó (73) 尖酸刻薄

"sharp acid cuts thin": a sarcastic person; a person whose sharp tongue can ridicule anything at any moment

líu-máng (74) 流氓

"a drifter": a man with no stable occupation

qīng-fú (75) 轻浮

"light and floating": a weightless person who acts restlessly

shū-dāi-ze (76) 书呆子
"book idiot": a bookworm

suěi-xìn yáng-hūa (77) 水性扔花
"water that flows up flowers": a sexually loose woman who indulges in seducing men; an unstable, fickle woman

wú-lài (78) 无癞
"no dependency": a person with no stable job or occupation

xià-liú (79) 下流
"lower stream": a lower-class man who takes advantage of others, especially of women. The term *liú* literally means river or stream, but refers to social class here.

xié-mén wài-dàu (80) 邪门外道
"lopsided/oblique door and illegitimate path": one who does not follow correct or legitimate ways in conducting one's affairs

yēn-qīang (81) 煙枪
"smoking gun": a heavy user of tobacco

zāu-qíng mù-chǔ (82) 朝秦暮楚
"morning Qing kingdom, evening Chu kingdom": a capricious person. This is taken from an ancient Chinese story of about the third century BC; a man who pledged his loyalty to the Qing kingdom in the morning and then switched to Chu, the opposing kingdom, in the evening.

4. Body Parts Provenance
A. Human

cái-mí xīn-qiào (83) 财迷心窍
"wealth blocks the heart aperture": a person who is so obsessed by greed that he or she loses his or her mind

càu-nǐ-mā-dè (84) 操你妈的
"fuck your mother's...": an insult to a person by implying the speaker having sexual intercourse with the person's mother. In some cases, the word *bī* ("cunt") is added to it to make a complete sentence.

cháng-shé fù (85) 長舌妇

"long-tongued woman" : a talkative woman who passes on gossip

chù-méi-tóu (86) 触霉头

"gore/bump into the mildewed head" : an act which brings bad luck to the receiving party

lā-pí-tiáo (87) 拉皮条

"pulling on strips of skin/leather thongs" : a pimp; one who lives by matching up adulterous men with women

máo-shǒu máo-jiǎu (88) 毛手毛脚

"hairy hands and hairy legs" : a man who intentionally touches a woman while making sexual advances

méi-zhǔng (89) 没种

"lack of seeds/balls" : a gutless coward; a man without the seeds to produce offspring. *Zhǔng* "seed, semen; testes"

pí-hòu (90) 皮厚

"thick skin" : a bold, audacious person

ruǎn gǔ-táu (91) 软骨头

"soft boned" : a pimp; a spineless person who lives off women

rǔ-còu wèi-gān (92) 乳臭未干

"milk stink not dry" : an immature person; a man who hasn't yet grown up

sān zē shǒu (93) 三隻手

"three-handed" : a pickpocket or thief

sě-pí lài-liěn (94) 死皮癞脸

"dead skin and blotchy face" : a shameless person who insists on making excessive demands on others. This is usually used by women to refer to a man who insists on having sexual adventures even after continuous rebuttals by the woman.

tān-zuěi (95) 贪咀

"greedy mouth" : a gluttonous person

xiǎng-rè fēi-fēi (96) 想入非非

"imagining to enter a hairy area" : a person who indulges in sexual fantasies. *Xiǎng* "imagining, longing for, wishing to, thinking of." The term for "hairy" originally referred to vulva.

xiǎo bái-liěn (97) 小白脸

"small, light-skinned face" : a gigolo; a male who lives off women through his good looks. The term "light-skinned" is a reference to persons of the upper class who don't get tanned skins as they don't work outdoors.

xiǎo-qì (98) 小气

"petty spirited" : a petty-minded, mean person

xiǎo-tōu (99) 小偷

"petty thief" : a pickpocket or thief

xīn-hěng shǒu-là (100) 心狠手辣

"cruel mind and hot hands" : a cruel person who enjoys inflicting physical injuries upon others

yīo-zuěi húa-shé (101) 油咀滑舌

"oily mouth and slippery tongue" : a glib person who manipulates words in such a way that he or she turns a serious conversation into a farce.

zéi-tóu zéi-nǎu (102) 贼头贼脑

"thief's head and thief's brain" : a person who behaves like a thief by sneaking behind other persons or by peeping at the activities of others

zuěi-cán (103) 咀馋

"craving mouth" : a gluttonous person

B. Animal

gǒu-pì (104) 狗屁

"dog's fart" : a worthless person; worthless words or opinions

gǒu tuěi-ze (105) 狗腿子

"dog's legs" : one who runs errands for villains. It used to refer to collaborators of the Japanese during World War II.

lán-xīn gǒu-fèi (106) 狼心狗肺

"wolf's heart and dog's liver" : a heartless, cruel person

mǎ-pì-jīn (107) 马屁精

"horse fart spirit" : a fawning flatterer

pāi mǎ-pì (108) 拍马屁

"petting a horse's buttock" : a fawning flatterer

shé-xiè xīn-cháng (109) 蛇蝎心肠

"snake's and scorpion's heart and intestines" : a cruel heartless person, often referring to women

xíung-xīng bào-dǎn (110) 熊心豹胆

"bear's heart and leopard's gall" : a bold, audacious person

5. Abstract Provenance

kē-fū mìn (111) 尅夫命

"against the husband's fate" : a woman who brings bad fortune to her husband

sàng jìn tīen-líang (112) 丧侭天良

"completely lost heavenly conscience" : a person who has lost all of his or her conscience

wàng-ēn fù-yì (113) 忘恩负义

"forgotten favors, betrayed justice" : a person who betrays friends who have done favors for him or her

wú-fǎ wú-tīen (114) 无法无天

"no law, no heaven" : a person who has no respect for any existing rules or laws

yú-xiào (115) 愚孝

"foolish filial piety" : a person who is foolishly loyal to undeserving parents or ancestors

yú-zhūng (116) 愚忠

"foolish loyalty" : a person who is foolishly loyal to an undeserving superior or an emperor

zāu-sān mù-sè (117) 朝三暮四

"morning three, dusk four" : a person who is not consistent. This is taken from an ancient Chinese story dating to the third century BC in which a man promised his monkeys three chestnuts in the morning and four in the evening. The monkeys objected, so he changed to four in the morning and three in the evening, and then they accepted. It is used to illustrate how to swindle one through clever tricks.

6. Activity Provenance

bān-lòn shè-fēi (118) 搬弄是非

"manipulating the truth and falsehoods" : a person who enjoys spreading gossip in order to create disputes

bān-mén lùn-fǔ (119) 班门弄斧

"handling/playing with an axe in front of the master craftsman Ban's front door gate" : an ignorant braggart. This is taken from a historical story which originated around the third or fourth century BC in which an ignorant person was bragging about how well he could handle his craftsman's tools, not knowing that he was bragging in front of the house of Mr. Ban, a real master craftsman.

chē rǔan-fàn (120) 吃軟飯

"eating soft rice" : a pimp; a man who depends upon women for a living

chuēi-máo qíu-cě (121) 吹毛求疵

"blowing hair to find a flaw" : a person who searches for trifling defects, as a person who looks for flaws in a piece of beautiful fur by blowing up the fur during the search

cīen-rén qí, wàn-rén iā (122) 千人骑,万人压

"thousands ride, ten thousands mount" : a whore who is mounted by thousands of men during her life

fǎn-fù wú-cháng (123) 反覆无常

"repeatedly turns around without consistence" : a person who changes his or her mind continuously; a disloyal subordinate who betrays the master

máng-chóng (124) 盲從

"blindly following" : a person who has no personal opinion or idea but rather blindly follows others

shù-diěn wàng-zhǔ (125) 數典忘祖

"thumbing through ancient scripts and forgetting the ancestors" : a traitor; a person who betrays his or her ancestors despite a proper training

tān-xiǎo (126) 貪小

"craving for small things" : a greedy person who seeks to obtain petty advantages over other people

tiǎu-pūo shè-fēi (127) 挑撥是非

"stirring up truth with falsehoods" : a person who spreads gossip in order to provoke conflict

tóu-jī qǔ-qiǎo (128) 投机取巧

"jump into opportunity for advantages" : an opportunist

7. Characteristics Provenance

bà-dàu (129) 霸道

"the way of might" : an unreasonable person who brushes his or her way over other persons' rights, in contrast to "the way of right"

bú yào liěn (130) 不要臉

"doesn't care about losing face" : a shameless person who doesn't care about losing face through misconduct

jīen-zà (131) 奸詐

"wickedly deceptive" : a person who is artfully fraudulent

jīn-jīn jì-jiǎo (132) 斤斤计较

"catty by catty/one by one counting" : a stingy person who argues with other people over trifling matters. The "catty" is a small weight unit equivalent to 1.33 lbs.

làn-huò (133) 爛貨

"rotten stuff" : a licentious person, usually referring to women

má-mù bù-rén (134) 麻木不仁

"numb and not kind" : a person who has no sentiment or feelings towards other human beings

méi jīa-jiào (135) 沒家敎

"without family teaching" : a ruleless, disobedient person

niáng-niáng qiang (136) 娘娘腔

"feminine vocal tones" : a man who speaks and acts like a woman; an effeminate man

pièn-ze (137) 骗子

"cheater" : a quack; a charlatan

shāu-huò (138) 骚货

"rank-smelling stuff" : a woman who seeks to attract the attention of men

shé-è bú shè (139) 十恶不赦

"ten crimes unredeemable" : a person who has committed all ten unpardonable crimes (rebellion, conspiracy against a ruler, treason, patricide, murder or mutilation, sacrilege, unfilial behavior, lack of harmony, insubordination, and incest); an unredeemable, guilt-ridden person

tān dé wú-yièn (140) 贪得无厌

"greed without tiring" : a greedy person with insatiable needs

wàng běn (141) 忘本

"forgotten origin" : one who has forgotten his or her own ancestry

wú-néng (142) 无能

"without ability" : a useless, impotent person

xǐ-xīn yèn-jiòu (143) 喜新厌旧

"love new, abhor old" : a man who abandons his old wife for other women, particularly younger women

xū-wǎi (144) 虚伪

"pretentiously unreal" : a person filled with vanity; a hypocrite

yī-lǎo mài-lǎo (145) 依老卖老

"depending on one's age to sell age" : an old person who insists on the superiority of his or her opinion or views merely because of greater age

yīn-xiěn (146) 阴险

"surreptitious danger" : a treacherous person who covers up his or her own emotion or opinion, but takes opportunities to damage other persons

yīn-yáng guài-qì (147) 阴阳怪气

"male-female confused essence" : a man behaving like a woman; a person with an unpredictable personality

8. Spirit Provenance

è-mó (148) 恶魔

"malicious devil" : one who commits a series of bad deeds

hú-lí-jing (149) 狐狸精

"female fox's/vixen's spirit" : a woman who has special talent in seducing men

jiǒu-guěi (150) 酒鬼

"liquor ghost": an alcoholic or drunkard. The "ghost" in this instance is malicious.

quóng gūang-dàn (151) 穷光旦

"poor as a bald egg" : a poor person

quóng-guěi (152) 穷鬼

"poor ghost" : a poor person

wú-yiào kě-jiù (153) 无药可救

"no medicine can save" : a hopeless person; a hopelessly ill, dying person

yiāo-jīng (154) 妖精

"female demon's spirit" : a woman who has special talent in seducing men.

MEET OUR COPY-EDITOR

Meet **Xiǎng-Rè Fēi-Fēi**, Ph.D., Dr. Aman's longtime collaborator. As *Maledicta*'s copy-editor, he transforms illegible, illiterate and uncouth manuscripts into the nifty material you read in these pages. Dr. FF, as he is lovingly called around here, is aware of human imperfection but nonetheless becomes livid at some of our contributors' sloppy manuscripts, which he has to clean up (as the caricature shows). While reading and preparing the manuscripts for Uncle Mal to typeset, he does not smile much, but instead curses a great deal and writes snide letters to

careless authors who submit their material in total disregard for the "Style Sheet" (MAL I/1). He waxes wroth at erasable and airmail-paper manuscripts and at submissions that have insufficient margins, are not double-spaced throughout, are full of typos, incorrect quotations, wrong footnotes, faulty names, titles, dates and page references, bloated with cacademic lingo, flawed by incomplete bibliographical data, incorrectly alphabetized glossaries, wrong foreign-language material by natives, lacking accents and other diacritical marks, etc., etc. — all of which force Dr. FF to waste untold hours on checking and correcting material supposedly submitted in "ready to typeset" form. He waxes even wrother at authors' last-minute changes and corrections in the galley proofs

Dr. XIǍNG-RÈ FĒI-FĒI

想入非非

— corrections to be made *after* the material had been painstakingly handset by poor Uncle "Two-Finger" Mal. Not wanting to die of a heart attack, he urges all authors to triple- and quadruple-check their manuscripts *before* submitting them and not to bug him with any further changes *after* the article was accepted for publication. To ward off an impending apoplexy and to balance his dreadful copy-editing vocation, Dr. FF engages in his favorite avocation, *xiǎng-rè fēi-fēi*, as the Mandarin Chinese (96) scrutably call it.

THE CORPORATE GLOSSARY
JOB TITLES AND WHAT THEY MEAN

John Hughes

Chairman of the Board: The highest corporate position. Involves sitting at a big desk, shooting in the low nineties, worrying about kidnappings, wearing dark suits, and placing blame.

President: The executive who sees to it that the other executives run the company properly. He apologizes for poor earnings and takes credit for favorable earnings. Also calls, cancels, reschedules, and misses meetings.

Vice-President: A job category designed to forestall pay increases for supervisors. Same function as supervisor, at same pay, but with free annual chest X ray compliments of the company.

Executive V.P.: A stalled presidential aspirant. Corporate purgatory at $235,000 a year.

Office Manager: In charge of office charity collections, time cards, coffee-machine complaints, unauthorized Xerox machine use. Gets longer lunch period and an extra phone button.

Supervisor: Someone who is given additional office responsibility with no extra compensation. Graduates from Bic accountant's-point pen to stainless-steel Cross pen. Wears tie but no sports coat.

Executive Trainee: Someone who spent four years in college and $50,000 to learn how to seek out a company with an executive-training program.

Sales Manager: A well-dressed salesman who doesn't sell anything.

Legal Adviser: University of Montana Law graduate.

Corporate Legal Counsel: Harvard Law graduate.

Executive Secretary: A typist who can screw.

Executive Assistant: A slut who can type.

Inventory Control Supervisor: An MBA who can use a calculator.

Purchasing Manager: Low-level executive who supplements his salary by selling supplier gifts.

Director of Planning: A Ph.D. who makes his mistakes a decade in advance.

Director of R&D: A scientist who convinces young researchers that developing a new room-freshener scent is as rewarding as searching for disease cures.

Chief Financial Officer: Corporate fall guy who is hired to take the rap if the company is accused of financial wrongdoing.

Production Supervisor: An employee who knows too much to work in the plant but not enough to work in the office.

Production Manager: A production supervisor whose good deeds were rewarded by a promotion and who will be fired before any of the production supervisors.

Controller: A guy who has a fun wife, a block of company stock, and a condo in Vail.

Marketing Director: A guy who isn't aggressive enough to sell anything.

Treasurer: An executive who spends thirty years trying to figure out a way to divert corporate funds to a bank account in Aruba.

Corporate Auditor: Works with the treasurer after he discovers the treasurer's attempts to divert corporate funds to a bank account in Aruba.

Key Computer Operator: A graduate of a G.I. Bill-approved technical school and a whiz at Asteroids who spends six hours writing a program on his Radio Shack home computer and diverts corporate funds to his interest-bearing checking account at the local Savings and Loan.

Director of Overseas Operations: An executive who knows where all the corporate bodies are buried.

Interoffice Communications Specialist: The switchboard lady who refuses to call her chair and board a "communications space."

Information Resources Director: The guy in the Xerox room with the *Hustler* beaver logo tattooed on his left palm.

Stockholder: A person who receives a handsomely printed booklet each spring explaining why the company will have a better year next year.

Printed with permission of National Lampoon, Inc. ©1981

"I'll have the Gazpacho, Leeks Vinaigrette with Shrimp, Marinated Zucchini, Orange Mousse, a bottle of Côtes du Rhône Rouge '59, and bring some shit for my fly."

THE CO(S)MICALITY OF SHIT

* Shirl Piperglow

Heard recently in a chemistry class: "What is the most common substance in the world, Professor?"

The professor makes a wry face. "Well, it isn't a very *pleasant* substance...."

In an English class: "What is the commonest word in the language, Professor?"

The professor's normally taciturn features twist into something of a grimace. "Well, it's not a very *nice* word...."

In a very refined discussion on literature: "You know, this piece is more than simply naive or fatuous. It's... I'm not sure I know how to express it... it's shit!"

"So that's the word you were looking for!"

Examination committee to a Ph.D. candidate in zoology: "Well, sir, what do you know?"

Student (sheepishly): "Sirs, I guess I know shit."

"All right then, tell us something about the composition of shit. Its bacterial content, for instance, by percentage and weight...."

An embarrassed silence – by which they proved that the poor guy didn't even know shit.

The scene shifts now to a discussion on medieval history, conducted by one of the world's supreme authorities on the subject.

"Professor, what is the real essence of the Middle Ages? Can you tell us the one thing that characterizes this period above all else?"

At this point the great man must pause to reflect. Ah, many things must be going through his mind now... the twelfth century, the thirteenth, the fourteenth, brilliant midday sunlight, glory and grandeur far flung into legend, the blare of trumpets, the clarion call, kings and kingdoms, cozy faraway lands, knights and maidens, beauty and the beast, *amor vincit omnia*, the Crusades, the Holy Grail, the True Cross, the long, long road, the dark, dark night, the clang of swords, the clank of gates, mighty castles, dread without, dead within, dank dungeons, awesome towering cathedrals, spirit veiled in flesh, through a glass darkly, magnificent temple of woman erected on pudendal sewer, moldy sanctity, malodorous moribund chastity, sickly beatific saints and virgins aspiring, expiring, flagellant monks in torturous ecstasy, *credo in unum Deum*, there is a cruel pain in my bowels, O Lord, but I believe, I believe, I am sick unto death, Lord, if only to come to Thee, O the deep purple hurt now made golden by Thy love and grace, blazing organs in flooding dusty sunlight, joyous sobbing release and relief, *sumer is icumen in, lhude sing cuccu*, huge-bellied laughter, jubilation, rejuvenation, boon companions, *bons vivants*, jinglers, jugglers, tower jumpers, fools, jesters, *beaux gestes*, lords and louts, heroes, *villeins*, village idiots, jolly giants, oafs, roughness, ribaldry, wenching, stenching, drinking, stinking, dancing peasants with the burgeoning vitality of their manhood scarce concealed neath their codpieces, endless jogs, jugs, jigs, *jeux, joie*, the high road, the low road, plainsong, plain singing, talking, loving *en plein soleil*, the common people, common law, communality, hustle and bustle, huddled huts and houses, bunched buildings, bright rooftops all in a row, London town, the majestic stinking Thames, gutters, ditches, narrow slops-clogged streets wider at the bottom than the space between buildings at the top, foul and pestilential vapors, pasty faces, clammy hands, itches and sweats, agues and plagues, festering sores, running pus, black blood, cartloads of waste, offal, human bodies, heaps of rot tumbling down upon piles of rot, *miserere nobis, nos habebit humus*, fire and brimstone, mutilations, amputations, stumps, deformations, defamations, oaths, vows, curses, maledictions, im-

precations, incantations, adumbrations, adulations, adora-
tions, into the light again, *gaudeamus igitur, juvenes dum
sumus, vivat academia, vivant professores*, Duns Scotus, Aqui-
nas, rhetoric, rigor, Dante, burning eyes, tight lips, Leonardo,
Michelangelo, transfixed to the Sistine ceiling, his spirit straining ever upward, his body mired in months of grisly sweat....

"The smell of shit," says the professor.

The title of this piece is to say that the substance referred
to is both comic and cosmic in its implications. It also happens
to be a number of other things. It is *cosmetic* (both this word
and the latter above derive from the Greek *kosmos*, "order")
and it is *comestible* under certain conditions, but, although
they are somewhat touched upon later, the full story of these
values is, as cacademics are wont to say, "beyond the scope
of the present paper."

II

If we think about anything long enough and hard enough, it
becomes strange and finally ridiculous. Why anything should
exist, why there should be something rather than nothing
anytime or anywhere to fill that void out there, is not only a
mystery but an absurdity. The entire cosmos as we know it,
with stars being born and dying all the time, celestial bodies
crashing into each other, blazing supernovae, dusty, icy comets,
villainous black holes, is like the bad dream of a mad scientist.
Granted, we may take it as a beautiful absurdity, one of those
things we like to contemplate, aesthetically, as ridiculous. A
good bad movie, the bad guy we love to hate.

And what of this world, the one we think we know even
better? Whoever or whatever created it could not have been
entirely serious. Was the dodo bird or the boogum tree in
earnest? Or the human body, for that matter? The act of copulation, considered by most to be the ultimate experience on
earth, and yet looking so ridiculous in practice. If it is so divine in feeling but in dispassionate observation by others so
improbable and humorous as the excretory organs wiggle and
dangle into such close proximity with each other, surely this
must be a kind of Jovian joke, the awful offal of the Almighty.

The human condition in general is of course the most ridiculous thing in the known universe, although again, to some it may be beautifully ridiculous. In the beginning, when God created man, maybe he was not only not supposed to live by bread alone but not by bread at all. That is, things purely of the spirit were intended to be his sustenance. And then, after he ate of that fatal and very material apple, God may have said to him, after that bit about eating bread only in the sweat of his brow, that he would be grunting in another way: "Henceforth ye will shit." And suddenly a puckered little hole appeared in each of their previously perfect bottoms. But the Lord certainly didn't stop there, did he? For the sin of their now knowing all about good and evil and wanting to hide in their nakedness, he gave them nakedness with a vengeance: he took a bit of clay and slapped those ridiculously dangling appendages on Adam, and he may just have taken poor Eve and, for her greater part in the sin, slit her with a jagged stone from her new asshole halfway up to what was to become, in those offspring to which she would give birth only in sorrow, a belly-button—thus rendering her a wound that would never heal, and, as some waggish engineer later said, perversely putting the intake next to the exhaust. And then — final wicked touch! — he put hair around the whole thing as if to brag about it, or perhaps so that the most sensitive and fastidious among us would recoil in disgust: Shaw, for instance, trying it once and then wanting to have nothing further to do with it; Ruskin, shocked into impotence at the grisly sight; Swift, in horror that "Celia shits" in the hirsute vicinity.

Woman is further advanced than man in one anatomical respect, though, and this is the separation of clitoris, urethral orifice and vagina (whose functions are known variously as "scream, stream and cream" or "flip, drip and grip"), where in man the parallel purposes are combined in one monolithic organ. But both are more advanced than lower forms of life which have a single cloacal orifice for reproductive input and output as well as excretion.

Consider the even lowlier earthworm, which is not thought of as sexual-reproductive at all but only ingestive-excretory.

Whatever goes in comes out, but loosening the ground to support life above: the plants that support the animals that support us. The most arable parts of the earth, its finest topsoil, is largely worm poop, a recycling through these innumerable rudimentary bodies and enrichment thereby of necessary raw material. On a somewhat higher level, we have the memorable comment of the wife of the governor of the fair state of Wisconsin that honey is just bee poop. Well, not quite, but on the right track anyway. But such organisms, and many others higher up the ladder, are not only shit-producing but shit-eating too: the animal world is largely coprophagous. It's inevitable, if only for entropic reasons, and extends to the top of the evolutionary heap. Just as our shit, which we never tire of saying is so odious to us, becomes a virtual delicacy for other creatures lower down in the animal kingdom, with all kinds of things thriving on it, we too get a lot of mileage out of *their* original products, even if we aren't always consciously aware of their provenance. Shit, now, becomes purified to the point of perfection as we derive life- and energy-giving chemicals and fuels by refining carbonaceous deposits, i.e., largely a matter of primordial excreta. Gasoline, gasohol, gasshole. And don't think we don't eat it in a much more direct way: we do, and plenty of it. Investigations keep turning up beetle shit, chicken shit, rat shit, pig shit, all kinds of animal and even on occasion human excreta in our grains, cereals, dairy products, ground meats and so on. We eat it and shit it back in turn, with a kind of vengeance. The Chinese and others use their own instead of cow or sheep manure on their gardens.

It's a good thing for archaeologists and anthropologists, at least, that enough human excrement has been preserved over the millennia so they may poke around in it to learn something about the way it was in previous cultures. The same applies to zoologists and forest rangers, of course: perhaps the most basic way to keep track of the movements and habits of animals is by a careful study of what they have dropped along the way. But then, the study of the animal world is only another way of studying man. Whatever we do in approaching this bottom line, this end game, we go and come in circles.

There are those who still like to think, in spite of all the scientific evidence amassed to the contrary, that human beings are in a class utterly by themselves, unrelated to the animal world except by the most tenuous theological considerations. These people deny any direct biological or evolutionary connection: animals are a matter of base materiality while man is divine, a thing essentially of the spirit. Again, the most "divine" thing we can experience with our physical bodies is thought of this way, while the activity of our other end is simply gross, by turns laughable and horrifying and repulsive. Thus you can go all the way around the world to get from vagina to anus, just as you can go to Russia from the United States by flying east from Alaska. But it's really just next door all the time, separated by the narrowest of straits. In one sense, a world of difference; in another, certainly not. What goes into one is very often the same as what goes into the other, whether finger or prick. (The so-called "normalcy" of one and "perversity" of the other is not really relevant here; for all we know, and by more than we know, that other is a consummation even more devoutly to be wished, secretly or openly. It's a relative matter in which the one is simply more acceptable in the broad spectrum of human affairs, just as we can say in polite society with George Carlin, "I pricked my finger," but not "I fingered my prick.") And what comes out of these respective if not respectable orifices? Out of an asshole comes shit, out of the vagina *we* come, *inter fæcem et urinam.* Is there an essential difference? Any bacteriologist would have a field day looking over even a Cheryl Tiegs. The skin of the most well-scrubbed young virgin would be absolutely crawling with the same kind of coprophilous parasites as found in that other horrific mass. In fact, repeated scrubbings would only expose deeper layers of the things.

III

As we have noted earlier, shit makes things grow. If this is plain biological fact, it might also be seen, in its symbolic ramifications at least, to pertain to the very highest cultures we know anything about: human ones. We grow out of, on top of, our own collective detritus. Rome, the Eternal City, is a particularly good example of a place where the mounds of shit from earlier centuries were never swept away but simply built upon. But all of us, in any town or city, still have to live with it and in it most of the time. As a well-known German tune has it, "Geld ist weg, Gut ist weg, Augustin liegt im Dreck." *Park* is *krap* spelled backwards. And sometimes, sweeping aside all symbolism now instead of the ordure, we are left with and have to face the real item. Even in this relatively antiseptic country, and in one of our most civilized cities, San Francisco, the dog shit lies so thick on the sidewalks of residential neighborhoods that you can hardly find a place clear enough to plant your foot. Watching people walk by is a veritable poor man's ballet, with some of the most neatly choreographed little dances in the world, and all for free. It's only recently that the citizens of some communities have risen up against this situation, mainly at the prodding of new ordinances (after all, there must be something inertial about being in a barrel of shit up to your neck), armed with their poop scoops and probably ready to attack other people as well as their dogs' doings. Something like the moral equivalent of war?

And with mention of *that* topic, we might turn things around here for a moment and recall one of our more illustrious heroes. It was George S. Patton who gave us the choice between taking part in the most glorious war in history and shovelling shit in Oklahoma. O.K., I guess we know where his sympathies lay, but really now, which is worse: the inestimable debris of the global warfare he so fervently espoused (he was even ready to take on Russia in the end), which hasn't yet been cleaned up but only overlaid with that from later wars, burying whole peoples and cultures, or a simple, honest shovelful or two of the stuff that can be more or less nicely and briefly disposed of, and put to good use at that if you dump it on your garden? However, to suggest that our general's heart wasn't in the right place might strike some even today as a bit unpatriotic. Let me merely suggest, then, that his asshole wasn't in the right place.

And so, back to that moral equivalent again. The ultimate state of warfare isn't just a matter of killing people; that's only the beginning. We'd like to blow everybody's shit away, sweep it all clean, forever. The question, of course, is whether we can clean up our act collectively, or whether we are inevitably, irrevocably and eternally doomed to foul our nest and remain like Chaucer's "shiten shepherde" trying to tend clean sheep. Even our noblest and furthest-flung aspirations cover us with their backfirings. Our propulsion, our exhaust in getting to places like the moon or Mars by rocket necessarily leaves behind on earth a certain detritus, a shit that keeps piling up as we try to move on. This is sometimes called progress. "We are drowning in our own excreta," says Philip Slater in *The Pursuit of Loneliness*. He sees this as a negative consequence of what he calls the "Toilet Assumption," the notion that anything we don't want around will disappear if removed from our immediate field of vision, just as our poop disappears when we flush it down a privy. But it's got to go somewhere. And now, in certain areas of greater Milwaukee, and I'm sure in many others around the country as well, the entire sewer system has to be redone.

The real sewer, though, is in our collective mind. We have not gotten rid of the dirt in our drive toward total antisepsis but simply kicked it upstairs. With all our soaps and sprays, our scrapes and wipes, our swabs and scrubs, most of them perfumed, we wouldn't be caught dead with a dirty body — and we have dirty minds. It's always the other guy who's covered with it and smells bad, not us. A flying bird deposits a tremendous load on a professor's hoary beard, and his horrified companion offers to run for some toilet paper. "Don't bother," sputters our professor, "he's probably miles away by now." Why don't we all form a great big circle at this point and hold hands and admit that we all have assholes, that part and parcel of our salvation is in a good honest crapper every now and then, in the realization and acceptance of the fact that our shit stinks. At least it did the last time I took a breath in the vicinity. Or could times have changed already?

Maybe they have, because it seems we'll do anything, climb

the walls, jump out of our skins in our desperation to get rid of the slightest hint of a foul odor. A certain guest at a motel, a fastidious professional man, finds on his morning of departure that his toilet is overflowing and so in his urgent need is forced to use a wastepaper basket. On later contemplation he decides this is pretty gross (what will the maid think?) and wonders what he can do to improve the situation. Take it out and empty it? No, somebody might see him and that would be embarrassing. His final solution is to bury the stuff by taking up a corner of the carpeting and depositing it underneath. But there is still an unsightly lump, and so he stamps on it and rolls the wastepaper basket over it.... Three days later, he receives an urgent telegram from the motel: ALL IS FORGIVEN. WHERE IS IT?

If we're a bit too squeamish in our attitude toward anything having to do with dirt or the natural odors thereof, it's curiously refreshing to know that in other parts of the world this situation does not obtain. There are still millions of civilized old-world denizens who have B.O., and plenty of it. Maybe they're even proud of it, because they've worked for and earned it. Travelling in most European cities is like being in a sea of effluvia, most of it still medieval, much of it shitty. In Russia, even in Moscow and Leningrad, toilet paper is virtually unknown among the natives, who generally use *Pravda* or *Izvestiya* for the purpose. It's not altogether impossible that this could be symbolic; after all, Russians like to say that "there's no news in *Pravda* ['truth'] and no truth in *Izvestiya* ['news']." In our own country, of course, we're far too fastidious for anything that honest and outright; to be caught without proper asswipe is distressing indeed. One man asks another occupying the next stall in a public john if he would please pass some paper under the partition, because he has discovered his own roll to be empty. "Sorry, I've just used the last of mine," is the answer. Comes back a whimper: "Well, do you have two fives for a ten?"

In still other, admittedly more primitive places of the world, there are those who not only never wiped their own bottoms in their life but use excreta for cosmetic purposes.

That "shiten shepherde" of Chaucer's may be only reluctantly covered with the stuff, but certain peoples of Africa and else-where do it willingly and gladly, sometimes bedaubing them-selves from head to foot. It's supposed to be good for the skin, among other benefits; the primary purpose is to make them-selves attractive. Is this any different in principle from the practice of some of our own high-society women who use musk or civet, substances secreted through the anus of cer-tain animals for purposes of territorial marking or sexual at-traction? And this to replace their own natural odors, which they would of course be horrified at owning up to. But even generals and kings, avers Norman Mailer in *Advertisements for Myself*, can't resist furtively sniffing their own.

IV

What we don't admit to ourselves consciously often shows up in the products of our imagination; that is, in the arts, even if only on a symbolic level. Consider, for instance, the case of Degas, who painted all those nudes in everyday unflattering positions, squatting around on the floor, getting in and out of bathtubs, etc. We suspect that he would love to have caught and pictured one or two in the outright act of sitting on a toilet and taking a shit. Maybe he did, and the rest of the world just hasn't seen it yet. The known pornography of other re-nowned artists, such as George Grosz with his grossly drawn figures, often reflects considerable coprophilic feeling. On the other hand, an artist such as Jacques-Henri Lartigue (a photo-grapher; *Diary of a Century*) has given us images of young and pretty women with their skirts flying up or their pants falling down to expose their bare protruding derrières, and one picture of his wife perched on a potty having what looks to be a very pleasant and satisfying crapper, and this rascal makes all of it look nice rather than grotesque. Maybe it is, or should be, finally a nice thing, pleasurable and cozy both to do and to contemplate, rather than something to make us throw up our hands in horror and disgust, or the contents of our stomachs in outright revulsion.

The needs of the human nadir may not only be "raw material," symbolic or otherwise, for such elevated matters as genuine art but also conducive to them. Among writers, Swift was supposed to have gotten many of his best ideas while "at stool"; he has Gulliver consider analyzing the products of this activity for the gems of wisdom that might be contained therein. Thomas Wolfe had an enormous privy erected where he spent a great deal of his time, the better to accommodate his Brobdingnagian frame while in the throes of creation. Schiller claimed that the smell of rotten apples from under his writing desk was a *sine qua non* for the working of his imaginative genius; we wonder to what giddy heights his muse might have taken him if these had been turd-apples instead. Let's not even begin to discuss those who have dealt more explicitly with the stuff in their flights of impassioned purple prose, from Chaucer and Rabelais through the Marquis de Sade and Restif de la Bretonne to Henry Miller and Norman Mailer.

Given an artist of sufficient imagination, the beloved substance under the piercing gaze of that genius may change hue and character entirely. In a short story by one of the most brilliant Russian writers of the 1920s, Yury Olesha, there is this interesting passage: "The realm of attentiveness begins at the head of your bed, on the chair which you moved up close to your bed when you were undressing before going off to sleep. You wake up early in the morning, the rest of the house is asleep, the room is filled with sunlight. Quiet. Don't make a move, don't disturb the stillness of the light. Your socks are lying on the chair. They are brown. But in the stillness and brightness of the light you suddenly notice in the brown fabric separate, variously colored little woolen fibers curling in the air: crimson, light blue, orange." The chair, of course, represents a toilet bowl, and the brown socks the pair of turds deposited therein, with the fascinated child-man discovering new worlds in the rapt contemplation of his own excrement. This at a time when the creative mind is trying to hold sway against the rising tide of Soviet collectivism which hardens everything out there into a kind of dross.

Even music, the most non-representational of the arts, is

not entirely exempt from the kind of connection we have been trying to make. At the very least, again, we know it's possible to compose masterpieces while sitting on the can. Never mind that the Germans didn't care for Tchaikovsky's music and used the *1812 Overture* for buttwipe during the war, or that Max Reger had this to say, after Voltaire, in retaliation against one of his many critics: "I am sitting in the smallest room of my house with your review before me. Soon it will be behind me." We wonder about Vivaldi, with about 600 concertos to his credit, or Bach, with all those cantatas — and they had to produce them, every week or so, for performance in school or church. Since no creative constipation was allowable here, they must surely on occasion have composed in a hurry, while at the same time giving vent to the stirrings of their other end. Here would come an urgent rush of bowel contents, and maybe at that moment an equally sudden rush of inspiration too, and a nice melisma or melodic run of crotchets would see the light of day.

V

"You can shit arpeggios if you like," Henry Miller sings in apostrophe to his beloved Tania in *Tropic of Cancer*, after she has in his mind taken the measure of his manhood through the back as well as the front door. Here, as elsewhere in his work, Miller shows an imaginative genius of the kind that relates the basest things we know to the vastest and most ethereal, to the music of the spheres. In *Black Spring* he compares, or rather reduces, the sun to a huge yellow anus up there in the sky. It takes quite a stretch to do this, of course, just as it does to picture Captain Ahab smiting the sun if it offends him, or Dostoevsky's Pawnbroker considering it dead after the light of his life has left him. But on these terms we could just as well turn things around and raise that anus to the greatness of the sun. Where it has at least the aesthetic stature of a "brown starfish" in a work such as that medieval Chinese classic of erotica, *The Love Pagoda*, now it is one with the ultimate source of life on this planet. Although a comparison with the vagina might seem at first a bit more apt here, the anus is just a minimal step removed, issuing a richness of its own which in turn, as we have seen, can give rise to new life. On the other hand, the vagina has been conceived as a symbol of death more dread than a mere anal orifice could ever be, a bottomless pit (and perhaps *dentata* as well) into which things fall, never to be seen again in the land of the living. A black hole, with enormous gravitational pull. World literature is full of the sexuality-as-the-kiss-of-death idea. For the Elizabethan poets, "to die" was a conceit for the sexual climax.

But fecal matter does not pull anything or anyone to it, unless you have the coprophilous tastes of a Marquis de Sade. Rather, its effluvia radiate outward in all directions, like the rays of the sun, and the stuff has already been seen as life-giving in a way that complements the sun's forces. And if you should happen to contemplate either one long enough, strange things would begin to happen. The sun would of course make you go blind. And the other — well, there was once a man who swallowed his glass eye while trying to take a drink of water in the middle of the night when half asleep. Later he has an obstruction in his rectum which he isn't quite able to figure out and so visits the doctor. That good man, after examining his patient, wanders into his secretary's office in a daze. "I've looked at thousands of assholes," he says, "and that's the first time one ever looked back at me!" Or perhaps we can best put it this way: there are times when you don't know whether to shit or go blind.

Of course, this is absurd. But again, anything we think about or do long enough and intensively enough is bound to be absurd. The very act of committing this thought to writing, for instance. Once on paper, and considered for what it really and ultimately is, *sub species æternitatis*, it becomes nothing more than an ejectum of the working, grinding mind, a kind of poop for which the stuff on which it is written serves as privy paper. I wipe off the effluvia of my mind, however carefully planned beforehand, with paper, and then I either push it away from me so that the rest of the world — my sewer — can have it, or I hang on to it for a while so I can contemplate it with morbid fascination. Perhaps ridiculousness of this kind has to be the natural overflow, the safety valve of intense seriousness, passion, concentration. I know a very intelligent man, for instance, who makes serious statements and punctuates them with farts. They are his commas, semicolons and colons (yes, an obvious connection here), exclamation marks, question marks and full stops. And what could be funnier or more appropriate than a well-timed fart in the midst of the platitudinous twaddle of a cacademic? There was once a windbag of this ilk on a bus who, having temporarily exhausted his own flatulence in spoken words and now feeling the need to jot down some more of the same, asked the student he was riding with if he had a piece of paper. "No sir, but if we pass close enough to a tree I'll try to grab a handful of leaves for you." And if it is true enough on a psychological level that those who can't laugh at themselves on occasion are in danger of cracking up, why wouldn't the same principle hold at a more basic physical level, or in a cosmic sense? Maybe if the world weren't basically or even basely funny, it would stop going around and drop into a black hole somewhere.

But here's another thought to top even that one, again voiced by Henry Miller. He speculates in *Sexus* that the ultimate reality out there may be nothing more than an enormous turd, going Nabokov's transformation of *le grand peut-être* into a potato at least one better. What now, if shit were not only the fecal but prime focal point of the universe? If the Prime Mover had succeeded only in moving his bowels? How gross, you might think, but how truly engrossed we would be in the unpleasant substance, so much so that we wouldn't even be able to sense it as unpleasant. There is the idea, not only toyed with by science-fiction writers but given more and more serious consideration by reputable astronomers, that there may be a great plurality of universes, one enclosed by or within another like nesting dolls. That is, what's a pebble or a grain of sand to us is a universe in its own right, its separate atoms becoming solar systems, just as the universe we know is no more than that pebble in the next larger universe — or that lump of excrement. When we become technological-

ly advanced enough to be able to see large and clear for the
first time just what this universe is a part of, perhaps some
astronomer will exclaim, "Why, my God, we're a turd, just
dropping from some asshole!"— although, the relativity of
space-time being what it is, there may be billions and billions
of years remaining to us before our universe makes it to the
sewer and is finally dispersed among other excreta.

VI

If current theories of space-time are correct, that our universe
is curved (and, considering the evidence that has been amassed,
very few would deny this today), so that you would return to
your starting point if you go far enough out there, we might
expect a word with as broad an application as the one under
discussion here to come "full circle" and be used in opposite
meanings. Where it is used aggressively, as a term of abuse, we
would also find it used caressingly, as a term of endearment.
And so it is, with many other things in between. In fact, the
word covers virtually the entire spectrum of language in its
usages as noun, verb, adjective, adverb, even conjunction and
particle—not to mention, of course, the interjection! There is
no doubt that it still has inestimable power in certain contexts,
in spite of this range of usage. But consider the refinement or
attenuation of, as well as the opposition to, its basic meaning
in the following contexts:

Wife: "Your old friend Bill just called, he's in town." Husband: "You're not shitting me, are you?" Or, more simply:
"No shit!" Student: "Professor, aren't there over a hundred
species of flatworms?" Professor: "Shit, there are thousands."
Football captain, after a disastrous first half: "Come on, guys,
let's get our shit together!" Spectator at a field-and-track
event, marvelling at the great distance achieved by a discus
thrower: "Holy shit!" Doting parent: "The little shit's going
to be in kindergarten this fall," or "My son just won an essay
contest in 7th grade. I'm so proud of the little shit!" Woman,
in the ecstasy of an orgasm: "Oh shit now, I'm coming!" And
then there is the case of Howard Fish, one of the most repul-

sive monsters in the annals of crime (the murderous atrocities he perpetrated against humanity in the earlier years of this century shall not be dignified by further elucidation here). Fish had an interesting personal habit or two. He would mortify the source of his excrement by stuffing gasoline-soaked plegets of cotton into his anal orifice and then lighting them. But the ensuing dance was more ecstatic than penitential. An extreme and pathological case, to be sure, but his final moments, just before they strapped him into the chair, are strangely illuminating. He asked for pen and paper to write a last testament of sorts, as if to redeem himself. Seized with passion, he wrote with astonishing rapidity, and what he wrote was an equally astonishing string of obscenities, hardly connected at all in any sensible or even grammatical way, in which the word "shit" was featured prominently.

I submit that this kind of thing is very great attenuation indeed—not to the breaking point, because there is none—but something that stretches far out into the known cosmos. Perhaps it is finally a matter of balance. Our wonder is sometimes so extreme, our feeling so towering that it can be expressed only by a word with the lowest center of gravity, in the same sense as when our eyes become fatigued by a brilliant blue, they see a yellow or brown after-image instead. That sun up there in the sky... and here we go in circles again.

EVOLUTION WITH A MORAL

Man is born, lives, dies. His body is then interred, becomes fertilizer, and helps make the grass grow green. Along comes a horse, eats the grass, digests it, and it becomes a horse turd.

MORAL
Never kick a horse turd.
It may be your uncle.

KAPEKAPE
CONTEXTS OF MALEDICTION IN TONGA

Harry Feldman

0.0. This paper attempts to provide a glimpse of the use of unacceptable language, *kapekape*, in the modern kingdom of Tonga. It is based primarily upon my own observations during a stay of some thirteen months on the main island of Tongatapu, but I am indebted to Margaret Craig, Cliff Goddard, and especially Thomas Riddle for their valuable comments and suggestions.

0.1. Section 1 consists of a brief overview of contemporary Tongan society. Section 2 is a glossary of terms for body parts, sexual activities, and excretion. And Section 3 discusses the range of social contexts and the relative levels of malediction that they tolerate.

1.0. Tonga is an archipelago of some 150 volcanic and coral islands lying at about 175° West and between 16° and 21° South. Approximately 100,000 people inhabit her 240 square miles of dry land. A nominal parliament ostensibly tempers the monarch's nearly absolute power. Tonga has, throughout her interesting history, managed to remain free of colonial rule (*see* Rutherford 1977 and references cited there).

1.1. Despite the profound and pervasive influence of the Wesleyan and other missionaries since the 1820s, many features of traditional Tongan social organization have persisted. Although the nuclear family is growing more important as the basic living unit, formal ceremonies, especially funerals (Kaeppler 1978), require the entire *kāinga* 'extended family' to participate in an intricate pattern of roles that the traditional kinship system determines.

1.2. While an analysis of the kinship system as a whole is irrelevant to this discussion (*see* Feldman, in preparation *a*) an understanding of the relationships of classificatory siblings will prove invaluable in the discussion of social contexts in Section 3. A synopsis of these, then, will serve to exemplify the kinship structure.

One calls any sibling, including cousins of one's own generation, of the same sex, *tokoua.* An older *tokoua* is called *ta'okete* and a younger one, *tehina.* A sister or female cousin of a male ego is called *tuofefine*, and a female ego's brothers are called *tuonga'ane.* It is the relationship between *tuofefine* and *tuonga'ane* that will prove of interest in Section 3.

Fefaka'apa'apa'aki 'mutual respect' is supposed to characterize the relations between brother and sister. This *faka'apa-'apa* has traditionally entailed almost complete avoidance behavior, particularly avoidance of physical contact and of eating in one another's presence. Male children ordinarily move out of their parents' house at about the age of puberty. Men customarily make their *tuofefine* gifts of their best produce and fish. In recent times the strictness of the avoidance has diminished. *Tuofefine* and *tuonga'ane* now frequently converse and sometimes eat together, but still rarely sleep in the same room.

1.3. The fundamentalist Wesleyan missionaries had no reason to find the manifestations of the incest taboo objectionable, and this may account for their survival. But in obliterating the pagan customs that did offend them, the missionaries achieved a gruesome success. Polygyny, for example, did not survive long after their arrival, nor did any of the traditional dances, nor the wrestling that was such an important pastime prior to contact.

It is hardly difficult to imagine the stigma that the missionaries must have attached to any kind of speech or behavior that lower middle class Victorian morality would have considered lascivious. The apparent enjoyment that many, if not most, Tongans derive from the use of *kapekape*, in appropriate contexts, may be a reaction to the strictness of Wesleyan dogma.

1.4. The Tongan language, along with Niuean and Niuan, comprises the Tongic branch of Western Polynesian. It is rigidly verb-initial and has straightforward ergative morphology (Churchward 1953; Feldman, in preparation *b*). As a guide to pronunciation I here provide a rudimentary sketch of Tongan phonology (but *see* Feldman 1978). Tongan has seventeen segmental phonemes: twelve consonants /p, t, k, ', m, n, ng, f, v, s, h/, and five vowels /i, e, a, o, u/. (The orthographic symbol ' represents a glottal stop, and *ng*, a velar nasal.) Vowels occur both long and short and there is a variety of diphthongs. Every syllable ends in a vowel and no syllable begins with more than one consonant; thus only open syllables of the form V or CV may occur. Main word stress falls on the second-to-last syllable if the last is short, and on the last if it is long or a diphthong.

2.0. This glossary comprises a selection of terms for body parts, sexual activities, and excretion. Each entry provides the usual word along with slang and euphemistic synonyms. Note that most words for body parts and bodily functions also have special synonyms applying only to persons of chiefly rank and a separate set for the royal family. These do not appear here.

2.1. BODY PARTS

2.1.1. **Penis:** *ule*; *me'a* 'thing', *mu'a* 'front', (*fu'u*) *'akau* 'tree', *fo'i siaine* 'banana'; *pū* 'uncircumcised' is a gross insult; *tefe* 'circumcised', *nuka* 'head of the penis.' Among the *kau fokisi* 'foxes; notoriously loose women', *menetete'e* 'outstandingly shrunken', is a commonly used insult (Tom 'Tomasi Fokisi' Riddle, in personal communication).

2.1.2. **Vagina, Vulva:** *pali, tole*; *manu* 'animal', *fo'i ava* 'hole.' According to Tom Riddle, *avangongo* refers to a vagina that frequent sexual intercourse has purportedly enlarged.

2.1.3. **Genitals:** *pī*, *'ao, fo'i 'ao*; *potu* 'place.'

2.1.4. **Pubic Hair:** *fulu*; *ali* 'beardless, lacking pubic hair.'

2.1.5. Scrotum: *laho, fuhilaho*; *lohofua* and *mahakivala* refer to testicles afflicted with elephantiasis.

2.1.6. Buttocks: *molū, tu'ungaiku*; *mui* 'back.'

2.1.7. Anus: *'usi, lemu, mata'usi. 'Usi* and *mata'usi* are interjections of annoyance. Young men also use these as a form of address expressing either hostility or solidarity.

2.1.8. Breast: *huhu*; *mata'i huhu* 'nipple' are not considered *kapekape.*

2.1.9. Semen: *hī.*

2.2. SEXUAL ACTIVITIES

2.2.1. Kissing: *kai 'elelo* 'eat tongue', *'uma fakapālangi* 'kiss European-style.' Many Tongans consider mouth-to-mouth kissing a bizarre practice rendering these terms quite dirty expressions.

2.2.2. Cunnilingus: *kai pali* 'eat vulva', *kai manu* 'eat animal', *kai pī* 'eat genitals.'

2.2.3. Fellatio: *kai mu'a* 'eat front', *komo'i mu'a* 'suck front.' Fellatio is not a popular activity among Tongan women although some of the *kau fokisi* do practice it. It is quite popular, however, among the *kau fakaleitī*, a group of extremely flamboyant tranvestites. They congregate at the Dateline Hotel and especially at Joe's Hotel in Nuku'alofa and often proposition European men, particularly those from visiting military vessels. They do not ordinarily have sexual relations with each other.

2.2.4. Sexual Intercourse: *fai* 'do', *mohe* 'sleep', *pongo* 'copulate', *hili* 'lay on top of.' Churchward (1959) gives also the following: *fe'auaki*; *mōhenga* 'go to bed to copulate', *tono* 'commit adultery', *tango* 'visit at night', *mohetō* 'habitually visit at night.' *Kopi* 'move up and down or back and forth in the act of copulation', *kopi tu'u* 'make one thrust, ejaculate immediately, stand up, and go away.' *Pusipusi* 'fuck' is probably derived not from *pusi* 'cat' but from the English *push*, or possibly Tok Pisin *puspus* 'fuck.'

    Tingi 'fuck' is a fascinating word. It arose, apparently out of nowhere, during my stay in Tonga and immediately replaced all other words for 'fuck.' Even old people and little children seemed to use it almost exclusively. On a recent visit to Tonga (26-30 June 1979), however, I noticed that its use had died down considerably. *Tingi* has no other meaning in Tongan nor is it an obvious loan from Fijian or Sāmoan. Cliff Goddard (in personal communication) suggests that it may derive from English *thing.*

2.2.5. Rape: *tohotoho, tohotoho'i.*

2.2.6. Petting: *ngaahi ngeli* 'make monkey.'

2.2.7. Anal Intercourse, etc.: *fai 'usi* 'fuck asshole', *fai faka-kulī* 'fuck dog-style'; *fai vaha'a va'e* 'fuck between legs' does not involve anal penetration.

2.2.8. Masturbation: *tukufule'i, fule'i, tukutoki, fule'ule.* *Fule'i* serves as an interjection of surprise or annoyance, and *Fule'ule!* corresponds roughly to *Fuck off!*

2.2.9. Cohabitation: *malimali* 'pretend to be married', *faka-suva* 'like a Suvan', 'cohabit without either being married or pretending to be', *nonofo* 'live together.' *Nonofo* makes no claims about the marital status of the participants. *Fakasuva* reflects the traditional hostility between Tongan and Fiji. *Fisi* 'Fiji' is a fairly productive derogatory suffix, e.g. *kumala-fisi* (=*kumala kovi*) 'bad sweet potato.' It is interesting that the Fijian word for unmarried cohabitation is also *vakasuva*, reflecting in this case perhaps the contempt that rural Fijians feel for the comparatively cosmopolitan center that their capital city has become.

2.2.10. Horny: *fie'uli* 'want to be dirty.'

2.3. EXCRETION

2.3.1. Defecate: *siko*; euphemistically, *tu'u mama'o* 'stand far', *'alu mama'o* 'go far.'

2.3.2. Faeces: *ta'e, te'e* in compounding, e.g. *te'epulu* 'cow shit.' *Me'a kovi* 'bad thing' is a common euphemism. *Fo'i kāsele* 'turd', from *kāsele* 'outhouse' (cf. *castle*).

2.3.3. Urine; Urinate: *mimi*; euphemistically, *tu'u ofi* 'stand near', *'alu ofi* 'go near.'

2.3.4. Flatulence: *te'epilo* (cf. 2.3.2.), *posī* 'hiss.' *Pilomotū* 'fart-smelling' is a common derogation.

3.0. In Tongan society, as elsewhere, there is a continuum of social contexts according to their relative toleration of swearing. In Tonga these range from contexts where *kapekape* is virtually compulsory to those where it is shocking, if it ever occurs at all. This section will focus on the contexts which in Tonga constitute the extremes of the continuum.

3.1. The single most permissive social environment for the use of *kapekape* is the *hopi* party. *Hopi* is a beverage concocted from water, sugar, yeast, and sometimes fruit. Because Tongan law proscribes its preparation, distribution, and consumption, *hopi* parties usually take place surreptitiously in the bush. Although the *kau fokisi* often drink the *hopi* that Peace Corps Volunteers prepare, women generally never participate in *hopi* parties.

3.2. The *faikava* 'kava party' approaches the *hopi* party as a context which tolerates *kapekape*. Garth Rogers (1978, 159) characterizes *faikava* conversation on Niuatoputapu as 'crude sex talk' and 'licensed ribaldry.' *Faikavas* may take place at an individual's home, in which case it is usually an unmarried woman who prepares the infusion from the crushed root of the *kava* plant (*piper methysticum*), or at a *kalapu kava-Tonga* 'kava club' (*see* Feldman 1980). Every village on Tongatapu has at least one such club and they tend to be all male, although a young woman remains the preferred *tou'a* 'mixer', if one is available.

3.3. Work situations vary in the degree to which they allow *kapekape*; some are comparable to the *faikava* while others are quite restricted.

Most Tongans earn their livelihood by subsistence farming. A group of related landholders commonly forms a *kautaha* 'company' working one man's garden one day, another's the next. When only adults are present the banter tends to center on sexual topics, but the strain of father-son relations (Rogers 1978, 159) would inhibit such discourse if a member's son is present.

In roadwork, dockwork, and similar enterprises, the ambience resembles that of the rural *kautaha*. Even office workers are free to indulge in sexually-oriented humor, with their female colleagues playfully flirting or loudly speculating among themselves as to the size of their coworkers' penes. In public places, however, like the bank or the post office, intercourse of this sort is severely restricted. In situations that tolerate *kapekape*, any crudeness directed towards the *tuofefine* of someone else who is present is a provocation to violence.

3.4. In general, there is a direct correspondence between the formality of a social situation and its toleration of *kapekape*. A schoolyard is therefore freer than a classroom, and a movie theater is more permissive than a church.

3.5. The restrictions on speech imposed by the brother-sister avoidance described in 1.2. cut across all other social contexts. As the actual avoidance diminishes, situations more and more frequently arise where a *tuofefine* and *tuonga'ane* are within earshot of each other. Not only a brother and a sister, but anyone else within their hearing, speaks circumspectly. Rogers (1978, 161) quotes a Falehau, Niuatoputapu youth as saying, "If someone swears or *speaks badly* when my sister is there, I must hit him or go away" (emphasis added).

The restrictions on speech in the presence of a classificatory brother and sister are very severe. It is not necessary to be sexually explicit to be offensive. This is what Rogers's youth means by "speaks badly." Words like *mafu* 'heart' and *sō*, both of which mean 'boyfriend/girlfriend' would not be heard in such a situation. Nor would *kaume'a* 'friend', even if it does not refer to a lover.

There is a popular anecdote in Tonga about a man who performed cunnilingus at Talamahu market in Nuku'alofa on a crowded Friday afternoon. To this day the mention of the names of the man or the woman involved will always raise a laugh. But if a *tuonga'ane* and *tuofefine* are within hearing one could hardly say anything more disgusting.

4. The aim of this paper has been to provide an overview of the way social context influences the level of dirtiness of speech in modern Tongan society. The following topics require a great deal of further research, and I hope that there will soon be native speakers of Tongan willing to undertake it:

(1) Compiling a more complete glossary of *kapekape*, including the chiefly and royal terminology and euphemisms.
(2) Formulaic expressions with sexual content, including, but not limited to, similes, e.g., *hange koe hoosi* 'like a horse', of penis size; *hange koe kosi* 'like a goat': horny.
(3) Nonce expressions and metaphors, e.g., *kai tofa kava* 'eat bearded oyster': perform cunnilingus.
(4) A more thorough survey of social contexts and the role they play in determining the relative acceptability of various types of malediction.
(5) Insults.
(6) Insulting and offensive gestures.

REFERENCES

Churchward, Clerk Maxwell. 1953. *Tongan Grammar.* London: Oxford University Press.

———. 1959. *Tongan Dictionary.* London: Oxford University Press.

Feldman, Harry. 1978. "Some Notes on Tongan Phonology," *Oceanic Linguistics* 17.2.

———. 1980. "Informal Kava Drinking in Tonga," *Journal of*

———. In preparation *a*. "Tongan Kinship Terminology."

———. In preparation *b*. "Tongan Verb Classes."

Kaeppler, Adrienne. 1978. *"Me'a faka'eiki*: Tongan Funerals in a Changing Society," in Neil Gunson (ed.), *The Changing Pacific: Essays in Honour of H. E. Maude.* Melbourne: Oxford University Press.

Rogers, Garth. 1978. "The Father's Sister is Black," *Journal of the Polynesian Society* 87.157-82.

Rutherford, Noel. 1977. *Friendly Islands: A History of Tonga.* Melbourne: Oxford University Press.

DISTURBING YOUR SEED
OR, GREATER LOVE HATH ONAN

Scott Beach

According to Eric Partridge's masterful *Origins*, "to mastur-bate" comes from the Vulgate Latin *masturbare*, whose past participle is *masturbatus*, whence "to masturbate." *Mas-* re-fers to the male seed (cf. *mas*culine, e*mas*culate), while *-tur-bate* has the same source as dis*turb* or per*turb*. Accordingly, when you jack off, assuming you're male, you're "disturbing your seed." If you're female, on the other hand, you should, by rights, have a word of your own. How about "cliturbate"? A neolojizm!

Now that we've laid the groundwork for this disquisition, let us consider the remarkable variety of terms, euphemisms, and phrases for autoerotism. Some are arcane and clinical, like **autoerotism**, some are pejorative, like **self-abuse**, and many more are simply ribald, like "**Yank my doodle**, it's a dandy!"

Probably the most popular of all expressions for this sub-lime activity is **jack off**, sometimes reduced to **j/o**. The "off" is clearly a reference to the climax of the ceremony. In other words, if you do it without having an orgasm, you merely jack. There are several other expressions with *off*: **jerk off, beat off, whack off, pound off,** and **do yourself off.**

A good many of these expressions incorporate terms of violence — *beat, whack, flog, pound, jerk, whip.* "An' there I was, **floggin' my log**, when. . . ." "There wasn't anybody else around, so I decided **to whip it**." "Wanna watch me **pound my pork?**"

Still others are more poetic: **make love with Mother Thumb and her four daughters; shake hands with the guy that stood up when I got married**. When a guy gets horny, and doesn't feel like having company, he can always **haul his own ashes**.

There is a controversial story in the Bible about Onan spilling his seed. In Genesis 38:9, we read: "And Onan knew that the seed should not be his; and it came to pass, when he went in, unto his brother's wife, that he spilled *it* on the ground, lest that he should give seed to his brother." In the very next verse, we read that this pissed off the Lord, wherefore He slew Onan. Verily, jacking off can be dangerous to thy health!

About 1590, somebody invented the coarse term **frig**. Apparently, it referred to friction, an indispensable ingredient in the act. Later, in the 18th century, someone else added *it*, as in "frig it!"

The French *se tapper la colonne*, meaning to tap, hit or pound one's column, has evolved into the usually insulting term *tappette*. If a Frenchman calls you a *tappette*, he means you're a jack-off.

Other English phrases are more rarified. **Prime your pump, stir your stew**, and **pound your pud** are cases in point. **Pull your wire** has an industrial connotation, and was possibly coined by an electrician experiencing a tumescence.

Many readers will recall the classic line: "Ninety-five percent of all males jack off, and the five percent who say they don't are damned liars." I, of course, have no way of proving that, one way or another. I suspect, however, that the author wasn't far off the mark.

What can we learn from all this? Well, what the hell do we *need* to learn? We're human. . . so we jack off! Big deal! It would be fair to say that if all the energy that goes into jacking off, world-wide, every hour of the day, could be harnessed, there'd be enough power to tell the Arabs and other oil producers to **go beat their meat!**

CHAUCER'S VIEW
OF THE
PROPER TREATMENT OF WOMEN

*John Davenant

I

Chaucer's interest in sex has been noted even by the least
intelligent of literary critics,[1] and has been celebrated[2] or
anathematized in accordance with each critic's prejudices. I
attempt in this paper to be more specific than usual about his
sexual philosophy. In doing so I take issue with Nevill Coghill,
whose translation of the *Canterbury Tales* smoothly obscures
one of Chaucer's most precisely described amatory incidents.

The reader may recall the scene in the "Miller's Tale" when
Nicholas approaches his landlord's wife

> And pryvely he caughte hire by the queynte
> And seyde "y-wis, but if ich have my wille,
> For derne love of thee, lemman, I spille,"
> And heeld hire harde by the haunche-bones... (A.3276-9)[3]

(And quietly he caught her by the cunt and said, "Clearly, unless I have my way, for secret love of you, lover, I shall die,"
and held her hard by the haunch-bones...) We cannot fail to
note that Nicholas's approach is somewhat sudden, not to say
violent. The vigour of the action is underlined by alliteration
and strong irregular stress in the last line—eight monosyllables
(but for the final *es*) of Anglo-Saxon origin. Separated pro-
sodically from what goes before by a combination of end-
rhythm, end of quotation and end of rhyming couplet at
lemman, I spille; separated from what is to follow by its own

153

slow cadence, and in particular the twin stresses of *haunche-bones*: this striking line stands alone, and recalls (in the middle of an adapted French tale) the rough, unpolished alliterative verse of an earlier England less influenced by continental courtliness.

Now if Coghill's translation is to be relied upon, Nicholas's boisterousness is soon effectively calmed. By the time this first embrace is over

> **And Nicholas had stroked her loins a bit**
> **And kissed her sweetly,**[4]

Alison might have concluded that she was being handled with kid gloves. But Coghill misleads us. Doubt arises, to begin with, over 'loins,' which translates *lendes*, although a study of the texts in which this latter word occurs in Middle English will soon show that it denotes 'bottom' rather than 'loins' wherever it is possible in context to distinguish the two. The real problem, however, is with 'stroked.' The original reads:

> **Whan Nicholas had doon thus everydel,**
> **And thakked hire aboute the lendes wel,**
> **He kiste hir swete... (A.3303-5)**

(When Nicholas had done this thoroughly, and *thakked* her well about the bottom, he kissed her sweetly. . .) 'Stroked' therefore is intended to translate *thakked*. But does it? Coghill may simply have been following Skeat, who in his edition of Chaucer's works[5] supplied two alternative glosses for the word, 'stroke' or 'pat.' Coghill chose the gentler alternative. What decisive evidence Skeat had that it might mean 'stroke' I do not know. But I doubt whether he had any. Certainly *this* passage cannot support him, for the context gives us no real clue as to what Nicholas was doing—only that it was something appropriate to Alison's *lendes.*

Fortunately there are texts where the precise meaning of *thakke* is not left in doubt. Now these passages suggest to begin with that Alison's bottom, not her 'loins,' is the part acted upon. This is clear enough from lines 140ff. of the *Land of Cokayne*, a Middle English satire on the morals of monks and nuns:

> To the maid dun hi fleeth
> And goth the wench al abute
> And thakketh al hir white toute.[6]

(Down they fly to the maiden, and all surround the girl and *thakketh* her white arse.) Lines 136ff. of the same poem are relevant, though *thakke* does not appear:

> [The abbot] takith maidin of the route
> And turnith up her white toute
> And betith the taburs with is hond
> To make is monkes light to lond.[6]

(The abbot takes a girl of the party and turns up her white arse and beats the drums with his hand to make his monks come back to earth.) The exactly similar contexts suggest that *betith* here and *thakketh* above are more or less synonymous. An amusing metaphor here likens spanking a girl's bottom with beating a pair of drums.

And, conclusively, Chaucer in the "Friar's Tale" writes:

> This cartere thakketh his hors upon the croupe... (D.1559)

(The carter *thakketh* his horse on the rump...) To urge his horse out of a muddy hollow, the carter *whips* it; surely, he does not *stroke* its hindquarters. I take this final example as proving that *thakke*, sometimes at least, means 'whip.' We must now work back to the experiences of the maiden in the *Land of Cokayne* and of Alison in the "Miller's Tale."

In these contexts *thakke* could mean 'stroke' or 'kiss' or 'pinch' or anything else that a man might conceivably do to a woman's bottom. But Occam's Razor discourages us from hypothesizing diverse and unprovable acceptations when we already have a proven meaning, 'whip,' which more or less fits. Admittedly the monks did not have whips with them when they went flying, so they could do no more than 'smack' the girl. But if we assume that *thakke* means 'beat (method unspecified),' we shall definitely be on the side of the evidence. The same applies to Nicholas and Alison. In the context of sexual play, and given the meaning we have deduced for *thakke* elsewhere, the best supported translation for it in the "Miller's Tale" will be 'smack' or 'spank.'

The length and prurience of the above argument is a pity, but the errors of Skeat and Coghill had to be set right.

II

We may now go on to examine some further relevant passages. And first of all, in case any doubt remains that sexual violence is in question in the "Miller's Tale," study of a later couplet will dispel it. Reflecting on the presents offered to Alison by her other suitor, Absolon, the miller comments:

> **For som folk wol be wonnen for richesse,**
> **And som for strokes, and som for gentilesse.** (A.3381-2)

(For some people are conquered by generosity, some by *strokes*, and some by courtesy.) What are *strokes*? Assuredly they are not caresses, for the word is not attested in this sense before 1665,[7] and it would in any case not form much of an opposition with *gentilesse*. *Strokes* means 'beating, corporal punishment,' as it already did in the contemporary *Gospel of Nicodemus*, lines 419f.:

> **Ane wane of fourty strakes**
> **With yerde falles hym be smyten.**[8]

(One less than forty strokes with the rod shall he be beaten.)

Here then are three different ways to conquer a woman. But Chaucer is not giving way to any urge to sententious, irrelevant moralizing. The "Miller's Tale" is colloquial, forceful and absolutely lacking in versifier's fluff: every line and every word has its point. Absolon tried the first way—money—and failed, as the reader is to learn. Alison's husband courted her as his wife—the third way—and is losing her. He is losing her to Nicholas, whose expression of his desire was boisterous and violent, and whose reward was the somewhat eventful night of love which the miller recounts.

Alison, then, was one of those who are to be conquered in the second way, by violence. As regards morality, she is quite lacking in commitment to her marriage or guilt at her promiscuity. She is amoral, in fact, and not in any word of the "Miller's Tale" is she criticized for it. Physically she is supremely desirable, and the skillful description of her in lines

A.3233-3270 is strongly erotic in its effect without being at
all coarse. Here and elsewhere she is likened to a wild animal
that requires taming. Alison's character as Chaucer gradually
develops it—her enjoyment of sex, her animal attraction, the
need to subdue her by violence—while not at all strained or
unconvincing certainly tells us something of Chaucer's own
sexual inclinations.

III

The miller's is only one of the *Canterbury Tales.* Alison is the
most sympathetic and the most desirable of Chaucer's young
women, but it is quite unjustifiable to draw conclusions about
any author from his creation of one character or one episode.

Further evidence that Chaucer considered violence between man and woman a central part of sexual relationships
is not difficult to find.

Passages implying that it was a man's right to beat his
wife in punishment are not especially interesting. After all,
this right has been generally acknowledged in Western societies,
and it was scarcely questioned in Chaucerian England. But
even in this context one remark in the "Shipman's Tale" is
particularly suggestive in its calculated ambiguity:

> For I wol paye yow wel and redily
> Fro day to day; and if so be I faille,—
> I am youre wyf—score it upon my taille... (C.1604-6)

(For I will pay you fully and willingly, day by day; and if I happen to fail, then—I am your wife—*score it upon my taille.*)
The most obvious meaning of the last phrase is 'mark it on
my tally,' that is, debit it to my account. The payment in
question is in any case sexual. The wife says that if she does
not, on any particular night, live up to her promise of sexual
satisfaction, she is at any rate at her husband's lifelong disposal
and they can make up the shortfall another night.

But Middle English *taille* is represented by modern 'tail'
as well as 'tally,' and 'tail' as a synonym for the buttocks is
not by any means only a recent usage: it has a long history.
Score it upon my taille thus equally, in the context, means
'mark it on my backside,' that is, give me a whipping. The

invitation, though disguised in ambiguity, is not meant to be missed by the alert reader. And the fact that the invitation is made suggests that corporal punishment between husband and wife can (in Chaucer's view) mean more to the wife than punishment alone.

A woman may indeed become emotionally dependent on chastisement, and accept it without complaint even when it is inflicted by someone other than her husband, guardian or lover. This is one of the reflections Chaucer intends to suggest to us in the long and little-read "Tale of Melibeus," in which Melibeus's enemies break into his house, beat his wife and severely injure his daughter. In the subsequent judicial arbitration Melibeus's wife pleads for the attackers and succeeds in saving them from punishment. The purpose of the tale is as obscure as the characters' motivations. While not claiming to have clarified it very much, I would suggest that *masochism* (to use an anachronistic term) is part of Chaucer's characterization of Melibeus's wife.

The Man of Law reminds his hearers with dry humour that women are subject to their husbands' whims for pleasure as well as punishment:

> For though that wyves been ful holy thinges,
> They moste take in pacience at nyght
> Swich maner necessaryes as been plesynges
> To folk that han y-wedded hem with rynges. (B.709-712)

(Wives may be very holy things, but at night they must accept patiently as their duties whatever may be the pleasure of the people that have married them with rings.)

IV

Chaucer's most cogent exemplification of his views of the relationship of woman to man comes, paradoxically, in the "Wife of Bath's Tale." The Wife of Bath is the proud and boastful personification of feminism triumphant:

> ... Jesu Crist us sende
> Housbondes meke, yonge and fressh abedde,
> And grace t' overbyde hem that we wedde;
> And eke I praye Jesu shorte hir lyves
> That noght wol be governed by hir wyves. (D.1258-62)

(Jesus Christ send us husbands that are obedient, young and fresh in bed, and give us grace to subdue the men we marry; and also I pray Jesus shorten the lives of men who will not be ruled by their wives.) This is her final prayer, shot through with the consciousness of power and success. Now the "Wife of Bath's Tale," the unashamed autobiography (within Chaucer's fiction) of a woman who has ruled five husbands and seen them die, is not written for us to admire the narrator. This goes without saying. But it is quite wrong to take the whole story as a satire on one small class of women—the masterful ones—for all women are implicated.

The narrator herself certainly does not claim to be unusual. Consider lines D.1037ff.:

> "My lige lady, generally," quoth he,
> "Wommen desyren to have sovereyntee
> As wel over hir housbonde as hir love,
> And for to been in maistrie hym above..."
> In al the court ne was ther wyf ne mayde
> Ne widwe that contraried that he sayde.

("My lady," he said, "generally, women desire to have sovereignty over their husbands, just as they do over their lovers, and to have the mastery over them..." In all the court there was not one wife, not one maiden and not one widow that contradicted him.) The statement that women desire to subjugate their husbands went entirely unquestioned by women in the audience. The Wife of Bath was simply a woman who had succeeded in this aim—or as she more picturesquely puts it,

> ...my self hath been the whippe. (D.175)

Yet although the Wife of Bath emerged from her eventful marriages the victor, she did not emerge unscathed. It is interesting and significant that the husband who came nearest to subduing her was the one who boxed her ears. The circumstances are themselves revealing. Jankin, her husband, had a book of tales from ancient history, with which he would sit by the fireside in the evenings reading tales of wicked wives and how they bullied and murdered their husbands. The Wife of Bath found this galling, and after hearing some particularly taunting recitation she sprang up and tore three pages out of his book. Jankin, unlike any of her other husbands, was brave enough to retaliate physically. He lost the war, needless to say: she recovered from concussion with all her wits about her.

> "O, hastow slayn me, false theef," I sayde,
> "And for my land thus hastow mordred me?
> Er I be deed, yet wol I kisse thee." (D.800-802)

("Oh, have you killed me, faithless thief," I said, "is it for my lands that you have murdered me? Still once more, before I die, let me kiss you.") To this mingled curse and endearment Jankin succumbed, became sympathetic and tearful, and never recovered the advantage.

In view of his spirited, if eventually doomed, resistance, Jankin is the only character in the "Wife of Bath's Tale" with whom the male reader can really sympathize; in the reversal of nature which the Wife of Bath's story is, he forms for a short time a reference point of normality.

The reversal of nature to which I refer is not the ambition and mercilessness of the Wife of Bath herself. It is clear enough elsewhere in the *Canterbury Tales* that women may be naturally cold and brutal: in the "Monk's Prologue," for example.

> By goddes bones! Whan I bete my knaves
> She bryngeth me the grete clobbed staves
> And crieth, "Slee the dogges everichon
> And breke hem, bothe bak and every bon." (B.3087-91)

(By god's bones! When I beat my apprentices she brings me the big knobbly sticks and shouts, "Kill the dogs, every one of them, break their backs, break every bone.")

The reversal of nature is in the fact that the Wife of Bath actually succeeds in dominating, if not killing, each husband in turn and even in convincing them that they are happy under her domination. Negatively here, positively elsewhere, Chaucer is showing us that women's unhealthy ambitions, sensual appetites and animal instincts need to be physically subdued if they are to be controlled at all.

V

It should be clear, though in the intellectual fog now surrounding sexual variation it may not be clear, that Chaucer is not here shown to be a *sadist*. The sadist derives sexual pleasure from activity which a partner finds painful. No philosophical view of human relationships is really consistent with sadism, except the sublime egotism and irresponsibility of the Marquis de Sade himself. Chaucer, by contrast, happily and perceptively observed society from its warm interior. He noticed that women, if they are to live peacefully with men, need to be kept under control, and that satisfactory control sometimes requires physical restraint or punishment. He noticed, moreover, that mastery of a woman by a man is often acceptable to both and may be a source of pleasure to both. Chaucer's view of the man-woman relationship is worth the attention of a good many confused thinkers of the twentieth century.

NOTES

1. Haldeen Braddy, "Chaucer: Realism or Obscenity?" *Arlington Quarterly*, 2 (1969), 121-138.
2. Peter G. Beidler, "Art and Scatology in the Miller's Tale," *Chaucer Review*, 12 (1977), 90-102.
3. Quotations from the *Canterbury Tales* are taken from the eight-volume edition by John M. Manly and Edith Rickert (Chicago: University Press, 1940) with minor alterations of punctuation and spelling.
4. Geoffrey Chaucer: *The Canterbury Tales*, translated by Nevill Coghill. Harmondsworth and Baltimore: Penguin, 1951. Page 114.
5. *The Complete Works of Geoffrey Chaucer*, edited by Walter W. Skeat. London: Oxford University Press, 1927. Page 111 of the Glossarial Index.
6. *Early Middle English Verse and Prose*, edited by Jack A. W. Bennett and Geoffrey V. Smithers. 2nd ed. Oxford: Clarendon Press, 1968. Page 143.
7. *Oxford English Dictionary*, s. v. Stroke *sb.*[2].
8. *Das mittelenglische strophische Evangelium Nicodemi*, edited by F. Klotz. (Inaugural dissertation: Königliche Albertus-Universität zu Königsberg i. Pr.) Königsberg, 1913. Page 54.

WORLD HEALTH ORGANIZATION REPORT : XII.1980

G. Legman

ASSUMING the present total population of the world to be about 4,000,000,000 (and doubling every 35 years or faster, from now on), that's four billion men, women, and children, of whom about one quarter are either too young or too old to have any sex life. The other three billion — making a billion and a half couples — have sexual intercourse an average of twice a week, making a total of *three billion acts of sexual intercourse on this planet weekly.*

Refining these figures a bit closer, since there are seven days in a week and 24 hours in a day (a total of 168 hours per week), that means that there are taking place *every hour,* seventeen million, eight hundred and fifty-seven thousand, one hundred and forty-two acts of sexual intercourse, or *297,619 per minute;* or using our smallest measure of time, *4,960 acts of sexual intercourse every second* of the time, since it is at all times a reasonable hour for it somewhere on the globe. Phrased more simply, at *5,000 acts of intercourse per second,* if it took you one minute to read the preceding two paragraphs, three hundred thousand acts of intercourse took place during that minute, meaning that six hundred thousand (other) people — or well over half a million — got fucked.

If we consider that during every act of intercourse, six inches of hot penis slip in and out of an equal and conjoined six inches of luscious wet vagina, for an average of two hundred strokes, that means one hundred feet — thirty-three yards — of combined trackage on the hot penis and luscious vagina, as above stated, per act of intercourse. Multiplying this by the 4,960 acts of intercourse per second (at godnose how many strokes?!?) we arrive at the total of 163,680 yards of hot cock, or exactly NINETY-THREE MILES lusciously slipping in and out of a separate And Equal NINETY-THREE MILES *of truly juicy pussy,* EACH AND EVERY SECOND of time that passes in this world. One question, friend: —

ARE YOU GETTING YOUR SHARE ???

BLASPHEMY IN "NOUVELLE FRANCE" YESTERDAY AND TODAY

Nancy Huston

According to Christian doctrine, speech constitutes an intermediary stage between thought and action; it is a kind of materialization of thought, the continuation of the same process being the "translation" of speech into action. An evil thought is already sinful but it escapes all forms of sanction, whereas the verbalization of this thought is subject to external judgment. As recently as the nineteenth century, tortures were inflicted on those bodies which contained particularly obstinate "evil tongues." (Etymologically, "blasphemy" indeed implies a form of gossip: it means to harm somebody's reputation and is derived from the same root as "to blame.")

In Québec, a law formulated in 1806 specified that: "All of the King's subjects, of whatever quality and condition, are very expressly forbidden to blaspheme, swear and detest the Holy Name of God, or to proffer any words against the honor of the Very Holy Virgin His Mother, or the Saints; and all those who shall be found guilty of having sworn and blasphemed the Name of God, of His Very Holy Mother or the Saints shall be condemned the first time to a pecuniary fine according to their means, and according to the magnitude and enormity of the Oath and Blasphemy, two-thirds of which shall be payable to the local Hospital, and where there is no Hospital, to the Church, and the remaining third to the denouncers; and if those thus punished should recommence the uttering of the said oaths, they shall be condemned the second, third, and fourth times to a double, triple and quadruple fine; the fifth time they shall be placed in fetters on Feast Days or other Sundays, and there remain from eight o'clock in the morning until one o'clock in the afternoon, where they shall be subjected to all insults and opprobriums, and in addition condemned to a considerable fine; and the sixth time, shall be led and conducted to the Pillory, and have their lower lip cut, and if by obstination and inveterate bad habit they continue, after all these punishments, to utter the said swearwords and blasphemies, they shall have their Tongue cut to the quick, so that in the future they can no longer utter them, and in the case in which those thus condemned should be unable to pay the said fines, they shall be kept in Prison for one month on bread and water, or longer, as the Judges see fit, according to the quality and the enormity of the said Blasphemies." [1]

One hundred and seventy years later, Québec lawcourts are still bringing people to trial for blasphemy; serious lawyers are still spending hours convincing serious judges that the Virgin Mary has really been offended, and thousands of Catholics are still signing petitions to protest against the public reviling of the name of God.

Three years ago, Québec feminist author and poetess Denise Boucher wrote the play *Les Fées ont soif* [2] (*The Fairies Are Thirsty*) whose three characters—the Mother, the Virgin and the Whore—denounce in terms at once crude and lyrical the condition of women in a Catholic society. The play was to be staged at Montréal's Théâtre du Nouveau Monde, but suddenly the Canada Arts Council withdrew its subsidies for the project. Throughout the fall, a lively debate as to whether or not the play should be censored was conducted in the columns of every newspaper in the province. *The Fairies* was famous before it even got onto the stage. It did, however, manage to get on, despite the obstacles. This provoked an unbelievable outlash of anger from right-thinking folks.

On December 4, 1978, after the play had already been running for a month, an "emergency" trial was held. The claimants, who claimed to represent 200,000 people (the Young Canadians for a Christian Civilization, the State Council of the Cavaliers of Columbus of Québec, Inc., the Catholic Parents Association of Québec, the Women Farmers' Circle of the Province of Québec, etc.) demanded the immediate interruption of the play as well as the total eradication of its printed version. They accused the accused (author, actors, director, editor, etc.) of having, among other things:

— Represented the Holy Spirit, the Third Person of the Very Holy Trinity, and God Himself, as being the rapists of all women including the Very Holy Virgin Mary;

— Incrusted in the skin and in the behavior of the rapist, that is to say of the Holy Spirit, words that are abject and vile, and gestures that are most disrespectful of the human body and in particular of the female body;

— Represented the Virgin Mary and all women as victims of the caricature that is made of God in this play;

— Claimed to liberate all women from the fetters in which the Very Holy Virgin Mary presumably has locked them through her virginal purity, this purity being a hindrance, according to the author and in the opinion of the defendants, to the experience of pleasure in their body and in their sex;

— Underlaid and explicitly situated the main thrust of the play entitled *The Fairies Are Thirsty* within the framework of a destruction of faith, morality, the family, laws, culture, and society as a whole. (...)

What is singular about the denunciation of blasphemy in general, whether the denouncer be the transgressor himself (as in the case of confession) or a third party (as in the present case) is that in order for the sin to be brought before a tribunal (be it religious or secular), it must be reiterated — which is to say, literally reproduced. No one expects a lawyer to commit murder in order to illustrate the gravity of the crime of murder, but crimes of language have always had an awkward and redundant status before the courts. This is why the transcripts and minutes of obscenity and blasphemy trials (cf. for example those of Lenny Bruce) have always made hilarious reading. The case in point is no exception: the "emergency trial" of *Les Fées ont soif* is in and of itself a stageable tragicomedy. Its cast is made up of three characters: Mr. Colas, the prosecution attorney; Mr. Sheppard, the defense attorney; and Mr. Reeves, the judge. Here are some excerpts from the more than forty pages of transcripts:

Colas: The statue is made to say: "I am the Desert that is recited grain by grain."

Reeves: Uh...what page are you referring to, please?

Colas: All right, I'll give you the page numbers, Your Honor, page 83. It starts and we see the statue speaking and it says: "I am the Desert that is recited grain by grain," and on the same page the author makes the statue — who obviously represents the Virgin Mary — say: "I am the Licking-up of Denegation." (. . .) One thing's for sure, when you make such blasphemies and such use of the litanies of the Virgin, you can't help feeling a certain nausea. (. . .) "I am an Image, I am a Portrait, I have both feet stuck in plaster, I am the Queen of Nothingness, I am the Doorway to the Void, I am the Sterile Marriage of Priests, I am the Nevershorn White Sheep, I am the Star over Seas of Bitterness, I am the Dream of Bleach Bottles, I am the Mirror of Injustice, I am the Seat of Slavery, I am the Unknowable Holy Vase, I am Obscurity and Ignorance, I am the Secret White Secretion of all Women, I am the Succor of Imbeciles, I am the Refuge of the Useless, I am the Tool of I am the Silence that is more oppressing and oppressive than any word, I am the Iron Collar imbedded with jewels of flesh, I am the Imagined Image, I am She who has no body, I am She who never loves herself." You see how far you can go in the transformation, not to say the parody, of the litanies of the Virgin which the majority of those here present have themselves recited at one time or another, during their childhood. (. . .) If this is how the liberation of women must be achieved, Your Honor, I must say that I feel sorry for those women who would obquire [*sic*] their liberty in such a manner. (*Pause*) There is a passage which — of course, it's written in a French that I apologize for having to use; it's just to show you to what extent it's possible to blaspheme — again, it is the Virgin Mary who is made to say....

Reeves: What page?

Colas: Page 111: "You done shaved your armpits with my d...
razor again, you crazy Christ." (*Tu t'es encore rasé l'poil d'en
dssour des bras avec mon m... rasoir, chrisse de folle.*) I apologize but after all, that's what it says—in a French that would
certainly not be accepted by the French Academy as being a
play that should be handed down to posterity as far as its
realism goes, and which obviously will not encourage Bill
101[3] to be recognized by all social strata. And then on page
113, there's this—and once again, Your Honor, this is an absolutely shameful blasphemy—: "I am the Immaculate One of
all their conceptions, I am the Disjointed One of all their ob-
sessions. Men are afraid of what blossoms between their legs,
that is why they batter you, that is why they invented me.
When they were afraid of the Void, they had already invented
God." (. . .) And then again—and once more in a French that
I apologize for, Your Honor, on page 137: "You gonna see
how I gonna wham into you, don't get up on your high horse,
I know you like it, you're made for it, you damnsweetcunt
Virgin of a Whore, come on, come, come!" (*Tu vas vo-ére que
j'av euh j'vas t'rentrer d'dans. Fa pas ta précieuse, chu sûr que
t'aime ça, t'es faite pour ça, mau-dite-bell' plott' Viarge de
Putain, envôye, jouis, jouis!*) You know, it's not easy, huh, I
mean, not just anybody could read something like that. It's
by a certain culture to even be *capable* of mastering that kind
of French, let me tell you. (. . .)
Reeves: . . . I don't think it claims to be French, but it is indeed a language that is spoken in Québec.
Colas: I see. Thank you, Your Honor...for clearing up such
an important point because I might have had my doubts....
These, then, are some of the passages. I could have read you
the whole play and believe me, we would have had some pretty hot stuff to show you in the course of the exposé.

*Mr. Sheppard, for the most part, refuses to deal with the con-
tent of the play; he orients his argumentation around questions of legal procedure:*

Sheppard: My erudite friends [the prosecution] claim that they
unfortunately had to wait for the publication of the script

before taking action. (...) What prevented them, if it was such an emergency, the play having been very noisily announced over the past several months and having opened more than a month ago, from sending emissaries—who would, I suppose, have been given absolution in advance for watching such a play...

Reeves: In your defense, you must be careful not to lay yourself open to a summons enjoining *you* not to indulge in blasphemy.

Sheppard: Oh, Your Honor, I don't think that receiving advance absolution is in danger of being a blasphemy. But I'll withdraw the remark, if that will give me immunity....

Reeves: Up until now you're doing fine; please continue.

(*Later*)

Reeves: Allow me to ask you a question, Mr. Sheppard. Supposing that in this play—we're going to do a bit of a cultural exercise here—it were Abraham, Sarah and other Biblical characters that were represented. That would have been just as valid as a symbol. (...) Which party would you be representing in this Court? (...) Given the general nature of the litigation submitted to me, what is your feeling? You're not obliged to answer.

Sheppard: I must say that I'm surprised to be asked what my feeling is, but since you ask me I'll tell you. If, instead of a play attacking the sensitivity of Catholics, it had been a play attacking the sensitivity of Jews or Protestants or any other religion or even my own principles, I would have no hesitation in defending the freedom of expression of the people I represent.

Colas, however, rejoins the fray and delivers the coup de grâce*:*

Colas: I'd just like to add, Your Honor, that...the whole play goes against the institution of the family. (...) On page 121, Mary Magdalene speaks of "unit, family unit, cell unit, living unit, family cell"— she rejects all of these fundamental values which are recognized even by the Canadian Declaration of the Rights of Man. There is really an attempt to debase not only religion but also all of the principles attached to it: "Fam-

ily family infamy infamy blues blues the family gives me the
blues bruise infamy bruise—uh—blues woman infamy infamy
family woman woman blues woman blues blues blues blues
blues a woman blues a family blues blues blues blues infamy
blues blues blues blues infamy blues blues blues blues little-
baby little-baby blues my little-baby blues blues blues blues
my little-baby blues my woman blues." (...) But you see —
it's not me, it's not me, I — it's not me that wrote that!

* * *

After deliberation, Judge Reeves hands down his decision:
The temporary withdrawal from circulation of all printed versions of the script. Although this judgment was subsequently
reversed in Superior Court (by a female judge), Colas & Co.
have appealed the new decision, and the scandal has done anything but subside.

MORAL: *In North America, almost twenty centuries after
the birth of Christ, the belief still prevails that—just as the
best way to keep a fish from smelling is to cut off its nose—
the best way to keep a fairy from being thirsty is to cut out
her tongue.*

NOTES

1. Robert-Lionel Séguin, *L'Injure en Nouvelle-France* (Ottawa: Leméac,
   1976), pp. 116-117.
2. Montréal, Québec: Éditions Intermède, 1978.
3. Law stipulating that French is the official language of Québec.

> ## YOU HAVE JUST
> ## INSULTED
> ## A WOMAN
>
> This card is chemically treated.
> In three days,
> Your prick will drop off.

MEDFLY CRISIS: GOVERNOR FORMS FRUIT POLICE

SACRAMENTO (AP) To combat the rapidly spreading Medfly infestation, Governor Jerry Brown has established a new corps of law enforcement officers known as the Fruit Police. The Governor, a renowned expert on California fruits, will take personal command of the Fruit Police.

The Fruit Police will go door to door and strip fruits in the Santa Clara Valley; they will set up roadblocks on highways leading out of the quarantine area, stopping all suspected fruit-carrying vehicles, ordering the fruits removed, and throwing them into the bushes to be dealt with appropriately.

The new officials will be clad in pink berets, lavender jumpsuits and chartreuse scarves, so that they can be readily recognized by motorists. Fruit Police will be issued State of California Flyswatters, carrying a photograph of Governor Brown on one side and Cesar Chavez on the other.

According to sources very close to the Governor, "Flight-trained Fruit Police will pilot helicopters that will drop massive quantities of *Brown for U.S. Senate* leaflets over the infested precincts—I mean areas—and our laboratory studies indicate that large doses of this literature make the Medfly nauseated and cause him to lose interest in mating." The source refused to confirm, however, reports that the material has the same effect on humans.

To assist the Fruit Police, there will be several volunteer auxiliary organizations, including the women's motorcycle patrol (Dikes-on-Bikes), the Swish Brigade, and The Faggots-against-Maggots.

Governor Brown insisted that his vigorous attack on the Medfly was consistent with his previous policies. "My administration has always given top priority to all fruits, nuts, and flakes," said Brown.

The new Fruit Police Commissioner, Gray Davis, was asked if the program was designed to help Governor Brown politically. Davis's only reply was noncommittal, saying, "Our sole motivation is to protect California's Number One Fruit."

— Submitted by Henry B., Colorado, Sept. 1981

THINGS BETTER LEFT UNSAID
PHOTOCOPY HUMOR

Cathy L. Preston *and* Michael J. Preston

If jokes are an index to popular attitudes, as has been asserted
in brief studies of sexual humor (Chapman & Gadfield 1976:
141-153) and of Nixon jokes (Preston 1975:233-244), then
it follows that, if one is attempting to assess those attitudes,
one ought not be seduced into ignoring non-oral jokes by the
rhetoric surrounding oral tradition. This is particularly true if
the group being scrutinized conventionally communicates on
paper (academics, bureaucrats, etc.) and prefers not to articulate the unpleasant or improper except in legally questionable
small-group discussions "that never happened." The parodies,
mock forms, jokes and cartoons which commonly appear on
bulletin boards or are circulated widely by hand before being
stuffed away in desk drawers and file-folders were first brought
to scholarly attention by a handful of articles, primarily Barrick (1972) and Preston (1974). The more recent efforts of
Dundes & Pagter (1975), Orr & Preston (1976), and Bell, Orr
& Preston (1976) make generally available a sizable quantity
of this material.

  Despite rather negative reviews of Dundes & Pagter, one
of which states condescendingly: "Much of the material—owing to its 'folk' genesis—is obscene and in poor taste" (Grider
1976:79), work continues. One difficulty with this material—
called, *inter alia*, "photocopy cartoons," "typescript broadsides," and "Xerox-lore"—is that redrafting cartoons for publication destroys as much evidence as it presents. Those in
Dundes & Pagter (1975) appear to have been so distorted that

Grider (1976:80) was led to comment that "many of these cartoons were apparently drawn by professional magazine cartoonists and have remained unchanged, without undergoing any 'folk' variation or embellishment." Simple inspection of an adequate sampling of these traditional cartoons reveals the opposite.

In the belief that—just as oral performances ought to be recorded by electronic means in order to capture more than just the text, so photocopied material ought to be reproduced by photographic means in order to reduce distortion—we are making our growing collection available through Xerox University Microfilms so that exact copies can be obtained for comparison with variants collected elsewhere. Our third installment of this material is presently being readied for Xerox-publication. A similar collection, that of P.S. and M.G. Smith of Sheffield University, is also being prepared so that, before long, both British and American "texts" will be available in substantial numbers to those interested in this kind of folklore. Variants cross both national and language boundaries. (Compare Herrera 1977:73-74 with four items in Orr & Preston 1976:114-117.) We have had items reported from Germany, Denmark, and Canada and would appreciate receiving any additional material from *Maledicta* readers, promising recognition or anonymity as desired in return.

Two pieces of Xerox-lore are appended. "Four Ways to Avoid Unpleasantness," an example of the not uncommon printed sheets which emanate from small print-shops, belongs in *Maledicta*, even though it strains our earlier attempts at delimiting the genre—at least until variants are located. (Our most ambitious definitional and analytical article is in preparation.) The second documents the near violent outrage of the thousands of academically displaced persons known euphemistically as unemployed or under-employed Ph.D.'s. Both examples were collected from an acquaintance who, upon receiving his M.A. in English literature, graduated into unemployment. The Modern Language Association *Job List* parody he obtained from, ironically, the University of Colorado Office of Admissions; the other from his brother in Louisiana.

REFERENCES

Barrick, Mac E. "The Typescript Broadside," *Keystone Folklore Quarterly* 17 (1972), 27-38.

Bell, L. Michael, Cathy M. Orr, and Michael J. Preston. *Urban Folklore from Colorado: Photocopy Cartoons.* Ann Arbor: Xerox University Microfilms, 1976.

Chapman, Anthony J., and Nicholas J. Gadfield. "Is Sexual Humor Sexist?" *Journal of Communication* 26 (1976), 141-153.

Dundes, Alan, and Carl R. Pagter. *Urban Folklore from the Paperwork Empire.* Publications of the American Folklore Society, Memoir Series No. 62 [Austin: University of Texas Press, 1975]. Reprinted as *Work Hard and You Shall Be Rewarded: Urban Folklore from the Paperwork Empire* by Indiana University Press, 1978.

Grider, Sylvia Ann. Review of Dundes & Pagter, *Western Folklore* 35 (1976), 79-80.

Herrera, L. [pseud.]. "How to Judge People's Character by Their Farting Styles," *Maledicta* I (1977), 73-74.

Orr, Cathy, and Michael J. Preston. *Urban Folklore from Colorado: Typescript Broadsides.* Ann Arbor: Xerox University Microfilms, 1976.

Preston, Michael J. "Xerox-Lore," *Keystone Quarterly* 19 (1974), 11-26.

———. "A Year of Political Jokes (June 1973-June 1974); or, The Silent Majority Speaks Out," *Western Folklore* 34 (1975), 233-244.

[*Editor's Note:* The two examples of photocopy humor presented here in typeset form look very different from the sheets one actually gets or sees: crummy-looking copies of copies of copies, barely legible, often full of errors, etc. The original copy of "Four Ways" is an 8½ by 11" white sheet, very professionally laid out and designed; with three line drawings of salesmen pointing to the coupon (deleted here for space reasons) and to the four sample sentences. The "Job List" parody is on an 8½ by 11" white sheet, typewritten, single-spaced throughout.]

FOUR WAYS
TO AVOID UNPLEASANTNESS

by George W. S. Trow

ESCAPE the ugly consequences of Straightforward Speech

Learn EUPHEMISM
The Language of Evasion

Do you need Euphemism? Read these sentences:

1. You're a Jew, aren't you, Mary?
2. Thank God I'm rich.
3. I'd like to take you out, Alice, but frankly, I'm a homosexual.
4. So many people of your age seem to be dead.

Did you spot the treacherous Straightforward Words (evocative of painful *reality*) in these simple sample sentences? If you didn't, you can expect endless difficulty and embarrassment in your pathetic little life. Let's *review* the FIVE MOST TREACHEROUS WORDS IN OUR MOTHER TONGUE, the words that cry out for translation into Euphemism, the language of evasion. They are (and, if you play your cards right, you need never face them again): "JEW," "RICH," "HOMOSEXUAL," "DEAD," and "FRANKLY." Learn Euphemism, the only language endorsed by the Department of Health, Education, and Welfare (as well as three leading Midwestern universities), and we'll tell you how to avoid these dread words, EVEN WHEN TALKING TO OR ABOUT MARCEL PROUST!*

*Our booklet, "The Lore of Euphemism," available for a nominal fee, tells the moving story of Euphemscholar Nancy Tmolin, who translated the sentence "Frankly, Marcel, you're a rich, dead, homosexual Jew" into Euphemism in ten seconds flat.

Now Look at the Subtle Problems Posed by this Second Group of Sample Sentences:

1. How come you don't have any children?
2. I have plenty of time, Mother, and I would come to see you more often, but actually I find you depressing.
3. I guess you're in the hospital for good this time.
4. How many toes do you have, anyway?

We'll teach you to defuse even these problem sentences.

1. You will learn ten ways to discuss the Middle Eastern Situational Conflict without ever mentioning the ugly word "Jew."
2. You will discuss *without blushing* people who are no longer alive!
3. You will learn the language secrets of the Carolinas (North and South), where absolutely nothing is said!
4. You will wear the miracle Eu-pho-phone (yew-foe-foe-nn), which automatically bleeps out offensive words in the speech of others.

ABSURDIST QUARTERLY: THE MLA *JOB LIST*

The October Issue

LOSTSWAMP COMMUNITY COLLEGE: We have one possible opening for a part-time, temporary Apprentice Instructor of English to be hired for a nine-month, non-renewable, non-tenure track, terminal appointment. The prospective candidate will replace four of our senior faculty members on sabbatical leave. We are looking for someone with the Ph.D. well-in-hand, a minimum of five years, post-Ph.D. full-time college level teaching experience, and with *significant* publications (i.e., they must be publications which have attracted international interest). The candidate will be expected to teach the following courses: 1 section of Film Studies for Fun and Profit, 1 section of Western American Literature of the Mohave Desert, 1 section of Remedial Grammar for the Educationally Disenrolled, 1 section of Old Icelandic Prosody, 1 section of the Bible as Literature: Leviticus and Numbers, 1 section of Bilingual Composition for Bi-cultural Day Care Center Trainees, 1 section of Cotton Mather: The Minor Sermons, and 4 sections of our 12-week introduction to literature course for engineers entitled Beowulf to Barth. (Please note that the courses for the second semester may vary slightly from those of the first semester as listed above.) Additional responsibilities will include: Director of the Writing Clinic, Chief Projectionist for the Campus Film Series, and Departmental Room Scheduling and Supply Officer. We would frankly prefer to hire a woman of highly mixed parentage who is bi-sexual and tri-lingual (i.e. English, Spanish, and Cajun—but not necessarily in that order of competency). However, since we are an Equal Opportunity and Affirmative Action Employer, by law we must also consider the applications of any qualified white males who want to waste their time submitting a dossier. Salary: $9,000 (but less for anyone lacking all the qualifications specified above). No moving expense provision; no health benefits. Interested? Write to Chairperson MaryLou Beauregarde, Lostswamp Community College, Whispering Glades, Louisiana 70001.

The December Issue

LOSTSWAMP COMMUNITY COLLEGE: Please be advised that our October listing resulted in 654 dossiers. We are sorting through the credentials of the many highly qualified candidates who have applied and will contact those we plan to interview at the MLA Convention by December 24. Don't call us, we'll call you.

The February Issue

LOSTSWAMP COMMUNITY COLLEGE: Since our December announcement—when we had already received 654 applications—over 150 additional dossiers have arrived. Frankly, we are inundated, so please do *not* send us any more. Also, we regret to say that there appeared to be some misunderstanding with regard to our original listing. Therefore, of the 125 candidates we interviewed at MLA, 78 had to be eliminated since, although they were over-qualified as *tri*-sexuals, they were, unfortunately, only *bi*-lingual. However, that still leaves us with 47 finalists. To all those who have been removed from consideration: good luck in finding suitable employment elsewhere.

The April Issue

LOSTSWAMP COMMUNITY COLLEGE: We regret to announce that due to severe budget cuts, we will not be hiring an Apprentice Instructor of English as planned. In fact, we are now involved in litigation over the dismissal of the four, tenured faculty members who had been scheduled for sabbatical leaves. But please keep your options open as we may have four junior appointments available during the 1981-82 academic year. We appreciate your interest in Lostswamp.

Come One!   Come All!

**OLD-FASHIONED
DONKEY ROAST**

Price $2.00

**EVERYONE
GETS A PIECE OF ASS**

Come Early!

MENOMINI MALEDICTA
A GLOSSARY OF TERMS OF DEPRECATION, SEXUALITY, BODY PARTS & FUNCTIONS, AND RELATED MATTERS

Reinhold Aman

The Menomini Indians, a Central Algonquian tribe, now have dwindled to about 3,000 people. They are centered around Neopit, Wisconsin, and are intermarried considerably with the French, with whom they generally sided during the French-British wars. There are few fluent speakers of Menomini (or Menominee) left, and within a few decades, this language will be most likely and unfortunately extinct.

The following glossary, culled from Leonard Bloomfield's 289-page *Menomini Lexicon*, is limited to our special concerns: words and expressions dealing with or considered verbal abuse, insults, sexual & excretory terminology, body parts and body functions, nicknames, ethnic slurs, negatively-valued nouns, verbs and adjectives, as well as taboo and other offensive terms.

Clearly, such a small percentage of the Menomini vocabulary taken from one source could mislead one to believe that the Menominis' concerns, value system and view of the world centered on the topics of this glossary. Obviously, there were many *more* important concerns, such as life and death, hunting and fishing, God and other spiritual matters. Still, this concentrated (and, if you wish, slanted) glimpse into the down-to-earth part of the Menominis' language shows us a side of their culture unlike the one presented by Hollywood's "Noble Brave": they are basically like you and I, expressing their displeasure for people who are "deviant from the norm" by being nasty, dirty in body or speech, insulting, quarrelsome, drunk, effeminate, big-nosed, sullen, stingy, stub-fingered — and who have anal hair. This last example is one of the many terms unique to cultures where members dress or dressed in scantier outfits than most of us do. By exposing more of their body, they see more of the other bodies and their shortcomings and, consequently, they have descriptive terms for such details and use them with a higher frequency than we would use our equivalents. Buttocks and genitals—neatly concealed beneath polyester pants by paleface—were in view of the other Menomini Indians who talked about them unabashedly, whether objectively, scornfully or in jest.

A few words about the arrangement of the entries and pronunciation. Lexicons of Menomini and other languages do not list verbs in the infinitive ("to go") but in the third person singular ("he goes"), as in this glossary. The colon (:) after a vowel indicates length, shown by Bloomfield as a single dot (·), and the open ε is shown here by ê. Pronunciation follows basically the IPA system, with a few exceptions: roughly, a ranges from *father* to *saw*; ê as in French *tête* or English *bad*; c as in ch*urch*; q is a glottal stop; and s ranges from s*ee* to almost sh*e*. Word stress basically falls on the next-to-last long vowel or diphthong.

Works consulted: Leonard Bloomfield, *Menomini Lexicon.* Ed. by Charles F. Hockett. Milwaukee, Wis.: Milwaukee Public Museum Publications in Anthropology & History, No. 3, 1975. (The late Professor Bloomfield extracted the vocabulary from texts collected in the 1920s.). Also, Leonard Bloomfield, *The Menomini Language.* Ed. by Charles Hockett. New Haven, Conn.: Yale University Press, 1962.

GLOSSARY

ake:now he lifts his leg and urinates against something
ana:qnem doglike person. *Plural* **ana:qnemok**
anê:cemyakosew he smells decayed
anê:m dog. *Archaic vocative, as insult:* **anêm**
anê:mikot! like a dog, dirty dog that he is!
anê:mo:hsêh little dog; puppy. *Note diminutive suffix* **-hsêh**

anê:mo:hse:hsêh tiny little dog; little puppy. *Note double diminutive suffix*

apê:qceketa:soq! how angry he is!

ape:saqnêm black dog

ape:s-wê:mêhteko:sew Negro. *Lit.,* 'black Frenchman'

aqsên, aqsan stone; *euphemism:* **ota:qseneman** his testicle(s)

aska:qnem glutton. *Plural* **aska:qnemok**

aska:qnemowew he is gluttonous

aske:pakaqnem green dog *(jest form)*

aske:h raw. ("Eskimo" is derived from this root)

aske:pow he eats raw things

a:nawehêhkiwê:w he fails to get a woman; he cannot get a woman

a:nemehê:w he makes things hot for him; he scolds him severely

a:pêhtawesew half-breed

a:pêhtawesiahkiw half-breed woman

a:poci:qkinamowêw he pulls back his foreskin for him *(med.)*

a:ya:nêqnêw he scolds him

a:ya:nehtah Scolds It *(man's name)*

awê:tok-apê:hni:hsak ugly dwarf spirits *(who dwelt on the rock called Death Door, near Green Bay, Wisconsin). From* **apê:hni:sêh** boy, lad *(dim.)*

ehsê:h! nasty! *Exclamation of disgust*

enê:kohkuahkosew he is so big around as a tree

enê:niahsêh little man

enê:ni:hsêh little man

ese:cehkê:qtaw he moves or places his buttocks that way

i:wê:w he (she) copulates with her (him)

i:yotowak they copulate with each other

kaka:pocehê:w he torments or afflicts him by teasing, insult or war

kaki:panakackow he is dumb

kana:skeqsa:hkwan he has a flat nose

kanêqsetam ese:kew, kanêqsetam otê:sekenan he is a troublesome person

kaska:mekopi:qtaw, kaski:kopi:qtaw he draws shut his anus

ka:qwekit Rough Face *(man's name)*

ka:skece:hkew his buttocks itch

ka:skenakê:w his penis itches
ka:skenê:qsewêw his testicles itch
kêqc-enê:niwew he is an old man; he is senile
kema:ceq-es-wê:pesem thou art indeed troublesome
kemo:têhkow he steals habitually; he is a thief
keni:qsahkwan he is long-nosed
keno:hkew he tells a lie
keno:htamew he thinks or calls him a liar
kenu:hkesi:hkiw he is a liar
kepuakomew he has a covering foreskin
kepi:hkihêw he gives him a swollen eye or black eye
kese:mê:w he angers him by speech
kese:qnenê:hkiw he washes his armpits
kesi:kopi:hsen he lies so as to rub his buttocks
kesi:mi:yahêw (or -how) he wipes himself after defecation
ke:hkamew he berates, insults or reviles him by speech
ke:hka:hcekew he is quarrelsome
ke:hka:hkow he berates or reviles people; he quarrels
ke:ma:pew he peeks, stealthily looks or watches; his glans
    shows within the foreskin (*medical*)
keto:ma:qnenim thou makest the Evil Gesture at me. *See*
    oma:qnenêw
ke:mena:qsow he carries on illicit love affairs
ke:menêciakan bastard
ke:menewê:w he secretly passes his hands over women; he
    carries on illicit love affairs
ke:ska:nowêhê:w he cuts off his tail; *especially as euphe-
    mism:* he castrates him (*bull, colt*)
ke:skenê:hciw he lacks a finger or hand
ke:skenê:hkiw he lacks an arm
ke:skesetê:w he lacks or has cut off a foot or toe
ke:wana:hpenêw he is insane
ke:wana:hpenêwetonê:skaw he talks insanely or deliriously
ke:wanêmê:w he speaks falsely of him; he slanders him
ke:wanêsew he acts crazily; he runs amok
ke:waskêpi:w he is drunk
ke:waskêpi:wahama:sow he sings a drunken song
ke:waskêpi:wenakosew he looks drunk

ki:hkenê:qsewê:hsen he hurts his testicles in falling

ki:qcenokan he limps; he is lame

ki:sapew he sits with his foreskin caught

ki:sekew he has no foreskin

ki:senekê:w he draws back his foreskin

ki:sketiq bob-tailed person or animal

konê:pa:ceqnêsew he talks wrongly or indecently

ko:hko:s pig

ku:ku:keciw fat person

macekehkwê:wes Silly Maiden *nickname and name of eldest of the ten women of the Eastern Sky (mythology)*

mace:q badly *and as prenoun,* bad

mace:q-awê:tok the evil one

mace:tonê:skaw he speaks in an evil way

maci:qsahkwan he has an ugly nose

mahke:nakew he is big at the genitals

mahke:qkow he is big-faced

mahki:qsahkwan he is big-nosed

mamasewê:w he (she) copulates

mama:hkêhtêw he has big ears

mama:hkesetê:w he has big feet

mama:kehsê:w, ma:ma:kehsê:w donkey; mule

mamu:qtapikên, mamu:qtapikat he is a bald, stringy creature

mana:skenê:qsewêw he is losing the skin of his testicles *(a coarse jest)*

maska:hsow lean, bony person

mata:qnem worthless cur *(dog or person)*

matê:sew he is bad, evil-looking, ugly

ma:ckêqnêw he has an erection

ma:ckêqnê:hkwamow he has an erection while sleeping

ma:hkekatê:w he has a crippled leg

ma:manêw he (she) copulates with her (him)

mêhkê:na:h (-kok) big turtle; dirty-spoken person

mêhkuahpenêweqkow he is red-eyed; he has sore eyes

meno:kosew he stinks

menu:kiton he has a foul breath

metê:mohsiahkasow he pretends to be a woman

me:cenêsow he befouls himself

me:cenêw he defecates or breaks wind on him

me:ceqtaw he defecates as he moves or works

me:ka:têhkiwê:w he fights or quarrels with a woman or with his wife

me:mena:skenêw he stuffs himself (with food) to the point of vomiting

me:me:cenanê:w he manhandles him to the point of defecation (*cf.* he beats the shit out of him)

me:qnakayê:w he (she) has pubic hair

me:qsece:hkêw he has anal hair

me:se:hê:w he causes or helps him to defecate

me:se:w he defecates

miana:ti:wê:qtaw he makes annoying noise

mi:h dung; piece of dung

mi:hêhkêw he gathers or works with dung; dung-beetle

mi:hece:hkew he is filthy on his buttocks

mi:henê:qsewêw he is filthy on his testicles

mi:si:wikamek privy. *Plural* **mi:si:wikamekon**

mi:tehkwamow he defecates in his sleep

mi:w he eats him or it

moqcecehkêw he is bare at the buttocks

moqceketê:hpêw he is bald-headed

nahê:neqnêsew he speaks in falsetto

nahê:qsenemow he is selfish

namê:h beaver

namê:pen sucker; carp; Norwegian; Irishman

nana:hehêw he reprimands or chastises him

nana:kwap between the legs

na:nawekahkwan Sagging Shins (*nickname*)

na:tawêw adder (*has spots behind head; its bite or a blow of its tail is deadly*); also, Iroquoian, *especially* Oneida

na:tawiahkiw Iroquoian woman; Oneida woman

nêhke:mê:w he angers him by speech

nêhke:nawêw he is angry or abusive

nêhku:hkipew he pouts, sulks

nêqnicenakê:w he has three penises (*nonce-form, for pun with* **nêqnoci:nekêw** he holds three of a kind (*at poker*)

nece:h my buttocks or anus

neka:san my vulva; **meka:san** a vulva

nemi:skanak my pubic hair

nena:wa:cenêniwakêsew he is a terrible man *(comical nonce-form)*

nenê:qseway my testicle

nenê:qsewaye:hsêh my little testicle *(jest)*

nepa:ceqtaw he exposes himself indecently

nepa:ka:nem my testicles. *Plural* -ak-. *From* **paka:n** large nut

nepo:hkesew he is taciturn or sullen or cross

nesa:kesekan my organ of excretion

neta:ta:skikatê:m short-legged person or creature

netê:tih my rectum

neti:n my thing; *also, euphemism:* my penis *or* my vulva

ne:cenakê:w my fellow penis-man *(jest)*

ne:cenê:qsewêw my fellow testicled one *(jest)*

ne:nak my penis

ne:nake:hsêh my little penis; *also,* my clitoris

ne:ta:hkasow my fellow dried-up one; my fellow skin-and-bones *(jest)*

ni:ciano:wêw he is childish. *From* **ni:cian** child

ni:skapetê:qtaw he angrily shows his teeth; he snarls

ni:skehewê:w he makes trouble for people

no:na:kan nipple; teat *(either sex)*

nu:hsi:qnemowew she is a bitch

oce:hkamekoh inside the anus

oma:qnenêtowak they make the evil gesture at each other. *See next entry*

oma:qnenêw he *(especially,* she) makes the evil gesture at him: *the closed fist is held out, with thumb underneath, and then the fingers are extended, with the words,* **Yo:m wa:pahtah** look at this.

oma:qnenewê:w he *(esp.,* she) makes the evil gesture at someone or at people

omê:ka:hpenêw he is scabby all over from a skin disease

omê:keciw he has scars or scabs on his belly or body

omê:kehcewê:w he has a scab or scar on his arm

omê:kekatê:w he has scars or scabs on his legs

omê:kenê:hciw he has scars or scabs on his hand

omê:kepê:hkwan he has scars or scabs on his back
omê:keqkow he has a scarred or scabby face
omê:keqsa:hkwan he has a scarred or scabby nose
omê:ketê:hpêw he has scars or scabs on his head
omê:keton he has a scar or scab on his mouth or lip
omê:ke:w he has a scar or scab
osa:manosow, osa:mehkama:w he smokes too much
osa:matimow he weeps too much
osa:ma:hpew he laughs too much
osa:mehkwamow he sleeps too much
osa:mehsemow he dances too much
osa:menawê:w he is excessively angry
osa:meqsew he drinks too much
osa:meton he talks too much; he is boastful; he is insolent
otê:hkomew he has lice; he is lousy
owaq! *Exclamation of contempt*
paci:skeqsa:hkwan he has a prominent nose
paka:cekamow he is nice and fat
paka:ceketa:sow he is in a fine rage
paka:cenawê:hê:w he gets him good and angry
paka:n large nut; testicle. *See* nepa:ka:nem
pape:ko:wew he is like a flea; he has fleas
pape:wesetê:w he has small feet
paqsanakeceh the fissure of the buttocks
patuanê:w he copulates with her
pa:hpakahê:w he repeatedly raps him; he knocks at *(as a door); coarse jest:* he copulates with her
pa:hpakekqsanê:hê:w he vigorously copulates with her *(related to:* to spank with or hit with a stick or switch*)*
pa:hpenahamasow he sings much and carelessly
pa:hpenawê:nehcekê:w he is confused in his mind
pa:hsekiw he swells up
pa:hseton he has swollen lips
pa:hsetonê:wak white people *(they have "swollen" lips)*
pa:kiqnêsew he talks noisily
pêqcetonêmow he makes a slip of the tongue
pê:ketow he breaks wind
pê:ketwan breaking of wind

pê:qsekomê:w   he speaks fault-findingly of him; he mentions his short-comings

pena:kehsen   he inspects without authorization; he noses about

pepê:hkeciw   he is pot-bellied

pê:pêhkêci:t   pot-bellied persons

pepê:hkeci:hsêh   little pot-bellied person (*nickname for the youngest of a set of brothers*)

pepê:kataneqkow   he has his face daubed up with dirt

pesku:qcikew   he is short of body

puaqcow   he is constipated

puh, pum, pu:q   *Sound of breaking wind*

pu:seciw   he is stingy, miserly

sa:kesew   he goes out of a place; he urinates; he defecates

sa:keto:hnêw   he walks out of a place; he steps out. *Polite expression for* he defecates or urinates

sa:qsaki:qsahkwan   he has a snub nose

seka:kimyakosew   he smells of skunk

seke:n, seke:na:poh   urine

seke:nê:w   he urinates on him or it

seke:w   he urinates

seki:hkwamow   he urinates in his sleep; he wets his bed

se:hkatênehtakosew   he is spiteful

se:pe:w   he acts long; he is long-winded, verbose

se:qsahowê:w   he pinches people

tê:skik   short person or creature

tata:skikatê:w   he is short-legged

tata:tekimow   he stutters

tati:hkeqsa:hkwan   he has spreading nostrils

ta:qtakacehkiw   he is lazy; lazy person

teki:sehkow   he is of bashful disposition

teki:sew   he is bashful, abashed

teme:ka:tê:w   he has a stub leg

teme:nêhciw   he has stub fingers

teme:nêhkiw   he has a stub arm

teme:setêw   he has a stub foot

tepa:ha:kaniahkiw   prostitute. *From* **tepa:ha:kan** thing for sale

tepa:ha:kaniahkiwikamek   brothel

to:hkopêka:powew   he stands with buttocks spread

to:hkopê:hsen he lies with buttocks spread

tu:hkopiahnêw he walks with buttocks spread

wane:nê:w he acts excessively or crazily; he is greedy

wane:nê:wesew he is foolish or mischievous or licentious; she is of loose conduct

wawa:kesetê:w he is pigeon-toed

wayê:semewê:w he cheats people

wa:ki:qnekew he is hunchbacked

wa:weyakeqnêsew he talks nonsense or gibberish

wa:wiaqna:têsew he is foolish

wa:wiaqnesew he is foolish; foolish person

wê:hcetawaqnem, wêhceta:qnem! truly doglike! *Exclamation, esp. accompanying the Evil Gesture; see* **oma:qnenêw**

wê:pesew he is unruly, troublesome, crazy

wes! Nonsense! Pish! He is silly!

we:c-mêhkê:nahkon his fellow foul-mouth

we:c-wa:wiaqnesewan his fellow silly one(s)

we:nahkamekêsew he is dirty in a big way; he dirties the whole place; he is dirty in his habits and surroundings

we:nanaq dirty fellow. *Plural* **we:nana:qsak**

we:napew it is dirty in his place

we:na:cemon dirty story

we:na:cemow he tells a dirty story

we:na:hpenêw he has a venereal disease

we:na:nake:qkow he has dirty eyes

we:nêhkawê:w he dirties or defiles him by foot or body movement, by presence or frequentation

we:nêhtêw he has dirty ears

we:nê:nemêw he thinks him dirty; he is disgusted by him

we:nehcekê:w he makes a mess

we:nehkêna:h *a species of winged beetle that appears on carrion;* a person of dirty habits or foul speech. *Plural* **-kok**

we:nekatê:w he has dirty legs

we:nemeneqtow he has a dirty eye

we:nenakosew he looks dirty

we:nenê:hciw he has dirty hands

we:nenê:hkiw he has dirty arms or armpits

we:nepow he dirties or defiles his mouth, especially by eating

we:neqtaw he works in a messy way; he botches his work
we:neqta:ckow he is a dirty, messy worker; he is a botcher
we:nesê:hkow he dirties up by spitting
we:nesew he is dirty
we:netanekomê:w he is dirty at the nose; he is snot-nosed
we:netê:hpêw he is dirty at the head
we:qsakakanamê:w he hurts him with a blow
we:qsakeketasow he is terribly angry
we:qsakenawê:mê:w he arouses his indignation by speech
we:y! *Exclamation at magnitude or distance; also, exclamation of disgust*
we:yaketonê:skaw he talks gibberish
we:yawekêh old woman. *Vocative:* **Weyawekêh!** Wife!
we:yawekêhko:hsêh little old woman
we:ya:cehêw he degrades or defiles him
wi:nahki:skawêw he dirties him by trampling
wi:necyanê:hamasow he sings through his nose
wi:necyanê:qnesew he talks with clogged-up nose; he talks through his nose
wi:nekasyamêw he eats him or it with dirty fingernails
wi:ya:ciahkawêw he defiles, injures or bothers him by coming or by frequentation
wi:ya:ciahkawekow he defiles, injures or bothers people
ya:h! *Woman's exclamation; also,* once more
ya:hpece:hsemêw he throws him to death
ya:hpetahê:w he knocks him senseless or dead with a club
ya:hpetê:hnaqsiw he burns him to death or ashes
ye:y! *Exclamation of horror*
yu:hwa:h! *Exclamation of severe pain.*

POSTSCRIPT

To see the reaction of a major god of linguistics to the preceding glossary, I sent an advance copy to a senior American linguist whom I shall identify here as "Old Chuckie." He did not like it, of course. Here is the gist of his letter of 29 Aug. 1981 to me:

"A worthwhile discussion of Menominee maledicta should turn first to ethnographic sources and determine—whatever still can be determined after three centuries of contact with the West—the Menominee's own inside view of such matters. The word list might then be much shorter, but it would be classified to fit Menominee folk-taxonomic notions, and the glosses on the individual entries would be more than just rough English tags."

While in full agreement with Old Chuckie, I maintain that our basic lists—gathered with great difficulty from sparse and Spartan sources—will have to serve until the experts start ploughing the virginal field of maledicta and submit the fruits of their learning for publication.

Then I politely asked him for permission to publish his reaction, above. *Oy, gevalt!* Now Old Chuckie became utterly pissed at me, even refusing my prepaid return envelope and putting on his own 18-cent stamp: that's social distancing, folks! Chuckie wrote that he finds "the whole idea unappetizing and unscholarly. It serves no purpose and I would prefer not to be associated with it in any way." But that was not enough. He added another page (20 October 1981):

"Your culling of words from Bloomfield's Menominee dictionary implies two things: first, that malediction is a human universal; second, that even if we can't be sure of just what sorts of remarks would constitute malediction in Menominee culture, a list made on the basis of what we know to be the case in various other cultures is at least a basis for further research.

Point one: we do *not* know that malediction is a human universal. [Yes, we know, and it is! *Ed.*]

Point two: an extracted list such as yours is, if anything, a step backwards from the more nearly complete lexicon from which the forms are taken. Knowing what little I do about Menominee culture, I could guess that if one man really wanted to insult another, he might say something like 'He talks to his mother-in-law.'

I consider your basic lists, made without any attention to

human cultural diversity and without reference to such ethnographic information as we have, a completely fake sort of scholarship. It is worse than that: it is just one more ethnocentric plowing-over of the historical and ethnographic record, making all human societies look much more alike than they actually have been. Even a large percentage of our so-called anthropologists engage in that sort of activity these days.

I am always prepared to grant that my own views may be mistaken. But I have to vote my own conscience, not anyone else's. I don't want to have anything to do with it."

Yes, Old Chuckie, you *are* mistaken, the main reason for which is that you don't even *try* to understand what MAL is about and what fascinating and useful information *could* be gathered if narrow-minded, uptight, humorless scholars like you would just *try.* But that's similar to arguing with a blind man about the hues of red—one blind by keeping his eyes shut reality-tight.

As to characterizing the glossary "a completely fake sort of scholarship," Chuckie engages in verbal abuse. Bless him. The glossary is *not* presented as "scholarship" but is a simple listing of appropriate terms taken *verbatim* from Bloomfield's lexicon and as edited by Hockett, neatly typeset and slightly improved upon by added cross-references, etc. If the glossary is "fake scholarship," then Bloomfield's and Hockett's original is fake scholarship, too—which it isn't. Oh, well. Maybe the genital references upset agèd Chuckie, maybe the few humorous touches. Whatever, this arch-learnèd man is a typical example of the opposition *Maledicta* faces from most of the professional linguists, anthropologists, sociologists, psychologists, philologists, folklorists, dialectologists, lexicographers, teachers of English and foreign languages, and others who make a living from "investigating the mind and language of mankind."

Actually, we are in good company, fake-scholarship-wise. Franz Boas, the world-renowned anthropologist & ethnologist and equally esteemed scholars compiled even simpler lists of swearwords, insults, etc. But: If Boas does it, it's scholarship; if Aman does it, it's fake. If it appears in the *Report of the Bureau of American Ethnology*, it's scholarship; if it appears in *Maledicta*, it's fake. Right, Chuckie? *Sheeyit!*

How can we get those bleeders to remove their blinders, or at least to open their eyes? We could offer them a $75,000 grant for one year of maledicta research. Suddenly, *thousands* of these cacademics would come out of their closets and drop their opposition to our "unworthy" topic! Suddenly, there would be a tumescence of uninhibited *Maledicta* fans! But I don't want anyone who does it for money only. Just intellectual volunteers wanted—no cacademic whores.

Uncle Maledictus, alias The Swearword Professor, illustrates the "negative finger" gesture meaning "May you die a virgin!" during his lecture on Verbal Violence at Northern Illinois University, DeKalb, 4 Nov. 1981. Even though he insulted the photographer, Connie Ricca, she kindly permitted publication of her photo.

ABUSES OF THE CLERGY

Clifford Mortimer Crist

I take this title from one of the major divisions under which Legman classifies limericks in his magisterial work *The Limerick*, the canon for all limerick composers and collectors. *The New Limerick* also uses these divisions. If it is not yet a canon, it is already a twenty-one gun salute.

There are over four hundred printed limericks dealing with these abuses of the clergy. Seldom in literature can one find such a hodgepodge, such a diversity of insults, of invective, of injurious remarks and dissolute behavior. Many of these limericks give a degrading idea of what the common man thinks the life of the servants of God really is. The curtain of mystery, the secrecy of the Church, are shredded and the raw flesh exposed. Such revelations are due to the dichotomy that persists between the need for the consolation and promises of salvation of the Church and the fears and overt animosity evoked by the severe restrictions levied against the pleasures of life, that is, against what some old spoilsport decided to call sin. The limerick is a direct outlet for pent-up rage, gleeful revenge, the conviction that religious folk are as weak and sinful as any ordinary person.

The most popular member of the clergy to be castigated is the Bishop. There are 75 limericks dealing with this venerable man. There are 50 about priests, 30 about nuns and 20 about monks. These four categories comprise the most popular subjects for limericks but very few of the many religious ranks escape the barbs and sharp tongue of the limerick composer. The list is a long and formidable one and includes, more or less in order of frequency of appearance in limericks, the following: Preacher, Vicar, Curate, Parson, Father, the Pope, Pastor, Reverend, Cardinal, Archbishop, Rabbi, Virgin Mary, Dean, Abbot, Brother, Divinity Student, God, Jesus, clergy in general, Rector, Saints, Friar, Quaker, Sister, Prior, Beadle, Missionary, The Church, Warden, Acolyte, Abbess, Minister, Deacon, Theological Student, Mormon, The Trinity, Mother and Father Superior, Prelate and Verger. Apologies to anyone who has been overlooked!

It is not surprising that the Bishop leads the popularity parade. Here is a representative of religion very much in the limelight, pontificating at public ceremonies, often married, highly placed in the sanctified pecking order, much more conspicuous and mouthy than such even more exalted ones as Archbishop, Cardinal and the Pope himself. The pomp and magnificence of these latter worthies tend to impose a modicum of respect and although there are a few limericks criticizing each of these, basically they are held in awe, as are also God, Jesus Christ, the Virgin Mary and the Holy Trinity. But they do not escape unscathed: the Pope cannot be buggered because he has piles, Jesus cures Matthew, Mark, Luke and John of syph, clap and gon, and a harlot boasts she will take on the entire Trinity. But major attention is reserved for the Bishop and the humble priests, nuns and monks.

Favorite adjectives for the Bishop are libidinous, lascivious, lecherous and bibulous. Once he is called fearless (with a whore with the clap). Whereas the underlings of the Church are often mocked for their puny endowments, the envied Bishop is given in one verse a 10-inch tool, in another an 8-inch one. In one instance he comes 10 times, in another he manages 13. Obvious penis envy! One Bishop's peter is a meter long (see the Bishop of Chichester, below) and another is said to have fathered 100 bambini. All in all, many Bishop limericks are, even if in a vulgar fashion, complimentary indeed. It is easy to spot the composer's jealousy, a bit of envy, but also considerable respect for the old Bishop and his powerful presence.

Insults are not far behind the faint praise. Bishops screw

girls, sisters, nieces, scores of whores (some with clap), innumerable nuns (the favorite pastime), a Dean's wife; even Saints in their niches are not exempt. Buggery is very popular. Bishops bugger young priests, choir boys, a tattooed man, even the Pope (evidently one without piles). The Bishop himself is frequently buggered, successfully except by one Pope, whose tool is too limp. The Bishop deflowers young owls, jacks off in the font; one has elephantiasis.

Priests, Nuns and Monks are the ordinary clergy. They are omnipresent, and far down on the clerical ladder, not worthy of much respect. Behind their closed doors and screened windows these lowly servants of God are made to act just like ordinary folk, that is, they do in secret all the obscene things the average person does or dreams of doing. Many are their weaknesses. Like the Bishop, priests are addicted to screwing, buggery and masturbation and they often make use of the confessional for performing these profane capers. Many priests are young, some are handsome, some are gay, some are proud of their equipment although actual statistics are not given. Priests are especially prone to clap. And why not? They habitually consort with whores. One priest screws a nun in her coffin, another exorcises a woman with his prick and still another kisses a menstruating nun. The priest leads a lecherous life. Priests must pay dearly for their sanctimonious airs and their daily preachments against lust and sins of the flesh.

The Nun takes her licks in many fashions. She is screwed by the Pope, by the Bishop, by the Dean, by priests galore and by sailors and soldiers. One sets herself up as a whore. One has shenanigans in the Sistine Chapel. Nuns freely pass on the clap to cleric and layman alike. They keep a supply of candles handy.

Monks get the least respect. They screw and bugger, including a Father Superior. They are dissolute, they stink, they have clap; they are especially fond of nuns, sharing with Bishop and Priest this predilection. One monk goes so far as to bugger a nun on the altar and another hangs a nun's cunt in a tree. Unfortunately no explanation is given for this whim.

As for the other members of the clergy, a few eccentrici-

194 - MALEDICTA V

ties will give some idea of what is thought about them:

> The congregation puts firecrackers up the behind of a long-winded Preacher.
>
> A young lady pulls down the Vicar's knickers and makes unladylike comparisons.
>
> A young fellow who shot three old maids is given a gun by the unmarried Curates.
>
> A Reverend jacks off during his sermon.
>
> A Cardinal seduces a prostitute.
>
> The Dean fucks the Bishop's wife but he keeps his old school tie on.
>
> God carelessly created the Marquis de Sade.
>
> A Prior rapes owls (this seems to be a popular sport) and also a green lizard, which bursts.
>
> A Missionary fucks baboons.
>
> A Mother Superior gives a Brother the clap.

Let us take a look at some of the most famous limericks, many of them immortal classics, so that we can observe more closely the abuses of the clergy.

Here is an amusing contretemps that illustrates the common bond between the highly-placed churchman and the ordinary Tom, Dick and Harry.

> *There never was anything neater*
> *Than the Bishop of Chichester's peter.*
> *In the heat of a clinch*
> *It would stretch from an inch*
> *To just a bit short of a meter.*

Frankly, this is wishful thinking on the part of the author. A meter! Do you know how long a meter is? Well, you should. It's in the neighborhood of 39.37 inches and that's a pretty sporty neighborhood. 'Just a bit short of' my eyeballs! Dr. Kinsey and his sexistants measured, I am told by a solid source, several hundred thousand male organs. Not only did they find no two exactly alike in all dimensions (scholars have suggested using sex organs instead of fingerprints for identification. Just imagine a female cop taking your organprint!), but it was also brought to light that five to seven inches is the average length of most male organs, in the United States and probably world-wide, despite all those stories about someone sweeping a dozen silver dollars off the bar in one fell swoop. Anything over seven inches is the beginning of affluence and anything under five is more to be pitied than scorned. But 39.37 inches! Had we not gone on the metric system, this cock-and-bull story might have slipped by unnoticed. This may be an example of poetic license. If so, the poet should have his license lifted.

Is this the same Bishop as the following?

> There was a young lady from Chichester
> Whose beauty made saints in their niches stir.
>   One morning at matins
>   Her breast in white satins
> Made the Bishop of Chichester's britches stir.

What an embarrassing moment for our Bishop. Does anyone notice his predicament? His wife in the front pew who has a nose for such things? The ushers giggling about something in the rear? Old Mrs. Pinchem, deaf as a post but with eyes like an eagle? The Bishop cannot help recalling the evil rumors about his old friend, the Bishop of Kew:

> Have you heard of the Bishop of Kew
> Who preached with his garments askew?
>   A lady named Morgan
>   Caught sight of his organ
> And fainted away in her pew.

What a scandal that would be! Quick! Think of something impure, like Sister Felicia's drawers, or Brother Flaherty's ill-timed farts during elevation of the Host, or getting a dose of clap from the Deacon's daughter. . . . There! That did it. Out of gear and back in neutral. Now on with the sermon, based this morning on Psalm 60,3: Thou hast showed thy people hard things.

A great classic and fine example of expert clerical problem solving:

There were two young ladies of Birmingham
And this is the story concernin' 'em.
They lifted the frock
And played with the cock
Of the Bishop while he was confirmin' 'em.

Two young *ladies*, indeed! People are much too careless with the use of this term. It implies virtue, standards, social values and a cold stare when displeased. And these two little hussies are anything but ladies, as can plainly be seen by their behavior.

There is a time and place for everything. Perhaps late at night, sneaking into the rectory, two such lewd creatures might have lifted the frock and so on from there, with a certain amount of cooperation from the Bishop himself. But during confirmation ceremonies! Is nothing sacred? In front of all those virtuous churchgoers. Such actions could easily destroy the most sacred rites or at least add something not in the original text. These young ladies should be punished severely, and I do not mean something like dipping their fingers in holy water, either.

What would *you* do in such a desperate situation as this? The harm has been done, Pandora's box has been opened, the dog is out of his kennel, and all that falderal. You may not have a solution ready; the Bishop does:

But the Bishop was nobody's fool;
He'd been sent to a large public school.
So he took down his britches
And skizzled the bitches
With his eight-inch Episcopal tool.

Never thought of that, did you? Well, you do not become a Bishop by just sitting around, daydreaming and resting your laurels. The Bishop had been to a large public school. There, on the laying fields of Eton or emulating the spires of Oxford, he learned the necessity for quick action. Here is something that has to be nipped in the bud. Teach these little sweethearts, I mean these little bitches a lesson and let them see what happens when you take the bird out of its cage. It is to be hoped that the choir master is on his toes and will accompany this *ménage à trois* with lusty song and pealing organ.

This moment might be appropriate to collect the Offering, while the congregation is cheering their Bishop on. The Lord loves a cheerful giver.

> *There was a young lady from Devon*
> *Attacked in a thicket by seven*
>   *Anglican priests,*
>   *Libidinous beasts;* —
> *Of such is the Kingdom of Heaven.*

We need more information before deciding whether she was a 'lady.' Some females who are far from being ladies claim to be. But ignoring that, what was she doing in that thicket? A thicket is a thick, dense growth of underbrush, full of thorns and pricks, as our young lady was soon to find out. Olay!

And aren't seven Anglican priests a bit of too much? Even in England, where they do proliferate. Devon is in Devon-shire, whose county seat is Exeter (in which town there re-sides another lady famous in limerick) and Devon is near Eton and were she laid low by some university lads out on a lark or looking for some kind of bird, no one would be surprised, ex-cept perhaps Mrs. Grundy. The Anglican Church is a power-ful institution, as every sinner knows, but *seven* priests, a real gangbang if I ever saw one and I have seen several. Perhaps there was a Syn-od taking place. Actually, I suppose, a num-ber that rhymes with 'Devon' leaves little choice for a com-poser. Variants to the middle lines include:

> *Episcopal preachers,*
> *The lecherous creatures*
>
> *Itinerant monks,*
> *The libidinous skunks*

which give Eliot and Moore little cause for worry.

I wonder if 'of such' is the Kingdom of Heaven. Not if you listen to some divines. Old Calvin, full of indigestion, piles and general malaise, thundered that only about 300,000 souls were going to be saved (including Calvin) and go to Heaven. Calvin was a nasty-tempered scold with not enough phallic endowment to make a Heaven on earth. He is probably still wondering why he did not make it to Heaven. It is a common erroneous belief that all good men and women of the cloth go to Heaven. Balderdash! The rocky road from Heaven to Hell is literally strewn, I have been told by sanctified sources, with discarded cassocks, cowls and chaplets, a surplice of cotton and silk, belonging to those clerics who have failed to find their names inscribed in the Holy Book of Saint Peter and thus been denied admittance through the pearly gates. The Mother Church, in its naive exuberance, has sold a great many more tickets to Heaven than there are places there. Unfortunately, these tickets are no good in Hell, not even for a seat away from the flames.

Devon is most famous for Devonshire cream, a delicious concoction.

> There was an old monk of Siberia
> Whose life grew drearier and drearier.
> So he did to a nun
> What he shouldn't have done,
> And made her a Mother Superior.

Siberia lies east of the Urals and comprises about five million square miles. It has a reputation for extreme cold, dozens of degrees below zero, and is a thoroughly unpleasant place as Stalin knew and Solzhenitsyn discovered. Doctors who prescribe cold showers for horny youth (and even those older) are talking through their stethoscopes. They should be forced to visit Siberia for an extended period in deepest winter and see how false this old medical nostrum really is. Fie on the A.M.A. and even worse.

Examine the following:

> A horny young monk of Citeaux
> Used to cool his hot rod in the snow.
> But no matter how frigid
> The thing remained rigid,
> Popping off when it got two below.

Can't you just imagine this horny young fellow, out in front of the monastery with his hard dong plunged in a ten-foot-high snowbank, holding in his hand a thermometer, anxiously watching (and praying) for it to hit two below! *Victoire! Triomphe!!* Back to his mean pallet, his ardor cooled and sinless as a babe.

Citeaux is in France. Larousse helpfully comments: *hameau de la commune de Saint-Nicolas-lès-Citeaux, cant. de Nuits (Côte-d'Or): 250 h.* An abbey was founded there in 1098 (Nostradamus was born in 1503), eventually occupied by the Trappists. Larousse fails to say the Côte-d'Or is the site of magnificent vineyards, such as La Romanée-Conti and Le Montrachet, among the greatest of the world. No wonder so many men became monks there.

But let us return to our original old monk of Siberia. Here's that nagging question again: what was the monk doing there in that nunnery? Or was the nun to blame? Blue with cold, did she slip into the monastery and promptly get her come-uppance? It might have been the short summer season when weather conditions are more conducive to social intercourse. We could do with some fervent research on Living Conditions of the Clergy in Sub-zero Climates.

There is something warm in the thought that this simple little nun, impregnated by a careless monk and inspired that it might perhaps be a Child of God, suddenly became officious and assertive enough to rise to the top post over older and wiser Sisters. As Mother Superior she might even be able to conceal the birth of her child and even if it was not another Holy Infant so gentle and mild, rear it until the child was old enough to become a nun. Stranger things have happened in such places before, I have been told in great secrecy.

What if it was a boy, you ask, which is not very nice of you. In such a case, long experience shows what must be done: hide the child in a shopping basket and leave him on the threshold of some local old maid, for spite as well as convenience. It is even more humorous if she is a Protestant. This religious prank goes back to medieval times and the nuns get quite a giggle out of it. This custom still survives, you may be surprised to discover, in greatly altered form in our sport of Trick or Treat at Halloween.

> There was a young monk from La Trappe
> Who found something wrong with his tap.
>   "Oh Pax! Oh vobiscum!
>   Oh why won't the piss come?
>   I fear me I've gotten the clap."

This is an ancient discovery that has dampened the ardor of millions of young men. And quite a few older ones, too! It is as depressing as a note from the I.R.S. that there is something wrong with your income (instead of your outgo). And in a monastery! It is not going to be very convincing to tell the Brothers he got it from the toilet, which is not a very romantic place to take a female (or a male) in the first place.

La Trappe is in Normandy. This is the original site of the Trappist order and dates back to 1664. Mozart was born in 1756. It is an ascetic order, noted for silence and abstinence. Silence and abstinence! This young monk is a considerable big mouth with his petulant complaints and his only-too-obvious lack of abstinence is what has brought him to his present lamentable state.

The monk's knowledge of Latin is at best sketchy, as anyone who has read Caesar, Cicero and Catullus will immediately perceive. All those 'Ohs' stuck in! Perhaps this ignorant whippersnapper translates *Pax* as 'Piece' and *Vobiscum* as 'Your come.' Stranger things have been done to Latin. Wait until the Father Superior and the rest of the monks get word of his clap, for it will spread (it always does) and rather fast, too. And perhaps far, also.

We have another account of this monk's predicament:

> There was a young monk of La Trappe
> Who had shooting pains in his jappap.
>   He said, "Jesus Christ!
>   This don't feel nice; —
>   Methinks Sister Maud has the clappe!"

Aha! So it's Sister Maud who has been spreading this around. This is valuable information for the rest of the monks and any Bishop spending the night. Sister Maud's popularity will take a catastrophic drop, a decline that will make even Spengler's look minimal.

The use of 'methinks' is a nice touch. It puts us back into medieval times, if not very chivalrous, and then there is the spelling of 'clappe,' as in Ye Olde Pharmaceutical Clappe Shoppe. One should not leave this limerick without pointing out how bad the fourth line is. The rhyme is bad, the scansion is bad, the grammar is bad. It's a bad line.

Clap, by the way, was a beastly nuisance in holy places and mendicant seats like an abbey, monastery, nunnery, convent, cloister, friary, priory and hermitage, where it was, unfortunately, almost epidemic at times. Some of the grievous howls occasionally heard emanating from these houses may not have been a poor indigent friar wrestling with his soul and God but an equally poor monk emptying his bladder. How sad that penicillin was right there on the daily bread and no one bothered to discover it. Such is fate! It is a comforting thought that soon after the discovery of the wonder drugs, informed medics told us in all confidence that clap would soon be a thing of the past. *Vive la médecine!* I have been told, very hush-hush, by a renegade doctor, that clap cases can still be found.

It is to be hoped that Sister Maud did not use the Lady Chapel for *matinées.*

> *There was a young monk of Kilkyre*
> *Was smitten with carnal desire,*
> *The immediate cause*
> *Were the Abbess's drawers,*
> *Which were hung up to dry by the fire.*

How little it takes to light the spark of lust! In all probability these drawers were made of cheap, coarse material, perhaps old flour sacks, with no lace trimming whatever and no enticing opening, fore or aft. What a contrast with those black lace panties modern monks (and others) can lust after. With these old garments, it was hard to tell which was front and which was rear, unless one looked carefully for faint yellow and brown stains.

Why did the Abbess have the gall to hang her shabby garments in front of the common fire where everybody sat to keep warm? She should have realized she might raise evil thoughts or something even more dangerous.

The important question is, what was the monk doing there anyway? Was it visiting day? Laundry Maundry? This is the room where afternoon tea is served and the Abbess should be severely chided for hanging such a mundane object up, for all to see, tea or no tea. The author of this limerick, classic though it has become, had a scanty religious background. Monks and abbesses do not cohabit, the same building, that is.

But it is a charming thought that this young, innocent monk can fantasize such ardor from such a homespun fetish. One hates to think what a copy of *Hustler* would do to this sensitive creature. But *Honi soit qui mal y pense*, which is roughly translated as "Horny is he who has evil there in his pants."

Carnal desire like carnal knowledge has a weighty, Biblical connotation. Casanova was said to have declared, "I may have a low I.Q. but I've had great carnal knowledge." Is it not much to be regretted that the quaint and lovely old way of expressing it, "He had carnal knowledge of her," has been replaced by so uncouth and unimaginative a statement as, "He fucked her." It certainly leaves us with the dirty end of the stick.

> *A rabbi who lived in Peru*
> *Was vainly attempting to screw.*
> *His wife said, "Oy vey!*
> *You keep on this way*
> *The Messiah will come before you."*

Of all the countries in the world, Peru is the most popular one for limericists. It is not because of the llamas (who may be *número uno*), nor the famed houses of Lima, nor the majesty of the Andes. It is because the *-oo* sound occurs in about a hundred English words (Proper and improper), making it a limerick composer's *Oo's Oo*, so superior to words like *elm* and *orange*.

The talented author of this classic limerick makes one dangerous blunder; he uses the word 'vainly' which unfortunately has several connotations. Is the rabbi trying to invent a new position (thirty-three?), deliberately showing egotistic admiration for his technique and performance, assuaging his *vanity*? Or is it a fruitless attempt, one quite *in vain*? Or is it just a frivolous pastime, like a *vain* hope? It is always necessary to avoid using words with one or more meanings. Ambiguity leads to bitter controversy. We do not know what acrimonious battles may yet be fought over this innocent limerick. Look at those words and phrases in the Bible, still being feverishly debated and splitting factions and sects and not a few heads, all in the name of God, too.

The comments of the wife do infer the rabbi was doing an inept job. She, instead of being grateful, shows no respect for her husband's valiant efforts, his constant striving upward. Her anguished "Oy vey!" is the universal Jewish cry of despair, handy for any occasion, from upsetting a jar of home-made gefillte fish to finding a daughter in bed with a distant cousin, in this case not distant enough. The wife has no respect for her hard-working spouse. Is she herself utterly blameless? Has she cooperated fully, instead of just lying there thinking of making tomorrow's chicken soup? Has she taken the trouble to inspire him? Women are often too quick to criticize the man and forget their own shortcomings.

Rabbis, by the way, do not fare well in limericks. One carelessly circumcizes the entire organ, another has intercourse with a sacrificial goat and still another is caught serving for lunch his collection of clippings.

How long has this screwing been going on? The author is remiss in not telling us. Two hours? Four hours? All night? Perhaps if the rabbi removed his *yarmulke* he would make better progress. Trying to keep one of those on your head during copulation is not unlike trying to do it standing up in a canoe out on a choppy sea.

Let us hope the rabbi achieves his end before dawn breaks on the over-advertised ruins of Machu Picchu. Of one thing we can be reasonably certain: there will be no Second Coming.

> *A flatulent nun from Hawaii*
> *On Easter Eve supped on papaya;*
> *Then honored the Passover*
> *By turning her ass over*
> *And obliging with Handel's* Messiah.

Flatulence is gas assembled in the intestinal tract. Handel was born in 1685. It does not seem likely that papaya would raise enough gas to render this musical masterpiece. Why, it would require a freight-car load. Have you ever listened to this thing? Competent authorities assert that even under a speedy conductor, like Zubin Mehta, it lasts one hour, forty-three minutes and fifty-seven seconds, mountain daylight time. No matter how you assay the facts, papaya seems a strange nourishment for Easter Eve. Passover, also called Pesach if you are interested, is a festival of seven days during which only *matzah*, unleavened bread, is eaten. Have you ever *tasted* unleavened bread? I *was* surprised. Not bad...not bad at all. Nowhere in the sacred scrolls does it say you can sup on papaya. It is well known that in Hawaii pineapple has the same end result as papaya, which is why, on a windless day, the little sail boats still make their way back and forth across the bay. It might be noted here that pineapple would raise Hell with the rhyme.

How does a nun turn her ass over? In fact, how does anyone turn his (or her) ass over? Doctors, surgeons and Walter Cronkite, assigned to study and probe this astounding exercise, have never gotten to the bottom of it. But the answer is simple. What rhymes with Passover? Ass over. Any asshole can work that out. No matter how you slice it, it's a clever rhyme and to Hell with verisimilitude. I once asked the President of the United States Toilet Seat Corporation to stick his nose into this embarrassment. He argued *a posteriori* that the astute nun was in bed (Easter Eve), assessing the delicious but forbidden meal (papaya) and being half asleep and in a religious stew (Passover) she turned on her side (turned her ass over) and exuberantly assailed the Handel, letting her astonishing wind instrument pour forth its *fortissimo assai* salute. But I assure you, this solution is a bum steer and a lot of hot air and it assaults common scents.

If the nun is in bed, that eliminates a sticky aspect: How does a fart, or a salvo of farts, a whole cadenza, find their weary way out of the heavy bloomers and voluminous depths and multiple folds of a nun's habitual habit? This nun and some of her assistants had already tried asbestos panty hose, promptly blowing their shoes off. Farts are born little stinkers and find it hard to get out of the habit. This can lead to disaster. Can't you just imagine those little musical devils darting and drifting around underneath all that raiment trying to ascend to freedom? When they do emerge, the final movement, I reassure you, has the bouquet of a vintage wine. All joking aside, they might circulate for hours, days even, perhaps weeks, so that it may be July Fourth before the Handel makes the airwaves, at which point an unmusical ear might liken the burst to firecrackers. Meanwhile, the good nun keeps bustling about, getting a little behind in her daily chores, often harassed by the Sisters, often the victim of vile character assassination, perhaps the butt of playful jokes and superior Mother wit, as she practices rump-titty-rump and assorted fundamental Dairy Airs, preparing for the Masses she aspires to render unassisted *a cappella* (in the chapel). A great talent may be at work here, even if you can't put your finger on it. Long may this flatulent nun continue to be the *sine qua nun* of the nunnery. No wonder they burn so much incense in holy places.

Research by dedicated scholars and other pitchmen has shown that the name of this noted nun is Grace, called Holey Grace and Amazing Grace by all her associates. She was born in Athol, Mass.

So much for Abuses of the Clergy. They really do seem

just like us, don't they? Further research will be needed to separate the true from the false, the imagined from the real. Perhaps there are some surprises ahead!

One very far-fetched possibility titillates the imagination. Much of our present knowledge about the men and the cultures of a mere thousand years ago is based heavily upon the few surviving bits of literature that have escaped destruction and decay. Let us imagine we super-intelligent creatures succeed, a few years from now, through universal greed and nuclear disaster, in blowing up the world as we know it, save for a small handful of chance survivors. These hardy souls by the year 3000 will have increased miraculously in numbers and also in knowledge and culture, so much so that they have begun to picture the world a thousand years ago even as we pictured another world also a thousand years ago. Historians are reconstructing the life of the Twentieth Century. They turn to the books in their libraries and museums to cull from this small collection surviving the nuclear fire the valuable information about us. The books are few in number. All of them are collections of limericks.

HUMOROUS NAMES FROM TORONTO

Jay Ames

Stimulated by Aman's comments on "funny" personal names ("New, Improved Dreck!" *Maledicta* III/2), I looked through my telephone directory—and could not stop reading until I finished the last page, with bloodshot eyes.

The following personal names have been culled from the Toronto (Ontario) phone book and may well bring a derisive grin, a good belly laugh, or a hearty chuckle to the reader.

Much less has been made of far more by classier experts.

Adcock	Bitze	Bull	Childerhose
Addercock	Blower	Buller	Chin-Fook
Allcock	Boddy	Bunger	Chuback
Arshoff	Body	Busch	Chui
Arson	Bomms	Bush	Chute
Assel	Boner	Bushey	Cocks
Asselin	Boney	Bushy	Conte
Babcock	Boocock	Butass	Cooney
Badcock	Boosey	Butkiss	Coontz
Bagg	Booze	Butts	Cooze
Baldick	Boyle	Butz	Cowe
Ballock	Bozo	Cann	Cox
Balls	Bottoms	Canns	Coxe
Bang	Bratty	Caunce	Crapper
Banger	Broad	Cauntz	Culos
Bastardi	Broadbent	Cheekes	Cuntz
Batcock	Browner	Cheeseman	Cuze
Batty	Brownie	Cherrie	Dick
Beacock	Bubass	Cherry	Dickey
Beaver	Bubber	Chick	Dickie
Berk	Bubers	Chicke	Dicky
Bitse	Bugger	Chicken	Dike

Diker
Dilcock
Dimcock
Dinger
Dingwell
Dodick
Dodo
Dong
Doucher
Dudu
Dumdum
Dungey
Dupa
Dyke
Dyker
Fairey
Fairy
Fartsalas
Feeley
Feely
Ficke
Ficker
Fickett
Fister
Foxall
Foxmale
Foxman
Foxwell
Freake
Fricke
Fricker
Fuchs
Fuks
Furdyk
Furrey
Furry
Fwx
Gaye
Gaylard
Gaylord
Glasscock
Goodboy
Goodfellow
Goodhands
Goodhead

Goodhugh
Goodreid
Groper
Gruntar
Grunte
Grusselfeunger
Gummer
Hagg
Halbfinger
Handcock
Hardness
Hardstaff
Harner
Haycock
Heathcock
Hedgecock
Hicock
Hircock
Hiscock
Hitchcock
Hole
Holman
Hooney
Horniblow
Horny
Hornyak
Hosegood
Hotts
Hotz
Hustler
Jancock
Johncock
Johncocks
Joncox
Kaka
Kishkis
Kister
Klinkers
Kokass
Koks
Konni
Kopstick
Kornass
Krawcock
Kreamer

Kuchs
Kummer
Kunce
Kuntz
Kunz
Lapper
Leaker
Leakie
Lecker
Lick
Licker
Lickfold
Lipman
Lipps
Longborrom
Longhorn
Longstaff
Loose
Loosely
Looser
Loosemore
Lovejoy
Lovelace
Loveless
Loverock
Loveseed
Lovsin
Lowcock
Lust
Lustgarten
Lusthaus
Lustig
Lusty
Maggott
Maycock
Meacock
Meaney
Meany
Milkereit
Mince
Mincer
Mintzer
Minett
Mistelbach
Mommo

Moonah
Moorecock
Moron
Mountjoy
Mucke
Muffitt
Mummie
Mummy
Mycock
Newlove
Nipper
Nuttall
Nutter
Peacock
Peaker
Peeker
Pekka
Pennicock
Pettibone
Pettypiece
Pinkas
Pizel
Pocock
Poots
Porco
Pork
Pottie
Prigg
Prikko
Pryke
Putz
Quimet
Raincock
Ramaswami
Ramdas
Ramdeholl
Ramdharry
Ramdin
Ramjohn
Ramlogan
Rampaul
Ramsammy
Ramsbottom
Ramson
Randy

Raybone	Stiff	Tremblee	Wetmore
Reamer	Studd	Tremp	Whang
Rear	Suckling	Trickey	Whitehorn
Reddick	Swallowell	Trimble	Wickwire
Reemer	Sweetapple	Truelove	Wiener
Rimmer	Sweetling	Tryon	Wilcock
Rowbottom	Szitas	Tucknott	Wilcox
Rump	Szitkus	Tuckwell	Willcock
Sapp	Tancock	Tugnutt	Windi
Scheithauer	Tietz	Tugwell	Winterbottom
Schimpfe	Tinkle	Tusher	Woodcock
Schwantz	Tinkler	Tushman	Woolcock
Schwanz	Tiplady	Upjohn	Worm
Shagass	Titis	Uprichard	Wurst
Sheety	Titus	Upshaw	Yakoff
Sillicock	Titz	Wacker	Yap
Simcock	Tode	Waghorn	Yankoff
Sitarz	Tool	Wagstaff	Yenta
Smellie	Tooley	Wang	Yoney
Smirmaul	Trebilcock	Wank	Yony
Spittle	Tredwell	Wart	Yuki

DÉFENSE DE PÉTER
FURZEN VERBOTEN

PROHIBICIÓN DE PEDAR
NO FARTING

ONE TOAST, NO FORK, NO SHEET
AN ITALIAN IMMIGRANT'S STORY

One day I'ma go to Detroit to da bigga hotel. Ina mornin', I go to da stair to eata breakfas'. I tella da waitress I wanna two pisses toast. She bringa me only one piss. I tella her I wanna two piss'. She say "Go to da toilet." I say "You no understan', I wanna two piss' ona my plate." She say "You betta no piss ona you' plate, you sonna-ma-bitch!" I'ma don't even know da lady and she call me sonna-ma-bitch.

Later I'ma go out to eat at da bigga restaurante. Da waitress bringa me spoon anna knife anna butta but no fock. I'ma tell her I wanna fock. She tell me "Everyone wanna fock." I tella her "You no understan', I wanna fock ona table." She say "You betta no fock ona table, you sonna-ma-bitch!"

Den I'ma go back to my room ina hotel, an' there isa no shits ona my bed. I calla da manager an' tella him I wanna shit. He tella me to go to da toilet. I say "You no understan', I wanna shit ona my bed." He say "You betta no shit ona bed, you sonna-ma-bitch!"

I'ma go check outta an' da man at de desk say "Peace to you." I'ma say "Piss on you too, you sonna-ma-bitch. I'ma go back to Italy!"

(Bill C., Miss., 1979)

COMMENTARY

The preceding tale is not a story ridiculing "stupid" Italians, even though popular, trashy books misrepresent such material as "Italian," "Polish" or "Irish" jokes. In fact, the story has nothing whatever to do with Italians.

It is an example of *linguistic humor*, using the convenient and easily-recognized Italian accent as a vehicle to illustrate the tremendous semantic difference vowel length can make. The three minimal pairs, contrasting the long (:) with the short vowels, are the key to this tale:

piece, peace /pi:s/ : *piss* /pis/
    fork /fɔ:k/ : *fock* /fɔk/
   sheet /ši:t/ : *shit* /šit/

Fork, here the *r*-less variety (New England? South Carolina? Cf. /ka:/ 'car') and pronounced with an open *o*, may be an indication of the geographic background of the originator of this story since *fork* and *fuck* are phonetically not sufficiently close, in most U.S. dialects, to be confused.

As native-born Americans and other cultured speakers of English distinguish very well between long and short vowels, and are aware of the vulgar meanings of the mispronounced words, the story has to feature a character with a poor command of spoken English, such as a recent immigrant or a visitor to this country. Why not a Russian, Portuguese or Albanian? Because their accents are very difficult to represent in writing and are not recognized easily by most readers (or listeners). The Italian accent is widely mocked and is understood by the masses who circulate such tales. The protagonist in this human drama (I used to teach literature, you know) could have been speaking another frequently mocked accent, such as German ("I vant two shitt in mine bett") but the story would have lost much of its warmth and charm since the stereotypical German is not funny.

There is much more to this apparently simple "joke." We can *identify* with the poor fellow. The originator wanted just a simple laugh caused by the mispronounced naughty words, but I'm certain that sociologists, psychologists, folklorists and philosophers (and not to mention Talmudic Scholars and Jesuits) could write long essays on the deeper meaning of this "simple" tale. Without trying to wax philosophical, I do sense an illustration of the Human Condition, a tale of everyday misery, a Kafkaesque nightmare beneath this tale: the outsider, trying to communicate simple requests, is misunderstood again and again, but he is determined to get his wishes across. Yet, because of lacking communication, he is helpless. He becomes frustrated, resigns himself to being misunderstood, and capitulates, finally saying, "To *hell* with it all! Who *needs* this hassle!? I'm going back to my kind, to where I'm understood."

Surely, each of us has been in such frustrating situations where we simply could not get our point across, be it in a foreign country or with co-workers, a spouse, child or parent. Finally, after too much frustration, we become resigned and say, "Oh, *fuck* it! (or civil equivalent) I'm leaving!" We can empathize with the tale's fellow-sufferer and therefore find it so appealing. It strikes a chord.

On a more mundane level, folklorists will recognize the ancient elements of folk tale and fairy tale: *three* events or situations (toast, fork, bedsheet) and *verbatim repetition* ("You no understan', I wanna..." and "You betta no..., you sonna-ma-bitch") which have been used for thousands of years. Unwittingly, the originator of this modern "urban folk tale" utilizes ancient story-telling techniques to which we respond, subconsciously.

The only modern touches are the "Peace" greeting of the desk clerk (?) and especially the blasé, callous, smart-ass or so-what's-new? reply by the waitress, "Everyone wants to fuck." Other than that, and with a change of locale, this tale could have been told in England several hundred years ago.   (R. A.)

MALEDICTA T-SHIRTS

During 1982, we will have a number of iron-on transfers of Maledicta-related matters. You will be notified when these iron-ons are actually available.

O.E.D. COCK 20

THE LIMITS OF LEXICOGRAPHY OF SLANG

Lorrayne Y. Baird

In a passage noted for its arch boldness, Chaucer's Wife of Bath anticipates a fallacy which appears six centuries later in *The Oxford English Dictionary* (1933):

> **Telle me also, to what conclusion**
> **Were membres maad of generation [...]?**
> **[...] To purge uryne, and eek for engendrure.**[1]

(Tell me furthermore, for what purpose / Were made the organs of generation [...]? / [...] To purge urine, and also for procreation.)

In her own direct and unforgettable way, the Wife refers to an intentional confusion of the two bodily functions performed by the organ of generation. The same confusion, though not deliberate, is seen in the *OED*, regarding the origins of *cock* in sense 20 ("penis") — a usage which, despite the *OED*'s late dating (1618) was known, I believe, in the fourteenth century, but which would have been out of place in the Wife's language. Though racy and even ribald, the Wife's performance never exceeds the boundaries of good taste. Likewise, even though preoccupied with the "tredefowel" propensities of the Monk and the Nun's Priest,[2] the Host, who might have used the term in an all-male company, refrains from this indecency, even though the context is such that the term *cock*, euphemized as "tredefowel," is clearly in his mind. (*Treadfowl* refers to the male bird in the function or act of copulation. Note that the German *treten* ["tread," "step," "trample"] in reference to fowl also means "to copulate.") Indeed, even in modern times when old taboos are weakening, the popular obscenity *cock* is so assiduously avoided in polite discourse, spoken or written, as to have infected and almost usurped the term in its primary sense of *gallus gallinaceus*, the less offensive term *rooster* now being commonly employed for *cock*, the domestic fowl.[3] For *cock* 20 the writers of the *OED* postulate an origin associated with "purgacioun of uryne" – to borrow the Wife's phrase – rather than with "engendrure." First appearing in 1730-36, according to *OED* records, the term *cock* as "penis" originates, the authors suggest, *post hoc ergo propter hoc*, from the name of an object similar in function first recorded in 1481-90: *cock* 12 (for "tap," "spigot," "faucet," "stop-cock," etc.), "a spout or short pipe serving as a channel for passing liquids through, and having an appliance for regulating or stopping the flow." To the crucial question concerning the *raison d'être* of the metaphoric use of *cock* for "tap," the lexicographers have not fully addressed themselves, though they are well aware of the problem:

> ...the origin of the name in this sense is not very clear; the resemblance of some stop-cocks to a cock's head with its comb, readily suggests itself; but some of the earlier quotations seem to imply that the power of closing the "cock" was no essential feature, i.e. that a *cock* was not necessarily a *stop-cock*, but that the word simply meant a short spout for the emission of fluid. . . .

In standard dictionaries and in popular slang the ideas and associations noted by the *OED* are widespread in Europe. Travellers to the northernmost regions, accustomed to the figures of the cock and hen as identifying signs on Scandinavian public toilets, are not surprised to hear as slang for "penis" the Swedish *kuk* ('cock') and Danish *kok* ('cock'), words not included in standard dictionaries with these meanings, nor, as one might expect, for "tap." Among other meanings in standard dictionaries, "tap," but not "penis," is given for Slovak *kohút* ('cock'), Czech *kohout* ('cock'), while the word in Serbo-Croatian, *kohot* ('cock') is officially recognized for both senses.[4]

The same is true of the German *Hahn* ('cock'), given extensive historical treatment in Grimm's *Deutsches Wörterbuch*

(1854-1960). According to Grimm, *hahn* 8 in the sense of "tap on a barrel," makes its first appearance in 1503, while *hahn* 4 (dim. *hähnchen*) for *männliches glied* ('male member') first appears in recorded use almost a century later, in 1591, in Frischlin's *Facetiae nomenclator trilinguis, graecolatino-germanicus*: "*hahn, membrum virile*" ('cock, male member'). Grimm conjectures that *hahn* 4 is connected with *hahn* 3a (*see* end of entry), used to designate the human male who distinguishes himself, like the cock, for his sexual prowess. Even more interesting is Grimm's further association of *hahn* 4 with *hahn* 1d, the *geiler vogel* ('lascivious bird'; 'treadfowl'), illustrated by a 1654 epigram by Logau — *An worten ist er mönch, an thaten ist er hahn* ("in words he is a monk, in deeds he is a rooster"; i.e., 'he talks like a monk but acts like a cock') — the implied criticism of the worldly monk couched in terms meaning precisely the same as those used by Chaucer through the Host, as noted above. Also of interest is *piphahn, piephahn*, which Grimm suggests as a comparison to *hahn* 4. The term in its primary sense, *ein piepender hahn* ('a peeping [or chirping] cock'), derives from *piepen* ('to chirp', 'cheep', or 'squeak') — compare German *Pieper* ('peeper,' 'young chicken') — and is used sometimes in derogatory contexts making use of some weakness, or ineffectuality of the immature bird. Playing upon *hahn* 4 and *piepe* 2 (i.e., a barrel spout or pipe with a *Dreh-hahn* [twistable spigot]), *piphahn* has a second meaning, "male member," documented by Grimm in a facetious quotation from *Maynhinklers Sack* (1612): *als im der alte biphaan aufgewacht* ('when his old cock woke up'). A cognate of Grimm's *piepe, pipe, pippe*, the Modern High German *Pfeife*, meaning "pipe," or "spout," is also used in an extended sense for "male member" or "prick."[5] Though well aware of these close relationships and the fact that in his sources *hahn* as "tap" substantially precedes *hahn* as "penis," Grimm stops short of suggesting that one originates in the other.

Although the French dictionaries do not list *coq* in the sense of *robinet* ('stop-cock'), Godefroy[6] does list a similar technical term, *coq*, the name for a part of the mechanism for discharging a pistol (cf. *OED cock* 13), oddly replaced in

Modern French by *chien* ('dog'). The term *coquille*, meaning "shell," "ornament with pearls in the shape of a bird's beak," "pilgrim's badge," or euphemistically, "female genitals," curiously becomes transvestite[7] in the 16th-century farce of *Frère Guillebert*, where it means, as Godefroy notes, "membre viril":

> Ha! s'il me prenoit en mercy
> Et qu'il prinst toute ma robille!
> Mais, hélas, perdre la *coquille*,
> Mon Dieu! c'est pour fienter partout.

(Ha! If he took mercy on me / And if he [merely] took all my clothing! / But, alas! to lose the shell/badge/cock, / My God! that is to void waste (urine, feces) everywhere [i.e., I'm up a creek]).

The hilarity of this passage is increased by the suggestion of the same doubleness of function referred to above: the *coquille*, a euphemism I believe for *coq* (unattested), when "lost" is good for nothing except *pour fienter* ('to void waste'). In both Old French and Modern French the sexual associations of *coq* are borne out abundantly in the derivatives: OF *coqueter*, "to act like a cock in the company of hens"; ModF *coqueter*, "to copulate with a 'chick'," or *coquer* (used around Lyons), "to kiss or embrace as the cock does the hens";[8] OF and ModF *coquelier*, "to lead a joyous life; to run after the young girls," and *coquellerie*, "dissipation," "libertinism";[9] ModF argot, *coquine*, "sexual mercenary," "prostitute," "homosexual,"[10] "sodomist."[11] Compare also *coq de village* ('village cock') or *coq de la paroisse* ('parish cock'), meaning "cock of the walk," used for a man who enjoys a great reputation among women of the locality; *un bon coq* ('a good cock'), used for a man having notable success with women;[12] *coquard* ('old cock'), used for a ridiculous old beau; *coquardeau* ('male flirt'); and the slang *coqueluche* ('ladies' man').[13] The homonymic *cocu* ('cuckold') is of disputed origin,[14] but may have also been associated in the popular mind with *coq* in the above senses.

Salvatore Battaglia, in his great historical dictionary of Italian[15] now in progress, lists *gallo* as used by Barbaro (16th century?) in the sense of *valvola di un rubinetto* ('valve of a tap'), but not *gallo*, the current Italian slang for penis. Various uses and derivatives of *gallo* ('barnyard cock'), listed in all standard Italian dictionaries, however, express ideas of virility, seduction, fertilization, etc.: *gallo*, used of a man because of his virility, authority over women, or role as a seducer (cf. *essere il gallo dalla checca*, "to be a lady-killer"; lit. 'to be a magpie's cock'); *gallismo*, used to denote excessive gallantry to women or aggressive virility considered typical of men in Latin countries, particularly the Southern Italian and Sicilian males, for their "preoccupation with the opposite sex and boasting of sexual success and prowess"[16]; *gallare* ('to fecundate' or 'to become fecund'); *gallatura* ('the act of fertilization'); *gallato* ('fertilized'), etc. Similar derivatives from *gallo* can be found in Portuguese and Spanish. In addition should be noted Sp. *gallarizo, -za* ('lustful'), from *propensión carnal en las personas y animales* ('carnal tendency in people and animals'),[17] and especially the euphemisms for "penis," Spanish *gallo* and (in Mexico) *gallito inglés*.[18]

Moreover, these ideas and associations are traceable to Latin from very early times: for example, *gallulasco, -ĕre* (from *gallus*), *pubesco*[19] ('of the voice of boys at the time of changing; to begin to sound manly'), as in *puer cujus vox gallulascit* ('boy whose voice is changing').[20] Used by the poet Naevius (†202 B.C.), the term expresses the similarity of the breaking adolescent male voice to the squawking of a cock and is thus doubly appropriate. Interpretative translations and mistranslations in the Vulgate are also revealing, not only of the generative connection of the cock, but also of the attitude toward it. Three separate Biblical Hebrew terms, none of which originally meant *cock* (rooster), were rendered *gallus* by Jerome. In the first passage, which he translated as *Dominus asportari te faciat, sicut asportatur gallus gallinaceus* ("Behold the Lord will cause thee to be carried away, as a cock is carried away" [Isaiah 22:17]), the Hebrew word גבר *géver*, which Jerome translates as *gallus gallinaceus*, denotes merely "male," "man," or "person," yet it was also probably used at that time as a euphemism for the male sexual organ,[21] a sense

_____

(Yoël Arbeitman supplied the words in Hebrew. *Ed.*)

which the word has in post-Biblical Hebrew—hence Jerome's interpretative translation, probably done in this way on the advice of his Hebrew instructor. In the second passage, translated in the Vulgate as *Quis posuit in visceribus hominis sapientiam vel quis dedit gallo intelligentiam* ("Who hath put wisdom in the heart of man or who gave the cock understanding?" [Job 38:36]), *gallo* is a complete mistranslation, since the original Hebrew שכוי *sekhví*, a *hapax legomenon*, apparently denotes "secret parts and hidden things," or "the reins and heart of man." The third term translated by Jerome as *gallus* occurs in an answer to a riddle: *tria sunt quae bene gradiuntur et quartum quod incedit feliciter leo fortissimus bestiarum ad nullius pavebit occursum gallus succinctus lumbos et aries nec ex rex qui resistat ei* ("There are three things which go well, and the fourth that walketh happily: A lion, who hath no fear of anything he meeteth, a cock girded about the loins, and a ram; and a king, whom none can resist." [Proverbs 30:29-31]). The Hebrew word זרזיר *zarzír*, which Jerome translates as *gallus*, may have been an onomatopoetic word for "starling" (and possibly also applied to the little-known cock), but it occurs in a very corrupt passage and is quite obscure. Greek, Peshitto, and Aramaic Targum texts, however, support the translation: "the cock which gallantly treadeth the hens," rendered by Jerome, in a complete reversal of the original idea, as *gallus succinctus lumbos* ("cock with the girded loins").

Linguistic evidence thus gives a rather convincing case for the widespread and long-standing association of the *gallus gallinaceus* with the male sex and its attributes, in particular, the generative aspects, for which the cock is remarkable—whence the old saying: *omne animal post coitum triste praeter gallum* ("After intercourse all animals are sad except the cock"). The cock, in fact, even came to be associated with Priapus himself, the god of generation and phallus personified. An awareness of this connection may have been current among classical Latin authors writing during the period of this god's decline and debasement. In a defense of his prurient verses, Martial argues that *Gallo turpius est nihil Priapo* ("Nothing is more disgusting than Priapus as Gallus").[22] In this line, *Gallo* obviously refers to Gallus, a eunuch priest of Cybele, since the context supports this sense. The same is true in one of the anonymous *Priapea*, in which Priapus, contemplating the prospect of castration and exile from his native land, is made to say: *Quae si perdidero, patria mutabor, et olim / Ille tuus civis, Lampsace, Gallus ero* ("If it [his member] is lost, I, a citizen of yours, O Lampsacus, shall change countries and become [that other?] Gallus").[23] Yet, in view of the fact that, while these poets could have chosen from a number of well-known mutilated gods, *Gallus* is selected, it seems quite likely that in these passages a pun on *gallus* ("cock") may be intended. Since I have been unable to find a contemporary literary example of Priapus as "cock," it is impossible to prove the case; the hypothesis is greatly strengthened, however, by the existence of several ithyphallic cock-headed figures of Priapus,[24] which, though not precisely dated, are thought to derive from early Roman times. Other figures, both ancient and modern,[25] of ithyphalli in the form of a cock — the shape of the bird lending itself easily to such caricature — also contribute to the linguistic and archaeological proof of the universal celebration of this animal for his erotic and generative powers rather than for his urinary powers.

Although Latin vocabulary reflects the fairly sophisticated plumbing systems for which the Romans are noted — *tubus, tubulus*, "pipe"; *canalis*, "conduit"; *os*, "spout"; *antlia*, "pump"; *cloaca*, "sewer"; *artifex plumbarius*, "plumber," etc., — there seems to be no form of *gallus* equivalent to "water-cock" or "stop-cock." The non-specific word *spica*, "pointed object," or "spike" from which *spicket, spigot* derive, may have been used at times for the spike-shaped *operculum* or *obturamentum*, "plug" or "tap." Plumbing in Northern lands lagged far behind the Roman state of development until very late, no significant advances being made until near the time of the Industrial Revolution.[26] Even so, simple devices such as pipes, spouts, and taps were known from early times; nevertheless words expressing the association of the barnyard cock with the tap seem not to have been in use in written records anywhere prior to the fifteenth century. On the other hand, phallic-shaped drinking vessels have survived from Greek and Roman times. Note also the *Priapus vitreus* mentioned by Juvenal (2,95): *vitreo bibit ille priapo* ("he drinks from a glass phallus").[27] Fountains from classical antiquity were sometimes supplied with water by fountain statues of urinating boys, now preserved in museums, for example, in Paris, London, Berlin, and Naples.[28] The most widely known is the "Pissing Boy" of Brussels (*Manneken-Pis*), a famous tourist photo object, near the City Hall. In ancient times images of Priapus were set up at wells and fountains to protect them and guard against defilers of water.[29] Like the *mingentes* ('urinators') mentioned above, even this god himself in the form of Priapus σπερμαίνων, *spermainōn* ('producing sperm') is said to have supplied fountains, as a sign of the life-giving power of water and its function as a fertility symbol.[30]

Thus, the idea of the water-cock appears to have originated in the idea of the phallus-cock, rather than the reverse, as the *OED* assumes.

Late in the fifteenth century, Albrecht Dürer playfully brought together all these ideas current in popular thought. In his woodcut, "Männerbad,"[31] depicting a group of men in a public bath, one man almost nude leans upon a post in such a way that his pelvic region is directly behind and in close proximity to a spigot attached to a post. In a triple visual pun, Dürer has placed atop the downward arching phallic-shaped spigot, which clearly serves as the appropriate anatomical part of the figure, a *Sperrhahn* ('stop-cock'), a tiny bird whose crest and plumage identify him unmistakably as a cock. This fowl, a venerable and long-accepted personification of the male generative organ, has come to represent not only the member in its urinary "office," but also, through similarity of function, the water-cock or spigot; and further, through association or extension, the stop-cock, or device for plugging the water-cock.

Complete and accurate lexicographical coverage for these matters will, of course, never be available, since it is axiomatic that a slang term, particularly an obscenity, finds its way into written expression much later than its first use in spoken language, where it is invented in poetic playfulness. On the other hand, important evidence is likely to be rejected or ignored, at least officially. Such is the case of the much-anthologized fifteenth-century poem, "I haue a gentil cook [cock]," which has until recently been considered as merely a brilliant little vignette of a gorgeous pet rooster, often compared to Chaucer's Chaunticleer,[32] despite the obvious phallic and amatory suggestion in the last two lines: & euery ny3t he perchit hym / in myn ladyis chaumbyr ("and every night he perches himself in my lady's chamber").

Finally, the bit of evidence which proves the existence of the cock-phallus in Chaucer's day again comes from art and iconography. In a mid-fourteenth-century French manuscript illumination (MS Douce 360, f. 162 r.), now preserved in the Bodleian Library, appears what at first glance seems to be one of the many typical representations of a fox carrying off a cock and being chased by someone with a distaff or club — in this case, a White Friar portrayed with an expression of chagrin.[33] The scene takes place in front of a castle, which may be allegorically and iconographically significant,[34] and in the background appear several barnyard cocks, all with the same peculiar expression, perhaps of smug relief or of pious supplication. Upon careful examination it becomes quite clear, however, that the fox has made no ordinary henhouse raid, but that the target of attack has been the Friar himself, since instead of the expected barnyard cock in the fox's mouth, the artist has substituted, in very clear outline, that other "cock," the male organ of generation.

ACKNOWLEDGMENTS

I am indebted to the University Research Council of Youngstown State University for financial aid to carry out research in Rome, and for support in typing the manuscript. I am also indebted to Reinhold Aman for notes on *Pfeife*, *Manneken-Pis*, Dürer's woodcut, Jiménez's *gallito inglés*, etc.

FOOTNOTES

1. *The Works of Geoffrey Chaucer*, ed. Fred N. Robinson (Boston: Houghton-Mifflin, 1957), III (D), 115-34. All references are to this edition.

2. Chaucer, *Works*, VII, 1945ff. and 3451.

3. H. L. Mencken, *The American Language* (New York: Alfred A. Knopf, Inc., 1945), Supplement I, comments on the squeamishness about using the word *cock* and notes, p. 480, n. 6, that the *NED* marks *rooster* as chiefly U. S. dialect.

4. Carl Darling Buck, *A Dictionary of Selected Synonyms in the Principal Indo-European Languages* (Chicago: University of Chicago Press, 1949), 4.492 and 3.52.

5. Edward Muret and D. Sanders, *Enzyklopädisches Englisch-Deutsches und Deutsch-Englisches Wörterbuch* (Berlin-Schöneberg: Langenscheidt, 1908), *Pfeife* 7. See also *Pfeife* 2d, "spout." This term is included among the more than 850 euphemisms and synonyms listed for "penis" by Ernest Borneman, *Sex im Volksmund* (Reinbek: Rowohlt, 1971), 1.73. He also includes *Hahn* and *Piephahn* (cf. *OED pillicock*, vulg. "penis"). [*Editor's Note*: In colloquial German, *Pfeife* means "penis" and "silly *or* stupid man." But, just as *cock* means "vulva/vagina" (not "penis") in parts of the U.S., in some German dialects, e.g. Central Bavarian, *Pfeife* does not mean "penis" but "vulva/vagina" and "dumb *or* silly broad." *See* entry *Pfaiffa* in Aman's *Bayerisch-österreichisches Schimpfwörterbuch* (Munich, 1973, 1979, 1981).]

6. *Dictionnaire de l'ancienne langue française et de tous ses dialectes du IXe au XVe siècle* (Paris, 1883; New York: Kraus Reprint Corp., 1961).

7. *Coquille* also means "penis" in Modern French. See Georgette A. Marks and Charles B. Johnson, *The New English-French Dictionary of Slang and Colloquialisms* (New York: Dutton, 1975). Published in Great Britain as *Harrap's English-French Dictionary of Slang and Colloquialisms* (London: Harrap, 1970). See *prison*. This tranvestite phenomenon is not completely unique. The use of the term *cock* in the southern part of the United States for "female pudendum" is a far more

remarkable instance. It is quite possible that this use originated from the AS *cocer, cocor, cocur*, ME *cocker*, meaning "quiver" or "case for arrows," and having cognates in French as well as in all the Germanic languages (e.g. Ger. *Köcher*). Bosworth-Toller's *Anglo-Saxon Dictionary* (1898) lists *cocor* also with the meaning "sword." Thus, even in Anglo-Saxon times, a word homonymic with *coc*, if indeed not derived from it, is in use for both an object universally recognized as having a "female" function and also one with a "male" function. Compare the modern custom of referring to electrical and mechanical connections as "male" or "female" (on the mechanical, *see* Norman Friedman, *Maledicta* I/2, p. 259, "Screws"). This fact suggests the possibility of an unwritten obscene meaning for the AS *coc, cocc, kok* and an explanation for the mysterious use of *cock* for the female organ in the linguistically conservative and predominantly Anglo-Saxon Southern U.S. For *cock* meaning "vagina," *see* e.g. Allen Walker Read, *Classic American Graffiti* (Paris, 1935 and Waukesha, Wis.: Maledicta Press, 1977), p. 42:

> **Ashes to ashes dust to dust**
> **If it wasnt for your cock my prick would rust.**

(Quoted verbatim from an outhouse graffito from El Centro, California, 27 June 1928.)

8. Godefroy, *coqueter*; Émile Chautard, *La vie étrange de l'argot* (Paris: Les Éditions Denoël et Steele, 1931), *coquer*.

9. Godefroy, *coquelier, coquellerie*; Algirdas J. Greimas, *Dictionnaire de l'ancien français jusqu'au milieu du XIVᵉ siècle* (Paris: Librairie Larousse, 1969), *coc*.

10. Gaston Esnault, *Dictionnaire historique des argots français* (Paris: Librairie Larousse, 1965), *coquine*.

11. Albert Barrère, *Argot and Slang: A New French and English Dictionary of the Cant Words, Quaint Expressions, Slang Terms and Flash Phrases* (London: Whittaker, 1889), *coquine*.

12. *Grand Larousse de la langue française* (Paris: Librairie Larousse, 1971), *coq*.

13. Étienne Deak and Simone Deak, *A Dictionary of Col-*

orful French Slanguage and Colloquialisms (Paris, 1959; New York: E. P. Dutton, 1961), coqueluche.

14. On the history of the word and the controversy, see Lucien Rigaud, Dictionnaire d'argot moderne (Paris: P. Ollendorff, 1888), cocu.

15. Grande dizionario della lingua italiana (Turin: Unione Tipografico, 1961).

16. The Cambridge Italian Dictionary, ed. Barbara Reynolds (Cambridge: Cambridge University Press, 1962), gallismo.

17. Martín Alonso Pedraz, Enciclopedia del idioma: Diccionario histórico y moderno de la lengua española (Madrid: Aguilar, 1958).

18. Camilo José Cela, Diccionario secreto (Madrid: Alfagura, 1971).

19. Alfred Ernout and A. Meillet, Dictionnaire étymologique de la langue latine, 3rd ed. (Paris: Librairie C. Klincksieck, 1951).

20. Ethan A. Andrews, A Copious and Critical Latin-English Lexicon (New York: Harper & Brothers, 1861). On this term and gallus, etc., see also Pierre Pierrugues, Glossarium eroticum linguae latinae (Paris, 1826. Reprint Amsterdam, 1965).

21. John P. Peters, "The Cock," American Oriental Society Journal 33 (1913), 366-70. I am indebted to this article for all the information on Jerome's translations.

22. Epigrams, I, 35, 15. For a similar comparison, see also XI, 72, 2.

23. Poetae Latini minores, ed. Aemilius Baehrens (Leipzig, 1879), p. 76.

24. Hans Herter, De Priapo (Giessen: Alfred Töpelmann, 1932), pp. 162-63, describes the major artifacts in the form of "Priapus gallinaceus."

25. A well-known example from classical antiquity is the phallic cock found on a late fourth or early third century pedestal near the shrine of Apollo on Delos. A photo of the pedestal appears in George Sackas and Maria Sarla, Delos Island: A Tourist Guide Book, trans. by J. Chryss (Athens, 1972). A good example of this style in modern grafitti is reproduced in Cela's Diccionario, p. 381.

26. J. Rawlinson, "Sanitary Engineering: Sanitation," in *A History of Technology*, ed. Charles Singer *et al.* (Oxford: Clarendon Press, 1958), vol. 4, p. 504.

27. On the modern controversy concerning this passage, *see* Herter, p. 166-67.

28. Balázs Kapossy, *Brunnenfiguren der hellenistischen und römischen Zeit* (Zürich: Juris, 1969), pp. 41, 44.

29. Herter, pp. 215, 247, 312.

30. Kapossy, p. 75. The cock as symbol of Priapus in this function, I believe, appears over the pipe of a watering trough in Pompeii, Reg. VII, INS VII.

31. *See* Edgar Wind, "Dürer's 'Männerbad': A Dionysian Mystery," *Journal of the Warburg Institute* 2 (1938-39), 269 to 271, for an interpretation, and plate 41 for a reproduction of the woodcut. A detail of the woodcut is shown below.

32. *See* Edmund K. Chambers and F. Sidgwick, *Early English Lyrics* (London: Sidgwick & Jackson, 1926), note, p. 377; William Tydeman, *English Poetry, 1400-1580* (New York: Barnes & Noble, 1970), p. 185; and Reginald T. Davies, ed. *Medieval English Lyrics: A Critical Anthology* (Evanston, Ill.: Northwestern University Press, 1964), poem 64, p. 334. Theodore Silverstein, *English Lyrics before 1500* (Evanston, Ill.: Northwestern University Press, 1971), p. 129, first notes the "amatory implication."

33. Reproduced in Kenneth Varty, *Reynard the Fox: A Study of the Fox in Medieval English Art* (Leicester: Leicester University Press, 1967), illus. no. 141.

34. *See* John V. Fleming, *The Roman de la Rose: A Study in Allegory and Iconography* (Princeton: Princeton University Press, 1969), p. 238.

Este es el gallito inglés,
Míralo con disimulo,
Quítale el pico y los pies
Y métetelo en el culo.

This is the little English cock,
Look at it with indulgence,
Take away his beak and feet
And shove it up your ass.

(From an advertisement for Jiménez's **Picardía Mexicana**)

Detail from Albrecht Dürer's "The Men's Bath," *ca.* 1497

SEX AND THE SINGLE SOLDIER

OR, THE LOVE BUG WILL BITE YOU
IF YOU DON'T WASH OUT

Daniel N. Weitzner

The following, within the Lore of *STD* (Sexually Transmitted Diseases), may be noted in any collection of medical paraterminology. With the advent of antibiotics and chemotherapy, the following expressions and aphorisms may soon be archaic or obsolete.

I. Pertinent to Syphilis Therapy

Riding the silver steed and **Taking the bayonet course**: Bismuth subcarbonate and neoarsphenamine were administered weekly over a period of years; however, it was the bismuth and not the *ars*phenamine which was injected into the *arse* muscles.

Three minutes with Venus; three years with Mercury: Mercurial salts were administered by inunction.

Take a trip with tryparsamide and see the world through a port-hole: Tryparsamide was used in the treatment of neurosyphilis. A common side-effect was narrowing of the visual fields, causing "tunnel vision."

II. Medical Student Concert-Dance

The band, featuring John Hunter and the Foreign Lesion, as well as the Condyloma Orchestra, played for Argyll-Robertson and his Pupils. Lues Gumma was M.C. "Saber Shins" was the keynote piece, played to the tune of "Wagon Wheels."

Notes: *John Hunter*: medical martyr who pioneered syphilology. *Hunterian lesion*: a primary lesion, a chancre fulfilling textbook requirements, a "rosebud." *Condyloma*: secondary syphilitic "wart." Take-off on Glenn Gray and his Casa Loma Orchestra. *Argyll-Robertson pupils* and *Saber shins*: symptoms of congenital syphilis. *Lues*: medical term for syphilis.

Gumma: secondary syphilitic lesion. *M.C.*: Master of Ceremonies and Medical Corps.

III. Miscellaneous

Clap (common), **cold in the dong, the dog, dripsy, gleet**: synonyms for gonorrhea.

Nine-day blues: Incubation period of gonorrhea after sexual contact.

Blue-balls: Buboes; testicular swelling.

Full house: Afflicted with syphilis, plus gonorrhea, plus . . . .

Short-arm inspection: Surprise inspection by Medical Department personnel for evidence of untreated or unreported venereal disease, crabs, or other infection, as well as personal cleanliness.

THE SPECIAL FORCES SOLDIER
AS SEEN BY . . .

... **The Military Assistance Command, Vietnam**: A drunken, brawling, jeep-stealing, woman-corrupting bum with a star sapphire ring, Seiko watch, and Swiss Army demo knife.

... **His Commanding Officer**: A fine specimen of a drunken, brawling, jeep-stealing, woman-corrupting liar with a star sapphire ring, Seiko watch, and Swiss Army demo knife.

... **The Department of the Army**: An overpaid, over-ranked tax-burden who is indispensable because he has volunteered to go anywhere, do anything as long as he can booze it up, brawl, steal jeeps, corrupt women, lie, and wear a star sapphire ring, Seiko watch, and carry a Swiss Army demo knife.

... **Himself**: A tall, handsome, highly-trained professional soldier, female idol, sapphire-ring-wearing, Swiss-Army-knife-carrying man of the world who is always on time due to the reliability and accuracy of his Seiko watch.

... **His Wife**: A filthy stranger who comes home once every six months with a rucksack full of dirty clothes, a crossbow, and a hard-on.

(S. Gregory, Mich., 1980)

IRANIAN VALUES AS DEPICTED IN FARSI TERMS OF ABUSE, CURSES, THREATS, AND EXCLAMATIONS

Soraya Noland *and* D. M. Warren

Farsi, the national language of Iran, belongs to the Indo-Iranian group of languages. It has been influenced by many different languages introduced to Iran over the past centuries by such migrant ethnic groups as the Mongols, Turks, Arabs, Greeks, Russians and, more recently, the Europeans. The numerous minority ethnic groups living in Iran, such as the Turks, Baluchis, Kurds, Bakhtiaris, Gilakis, and Arabs all speak their own languages, with Farsi learned as a second language through the public school system, as Farsi is the national language for instruction in schools. Non-Muslim religious minorities in Iran, such as the Armenians, Jews, Baha'is, and Zoroastrians are other distinct groups within Iran, although only the Armenians continue to speak their own language as a first language. Farsi is also spoken in Afghanistan where it is referred to as Dari. The abusive terms listed in this article are used by the Farsi-speaking Muslims of Iran, although the very use of most of the terms is considered improper behavior by the majority of Iranians.

Many of the Farsi abusive terms focus on the values of honor and prestige. The concepts of honor and modesty are well discussed by such authors as Abu-Zeid, Antoun, and Bourdieu. The honor of an individual may be stained through his or her act and/or through his relatives' (female and male) immodest behavior. Furthermore, the rôle one assumes in the sexual act itself may be an issue of social dominance. In both heterosexual and homosexual relationships, the individual who assumes the "male" rôle dominates the individual who assumes the "female" rôle. The "male" partner is superior in a social power sense to the "female" partner. Therefore, an abuse which focuses upon having intercourse with the addressee's relatives is a statement of superiority by the abuser. As such, it is considered an insult to the addressee.

Abusive terms are usually used by individuals of a higher social status and/or by an older person in relation to the addressee. Individuals of the same age also exchange abusive terms. Unless otherwise stated in the following list, the terms may be used by both males and females to abuse either other males or females. However, an individual of a lower social status and/or a younger individual would rarely use such terms in a face-to-face situation with individuals either older or of higher social classes.

Another category of abusive terms consists of wishing one ill or dead. It is assumed, regardless of the age of the individual, that his/her parents are responsible for his/her shortcomings in terms of personality. Attributing animal qualities to individuals comprises another category of Farsi abusive terms. As Huang and Warren (1981) mention with regard to Mandarin abusive terms, animals are considered inferior to human beings in Iranian culture, too.

Romanization of the Farsi terms in this article follows the English Transliteration System as published in the *International Journal of Middle East Studies*. The circumflex (^) is used in this glossary, instead of the customary diacritical mark indicating a long vowel, the macron (ˉ).

REFERENCES

Abou-Zeid, Ahmed. 1974. "Honour and Shame Among the Bedouins of Egypt." In J. G. Peristiany (ed.), *Honour and Shame: Values of Mediterranean Society* (Chicago: University of Chicago Press), 241-259.

Antoun, Richard. 1968. "On the Modesty of Women in Arab Muslim Villages: A Study in the Accommodation of Traditions." *American Anthropologist* 70 (4), 671-697.

Bourdieu, Pierre. 1974. "The Sentiment of Honour in Kabyle Society." In J. G. Peristiany (ed.), *Honour and Shame: Values of Mediterranean Society* (Chicago: University of Chicago Press), 191-241.

PRONUNCIATION GUIDE

ai as in 'tail'; **ch** as in 'change'; **gh** has no English equivalent but sounds approximately like **g** in 'girl'; **h** as in 'hat'; **j** as in 'jam'; **kh** has no English equivalent but sounds approx. like Scottish 'loch'; **q** approx. like **qu** in 'quick'; **s** as in 'sand'; **sh** as in 'shower'; **th** is Arabic *th* but in Farsi sounds like **s** as in 'simple'; **v** as in 'vicious'; **w** in Arabic *uww* as in 'wound'; **u** as in 'road'; **y** as in 'ink'; glottal stop ' sounds approx. like Scottish *bo'l* 'bottle.'

FARSI VERBAL ABUSE

I. INSULTS ATTACKING PHYSICAL DEVIATIONS AND SHORTCOMINGS

chishmit kûr (1) چشمت کور

"may you become blind!"

chulâgh (2) چلاق

"arm": a clumsy person

dandit narm (3) دندت نرم

"may your ribs get crushed!"

dirâz-i-bi-aghl (4) دراز بی عقل

"tall and without brains." Tall individuals are considered dumb.

fîl (5) فیل

"elephant": a fat and stupid person. Fat persons are considered stupid.

gardan dirâz (6) سَرِدَنِ دِرِرَازِ

"long neck": a clumsy person. Used for tall persons, it is a general reference to the camel which is considered clumsy.

khirs (7) خِرِس

"bear": a fat and lazy person. Fat persons are considered lazy.

kus gundih (8) کُس گُنده

"big cunt": a lazy woman. This term is used only against women.

kus qushâd (9) کُس گُشاد

"wide/big cunt": a lazy woman. A term used only by and against women.

kusi zanit (10) کُس زِنِت

"your wife's cunt." This term is used only by men.

kûtah-i-mûzy (11) کوتاه مودی

"short and sneaky." Short individuals are considered to possess a sneaky trait.

ling dirâz (12) لِنگ دِراز

"long legs": a tall and insensitive individual. Tall individuals are considered insensitive.

murdanî (13) مُردنی

"you who look like you are dying": you weakling. Addressed to physically weak, feeble and pale-looking persons.

shamshîr az kûn-i-sag dar âmadih (14)

شمشیر از کون سگ در آمده

"a sword pulled out of a dog's ass": a feeble or pale-looking or skinny person

shutur (15) شتر

"camel": a tall and clumsy person

II. INSULTS ATTACKING INTELLECTUAL AND MENTAL DEVIATIONS AND SHORTCOMINGS

bû ghalamûn (16) بوقلمون

"turkey": an unstable personality; a person who is ideologically unstable. The neck wattle of turkeys is considered to change colors; this term refers to persons who continually change their positions or attitudes.

dirâz gûsh (17) دراز گوش

"long ears": a donkey; a stupid person

gâv (18) گاو

"cow": a stupid person; an insensitive person; one without manners

kurih khar (19) کره خر

"donkey's child": a stupid person. The donkey is a symbol of stupidity.

kusish khulih (20) کس خله

"her cunt is crazy": a stupid woman. Used by both men and women to abuse a woman.

tukhmih jin (21) تخم جن

"testicles of the *jinn*": a clever but dishonest person. The *jinn* (supernatural beings, spirits, demons) are believed to have superior intelligence in the Iranian culture. The abuse also means that the person addressed is not the son of a human male, but rather the son of a *jinn*.

III. INSULTS ATTACKING INDIVIDUAL AND SOCIAL DEVIATIONS AND SHORTCOMINGS

aghrab zîr ghâly (22) عقرب زیر قالی

"scorpion under the rug": a sneaky person

avazi zâidan rîdî (23) عوض زاییدن ریدی

"you shat instead of giving birth": a hopeless person. This term is addressed to the mother of an individual who is considered incapable of doing anything correctly.

az sad tâ aghrab-u-mâr bad tarih (24)

از صد تا عقرب و مار بدترہ

"worse than a hundred scorpions and snakes": a sneaky person

bâbât bi kûnit (25) بابات بکونت

"your father is in your ass!" A general abuse addressed to both men and women.

bad asl (26) بد اصل
"evil nature": an evil man

bad bakht (27) بد بخت
"unfortunate": an unfortunate person

bad-i-damagh (28) باد دماغ
"wind in the nose": an arrogant person. The term refers to wind blowing into a person's nose, swelling up his or her head.

bî asl-u-nasab (29) بی اصل و نسب
"without origin or title": a low-class person

bî band-u-bâr (30) بی بندوبار
"without any moral standards": an immoral person

bî chârih (31) بیچاره
"without any choice": an unfortunate person

bî chishm-u-rû (32) بی چشم و رو
"without eye and without face": a shameless person

bi damâghi bâbât rydam (33) بدماغ بابات ریدم
"I shit on your father's nose!" A general abuse addressed to both men and women.

bî hayâ (34) بی حیا
"shameless" : a shameless person

bi jahanam (35) به جهنم
"go to hell!" A general abuse addressed to both men and women.

bî sar-u-bî pâ (36) بی سرو بی پا
"without a head and without feet" : a low-class person; one without roots

bih kûnish mygih bâ man niâ ki bût myâd (37)
به کونش میگه با من نیا که بوت میاد
"he/she tells his/her ass, 'do not come with me because you stink'" : an arrogant person

bimyr tâ kasy na murdih (38) بمیر تا کسی نمرده
"die before anyone else does!" : drop dead!

biry kih bar na gardy (39) هری که برنگردی
"go somewhere so you won't return!" : get lost!

châki dahanit biband (40) چاک دهنت به بند
"shut your mouth!"

chinan myzanam tûyi dahanat ki sarit bi aqab bar gardih (41)
چنان میزنم توی دهنت که سرت به عقب برگرده
"I will hit you in the mouth so hard that your head swings back!" : I'll knock your block off! This is a threat which becomes an insult if used by someone of low status against someone else of higher status or age.

chishm charûn (42) چشم چرون
"grazing eyes." Used against a male who stares at women too much.

chishm tang (43) چشم تنگ
"narrow eyes" : a greedy person

chus khur (44) چس خور
"fart-eater" : a stingy person

dahan lagh (45) دهن لق
"loose mouth" : one who can't keep a secret

dast kaj (46) دست کج
"crooked hand" : a thief; a dishonest person

dayuwwth (47) دیوث
"pimp"

falak zadih (48) فلک زده
"being beaten by the world" : an unfortunate or hopeless person

gaum shu (49) گم شو
"get lost!"

gidâ zâdih (50) گدازاده
"son of a beggar/born of a beggar" : a low-class and stingy person. Addressed to individuals from low status who are not generous.

guh bi gîsit (51) گُه به گیست

"may shit be on your hair!" A term of disrespect used by males or females against women.

guh bih gîsih mâdarit (52) گُه به گیس مادرت

"may shit be on your mother's hair!" : you worthless person!

guh lûlih (53) گُه لوله

"rolled in shit" : a worthless person

gurbih kûrih (54) گربه کوره

"blind cat" : an ungrateful or unkind person

gûshti rûnih ni mykhurih mîgih mâlih dar kûnih (55)
گوشت رون نمی خوره میگه مال درکونه

"he/she does not eat the rump roast because it is close to the ass" : an arrogant person. *Kûn* is a single term in Farsi which is used to refer both to the anus and the buttocks.

gûz bi rîshit (56) گوز به ریشت

"may a fart be on your beard!" A term of disrespect used by both males or females against men.

har jâî (57) هرجائی

"sexually loose" : a sexually loose woman. This term is milder than 'prostitute' and is used by women to refer to other women.

harâm luqmih (58) حرام لقمه

"a person who eats stolen food" : a dishonest person. *Harâm* is a term which refers to unclean or unlawful items or acts according to the teachings of Islam.

harâm zâdih (59) حرام زاده

"bastard" : a tricky or malicious person.

jâ kash (60) جاکش

"pimp"

jûni marg bishî illahî (61) جونمرگ بشی اللهی

"may God kill you in your youth!" Addressed to young people. In Persian culture, wishing one to become old is a compliment.

jûnit dar birih (62) جونت دربره

"may your life end!" : I wish you were dead!

kam az anish bi khur (63) کم از عنش بخور

"don't eat his/her shit so much" : a flatterer; a brown-noser

kam az kûnish bi khur (64) کم از کونش به حور

"don't eat his ass!" Addressed to individuals who stick up for someone else too much.

kâsh kamar bâbât khushg shudih bûd (65)
کاش کمر بابات خشگ شده بود

"may that your father's back had been dried up!" This phrase is used in situations where it is wished that the addressee had not been born at all. In Persian culture, it is believed that semen originates in the back of a man's waist. The term 'back' refers only to the back portion of one's waist.

khabîth (66) خبیث

"evil nature" : an evil man

khafiqân bigîr (67) حفقان بگیر

"shut up!"

khâharit gâîdam (68) خواهرت گاییدم

"I fucked your sister." This phrase is used only by men.

khâk bar sarit (69) خاک برسرت

"may soil/dirt be on your head!" This phrase is used when wishing someone dead or wishing someone's father dead. Dirt is put on the head as a sign of grief during the Persian funeral ceremony.

khodâ tu râ bikushad (70) خدا تو را بکشد

"may God kill you!"

kîram bi kusi zanit (71) کیرم به کسی زنت

"my prick is in your wife's cunt!"

kûn goshâd (72) کون گشاد

"wide anus" : a lazy person. A term addressed to both lazy men and lazy women.

kûn gundih (73) کون گنده

"wide buttocks" : a lazy person. A term addressed to both lazy men and women.

kûn kuluft (74) کون کلفت

"big ass" : a lazy person. A term addressed to both lazy men and women.

kûnî (75) کونی

"queer." In Farsi, this term refers only to the male who assumes the female rôle in homosexual intercourse. Both males and females may use this term to abuse a male.

kus kash (76) کس کش

"a person who trades in cunt" : 'a cunt-trader,' pimp

kyram bi kûni khâhar/mâdarit (77)

کیرم به کون خواهر مادرت

"my prick is in your sister's/mother's ass!"

kyram tûyi dahanit (78) کیرم توی دهنت

"my prick is your mouth!"

lakâtih (79) لکاته

"whore"

lingi kafsh kuhnih (80) لنگ کفش کهنه

"an old shoe" : a person who stands up for somebody else too much

lingit pârih mykunam (81) لنگت پاره می کنم

"I will tear your crotch apart!" A term used only between /among women.

mâdar sag (82) مادر سگ

"your mother is a dog" : a low-class person. In Iranian and Islamic culture, the dog is considered unclean.

mâdarit au khâharit (83) مادرت و خواهرت

"your mother and your sister!" This is a shortened version of "I fuck your mother and I fuck your sister!" Even the naming of the mother, sister, or wife by a man to another man is considered an insult in Iranian culture.

mâdârit bi azâyat bishînih (84) مادرت بجزا یت به نشینه
"may your mother mourn for you!" A phrase used by someone wishing that the addressee were dead.

mâdarit mygâm (85) ما درت می گام
"I fuck your mother!"

maymûnih har chî zishtarih bâzîsh bîshtarih (86)
میمونه هرچه زرشت تره با زریش بیشتره
"the uglier the monkey the more active he/she is." This phrase is used to refer to individuals who are physically ugly or of low social status but who behave arrogantly.

misli chusih — na bû darih na khâsiat (87)
مثل چسه نه بو داره نه حاصیت
"just like a fart — it has neither smell nor use" : a useless person. The term *chusih* in Farsi refers to soundless, odorless farts; the term *gûz* refers to the type of fart which has both sound and odor.

misli sindih kih az kûni sag bi kashî bîrûn (88)
مثل سنده که ازکون سگ به کشی بیرون
"just like shit pulled out of a dog's ass" : a feeble person; a hopeless person

'mrit sar birih (89) عمرت سربره
"may your life end!" : I wish you were dead!

mûsh-i-murdih (90) موش مرده
"dead mouse" : a sneaky individual

myzanam tûyi lingit (91) میزنم توی لنگت
"I will hit you in your crotch/cunt!" This phrase is used only between/among women.

myzanam tûyi mukhit ki biry zîri zamyn (92)
میزنم توی مخت که بری زیرزمین
"I will punch your brain so that you will be buried under the ground!" A threat which can become an insult (*see* No. 41).

nafasit band birih (93) نفست بند بیاد
"may you stop breathing!" : may you die!

qirtî (94) قرتی
"gigolo"

pâ bidar (95) پا بدر
"loose" : a loafer

pâ kaj (96) پاکج
"crooked foot" : a sexually loose woman

pufyûz (97) پفیوز
"pompous." This term is addressed only to men.

rîdam bi gûr-i-pidarat (98) ریدم بگور پدرت
"may shit be on your father's grave!"

rûhi bâbât sag rîd (99) روح بابات سگ رید
"may a dog shit on your father's grave!"

sag (100) سگ
"dog" : a feisty or quarrelsome person

sag pidar (101) سگ پدر
"your father is a dog" : a low-class person

salîtih (102) سلیطه
"loudmouth" : a woman who brawls often and screams
too much

sari khar tûyi lingit (103) سر خر توی لنگت
"a donkey's head is in your cunt" : you dumb cunt. This
term is used only between/among women.

shilakhtih (104) شلخته
"messy person" : a woman who does not take proper
care of her children and household

shul-u-vil (105) شل و ول
"loose" : an incapable person

tukhmi harâm (106) تخم حرام
"bastard" : a dishonest person; literally, "unclean semen
or testes." *Tukhmi* refers both to the testes and to semen;
harâm means unclean in the religious, Islamic sense.

tûlih sag (107) سگ لوله

"puppy" : a low-class person

vilgard (108) ولگرد

"loose" : a man who meanders without apparent aim and who goes anywhere even without invitation; i.e., a man who acts as if none of society's norms applied to him.

vilingâr (109) ولنگار

"loose": a woman who exhibits loose (non-sexual) behavior. The female equivalent of *vilgard* (*see* No. 108).

zabân dirâz (110) زبان دراز

"long tongue" : an outspoken person

zabân tîz (111) زبان تیز

"sharp tongue"

zabûnit mâr-u-aghrab bi gazih (112)

زبانت مار و عقرب بگزه

"may your tongue be bitten by a snake and a scorpion!" A phrase used in wishing the other dead or speechless.

zahri mâr (113) زهرمار

"snake poison." A term used in wishing one dead.

zahri mâr ham nimydam (114) زهرمار هم نمیدم

"I don't even give snake poison." A phrase which indicates that 'I would not give you anything.'

zani jindih / zani qahbih (115) زن جنده / زن قحبه

"your wife is a whore." Both men and women use this phrase to abuse a man.

zani kusdih (116) زن کس ده

"your wife is a cunt-giver" : your wife is a whore. Both men and women use this phrase to abuse a man.

A LETTER TO DR. RANDY QUIRK

Dr. Randolph Quirk
Quain[t] Professor of English
University College
Gower Street
London, WC 1, England

Dear Professor Quirk:

Perhaps you have heard of me and my nationwide campaign in the cause of temperance. Each year, for the past 14 years, I have made a tour of Florida and Southern Georgia, and as far north as Indiana, Iowa, Illinois and Wisconsin, and have delivered a series of lectures on the evils of drinking. On these tours I have been accompanied by my friends and assistants Ian Hamilton and D.J. Enright. These friends, young men of good family and excellent background, are pathetic examples of life ruined by excessive indulgence in whiskey and gin.

Ian and D.J. would appear with me at my lectures and sit on the platform, drooling at their mouth, wheezing and staring at the audience through bleary, bloodshot eyes, sweating profusely, picking their nose, passing gas, and making obscene gestures, while I would point them out as examples of what overindulgence in the Devil's Brew can do to a person.

Last fall, unfortunately, both my assistants passed away. Dr. Freddy Cavity, a mutual friend, has given me your name, and I wonder if you would be available next spring to accompany me on my tour, taking the place of my former assistants?

Yours in Faith,

Rev. C. Calhoun

The Reverend Clevite Calhoun
Rescue Mission, Intercourse, PA

[*Editor's Note*: The above letter is part of American Folklore, circulated widely, with different names and places, and generally sent to one's friends as a joke. It is briefly annotated in Dundes & Pagter's *Work Hard*, pp. 31-32. Several of our readers submitted different versions of this letter. Any resemblance to living cacademics, in the above version, is purely intentional.]   (*J. Vriend, G. Wood, Henry B.*)

FIVE YEARS AND 121 DIRTY WORDS LATER

Wayne J. Wilson

Assuming that, unlike jargon or slang, well-known dirty words become essential to strong verbalizations and to the reinforcement of sexual roles, I propose that sex differences in using familiar obscenities should remain stable. Since neither obscene usage nor the psychology of sex differences enjoys a standard definition, each concept requires a practical interpretation in the present study. I define dirty words as taboo expressions of a sexual, scatological or religious denotation, familiar to most college students in American society.* And I define sex differences as the preferences of male and female students for using these words.

Gass (1976:24-25) speculates that popular obscenities represent an impoverished lot: they are few in number, poorly defined, they resist change, and novel obscenities appear unable to crack their exclusive club. Although Gass emphasizes the failure of dirty words to exhibit clarity and subtlety, my paper focuses instead on their stability, on their perennial usage. As for sex differences, Jay (1980:614) indicates through his literature review that males and females vary in how and why they use dirty words. Research findings particularly favor males as more prolific in producing and voicing obscenities (Foote and Woodward, 1973; Kutner and Brogan, 1974; Walsh and Leonard, 1974).

To test the assumption that stable sex differences exist in voicing familiar obscenities, I asked human sexuality students

---

*See NOTES for qualifying remarks on this definition.

in 1975 and again in 1980 to record their usage of dirty words. If stability in expressing obscenities poses a reasonable assumption, then few prominent changes in usage, or changes in attitude about usage, will occur. But if the self-reports in 1975 and 1980 disagree, and the mechanics of testing appear valid and reliable, then the stability proposition will not seem so reasonable after all.

THE TASK

With the happy assistance of psychology faculty and students, I composed a list of 121 dirty words and organized the terms according to body products, male and female anatomy, body functions, male and female character, and religion. I introduced four control items to the list, invented to check the honesty of student answers: *shit away, shit fuzzy, dicky do*, and *liver lips. Shit fuzzy* denoted a sentimental choice because I recalled using it, indeed overusing it, as a grade schooler. We would shout *shit fuzzy* this and *shit fuzzy* that, taking every opportunity to voice an expression that no one fully understood. After a brief sojourn, the term disappeared from our blue vocabularies. Students today occasionally recognize the expression, or think that they do, but seldom use it.

My inventiveness deserted me however, when I decided to include *liver lips*. Students informed me later that this expression enjoys a limited circulation with reference to the genitalia of black females. I left it in anyway. The value of these control items concerns usage more than recognition. Students may claim recognition of a novel obscenity, especially if it appears partly familiar, but most of them should report low usage.

Students rated their personal knowledge and use of each expression according to this scale: I don't know the word (?); I don't use the word (0); I rarely use it (1); I occasionally use it (2); I frequently use the word (3). The figures cited in Table 1 do not represent percentage of students but percentage of *usage.* An expression attains 100% usage only if every student assigns that expression a maximum rating of 3.

A second exercise consisted of seven dirty words, chosen

rationally but not empirically, that seemed more offensive than most dirty words: *shit eater, mother fucker, cock sucker, goddamn, bitch, whore,* and *son of a bitch.* Note that *mother fucker* and *son of a bitch* carry a masculine denotation, whereas *bitch* and *whore* share a feminine label. The remaining terms, *shit eater, cock sucker,* and *goddamn,* though technically neutral, possess a masculine bias in our society. I asked students to use a scale of low anger (1) to high anger (10) and judge their feelings upon hearing these expressions in casual speech from other males and females. Assuming that the speaker and listener are friendly rather than intimate, each student imagined himself or herself listening to someone of the same sex and of the opposite sex: a male speaking to a male, male to female, female to male, and female to female.

SAMPLING AND PROCEDURE

Jay (1977:234) avows the need to articulate context when researching dirty words. This need becomes apparent upon testing females, since they show greater inhibition than males in expressing dirty words if asked to do so orally (Foote and Woodward, 1973), in the presence of a male experimenter (Kutner and Brogan, 1974), and when they hold religious beliefs against using obscenities (Mabry, 1975). I conducted research in 1973 to find, serendipitously, that knowing the investigator may increase the output of dirty words. Students wrote dialogs to their best friend, using the slang phrases and obscenities that normally pepper such conversations. Knowing the investigator and given the opportunity to write their dialogs privately, 69% of the males and 42% of the females included at least one obscenity. Yet when other students faced a strange investigator and he asked them to write their dialogs in class, 62% of the males but only 23% of the females inserted an obscenity (Wilson, 1973:424).

Although students in my present study participated in class, they knew the investigator and the exercise reflected an informal, relaxed session. Also, since students had only to record their rating of different terms, females probably felt freer to respond. Participants included 41 males (72%) and 75 fe-

males (85%) of those students enrolled in a 1975 human sexuality course; 64 males (67%) and 81 females (70%) comprised
the 1980 sample. Students performed voluntarily, anonymously, and without extra credit. Absentees during testing account-
ed for nearly all the students not participating. The human
sexuality course represents a popular elective, drawing from
all majors. Allowing four years for matriculation, this offering
involves approximately 1 of every 3 students on campus. The
2 of 3 students showing no interest in the course, unfortunately, depict a silent sample that remains inaccessible and un-
testable. Whether their usage of obscenities differs from the
students tested becomes a moot point.

RESULTS

Relying on descriptive statistics to convey the results, males
in 1975 scored higher than females in using 117 of 121 terms;
and males in 1980 continued to score higher on 115 of 121
terms. To index a genuine change in expression not due to
sampling error, I arbitrarily declared a usage difference of 20%
that had to occur for males or females between 1975 and
1980. Considering the 121 dirty words in Table 1, only 4 expressions met my criterion. Males and females decreased their
usage of *balling* by at least 20%; males alone decreased their
reference to *piece*, and females increased their usage of *ass
hole* and *tough titty.* No remaining terms for males or females
achieved the 20% change criterion.

Now, instead of frequency of usage, consider applying the
20% change guideline to the number of males and females who
believe that they recognize certain obscenities. Thus, a 20%
difference here refers to percentage of students rather than to
a percentage based on frequency of usage. From this perspec-
tive, males persisted in recognizing a greater number of obscenities. Females in 1975 recorded higher recognition for only 7 of 121 terms; in 1980 this figure fell to 6 terms. Nor did
females achieve a superior recognition difference of 20% over
males for any of these expressions.

Examining the number of obscenities for which all males
and all females indicated recognition, the entire sample of

males recognized 46 of 121 terms in 1975 and 49 such terms in 1980; total female recognition included 27 of 121 terms in 1975 and an identical number in 1980. Students tended not to recognize, or if declaring recognition, not to use the four control items described earlier: *shit away, shit fuzzy, liver lips,* and *dicky do.* Combining the categories of nonrecognition (?) and nonuse (0), the percentage of males ranged from 83% to 97% for these terms in 1975, and 82% to 94% in 1980; the percentage of females varied from 98% to 99% in 1975, and 93% to 99% in 1980. It appears that neither a prevalent number of males or females claimed usage of these planted items.

Students, however, did show a few marked differences in recognizing obscenities after 1975. Continuing to apply the 20% criterion, fewer males and females recognized *shit hook* in 1980, and fewer males showed familiarity with *dink.* By contrast, more males in 1980 recognized *keester* and *twat;* more females became familiar with *keester* and *beaver.* These changes involve novel obscenities which possess a greater capacity for shifts in recognition than do the more familiar obscenities listed in Table 1.

Another index of stability concerns the relative expression of obscenities between males and females. Returning to frequency of usage once again, I applied a more restrictive criterion of 40% to judge extreme differences in male and female usage. *Tits, fuck up, pussy, piece, mother fucker, nuts, jack off, cock sucker, cunt,* and *knockers* represent obscenities which produced at least a 40% difference in usage, favoring males over females in 1975. These terms denote male-female anatomy and body functions, excluding references to body products, male-female character, and religion. But in 1980, only *pussy* retained a 40% difference. Although disparities in male-female usage fell below 40% for the other nine terms in 1980, their margin of difference remained decisive and males continued to dominate.

Measures in the second exercise included mean anger ratings, with higher ratings indicating greater anger; and the standard deviations of these ratings, with higher deviations expressing less agreement among raters. First, because I asked students to pose as listeners, remember that males rated their feelings for only the male-to-male and the female-to-male relationships; females registered their anger for the male-to-female and the female-to-female conditions. Without exception in 1975 and 1980, male students recorded greater anger when they imagined hearing the seven expressions in Table 2 from females rather than males. Males in 1975 and 1980 reserved their greatest anger at the prospect of females using *cock sucker* and *mother fucker* in casual conversation. Female students recorded greater anger at males for using the dirty words in Table 2, but females, unlike males in their conditions, did not distinguish sharply between male-to-female and female-to-female relationships.

Judging the consistency within each relationship from 1975 to 1980, *goddamn* in the male-to-male condition, and *cock sucker* in the male-to-female and the female-to-male conditions produced the highest anger ratings for both years. The high standard deviations accompanying *goddamn* across relationships in 1975 and 1980 imply that the presence and absence of religious beliefs may have prompted students to give extreme ratings in both directions.

To summarize, the overall results confirm a familiar theme in obscenity research. Female students recognize fewer obscenities, use fewer obscenities, and use them less frequently than males. The scattered changes in recognition and usage which transpired since 1975 do little to threaten the stability of how males and females acknowledge their swearing. Males expect other males to swear, but become angry when females "step out of character" to casually voice offensive expressions in the male's presence.

CONCLUSIONS

Certainly these data supporting the stability assumption do not stand unchallenged. Jay (1977:247), for example, lists 28 obscenities that males and females frequently hear in student conversations. Twenty of the 28 terms also appear in Table 1 of my study. Jay's list shows that females recorded a higher frequency than males in hearing 10 of the 20 dirty words, whereas female ratings rarely exceeded male ratings in my project. One explanation for this discrepancy concerns what we ask students to do. Jay instructed his group to judge how frequently students use dirty words in everyday conversations. I directed students to record their personal usage of obscenities – a different frame of reference which probably made a considerable difference in outcome. Sex differences may become more apparent when students judge their personal usage than when they estimate how often other students use dirty words, although this possibility remains untested.

Another challenge involves those perennial problems that plague most social scientists. Will students, say, elsewhere in America and in other English-speaking countries, compare with my sample and display the same sex differences in using obscenities? Will females record a higher usage of dirty words if allowed to do so privately, or in a session with only females present? Do five years encompass sufficient time to evaluate changes in dirty word usage? And does the artificiality of listing individual obscenities cause less valid ratings because some students customarily swear using combinations, such as *that muthafuckinsumbitchinasshole*? These questions need attention before researchers of dirty words can feel more secure in generalizing from sex differences.

The psychology of sex differences, in fact, represents a bottomless pit, scientifically. So many fronts exist in this verbal battle over the sexes that no investigator can make much progress by remaining abstract about such an ambiguous puzzle. It helps instead to find a less confusing issue, a more testable issue, and relate findings from this simpler notion to the catchall concept of sex differences.

Henson (1980:68), for example, defines a taboo as "a ritualistic exercise in control." Drawing on this definition, consider the possibility that dirty words not only allow us emotional release when we need it, but that merely saying dirty words affords us a sense of control. Strong emotions can overwhelm, can cause us to lose control and feel that we cannot master a very intense moment. Martha drops a pot pie and, temporarily shocked, she stares down at her splattered dinner.

Ohh, shit! Shit, shit, shit! Ohh, SHIT! Afterwards, Martha's unpleasant mood lingers but she quickly regains her composure and begins to clear away the pot pie. Bellowing forth her string of *shits* gives Martha the brief release she needs to resume emotional control and come to terms with her clumsiness. For Martha at least, *Oh shucks!* or some other benign expression hardly suffices to register her dismay.

Turning to higher stakes, Johnston (1976:62) reports on the last words of airline pilots just prior to a crash: "When pilots do realize they have lost control, they generally respond with frustrated resignation. Though the tapes are always edited for the sake of the surviving families, the pilot's last words on the cockpit voice recorder are often 'Oh shit!' as though he had just hit his thumb with a hammer or missed the last train." Despite losing control of the aircraft, a pilot voicing obscenities in his final seconds may afford himself some semblance of composure by aptly punctuating such a tumultuous moment.

Saying dirty words therefore, whether in exultation or despair, permits individuals to address and manage strong emotions. Control, however, does not represent a concept for all seasons. A sense of control through obscene expressions seems plausible for anchoring intense encounters, but this idea cannot account for all the contributions that dirty words make to communication. Irving glances up nonchalantly as Buford enters and says, *Hey, fartface, where you been?* He delivers a greeting that implies familiarity and (we hope) friendship, yet without the strong emotion which heretofore related obscenities to self-control. The absence of intense feelings makes the idea of control less feasible as a purpose for using dirty words.

Because my results indicate that females know fewer obscenities and use them less frequently than males, the possibility arises that females may have less need to use dirty words in controlling their behavior. The female's sexual role allows her greater latitude for exhibiting despair and joy through crying or other outlets not commonly acceptable to the male. Males, however, appear to cherish dirty words as a traditional and comfortable masculine style of handling elation and distress. Recall that males, in Table 2, recorded higher anger when confronted with hearing females use obscenities in casual conversation. Perhaps their anger stems from the belief that females can justify swearing only under select circumstances, such as during instances of intense emotion.

If so, then genuine changes in sexual roles will alter the need to maintain control through swearing. Males evaluated as androgynous, for example, will feel freer to express their emotions by crying or other means, and rely less on obscenities. Androgynous females will show greater inclination to voice dirty words on more public occasions than will other females. These propositions have no empirical support at present, but assuming a reasonable determination of androgyny, this group of males and females should reflect fewer sex differences in using obscenities.

And if, as my findings suggest, the stability assumption has merit, then the male's monopoly on recognizing and using obscenities may relate to his particular need for self-control. If a sense of control means that dirty words become important to achieving emotional release, especially for males, then stability in using obscenities can serve as one index of that control. Control, in turn, offers a testable concept for speculating on the differing ways that males and females choose to express their emotions.

NOTES

Through Dr. Aman's thoughtful editorial comments, I am reminded that religious violations properly refer to blasphemies, not obscenities. Indeed, Table 2 in my study indicates that *goddamn* may have prompted bipolar ratings among some students, depending on their religious beliefs.

For this paper however, I have not pressed the distinction between obscenities and blasphemies; and, with a few exceptions, I have used "dirty words" and "obscenities" interchangeably. I have done so for the convenience of exposition, and because only a few of my 121 terms qualify as blasphemies.

TABLE 1

Frequency of Using Dirty Words Expressed in Percentages

*Indicates a 40% difference in male and female usage. C = control item

	1975 M	1975 F	1980 M	1980 F		1975 M	1975 F	1980 M	1980 F
Hell	85	74	83	70	Prick	47	17	50	19
Bull Shit	85	52	81	67	Shit Ass	46	32	40	32
Fuck	84	47	82	50	Jugs	46	6*	33	10
Shit	83	76	89	79	Tough Titty	46	16	28	36
Pissed Off	83	70	78	70	Good Shit	43	15	35	12
Damn	82	74	87	80	Shit Hits Fan	42	24	47	39
Tits	82	31*	73	43	Shit a Brick	42	24	42	26
Piss	78	46	76	53	Suck Ass	42	4	35	10
Dumb Ass	75	63	75	67	Tail	42	12	25	10
Screw	75	55	64	48	Humping	41	8	31	12
Bitch	74	58	72	64	Shit Head	39	18	41	28
Son of a Bitch	73	48	76	47	Bad Shit	39	11	30	7
Ass	72	54	72	58	Cherry	37	9	32	11
Fuck Up	71	29*	64	31	Hot Damn	36	13	38	28
Pussy	68	13*	64	12*	Snatch	36	4	37	3
Piece	68	17*	48	21	Pecker	35	14	40	15
Mother Fucker	67	26*	67	28	Jerk Off	33	8	36	12
Ass Hole	67	40	73	61	Hot Shit	33	9	35	16
Fuck Off	66	28	63	31	Shit-eating Grin	33	12	32	16
Balls	66	35	64	30	Shit House	33	3	29	10
Boobs	66	56	51	54	Piss Ant	33	13	27	18
Smart Ass	65	64	65	61	Holy Shit	31	12	35	28
Goddamn	63	34	51	28	Fart Face	31	27	22	22
Nuts	63	23*	58	25	Peter	30	18	34	18
Balling	62	27	31	7	Turd Face	30	14	22	24
Bastard	62	52	63	52	Crock of Shit	29	8	39	19
Screw Up	61	48	56	51	Horse's Ass	29	17	33	20
Chicken Shit	61	36	53	39	Shit Face	27	12	36	23
Whore	59	31	57	41	Twat	24	6	33	12
Jack Off	59	19*	47	23	Beaver	24	1	24	2
Fart	58	46	64	44	Tube Steak	23	1	18	4
Cock Sucker	57	7*	45	11	Fuzz	23	4	15	6
Dick	56	25	58	23	Furburger	22	1	27	2
Tough Shit	56	46	58	53	Family Jewels	21	4	33	11
Prick Teaser	55	22	51	21	Dork	21	14	25	24
Up Shit's Creek	54	36	57	38	Hell Fire	21	17	23	12
Cock	54	16	50	13	Tool	21	4	18	5
Cunt	53	5*	45	7	Shit Hook	21	4	8	1
Knockers	53	11*	37	12	Nurds	20	11	24	24
Blow Job	53	14	54	27	Hell's Bells	20	30	23	19
Pile of Shit	50	27	41	34	Shit on Shingle	20	6	17	8
Turd	48	43	39	35	Skin Flute	20	1	12	0
Beat your Meat	48	4*	38	7	Pie	19	0	7	1

(cont'd.)

	1975		1980			1975		1980	
	M	F	M	F		M	F	M	F
Shit Hole	18	4	21	9	Bat Shit	8	4	14	3
Lungs	18	3	20	4	Dink	8	2	9	3
Peter Eater	17	3	15	5	Muff Diver	7	1	18	3
Hell Hole	16	6	19	9	Bearded Clam	7	0	8	1
Dong	16	3	18	3	Shit Knocker	7	1	6	1
Shit on a Stick	16	4	16	5	Liver Lips (C)	7	1	5	1
Yang Yang	16	5	14	4	Twat's Hair	6	0	12	1
Shit Eater	15	5	23	6	Shit Nose	6	1	8	1
Poot	15	26	21	19	Hide	5	3	8	2
Fart Knocker	15	4	9	3	Fern	5	0	5	0
Tallywhacker	13	8	15	7	Shit Away (C)	3	1	9	3
Muff	12	1	21	4	Shit Fuzzy (C)	3	1	2	1
Fuck Stick	12	2	8	2	Tinker Toy	2	0	7	2
Hot Ass	11	2	17	7	Shit on String	2	1	6	2
Cold Shit	11	2	17	3	Keester	2	1	3	7
Whip your Willie	11	1	9	2	Shit Stopper	1	1	5	2
Wooter	10	2	7	1	Dicky Do (C)	1	1	4	0
Pissed Out	9	1	8	3					

TABLE 2
Mean Anger Ratings with Standard Deviations
*Highest mean anger rating within each of four categories

1975	M & M		M & F		F & F		F & M	
	Mean	SD	Mean	SD	Mean	SD	Mean	SD
Shit Eater	2.02	1.99	3.70	3.01	4.10	2.15	5.28	3.05
Mother Fucker	2.29	2.37	4.95	3.22	4.85	3.25	6.24	3.59
Cock Sucker	2.20	2.15	5.30*	3.46	5.64*	3.55	7.21*	2.49
Goddamn	3.46*	2.56	4.17	3.32	3.96	4.17	4.87	3.82
Bitch	1.61	1.24	2.80	2.26	2.50	1.62	3.85	3.37
Whore	1.70	1.69	3.39	2.87	2.63	2.65	4.60	3.44
Son of a Bitch	1.61	1.09	3.37	2.76	2.31	2.48	3.44	3.08

1980	M & M		M & F		F & F		F & M	
	Mean	SD	Mean	SD	Mean	SD	Mean	SD
Shit Eater	2.48	2.00	6.00	3.78	3.84	3.01	5.85	3.29
Mother Fucker	2.81	2.38	7.05	3.91	5.04	3.40	7.24	2.90
Cock Sucker	2.84	2.43	7.33*	4.04	5.98	3.44	8.04*	2.74
Goddamn	4.69*	3.71	6.53	4.03	6.37*	3.69	6.93	3.39
Bitch	1.95	1.58	3.83	2.95	2.20	2.18	4.69	3.14
Whore	1.94	1.54	4.41	3.30	2.74	2.52	4.95	3.04
Son of a Bitch	2.22	1.99	4.73	3.49	2.53	2.31	4.27	3.12

REFERENCES

Foote, R., and Woodward, J. "A Preliminary Investigation of Obscene Language," *Journal of Psychology* 83 (1973), 263-275.

Gass, W. *On Being Blue.* Boston: David R. Godine, 1976.

Henson, S. "Female as Totem, Female as Taboo: An Inquiry into the Freedom to Make Connections," in E. Sagarin (ed.) *Taboos in Criminology.* Beverly Hills: Sage Publ., 1980.

Jay, T. "Sex Roles and Dirty Word Usage: A Review of the Literature and a Reply to Haas," *Psychological Bulletin* 88, no. 3 (1980), 614-621.

–––. "Doing Research with Dirty Words," *Maledicta* 1, no. 2 (1977), 234-256.

Johnston, M. "The Last 77 Seconds of Flight 981," *Psychology Today* (November 1976), 58-62.

Kutner, N., and Brogan, D. "An Investigation of Sex-related Slang Vocabulary and Sex-role Orientation among Male and Female University Students," *Journal of Marriage and the Family* 36, no. 3 (1974), 474-484.

Mabry, E. "A Multivariate Investigation of Profane Language," *Central States Speech Journal* 26, no. 1 (1975), 39-44.

Walsh, R., and Leonard, W. "Usage of Terms for Sexual Intercourse by Men and Women," *Archives of Sexual Behavior* 3, no. 4 (1974), 373-376.

Wilson, W. "Secrecy and Written Dialogue," *Psychological Reports* 32 (1973), 419-425.

GLOSSARY

Dink, Dork: penis
Fart Knocker: a braggart; one who does not know what he is talking about; also used affectionately.
Fern: female genital region and pubic hair
Fuzz: 1: female pubic hair. 2: young male, especially around the age of puberty
Hell's Bells: exclamation of surprise. WW II usage.

Hide: vulva and surrounding genital area
Lungs: female breasts
Nurds: testes
Pie: vulva. Used in "pie taster" = cunnilinctor
Poot: excrement (wet). Used with and by children; variant of *poop, poo-poo.*
Shit Hook: going through a hard time or being taken advantage of
Shit on String: something difficult or impossible to do
Shit Stopper: a prank, a funny scene, an escapade
Tube Steak, Wooter, Ying Yang: penis.

KNOW YOUR FRIENDS

A nonconforming robin decided not to fly south for the winter with the rest of his friends. After a few weeks of rather cold weather, he decided he had better make way for the south. But as he flew along, the weather became worse, and ice began to form on his wings. He fell to earth, almost frozen, on a small barnyard. Shortly thereafter, a cow passed by and shat on the robin. The manure warmed the bird, and as he began to thaw out, he felt much better and began to sing. A cat passing by heard the chirping and decided to investigate. He promptly dug the bird out of the manure and ate him.

THE MORAL OF THIS STORY IS:

— *A person who shits on you isn't necessarily your enemy.*
— *A person who digs you out of the shit isn't necessarily your friend. And,*
— *If you are warm and comfortable in a pile of shit…keep your mouth shut!*

(M. Cornog + R. Lederer)

An example of crude, often aggressive photocopy humor circulated widely. The original is 8½ by 11 inches. Cleaned and slightly modified by R.A. (G. Wood, Texas, 1981)

A FRENCH MENU

G. Legman

RESTAURANT BITENLAIR
— MENU —

Potage
Urine de pucelle
Julienne aux fleurs blanches

Entrée
Têtes de nœuds à l'huile
Cons d'allouettes en papillottes
Ragoût de matrices

Rôtis
Couilles de sapeur sautées
Filet de pucelle au cresson
Morpions à la broche

Poissons
Maquereau au copahu

Légumes
Purée de mer[de]
Laitues à la conflante

Dessert
Chaudepisse à la savoisienne
Chancres à la vanille

Vins et Café
De Bordel, Veuve Poignet, Clos
De Suresne, Cliquot, Lance échauffée

Personnel:
Cuisinière: Kamalosqu, Mepaquela, Guimét
un nœud à la sauce blanche

Caissière: Mme N. Laplu. Garçon: Baize-alleuil

Directeur,
CALEVITFORT

PRICKINAIR RESTAURANT

— MENU —

Soups
Virgin's Urine
Vegetable Soup with the Whites[1]

Entrée
Prick-Heads in Oil
Lark-Cunts in Buttered Wraps
Womb Stew

Roasts
Browned Fireman's Balls
Split Vagina with Watercress
Crablice-on-the-Spit

Fish
Sweetpimp with Clap Sauce[2]

Vegetables
Strained Sh—t
Cuntified Lettuce

Dessert
Running Clap (Italian style)
Soft Chancres with Vanilla Sauce

Wines & Coffee
Whore-Alley, Widow Fist,
Suresne Field, Cliquot, Hotprick

Staff:
Cooks: Rottenprick, Stickitinthere,
Gimme-a-Jock-in-White-Sauce[3]

Cashier: Madam N. Laplu. Waiter: Grannyjazzer[4]

Director,
STIFFPRICK

---

[1] Gonorrhea. [2] Being treated with copaïba for gonorrhea. [3] Semen.
[4] 'Fuck-grandfather'

NOTES

Provenance: Collected in Paris, 1960, in the form of a printed slip reproduced by alcohol-gelatine plate process (like authentic menus in small French restaurants), from copperplate-style handwriting. All misspellings as in original. Had been owned by source since 1937, and another item in same group of these pre-Xerox materials is dated 1924. Source (male) read "Menu" aloud, laughing continuously.

In Thomas Pynchon's *Gravity's Rainbow* (New York: Viking, 1973), a Götterdämmerung novel concerning the launching of the Ultimate Bomb by U.S. forces in Germany, Book 4, "The Counterforce" (Bantam ed., pp. 832-36), a food-dirtying "Menu" of this type is shown in the process of being elaborated by presumed "communal improvisation" by the guests at a banquet *de grand apparat*, featuring "*scab sandwiches with mucus mayonnaise*," etc. See further my *The New Limerick* (More Limericks: 1977) chapter IX, "Gourmands," and Note 2:1511; also and more fully *Rationale of the Dirty Joke*, Second Series (*No Laughing Matter*) 12.IV.4, "Sexual Smörgåsbord," pp. 376-78; and Mac E. Barrick, "The Typescript Broadside," in *Keystone Folklore Quarterly* 17 (1972), pp. 30, 36-37. Also relevant is the totality of the purposely disgusting dishes served, beginning with "*fried shit choplets*," in the Negro toast recitation, "The Ball of the Freaks," in *The Life*, ed. Dennis Wepman, *et al.* (University of Pennsylvania Press, 1976) p. 12; and the long, spontaneous fantasy of a 7-year-old American boy, "Nixon's Favorite Menu: UnAppetizers," beginning with "*Cross-eyed Goose egg broiled in butter made with mustard*," in Brian Sutton-Smith & David Abrams, "Psychosexual Material in the Stories Told by Children: The Fucker," presented at the First International Conference On Sexology (Montréal, 1976) 31 f. 4to, at ff. 25-27. Compare also the aggressively food-dirtying "pie-throwing" comedies.

MORE REPULSIVE MENUS

Reinhold Aman

I

A GERMAN MENU

MENU

Gebaermuttersuppe mit Haemorroiden-Kloesschen
Saure Nachgeburt in Kaltenbauer mit Meesenschleimtunke
Klabusterbeeren-Salat in Scheismajonaise
Negernillen-Kaese / Mitesserqualster / Augenbutter
Gefuellter Nasenpobel-Pudding und Fotzenschaum-Gelée

MENU

Womb Soup with Hemorrhoid Dumplings
Sour Afterbirth in Come with Pussy-Juice Gravy
Dingleberry Salad in Shit Mayonnaise
Negro-Dick Cheese / Blackhead Slime / "Sleep"
Filled Nosebug Pudding and Cunt-Foam Jelly

NOTES

A copy of this menu was submitted by Rainer G. Feucht, an antiquarian and folklore bookdealer in Germany who found it in the Supplement (*Ergänzungsheft*) to Magnus Hirschfeld's *Sittengeschichte des Weltkrieges* (Leipzig / Wien: Verlag für Sexualwissenschaft Schneider & Co., 1931), p. 28. The menu in this History of the Morals of the (First) World War is reproduced above with all its misspellings as in the original. Corrected and modern spellings, with explanations: *Gebärmutter*,

Hämorrhoiden, Klößchen 'small dumplings,' *kalter Bauer* 'ejaculate'; *see* MAL IV/2:249-51; *Möse* 'pussy'; *Klabusterbeeren* 'dingleberries' (or *dingbats* in Australian English) are the small hardened balls of feces clinging to the anal hair of unhygienic people and animals; *Scheißmayonnaise*; *Nille* or *Nülle* 'dick, pecker'; *Nillenkäse* 'smegma'; *Mitesser*, lit. "with-eater," 'blackhead' or 'comedo'; *Qualster* 'expectorate' or 'oyster'; *Augenbutter*, lit. "eye-butter" or 'sleep,' the slimy yellow excretion in the corner of one's eyes.

II

Professor Mac Barrick, a leading folklore scholar, informed us that another version of our *Pussy Café* Menu (MAL IV, No. 1, p. 116) appeared in his article quoted by Mr. Legman, above. Among the variations of dishes listed are: *Smoked Quiff; Ass Holes in Jelly; Cocky Leeky; Stewed Boo-Jess Ass with Hole; Roast Kosher Kock mit Fancy Trimmings; Cremated Bitches, Ozone Park Nooky Sauce; Sliced Ass Cheeks à la Asshole Inn; Fried Redsnapper, Period Sauce; Toilet Seat Crabs on Toast, Blue Balls Butter; Grilled Split Pussyfoot, Piss Clam Sauce; East River Condoms, Cream Sauce; Mashed Nuts; Reamed Spinach, Butt Butter; Screwed Carrots; Lettuce Turnip & Pee; Canada Dry Splits; Poop Cocktail; Flung Dung Pudding;* and *Ladies' Whole Fingers.* This menu circulated in mimeographed form among Dickinson College (Pa.) students in 1953 and 1954.

Dr. Barrick also pointed out that our *Dinner Dansant* Menu (MAL IV/2:202) was circulated as an Adult Greeting Card in Pennsylvania, produced and copyrighted in 1973 by Peppermint Stick Greeting Cards.

III

As disgusting as these and other menus printed in earlier issues of MAL are, they are significant for folklore and cross-cultural studies and at least as important as the study of embroidery of Tyrolean peasant dresses or Kwakiutl fishhooks. As Allen Walker Read wrote in 1935, "No emanation of the human spirit is too vile or too despicable to come under the record and analysis of the scientist" (*Graffiti*, p. 6). Some of the psychological aspects of this "food-dirtying" have been explored by Mr. Legman, but questions remain: what is the relationship between these repulsive menus and wartime or soldiers? Are such menus in existence in societies where food is far more scarce and vital than in America, France and Germany, from where we have such menus? Do such menus exist in Japan, China, Tibet, Nigeria? If not, is it caused by the traditional oral transmission (few written records, even now in Xerox days)? Or do the members of other cultures, close to chronic starvation, value food too much to degrade it in such a way? Are adults in other cultures less inclined to "gross out" other adults with such crude, childish travesties?

We are not going to publish further variations of English menus but we would welcome such menus from Russia and especially from Africa, Asia and Oceania—if they exist.

IV

Finally, Mr. Roy West, Philadelphia, submitted a classic of such menus, authored as a Dining Car Menu by Elliot Springs, in 1953, owner of the Lancaster and Chester Railway Co. of South Carolina, a mere twenty-mile single-track connecting line between the two cotton plants of Springs Mills. This four-page menu is quite witty, full of word plays, and contains no vulgarities. Among the dishes listed are: *Low Calorie Juice / High Voltage Juice; Green Turtle / Red Herring; Split Pea / Split Infinitives / Split Dixiecrats with Frozen Assets; Fillet of Flounder / Floundering Filly; Pâté of Young Shrimp / Pinch of Old Shrimp; Deep Sea Scallops with Salty Accent / Back Bay Trollops with Harvard Accent; Breast of Peasant Stuffed with Russian Propaganda; Domestic Lamb Chops with Imported Pants / Imported Mermaid without Pants; Jerked Deer stewed in Chestnuts / Dear Jerk stewed in Chestnut Hill; Imported Bustard stuffed with Domestic Snipe / Domestic Bastard stuffed with Imported Tripe; Alligator Pear / Pair of Alligators; Pie with Cheesecake, filled Up to Here / filled Up to There; Pitted Grapes / Potted Dates (New York $20, Palm Beach $40); Assorted Nuts and Nuts à Vous.*

BY ITS SLANG, YE SHALL KNOW IT
THE PESSIMISM OF PRISON LIFE

Hugh Morgan

Prison inmates have little choice but to accept the rules which regulate their lives. They eat, rest, and work on orders from guards, whose enormous power represents society's grasp over the prisoners. To reassert their independence, convicts create a subculture with its own mores and language. One way to get a glimpse into this prison culture is by examining this vocabulary, which is charged with cynicism, suspicion, gloom, and coercion. This pessimistic world view, one without wholesomeness or cheery humor, will be revealed in this paper. Two-thirds of the words do not appear in the second supplemented edition of the *Dictionary of American Slang.*[1] The terms were gathered at Vienna Correctional Center, a minimum security state prison in Southern Illinois, where inmates are sent after serving time in an institution with more rigorous restrictions. A white[2] inmate prepared the list in December 1979 at the request of this writer, at the time an instructor in a journalism class conducted through an extension service of Southern Illinois University.

The murky prison life has no folk heroes who represent the traditional values that are so much a part of the American conception of the courageous individual. The cast of prison characters contains guards, who are the enemy or crooked conspirators, and inmates, who seek advantage by informing, who show their conception of virility by boasting of their own criminality and by deprecating many fellow convicts, and who are often the victim or the aggressor in the homo-

264 - MALEDICTA V

sexual way-of-life. Daily life is filled with words that display
a warped view of honor, a glorification of intimidation, and a
chorus of threats used to protect personal space. Even the vocabulary for dining contains no delicacy, but it represents a
crude sense of humor. Positive words crop up now and then,
but the concern is with the self.

While slang serves as a means to achieve identification with
a group,[3] it is also used to keep outsiders from participating
in society. The following scene from prison life shows how a
code word is used: as a prison guard approaches three convicts who do not want to be overheard, one prisoner casually
inserts into his conversation the word **radio**. The guard, who
had inspired the term from the two-way radio he carries, does
not realize that the prisoners were referring to him in time to
tone down their conversation. The term, however, took on a
meaning beyond a word for a guard as it became a synonym
for "shut up." An inmate demanding quiet yells **Radio that!**
or **Radio that shit!** Inmates have other terms for guards, i.e.,
the *screws,[4] as every television viewer knows. Prisoners try
to locate a *horse or *mule to smuggle contraband, usually
drugs or cash, into prison. All inmates have stories of how
they were arrested by a **roller**, a policeman. When fighting
breaks out in prison, the inmates seek to avoid the **big six**, an
emergency riot squad of prison guards. They also shun a
crank, a veteran guard or prisoner who likes to give them a
difficult time, just for the "fun" of it.

The inmate who draws the resentment from most of his
peers is the informer. The **snitch** goes up to a guard and he
drops a dime, **flips** or **turns over** on a fellow inmate. Sometimes, an inmate goes the route of **dry snitching**, in which he
accuses another of infractions by innuendo, whether intentional or not. An inmate **hangs a jacket** on another convict
by accusing him publicly of being an informer. When an inmate just **burns bread** on another, he rails against him for any
reason. Then, there's the segment of prison society that seeks
favor with the authorities or with anyone holding power
over it. They **stroke** or **grip** the power brokers by playing up
to them in hopes of receiving favors, now or in the future. A

prisoner who adheres to the rules and does his assigned duties so he can get as favorable a break on his parole record as possible is following his **program**. "I'm programming," a prisoner says in refusing to join in a petty prank.

Other terms used by prisoners to describe themselves are derisive, suspicious, or boastful of a criminal past or ability to be tough. Some slang terms have been around for decades, such as the word *fish to denote a new inmate. It came into vogue around 1900 as a term for a college freshman. It was appropriated by 1915 to refer to an imprisoned first offender. [5] **Fish** is mild enough compared to other terms for prisoners. The average inmate, if such a person exists, looks down upon a *lame, *duck or *lemon because he is simple-minded and vapid. He also steers clear of a **half-stepper**, who does things half way, or a **sometime**, who is a person one cannot depend on. And he does not want to live or work with a **crank gang** because it is made up of prisoners who are eccentric or lazy. He's wary of the prisoners comprising the *goon squad,[6] who assist guards in disciplining other inmates, and also of the **gang-bangers**, gang members who enjoy a rousing fight. He's at ease with a **hood** or a *homey, a friend from the same hometown and neighborhood. A convict seeking a **rappie** wants to enlist a partner in committing a crime. His **ride** is a companion, especially a fellow gang member.

Power, rather than love, emerges from an examination of the sexual slang terms. An aggressive homosexual, a *jocker, forces himself upon a **gump**, a passive homosexual, or a *punk, a weak person used for sex. A homosexual may **flip-flop** with a fellow **bitch** by reciprocating sexually. An inmate **pulls the covers off** another person by exposing his sexual preference or he *turns out[7] another inmate by enticing him to become gay. The men refer to lesbians as **jaspers**. Males, bereft of female comfort, sometimes resort to a **fi-fi bag**, a plastic sack containing a warm, wet towel used as a vagina.

The sample of non-sexual phrases used in daily conversation illustrates not only the violence, defiance, and threats in prison life, but also the prisoners' conception of manhood. Violence occupies a prominent place in prison vocabulary. A prisoner calls his fists **guns** and when he **guns up**, he puts up his fists or arms himself with a weapon. He **fires up** another prisoner when he thrashes him or he ***fires on** a person when he throws a sucker punch. A prisoner **hooks up** with a gang and he **rides with** or sides with someone during a fight. By **dragging** an acquaintance, the prisoner leads him on, and by **getting over** the person, the inmate makes himself look good by taking advantage of the other. But if he **drags** or **gets over** another **by way of no harm**, he's doing so without any malicious intent to hurt or to offend the person. If the prisoner **peeps the holecard** of another, he discovers the person's inner motivation. A prisoner threatens another by **selling a wolf ticket** or ridicules by **signifying**, usually in rhyme. Some common sayings: "I know you from the street. You were so hard up, the cockroaches went next door to eat," or "He's so old, he could have been a waiter at the Last Supper," "He's so thin, he has to drink chocolate milk to cast a shadow." Fury is implied in requests to **pull up**, as in "Why don't you pull up, mister? You're bothering me," or "Give me some air" and "Give me some space." A person who breaks down under pressure or slinks away from a threatening situation is said **to go out the back door.** Convicts told **don't do out like that** are being asked not to react in a way that will draw the scorn of fellow inmates. This phrase arose perhaps from the custom of taking a convict, who died in prison without any family, out of the cellblock without any fanfare to a prison grave.

The list contains many words for prison facilities and for the system's policies. The media have popularized the term *****joint** for prison and *****hole** for solitary confinement. More unfamiliar are the expressions **to bank off** or **to lay down** to describe a prisoner being placed in a punishment cell. Quite possibly, **bank off** stems from the fact that some solitary confinement cells resembled a bank vault, and **lay down** derives from the time cells were so cramped that inmates could not stand up in them. A **gladiator school** is a maximum-security prison. In his view of the judicial system, a prisoner is given a *****bit**, as in a **one-year bit**, by the judge who sentenced him to prison. Once there, the prisoner seeks to avoid a *****ticket**, a disciplinary report, which could go on his **jacket** or prison file, and thus earn him a **set** or continuance of a parole hearing. The inmate's **papers** are his documents dealing with his parole application which, when approved, makes him *****short**. A happy time is when he has **one and a get up**, just one more day to serve and when he awakens the next morning, he can depart.

Some of the words referring to food, drink, or cigarets are too uncouth to be used in a gourmet restaurant or even in a fast-food emporium. The late Colonel Sanders undoubtedly would have shuddered if he had heard inmates refer to fried chicken as **barnyard pimp**. In the same manner, prisoners call any fish dinner in prison **sewer trout**. Sugar is *****sand** and salt and pepper are **glitter** and **sneeze**. The latter term is especially applied to red pepper, which is contraband in some prisons for fear that it will be used to blind a person temporarily. Other illegal items are *****hooch**, a familiar term for alcohol, especially the homemade variety, and **stinger** for an electrical device used to heat water in a *****crib** or cell. The **stinger** consists of wires with both ends exposed. One end is inserted into an electrical socket and the other is placed in the water to heat it, to prepare coffee. An inmate will **flash the gallery** or **flash the range** by using a shiny object to look for the reflections on it of any guard while he is doing the illegal boiling. If a guard approaches, the **stinger** can be removed easily. A phrase that must have been conceived by a person with a playful imagination is **zoo-zoos and wham-whams** for confections, usually small packaged cakes, pies, candy or gum obtained from a vending machine. In prison, cigarets serve as a universal means of exchange, with a **brick** being a carton, **Double O's** for Kool cigarets, and **red head** for match. Other terms commonly heard in prison life are **shank**[8] for knife, *****kite** for message or letter, sometimes a secret one, **box**[9] for television, *****bricks** for the street, *****beef** for complaint, **scrap iron** for weights for exercising, and **reggin** for a black person. The latter does not carry the same ugly meaning as it does when spelled in reverse. It is more of a non-controversial term used by both races in the Vienna Correctional Center. Other neutral terms are **off into** for being deeply involved with something and **24/24** for all day, as in "Are you going to be in your crib tomorrow?" Answer: "24/24."

There are a few positive words on the slang list, although they deal with little but the personal concerns of the prisoners. The truth is **square business** and being **straight up**, as in "that's straight up, brother," is being truthful. A prisoner joking with another is **jeffin** with the person. A person proficient at something is *****down**, as in "He's down in handball." A well-dressed man is **clean** or **pressed to the max**.

Perhaps a word should be said about what the list does not contain. No words appear for family, for religious beliefs, or for a contribution toward helping society. The slang illustrates the concern with the self and with how to gain the best advantage in prison. The overwhelming pessimism and vileness in these words indicate that the prisoners help create their own shabby environment where altruism has no place.

NOTES

1. Harold Wentworth and Stuart Berg Flexner, *Dictionary of American Slang*, 2nd supplemented edition (New York: Thomas Y. Crowell, 1975).

2. Wentworth, p. 477. The term "signify" is an example of a term originating in black culture which became part of the common language inside prison. Other terms, such as "wolf ticket," do not yet appear in the *Dictionary of American Slang* but have been in widespread use in the black culture. No attempt will be made, however, to trace the racial origins of the words. This is mentioned to point out that terms from both white and black cultures become part of the common argot inside prison.

3. Julia S. Falk, *Linguistics and Language*, 2nd edition (New York: John Wiley, 1978), p. 66.

4. Wentworth. All words relating to terms found in the *Dictionary of American Slang* are preceded by an asterisk.

5. Wentworth, p. 184.

6. Wentworth, p. 224. The dictionary term related to a gang

of thugs used to break up a labor dispute. In prison, "goon squad" came to be applied to the convicts used by prison authorities to punish unruly inmates.

7. Wentworth, p. 752. The phrase outside prison had been used to denote turning a woman into a prostitute. Inside prison, it took on a homosexual connotation.

8. Wentworth, p. 462. In the slang dictionary, "shank" is defined as a verb, meaning to stab a person, whether in the leg or elsewhere. It derives from the term, "ride shanks' mare," meaning to walk. In prison, "shank" also became a noun, meaning a knife.

9. Wentworth, p. 686. The slang dictionary defines "box" as a radio. In the prison slang list, "box" was used for a television set.

A TALMUDIC CURSE

Alexander Feinsilver

Professor Leonard Ashley inquired about the following quote found in Will Durant, *The Story of Civilization: The Age of Faith* (vol. 4; New York: Simon & Schuster, 1950, p. 359): "On that day [Purim], said Rab[bi] Raba, a man should drink until he could no longer distinguish between 'Cursed be Haman!' and 'Cursed be Mordecai!'" Not only is this quote wrong, but also Durant's reference to Moore. In his book, Rabbi Emeritus Feinsilver, who recently published his fascinating and recommendable *The Talmud for Today* (New York: St. Martin's Press, 1980), discusses—among many other interesting topics—the use of wine. Below is Rabbi Feinsilver's reaction to the above misquotation, with the opening quote from his book, p. 91, No. 283. (*Editor*)

Rabba said, "A man is obliged to drink enough [wine] on Purim so that he cannot distinguish between 'Cursed be Haman!' and 'Blessed be Mordecai!'" *The Talmud, Megillah, 7b.*

Jewish literary sources prohibit cursing. The Bible states "Thou shalt not curse [even] the deaf" (Lev. 19:14). Nonetheless, cursing Haman was an acceptable catharsis of rage against the Prime Minister of ancient Persia, who sought to destroy the Jews because Mordecai refused to bow before him. As detailed in the Biblical story of Esther, Haman's plans were foiled by Queen Esther's intercession with her husband, King Ahasuerus, at the request of Mordecai, her cousin, who had saved the king's life.

The Book of Esther is read aloud in the synagogue on Purim. At each mention of Haman, children twirl *gragers* (noisemakers, rattles) to drown out his name, and adults may respond with *Arur Haman!* ('Cursed be Haman!'). At the mention of Mordecai, *Baruch Mordecai!* ('Blessed be Mordecai!') may be uttered. Because the Megillah (Scroll) of Esther is a long story (that's the origin of the Yiddish-American slang *a gantse megille*), a worshiper who had drunk too much wine might mistakenly respond with the wrong phrase as time wore on.

LEXICOGRAPHY
(A TROUGH OF LOW PLEASURE)

Gavin Ewart

Like a lepidopterist with a fine new specimen
Carried carefully home from a successful sortie,
What did I do with this marvellous trophy?
    Spread it out and put it under the microscope!

This, the *O.E.D.* in its Compact Edition,
Carried a reading glass, a standard extra.
What did I search for? Just like anyone,
    Looked up CUNT, to see it under the reading glass

(The same would have been done by the magazine editors
And by all the publishers, including Virago,
It's an important word and basic in folklore,
    Known about and spoken, over the hemispheres),

Keats's friends drank to it as Mater Omnium,
It's full of sexual overtones and sensual undertones,
It has a kind of inwardness that some call mystical.
    So I crept, so slowly, over the printed mass,

Not wanting to disturb it as it basked in the sunshine,
Tiptoeing in to net it. I reached CUNCTATION,
Which means delay, delaying, or tardy action;
    Turned the page, to CUNNING, under the reading glass.

I was sure I should see it, what a triumph! Quietly
I moved on to CUNSTER, a conner once in Scotland . . .
And then, in upper and lower case, I saw it:
    Cunt —: see CONT. Injustice! Under-represented!

When COCK is there in glory with words like CLAPPERDUDGEON
(Meaning a man who was born and bred a beggar).
So I turned to CONT, in a mood of disappointment.
  It's "To punt (a boat, or barge)" over inland waterways!

PUNT for CUNT! That dictionary was joking!
Surely some scholar was laughing his head off!
I passed on, to the Supplement (CHIP-SPARROW, CLEAVAGE).
  Still not there! What sadness, under the microscope.

No wonderful butterfly opening wings and closing
Or even frozen timelessly in grave lexicography —
Absent without leave, as they said in my Army days!
  Shut the book and put it back, with the reading glass.

STILL READING YOUR FRIEND'S *MALEDICTA*?

BUY YOUR OWN COPY, CHEAPO, OR UNCLE MAL'S LITTLE DICKY WILL GET YOU!

Dicky

"THEY ARE A HAIRY, CRUEL, SAVAGE NATION"
ETHNIC SLURS ANNO 1774

Reinhold Aman

I

Compilers of dictionaries, lexicons and encyclopedias show not only their own likes and dislikes but also reflect the prejudices of their times. Ideally, a compiler or editor should strive to present the information as objectively as he or she can. Sometimes, he is forced by political pressures to mouth the propaganda of his masters, as seen in reference works published under the Nazi regime and in today's Communist countries. Take Communist East Germany — please. Almost all scholarly (reference) works, often put out by an *Autorenkollektiv*, knock the enemies of the State, especially West Germany and the United States, whenever they can. (Most scholars behind the Iron Curtain *have* to sell their soul and work slurs into their works, not wanting to end up in a saltmine in Siberia.) For decades, the Chinese Communists called Americans "Imperialist Running Dogs," in print and on shortwave radio broadcasts. Because of better political relations nowadays, this slur is no longer hurled at us. Publications put out by a militant Arab group *must* contain slurs against Jews. But we have such slanted reference works right here: the most militant blacks knock Whitey (just as Whitey has slurred the blacks for centuries), and some American ultra-feminists cannot write a decent sentence referring to yucky Man without foaming at their labia, and going as far as using "she" in definitions.

This Us-Against-Them division ranges from the largest concepts (Earthlings vs. Aliens and Continent vs. Continent) to all other distinct groups: White vs. Black, Old vs. Young, Rich vs. Poor, Educated vs. Uneducated, Christian vs. Non-Christian, City Dweller vs. Rustic, Man vs. Woman — down to the animosity of Parent vs. Child.

The ubiquitous dislike for, or fear of, others (who deviate from the norm—us) exists in the animal world and has existed in man from the moment he met another troglodyte. The most primitive types clubbed or stabbed the perceived enemy or stranger to death—a million years ago (just as today). The cultured and powerless, individuals or minority groups, used and still use verbal weapons instead.

The pen is often used as an unfriendly weapon. Many editors and publishers use and abuse their position to play to the prejudices of their readers by abusing ethnic groups, etc., thereby increasing their own income, while other editors flaunt their likes and dislikes, not caring how many readers = money they lose (*ahém*). Yet, aside from personal prejudices of editors, compilers or publishers, there are the prejudices caused by the times, by society, by the state of knowledge in a given epoch.

Limited or hearsay knowledge of another group in a given time and place obviously slants the information presented, as in the work discussed below. In other cases, the author had unpleasant personal encounters with the "natives," and his slanted or slurring report of other groups is seen clearly, even in grammars and textbooks ("Change to the future tense: *My servant Ahmed stole my watch.*"), and especially in reports of expeditions and travels abroad, also often caused by unfortunate events experienced by the writer. (In a future Maledicta Press book, Gert Raeithel's *Awful America*, we shall see what Europeans have had to say about the United States during the past 200 years, much of the slander being the result of ignorance, jealousy, or unfriendly encounters with the natives.)

II

The ethnic slurs found in the work now discussed generally stem not from the compiler's personal prejudices caused by personal encounters with the foreigners but reflect the pre-judices of a society and an epoch.

In his *English Dictionary* (1774), Jacob Barclay describes ethnic groups as perceived by the Protestant British of *circa* 1774, and based on the state of knowledge of the later part of the 18th century. Some of Barclay's personal likes and dis-likes show through, to be sure, but he basically reports what his contemporaries knew. For example, the Australians and their country are not listed in this lengthy encyclopedic dic-tionary, as Cook had just discovered the East Coast in 1770, four years before Barclay's *Dictionary* was published. North Americans did not fare much better, since the British had not had too much contact with the natives of the Colonies and Canada, and as the New Americans and New Canadians were emigrants with well-known characteristics.

Other countries and their inhabitants are not mentioned at all in this dictionary, for various reasons, such as the Arme-nians, Croatians, Hebrews and Israelis (but Palestinians), Ko-reans, Latvians, Lithuanians, Mongols, Slovaks, and Walloons.

Another group of foreign countries is mentioned and de-scribed, often in great detail, but Barclay fails to mention any characteristics of the inhabitants of Austria, Belgium, Den-mark, France, Holland (but Flanders), Norway, Persia, Poland, Portugal, Scotland, Turkey, and Wales.

Just as reading a foreign-language dictionary lets one peek into another cultur's soul, reading old dictionaries and ency-clopedias transports one back to another century. When read-ing the descriptions of the following ethnic groups, *you are there* with the British, back in 1774, looking at the world with a completely different frame of reference than today's. It is a fascinating experience to travel in time and space without leaving one's chair. One gets an impression of the limited world-view of our ancestors, of their political and religious affilia-tions and enemies, of the relative importance of ethnic groups quite unlike that of today.

Normally, and world-wide, ethnic groups sharing a com-mon border dislike their neighbors and show their dislike or fear of them by slurring epithets and proverbs, as Roback's

276 - MALEDICTA V

Dictionary of International Slurs amply proves. The foreigners' speech often is likened to animal sounds or considered no language at all. The ancient Greeks, for example, considered the language of their Persian neighbors to the east "barbaric," i.e., 'non-Greek, foreign, rough-talking, wild, cruel,' just as the Poles denounced the language of their German neighbors to the west as being no language at all: *niemy* "mute," whence *Niemiec* "German," literally, a mute person. The Malayans liken the language of the Tamils to "the rattling of coconuts." When American soldiers were first encountered in Germany, in 1945, we youngsters made fun of their language by saying that the Americans talk as if they had a dumpling in their mouth. Barclay comments very little on the language of the ethnic groups he describes, and when he does, he usually is wrong.

One need not cross international borders to find dislike, ridicule or fear of others. Within one country, different ethnic groups, tribes, or even smaller social, racial, religious and other groups are targets for verbal abuse. See, for example, Charles Kauffman's glossary of ethnic slurs (*Maledicta* 4/2, pp. 283-86) used by the Russians against their own minorities (Armenians, Turks, etc.). This is probably the first list of its kind ever published. Now our boys in Washington can handle the Soviets' hypocritical berating of America's treatment of her minorities: we use slurs, but we don't — like the Soviets — characterize whole ethnic groups as "pricks" or "ass-fuckers."

On a larger scale, one finds the animosity between the Walloons and the Flemish in Belgium, the German-speaking vs. the Slovene-speaking Austrians, the French-speaking vs. the English-speaking Canadians, the Northern Irish Catholics vs. the Protestants, the Northern and Central Italians vs. the Italians south of Naples, the East Frisians vs. all other Germans — the list is nearly endless.

In the U.S.A., and remaining within the WASPs, we find larger groups (Southern "rednecks," Midwestern "hicks" and Texan "braggarts") and smaller ones, such as New York City "perverts," down to certain boroughs, sections or neighborhoods whose inhabitants are ridiculed. This phenomenon, too, goes way back. In Ancient Greece, the "foolish" inhabitants of Abdera in Asia Minor were derided, just as in other countries the inhabitants of the Polish town Chelm, the Dutch Kempen, the Italian Cuneo or the foolish folks of Germany, the *Schildbürger*. Our deep-seated prejudices and fears, most likely the result of biological survival mechanisms carried in our genes, have always existed and probably will always exist, and no amount of bureaucratic bubble-brained busing will change our intolerance toward those who are not like us.

III

But back to Barclay. The relative importance of certain foreign countries to England in 1774 becomes evident when one compares the length of the entries, here limited to the inhabitants, and disregarding often lengthy excursions into their political organization and geography. Barclay's descriptions and characterizations of ethnic groups range from the pithy and positive (Flemish) to the short and useless (Finnish, Mexicans). In other cases—Chinese, Japanese, Italians and Spaniards—the descriptions are unusually long. The former two Asian countries and their inhabitants were a novelty then (as now), and the reader is given a fairly extensive impression. In the latter two Mediterranean countries—also described unusually extensively—it must have been the British political and religious relations with Catholic Italy and Spain at that time that caused the long descriptions and excursions into the immorality of the Italian and Spanish males.

Contrary to today, the Laplanders, Cossacks and Tartars were relatively important, whereas Africa and South America receive short shrift. Among his own English-speaking neighbors, the Irish are treated fairly well, while the Scots and Welsh are ignored altogether. Of all ethnic groups described below, verbatim, only the Flemish, Germans and Swiss are presented without any negative characteristics, for whatever reason.

IV

Abyssinians: The inhabitants are black, or very near it; but they are not so ugly as the negroes. (*See also* **Africans**)

Africans: There are wild Arabs, and other people, who rove from place to place, partly in search of pasture, and partly to lie in wait for the rich caravans that travel from Barbary and Egypt to Negroeland and Abyssinia.

Americans: All the men, except the Eskimaux, near Greenland, seem to have the same original; for they agree in every particular from the Straits of Magellan in the South to Hudson's-bay in the North. Their skins, unless daubed with grease or oil, are of a red copper colour; and they have no beards, or hair on any other part of their bodies, except the head, where it is black, straight, and coarse. (*See also* **Canadians, Eskimos, Irish, Mexicans, New Englanders**)

Canadians: The original natives of this country speak four different languages, and may be divided into as many different tribes, viz. the Siouse, the Algongiere, the Hautonne, and that of the Eskimaux. Most of them live a wandering life, and maintain themselves by hunting. Their complexion is of a red copper colour, like the rest of the Americans, with coarse hair, and no beards, except the Eskimaux, who are a hairy, cruel, savage nation. They are very fond of brandy; and, when they are drunk, they become almost mad. (*See also* **Eskimos**)

Chinese: The complexion of the Chinese is a sort of tawney, and they have large foreheads, small eyes, short noses, large ears, long beards, and black hair; and those are thought to be most handsome who are most bulky. The women affect a great deal of modesty, and are remarkable for their little feet. The men endeavour to make as pompous an appearance as possible, when they go abroad; and yet their houses are but mean and low, consisting only of a ground floor. They are addicted to all sorts of learning, particularly to arts and sciences. . . . There is no country in the world where the inhabitants are so ceremonious as here; and yet, notwithstanding their seeming sincerity, they cheat as much in their dealings as in the most uncivilized countries. . . . All their cities and towns are so much alike, that those that know one are acquainted with all. . . . They have laws which regulate their civilities and ceremonious salutation they pay each other, for which reason they always appear to be extremely good-natured;

and yet there is but little dependance on their friendship, for they are as deceitful, and as great hypocrites, as any people in the world.

Cossacks: They live on husbandry, fishing, and their cattle, but rob their neighbour as often as they have opportunity.... They are large and well made, have blue eyes, brown hair, and aquiline noses; the women are handsome, well shaped, and very complaisant to strangers. (*See also* **Ukrainians**)

Egyptians: The inhabitants are of four sorts, Turks, Moors, Arabs, and Christians, Cophts, or Cophtis, besides Greeks, Jews, and other foreigners. With regard to the complexion of the Egyptians, it is tawny, and the farther South, the more dark, insomuch that those on the confines of Nubia are almost black. They are most of them very indolent and cowardly, and the richer sort do nothing all day but drink coffee, smoke tobacco, and sleep; besides this, they are extremely ignorant, proud, haughty, and ridiculously vain.

Eskimos: [The inhabitants of New Britain, called also Terra Labrador, and Eskimaux, are] a rude savage sort of people, called Eskimaux, who have neither laws nor religion. They have no houses, but live in caves and holes in the side of hills, and are the only people in America that have beards, which almost hide their faces. (*See also* **Canadians**)

Finnish: The inhabitants differ from the Swedes both in their manners and language.

Flemish: The men are heavy, but laborious, and lovers of good cheer; and the women are reckoned to be very handsome.

Germans: As to the disposition of the people in general, they are robust, brave, good soldiers, free laborious, inured toward labour, dexterous in manufactures, and fruitful in inventions.

Greeks: Greece...produced a vast number of famous men, who performed very great actions as soldiers, as well as others, who were eminent for their parts and learning. But it now groans under the tyranny of the Turks, and is but the shadow of what it was formerly, being over-run with ignorance and barbarism, and almost all the fine towns quite destroyed. It is inhabited by Mahometans and Christians.

Hungarians: The inhabitants are well-shaped, brave, haughty and revengeful.

Icelanders: Their houses...are all miserable huts covered with skins. They are mostly cloathed with the skins of beasts. ... They are said to live 100 years, without either physicians or medicines.

Indians (East): The Indians are generally well made and robust, but they do not love labour, nor do they make good soldiers. They are very fond of women, and in other respects are civil, kind to strangers, and very ingenious.

Irish: The common people are so poor, and it is so hard for them to get a livelihood, that they frequently go into other countries to seek their fortunes; and, particularly, great numbers go over to the plantations in America. That part of the inhabitants called the Wild Irish were formerly as savage as the native Americans; and like them, lived in huts, making a fire in the middle of them; but it is to be hoped, that all the rude and barbarous customs so common among them will in a short time entirely cease.

Italians: The inhabitants have a great many good qualities as well as bad ones; they are polite, active, prudent, ingenious, and politic; but then they are luxurious, effeminate, addicted to the most criminal pleasures, revengeful, and use all sorts of artifices to destroy their enemies; which produce a great number of assassinations. Add to these, that they are extremely jealous, and keep their wives and daughters always shut up, insomuch that they cannot go to church without somebody to watch them. However, there is no place in the world where impurity abounds so much as in Italy; for there are great numbers of bawdy-houses and courtezans, who are tolerated by the magistrates. (*See also* **Sicilians**)

Japanese: The inhabitants are naturally ingenious, and have a happy memory; but their manners are diametrically opposite to those of the Europeans. Our common drinks are cold, and theirs are hot; we uncover the head out of respect, and they the feet; we are fond of white teeth, and they of black; we get on horse-back on the left side, and they on the right; and they have a language so particular that it is understood by no other nation. They value their lives so little, that when a lord makes a feast, the domestics dispute who shall have the honour of cutting open their bellies before the guests. ... They treat the women with a great deal of severity, and punish adultery with death; yet a man may take as many wives as he pleases. On the other hand, bawdy-houses are very frequent, and they tolerate sins against nature. Those that have too many children make no scruple of destroying some of them; and there are many women who kill them before they are born, especially if they suspect they are of the female sex.

Laplanders: They are very poorly clad, and often lie upon the snow. They are of a short stature, with a large head, broad forehead, blue eyes, short flat noses, and short, straight, coarse, black hair. They are a rude, brutal sort of people, though some of them have embraced Christianity, which has not mended their morals. They live a great while without the assistance of physicians, and their hair never turns grey. ... They are very fond of spirituous liquors, and are never sober when they can purchase them.

Mexicans: All the people are Papists, or at least profess to be so, on account of the Inquisition.

New Englanders: Nothing need to be said of the manners or disposition of the inhabitants, as they all originally came from England.

Palestinians: Palestine...is a poor, barren country, which perhaps may be owing to the indolence of the inhabitants.

Russians: The habitants in general are robust, well shaped, and of pretty good complections; they are great eaters, and very fond of brandy. They were formerly the most ignorant, brutish people in the world; but they are making a rapid progress in every social and elegant improvement and refinement.

Sicilians: Sicily... is said to contain one million of inhabitants, who in general have a very bad character. (*See* **Italians**)

Spaniards: The Spaniards are very moderate in their eating, and can make a meal of olives, of sallad, a little garlick, or a few roots. They seldom invite their friends to dinner, and the women in general are very bad cooks. The men dine by themselves, and their wives and children eat together. The general vice of the nation is pride and haughtiness, and the very peasants keep genealogies of their families, like the Welsh; for this reason, they have gravity in their looks, and when they walk. This disposition renders them very indolent. The women are generally very clean, and very amorous; they have black eyes, flat bosoms, little feet, and wear long garments. When they make visits, they sit on carpets, in the manner of taylors, as well as at home; which custom they have derived from the Moors. They are greatly addicted to painting, and are kept very much at home, through the jealousy of their husbands. Neither men nor women often change the fashions of their garments, and the men generally wear their own hair, without powder, and long swords by their sides. With regard to their religion, they are the strictest Papists in the world, and yet for fornication and impurity, they are the worst nation in Europe.

Swedes: The Swedes live a long while; and it is not uncommon to see ten people at the same table, whose ages make up 1000 years. The inhabitants are of a robust constitution, and able to sustain the hardest labour. They are much more polished than what they were. . . . There is no country in the world where the women do so much work; for they till the ground, thrash the corn, and row the boats on the sea.

Swiss: The inhabitants are all strong robust men, for which reason they are generally chosen by several nations for the military service, and even the Pope has his Swiss guards. The women are tolerably handsome, have many good qualities, and are in general very industrious. The peasants retain their old manner of dress, and are content to live upon milk, butter, and cheese. Some of the mountaineers never have any bread.

Tartars: In general, the Tartars are a robust people, have a good constitution, and are capable of undergoing hardships. They have broad faces, short chins, large whiskers, and noses even with their faces. They are dextrous in handling their sabers, and shooting with bows and arrows. The men have no other business than that of going to war, and the women take care of domestic affairs.

Ukrainians: The Ukrain...is inhabited by the refuse of several nations, who came from the neighbourhood of the Black Sea, among whom are Poles, Russians, Hungarians, Turks, and Tartars, who, however, pretend to be Christians. They are usually Cossacks, are noted for their cruelties, and there is no sort of crime they are not ready to commit: however, these Cossacks are distinguished into two sorts, the Zaporavians, and the Donskians, which last have always been tributary to the Russian empire. (*See also* **Cossacks**)

And what does Barclay say about his fellow Englanders? "As for the manners, customs, and abilities of the inhabitants, nothing need be said, because they fall under everyone's own observation."

ACKNOWLEDGMENT

The preceding descriptions are taken from Jacobus Barclay's *An English Dictionary Upon a New Plan* (Edmonton, 1774), a rare copy of which was donated to the Maledicta Archives by Dr. Weston La Barre (Chapel Hill), to whom I wish to express my deepest gratitude.

DON'T
REMAIN
IGNORANT

EXPOSE
YOURSELF

TO
MALEDICTA

FRUSTRATION → AFFECT → RELEASE
AN OPEN LETTER TO A GREEDY COMPANY

Pitney Bowels Co.
Walter H. Wheeler, Jr. Drive
Stamford, CT 06926   10 November 1981

Dear Mr. Chairman:

Of all the greedy companies I have to do business with, such as IBM, your outfit is the most shamelessly greedy, blood-sucking monopoly.

I'm already paying over $200 a year rental fee for your little Touchamatic Postage Meter. Now you want $2.00 more every month, due to "rising costs." Bullshit! If $205.92 per year is not enough for your greedy hands, you'll get <u>nothing</u> from me.

I'm appalled by your company's incredible greed. In the past four years, you have received from me over $800 in rental fees for a rinky-dink machine that cost you perhaps $30 to build. Every time the postal rates go up, your pushy Marketing Vice President wants me to buy a new rate sheet, a 3½-square-inch piece of paper for $4.00 (your cost: 2 cents). You charge $10 for two ink rollers worth 25 cents, and over $2.50 for a few slips of meter tape worth 5 cents. And when your highly-trained salesman dropped off the postal meter, your company greedily charged me $50 "installation fee."

And now your obnoxiously greedy outfit wants another $24 a year from me, so that you can make ends meet.

Enough is enough! I will go back to licking stamps. When my contract expires on 31 December 1981, you can take your Pitney Bowels Postage Meter and shove it up your colon! No installation fee. Or better, why don't you and your pushy V. P. take your meter, stick in your little peter, and stamp it until your glans drops off.

Sincerely Up Yours,
(Signed) Reinhold Aman

VERBAL AGGRESSION
IN DUTCH SLEEPTALKING

Frank Heynick

*Sleep-speech is always the expression of our inner-
most feelings—the mind freed of restraints stem-
ming from reality, conscience, education and consciousness, reveals itself 'in the nude.' As the
dream is the life of the unconscious, sleeptalking is
its voice.*
— G. Andriani
Fisiologia psicologica del somniloquio (1892)

SLEEP THOUGHT: CONTINUOUS OR
COMPLEMENTARY TO WAKING THOUGHT?

Since the advent of scientific sleep/dream research around the
turn of the century, and even long before, there has existed
the global question of how sleeping mental activity relates to
waking mental activity. In recent times, this has come to focus
on an issue of continuity vs. complementarity. Cartwright
(1977, 1978) points to various historical authors, the most
prominent being Adler, who theorize dreams to be extensions
of conscious waking thought. These Cartwright places in opposition to Freud, for whom dreams are hallucinatory gratifi-
cation (albeit often in disguised form) of instinctual wishes
repressed into the unconscious in waking life. (Jung's model
allows for both continuity and complementarity between
sleeping and waking thought, depending on the psychological
circumstances of the individual.)

In the last decade, research based on data assembled on
the beds of sleep laboratories, rather than on the couches of
psychiatrists, has sought to resolve this issue empirically. What

can the disciplines of psycholinguistics, sociolinguistics, and the transdisciplinary work of maledictologists contribute to this research?

SLEEP-SPEECH

At first thought, one might reply "nothing." After all, a traditional dictionary definition of "dream" often reads "a vision in sleep," and modern sleep research into the cognitive content of dreams has indeed placed overwhelming emphasis on the visual. Yet, sleeping mental activity need not be silent. There has always existed the phenomenon of somniloquy, commonly known as sleeptalking.

Few historical authors on sleep and dreams have ever made more than passing reference to sleeptalking. Andriani, whose quote above we will soon consider in more detail, was an exception, yet even his article was based solely on anecdotal data. However, the development of sociolinguistic and psycholinguistic models of verbal behavior in recent years offers the possibility that systematic research into sleeptalking might prove most rewarding. Indeed, Arkin (1966, p. 119) points out in a review article that, in contrast to reports on sleeping mental activity obtained from awakened subjects:

> Sleep-speech is a spontanious, subject-emitted phenomenon which conveys details of mental content without...interferences [inherent in reporting]. Furthermore, aspects of sleep-speech are subject to measurement, e.g. frequency, duration, word and syllable count, volume, clarity, rate, and the like.... The data collected may be suitable for linguistic and content analytic procedures which have been highly developed in recent years.

Yet, prior to our own research, there seems never to have been a linguistically-based study of sleeptalking.

THE EXPERIMENT

During the period September 1976 through December 1977, a corpus of 83 sleeptalking utterances was obtained from 15 subjects by means of a take-home experiment using cassette-recorders and acoustically-triggered ("Watergate") microphones. The subjects, all native speakers of Dutch, were unremunerated volunteers chosen from over 150 people who responded to our call on the radio and in the newspapers for chronic sleeptalkers. Although no electroencephalographic monitoring was feasible to determine whether a given utterance was associated with REM ("dreaming") sleep or NREM ("thinking") sleep, it was hoped that the absence of a laboratory environment would have a less inhibiting effect upon the sleeping subjects (cf. Snyder 1970) and would indeed, in Andriani's words, allow the mind to reveal itself — via sleeptalking — "in the nude." At an interview following approximately 2 weeks of home recording, each sleeptalker was asked (when awake) a series of some 25 questions and sub-questions about his/her verbalizations. The general purpose was to compare sleeptalking verbal behavior to waking verbal behavior. The questions sought to establish, among other things, whether the utterances were deemed: (a) to be grammatical, (b) to be in the language or dialect most often used by the waking subject, (c) to contain any neologisms or language-mixing, (d) to have been spoken during a concomitant dream (etc., etc.). The corpus was further subjected to analysis by various linguists and psycholinguists. Subsequently, the combined data from these analyses along with the interview responses were evaluated within a framework of competence/performance (cf. Chomsky 1965), especially as this relates to the psychoanalytic model of dream-speech generation (Heynick 1981b). Competence/performance models have been applied to some extent to the deviant speech of aphasics (cf. Lesser 1978) and even, in passing, to schizophrenics (cf. Wales & Marshall 1965, Masters 1970), but never to sleep-speech.

RESULTS

Here we will consider the results of interest to maledictologists. The broader conclusions are presented elsewhere (Heynick 1981a) and a complete corpus transcription appears in Arkin (1981).

Although many of the 83 utterances in our corpus were peevish or spoken with obvious irritation, only 5 of these (from 4 subjects) were found to contain terms of abuse or profanities. The utterances, in English translation, are as follows (our corpus numbers have been retained). The original Dutch maledictions are given in parentheses:

(3) *Keep your hands off the vinyl, and keep your hands off that...uh* [mumble] *tiles! Come on! What are you, completely crazy!? Vermin!* (Ongedierte!)

(Subject N. T., ♀, 31 years old)

(47) [unclear sentence +] *goddamn!* (Godverdomme!)

(Subject F. v/d I., ♀, 13 years old)

(57) *Th..there he comes. Yeah, there he comes...uh... What! He's riding past!... bah ... To..to... Come, l..let's walk it. Idiot!* (Idioot!)

(Subject D. N., ♀, 25 years old)

(59) *Do it completely differently. Th..this way...Quite... No. Damn!* (Verdomme!)   (Same subject)

(68) *Serpent* (serpent) *that you are!*

(Subject L. N., ♀, 23 years old)

These 5 instances of verbal aggression are not without interest despite (or, should we say, aside from) their low frequency of occurrence.

Even without referring to the interview data, we can make two noteworthy observations. All maledictions were uttered by female subjects; 5 of the 15 subjects were male, and these did no swearing in their sleep. There were no sexual profanities (very common in Dutch), nor scatological profanities (far less frequent anyhow than in German or English).[1]

Verbalization (47) was not the subject of interview questions, due to its general lack of clarity, although the expletive itself was well articulated. In response to the interview questions, the speakers of (3) and (68) claimed that the respective expletives were not part of their waking malediction vocabulary. Rather, they would have used words like *mormel* "monster" and *mispunt* "good-for-nothing" respectively.

The speaker of (57) could recall a concomitant dream, and claimed that although in the dream-scenario it was she who had produced most of the utterance, it was her sister, and not herself, who had said *idioot*. (They has been waiting at a bus-stop, and the bus-driver went by without stopping for them.) For (59), the same subject felt that in general she would have been the one to make this utterance in her dream (she did not have recall of any specific concomitant dream), but that while the first half of the verbalization would have been addressed aloud to someone else, the second part (which contains *verdomme*) would have been muttered to herself under her breath.

DISCUSSION

To return to Andriani's (1892) quote, with which we began this article: to the extent we accept that "as the dream is the life of the unconscious, sleeptalking is its voice," we can, by looking at our corpus and interview data from a maledicta point of view, offer some tentative conclusions about mental activity in sleep in general.[2]

On the one hand, judging from the infrequency of malediction, mental activity in sleep does not appear on the face of it to be a welling-up of aggressive or sexual feelings, and is therefore more continuous than complementary vis-à-vis waking mental activity. This observation seems to be supported by Arkin *et al.* (1970), where a corpus of 40 sleeptalking utterances from 28 subjects, presented in connection with a purely non-linguistic experiment, reveals only one specimen of verbal aggression (utterance 8 in Arkin's corpus):

(8) [with anger] *You'll have to—you're gonna have tuss* [sic] *—(if you don't* [?]), *I'll lay a chair over your head*...[mumble]...*leave them up—you leave them up! I'll bust your butt!* ... [mumble]

Yet, it should be mentioned that these data would not cut much ice with Freudians. While Freud in his *Traumdeutung* (1900) would agree with Andriani who eight years before wrote "the dream is the life of the unconscious," he would qualify the statement that via sleep-speech (or however) "the mind...reveals itself 'in the nude.'" Freudian dream theory seldom takes signs—be they words or images—at face value.

The sleeping, or sleeptalking, mind may for the Freudians express our "innermost feelings," but then usually in drag rather than naked. Psychoanalyst Jones (1927), for example, interpreted "shawl" in what might be called the "surface structure" of a sleeptalking utterance by a young girl, as having a "deep structure" meaning of 'penis.' In the Freudian model, many of our 83 utterances could then take on sexual or aggressive meanings. [3]

But even when we restrict ourselves to our empirical interview data relating to those infrequent specimens of overt malediction which appear in our corpus, we find distinct indication that, when such verbal behavior does occur, the waking subjects tend either not to recognize these words as being part of their daytime lexicon (although not necessarily because of their harshness), or to dissociate themselves from having (actively) used such words in a recalled or postulated dream-scenario. This argues for some complementarity relationship between sleeping and waking mental activity.

We can round off this article with a passage from Skinner (1957, pp. 388-90). It boils down to something very much like Andriani's quote with which we began, although the terms are different (Skinner speaks of 'editing,' as yet more recent authors speak of 'monitoring'). And like Andriani, Skinner seems to have based himself on anecdotal data only:

> An inability to respond to one's own verbal behavior or to controlling variables is most marked in certain conditions of the organism, of which sleep is the commonest example. Most people speak occasionally while asleep; but the behavior does not affect the speaker as listener and is not edited.... When feed-back from verbal behavior has been lacking at the time of emission and when the speaker ...is presented with evidence of that behavior, he is likely to attribute it to another person. He not only has no memory of having produced it, but the unedited material may be so strange or objectionable as to be unrecognizable.

For most of our 83 sleeptalking utterances, this was hardly the case. The majority were not particularly strange, and, as we have seen, only a handful were in any way objectionable. Yet, the subjects' interview responses upon hearing the few instances of malediction which did occur lead one to speculate that, after all, sleeptalking may—at least occasionally—be the voice of what Andriani called "the mind freed of restraints," or, in Skinnerian terms, "the other one."

POSTSCRIPT: VERBAL AGGRESSION IN HALLUCINATED DREAM DIALOG

Sleeptalking is of course not the only kind of language behavior to be found in sleep. Most dreams are not like silent movies, but rather have auditory as well as visual content, often in the form of dialog between the "actors." (This has been recognized since antiquity: the first dream in the Bible, that of Jacob's Ladder, involves a "message" delivered verbally to the dreamer.) Such language behavior in sleep is referred to as 'recalled verbal material' (RVM): since it is only hallucinated in the dream and (in contrast to sleeptalking) not actually articulated outloud, it can only be reported by the subject as he or she remembers it after awakening. Herein lies its unreliability. (While sleeptalking avoids this problem, its 'sleep-associated' status has its own disadvantages, as discussed in footnote 2.)

Although RVM has gone unmentioned in the present article, there are nevertheless some relevant data to be reported. In a recent experiment, we awakened by telephone on random nights and at random hours 71 volunteer subjects in order to elicit verbal material from their dreams. 358 awakenings yielded 107 dream-like reports, 72 of which contained immediately-recalled dream utterances or dialog. Of these 72 'sound-tracks,' only two display any overt verbal aggression:

(a) *Dirty prick!* (Vuile klootzak!)
(b) *Let go of my leg, damn!* (verdomme!)

The following verbal exchange from another dream was not reported immediately upon awakening, but appeared somewhere around the middle when the entire dream was reported:

(c) [said to the dreamer] *Prick!* (Klootzak!)
   [the dreamer replies] *What d'ya mean 'prick'!? You're*

> *a prick! You didn't bring the loop around the back,*
> *but around the front, thanks to which we'll both fall.*

Since the corpus in which the above specimens appear is almost as large as our ST corpus, there seems to be indication that overt RVM aggression shows up with about the same — rather low—frequency as overt sleeptalking aggression. There are, however, also a few contrasts: the sexual expletive *klootzak* is a common one in Dutch, as is the ubiquitous *verdomme*. (*Klootzak*, lit. "ball-bag" = 'scrotum' and the short version, *zak*, are equivalents of English *prick, bastard, cocksucker.*) Two of the three specimens, (a) and (c), were due to male subjects, although most of the subjects in the experiment were female. In each case, the subject recognized having said the expletive himself/herself in the dream. Furthermore, it seemed appropriate to the circumstances in each instance: (a) the dreamer was involved in a near-accident with a car, (b) a character identified as Alfred Hitchcock, but no larger than a child, latched onto the dreamer's leg due to his being frightened, and (c) the dreamer and a soldier were involved in a military operation which ran into difficulty.

The psychoanalytic distinction between overt and camouflaged aggression would of course hold as well for RVM as for ST utterances. The following specimen from our RVM corpus, said by the dreamer (female) to her father, would probably have been a Freudian delight for Jones (footnote 3):

(d) *I'll cut a piece off it soon.*

The dream context would, on the face of it, seem innocent enough: the cutting off refers to the limp and yellowed ends of the stems of flowers before putting them into a vase.

More recently, the Paris and Bologna-based Italian sleep researchers, P. Salzarulo and C. Cipolli (personal communication) have supplied us with a corpus of the RVM of 13 subjects: 59 utterances or 'dialogs' from REM periods (dreaming sleep) and 17 from NREM periods (thinking sleep). (It should be noted that, in contrast to our own RVM experiment, all subjects in this laboratory research were male, and they were asked upon provoked awakening to simply report everything which was "passing through their minds." Some of these reports included recalled verbal material, and this is what constitutes the corpus.)

Of the 76 Italian corpus specimens, there are four from two subjects which contain swearing. The "verbal aggression" varies from the polite to the not-so-polite, and this is the order in which I have arranged the specimens. (The original corpus numbers have been retained.):

(32) *That's OK; I'll take the books and I'll go; it's no problem. Heck!* (Acciderbole!) *If I have to take away all the books, I'll go crazy, because I've got very many of them. — Yes, yes, don't worry; now I'll put all this stuff away.* (Subject D.S., stage I REM)

(30) *But look at all those idiots* (idioti), *what they're doing. Darn!* (Accidenti!) (Same subject, stage I REM)

(7) *I'm unwell. — You're not unwell....; you want to stay there; you're a parasite* (parassita), *but I want to give it to you.* (Subject Q.T., stage III NREM)

(8) *What an ass-face!* (faccia da cullo!) *— Excuse me, gentlemen, leave the change. — No.* (Same subject, stage II NREM)

While the following witty specimen shows no externally-directed aggression (assuming the 'actor' in the dream-scenario who uttered it was the dreamer himself), it may be sufficiently off-color to deserve mention here:

(18) *Come on, cover yourself! — You can't come under the blankets, but I can because I'm in bed. — Since I'm a toilet* (cesso), *I knock to see if I'm free. I knock because.....* (Subject N.H.Q., stage I REM)

We hope eventually to assemble a total of over 1000 specimens of RVM from a large population, and this should enable a statistically significant calculation of the nature and frequency of verbal aggression in dream dialog. The results we shall gladly report in a future article.

NOTES

1. It would seem that Dutch malediction is fully advanced into the genital phase in Freud's scheme of libidinal infantile development, while English, German and many other languages remain partially arrested at the anal level. Some examples: Exclamations like *shit!*, *Scheiße!*, and *merde!* know no literal equivalent in Dutch (**schijt!*). (The English *shit!* is gaining some currency in the Netherlands—especially among children —but without having any scatological associations.) Instead, Dutch is fond of employing *kut!* "cunt!"

Similarly, although Dutch has aside from *schijt* another common impolite term for excrement, *stront*, neither is to be found as modifiers in compound nominals. This is unlike German and English: *Scheißwetter*, *shit-weather*, but **schijt-weer.* (Only among some young children do you find *poep-* "poopy" used in such positions.) For these purposes, Dutch makes compounds with *rot-* "rotten," e.g., *rotweer*, but also commonly with the two abovementioned sexual words, *kut-weer* and *kloteweer*, "cunt-weather, ball-weather."

2. We are reluctant to draw from our data any sweeping conclusions about mental activity in sleep in general. This is due partly to the size of our corpus and our limited number of subjects. (Let it be added though that chronic sleeptalkers as a group do not seem to differ psychologically from the over-all population; *see* Arkin 1966.)

More importantly, on various physiological, psychological, and philosophical grounds, several authors prefer to classify sleeptalking not as a strict sleep phenomenon, but as "sleep-related," somewhat intermediate between pure sleep and waking. It should also be noted that only one fifth to one quarter of sleeptalking incidents occur during REM periods ("dreaming sleep"), the rest taking place during NREM periods ("thinking sleep").

3. Arkin (1966, p. 113) writes:

A girl of 20 years, after hearing Jones's lecture, queried him as to the meaning of an episode which occurred when she was 12. While she was asleep in her parents' bedroom, she arose and walked. Her father asked her what she was going to do, and she replied, 'to fetch a shawl to crack' (as in a nutcracker). Jones speculated that the phrase was derived from erotic and aggressive wishes toward the father's penis. The latter was symbolized by 'shawl'—an example of mantle symbolism signifying the male genital.

To give just a few examples from our corpus of utterances open to sexual interpretation according to the Freudian model:

(1) [...] *I laid it all out on your bed ... and it's there ... it's there this evening too* [...].

(2) *I want to decorate a tree, and then I'm going to decorate another tree, and then I'm going to decorate another tree, and then I'm going to see how that tree is being decorated, and how it's being maintained....* [The Dutch word for "decorate," *versieren,* also means "seduce."]

(4) *Jake with two cuffs on and one cuff-link. Where's the shirt* [...]?

(23) *Can't you stoke a little harder?*

(32) *It's always that way. — Oh. — Then we used to call it a shaving-brush.*

(46) [...] *fling it to you. Cut this in two.* [...]

(53) *Telescope, yes.*

(58) [sigh +] ... *Now, hurry up man, o...otherwise we'll get there too late. Now get moving ...* [+ groan]

(64) *I don't intend to throw some sort of party or reception for you. Leave the bottle alone, leave the bottle alone.*

(67) [...] *pushed the tap on. You said yes.*

(71) *If it keeps turning, that thing, then bed.*

Most utterances could not be associated by their speakers with a concomitant dream or other sleeping mental activity, so the situational contexts (and any interpretation of them, Freudian or otherwise) were unavailable to us. Of the few utterances (10 of the 83) which could be clearly associated, only one had to do with a dream which was overtly sexual (involving intercourse):

(9) *No, don't! That can never be. That can't be.*

(Subject N.T., ♀, 31 years old)

REFERENCES

Andriani, G. (1892). "Fisiologia Psicologica del Somniloquio," *Annali di Neurologia* (Torino) 10. (Quoted in Arkin 1966)

Arkin, Arthur M. (1966). "Sleeptalking: A Review," *Journal of Nervous and Mental Disease* 143, no. 2, pp. 101-122.

———.(1981). *Sleeptalking: Psychology and Psychophysiology.* Hillsdale, N.J.: L. Erlbaum Associates.

Arkin, A.M., M.F. Toth, J. Baker & J.M. Hastey (1970). "The Degree of Concordance between the Content of Sleeptalking and Mentation Recalled in Wakefulness," *Journal of Nervous and Mental Disease* 151, no. 6, pp. 375-393.

Cartwright, Rosalind D. (1977). *Night Life.* Englewood Cliffs, N.J.: Prentice-Hall.

———. (1978). *A Primer on Sleep and Dreaming.* Reading, Mass.: Addison-Wesley.

Chomsky, Noam (1965). *Aspects of the Theory of Syntax.* Cambridge, Mass.: MIT Press.

Freud, Sigmund (1900). *The Interpretation of Dreams.* Harmondsworth: Pelican Books (1976).

Heynick, Frank (1981a). "Freud and Chomsky: Our Linguistic Capacities During Dreaming." In W.P. Koella (ed.), *Sleep 1980.* Basel: Karger, pp. 373-376.

———. (1981b). "Linguistic Aspects of Freud's Dream Model," *International Review of Psycho-Analysis* 8, pp. 299-314.

Jones, Ernest (1927). "The Mantle Symbol," *International Journal of Psycho-Analysis* 8, pp. 63-65.

Lesser, Ruth (1978). *Linguistic Investigations of Aphasia.* London: Edward Arnold.

Masters, J.M. (1970). "Pushdown Automata and Schizophrenic Language." Unpublished report. Sidney: University of Sidney.

Skinner, B.F. (1957). *Verbal Behavior.* New York: Appleton-Century-Crofts.

Snyder, Frederick (1970). "The Phenomenology of Dreaming." In L. Madow & H. Laurence (eds.), *The Psychodynamic Implications of Physiological Studies of Dreams.* Springfield, Ill.: Thomas Publishers.

Wales, R.J. & J.C. Marshall (1966). "The Organization of Linguistic Performance." In J. Lyons & R.J. Wales (eds.), *Psycholinguistic Papers: The Proceedings of the 1966 Edinburgh Conference.* Edinburgh: Edinburgh University Press, pp. 29-95.

UMI-UMI : PUS-SEA

*"The Sea Has Already
Been Reduced to Pus"*

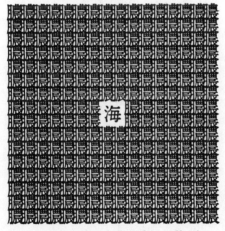

An eloquent attack on the pollution of our oceans, by an unknown Japanese artist, *ca.* 1975. The Chinese ideograms *kai* and *nō* are pronounced alike in Japanese:

海 *umi* 'sea, ocean'

膿 *umi* 'pus, discharge'

HEUTE BLEIBT DIE KLOWAND KALT
ADVERTISING, RHYMED COUPLETS, AND GRAFFITI IN GERMAN

Charles J. James

One of the most common rhetorical devices in use in Modern German is the rhymed couplet. It is used not only by poets and other real or imagined literati, but also by commercial advertisers. It is short. It does not require much creativity. It does, however, give the user the opportunity to show off his or her linguistic skills without straining language proficiency or semantic credibility. Even such internationally known products as McDonald's hamburgers are advertised by means of rhymed-couplet ditties. One ad, for Big Mac (written **Big Mäc** in German), is almost an epic poem, consisting of fifteen rhymed couplets!

It is thus no surprise that the rhymed couplet is also a popular vehicle for toilet graffiti and that often the starting point is some advertised product, whether or not the product is known through a slogan which is a rhymed couplet. The following is a sample of products and their renderings as scatological poetry. All examples have been gathered "in the field," specifically from the john walls of the Philosophisches Seminargebäude of the Universität Erlangen-Nürnberg in Erlangen, West Germany.

Insurance: One of the better-known insurance companies in Germany is Allianz. Its advertising slogan is also well known: *Hoffentlich Allianz versichert* (Hopefully insured by Allianz). This slogan has generated the following extension of coverage:

> *"Schwanz verbrannt?" die Nutte kichert*
> *"Hoffentlich Allianz versichert."*

("Cock burned?" the hooker chuckles / "Hopefully [you are] insured by Allianz.")

Clothing: There are several chains of clothing stores in Germany whose names consist of only one syllable (Wöhrl, Frey, etc.); although none has a slogan resembling the following, one has to wonder why this thoroughly original rhyme has not moved more underwear:

> *Selbst Eunuch der Hodenlose*
> *Kauft bei Frey 'ne Lodenhose.*

(Even Eunuch the gonadless / Buys a pair of "Loden" trousers at Frey.) "Loden" is reconstituted, i.e. nonvirgin wool. It is normally more durable and warmer than virgin wool.

Detergent: Soap, hygiene, and sex go together well. Three variations on this theme were found together on the same wall, in three different hands, with three different name brands of dishwashing/laundry soaps. In order to appreciate what follows, one must know that the German word *Becken* means not only a wash basin or sink, but also refers to the pelvis and lower abdomen.

The first product has no particular advertising slogan behind it:

> *Die Pille ist ein fauler Zauber*
> *Nur Ajax hält das Becken sauber.*

(The pill is humbug; only Ajax keeps the sink/pelvis clean.)

There is, on the other hand, a slogan for the following, an alliterative *General gereinigt* ("cleaned by General," a brand):

> *Und riecht das Becken noch so schal,*
> *Gereinigt wird's vom General.*

(And regardless how stale the sink/pelvis smells / It will get cleaned by [the] General.)

The last of the trilogy is not, unfortunately, in a rhymed couplet, but is still a fertile graffito worthy of passage:

> *Pril: ein Schuß ins Becken und die Hausfrau glänzt.*

(Pril [a detergent]: a shot in the sink/pelvis and the housewife sparkles/beams.)

The title of this mini-article refers to a slogan which is itself a rhymed couplet, advertising the ubiquitous *Wiener*

Wald chicken restaurants, which made Friedrich Jahn the Colonel Sanders of Western Europe. The slogan:

> *Heute bleibt die Küche kalt,*
> *Wir gehen in den Wiener Wald.*

(Today the kitchen will remain cold / We're going to [eat in]
the Wiener Wald). The not-so-appealing alternative is:

> *Heute bleibt the Klowand kalt,*
> *Wir pinkeln in dem Wiener Wald.*

(Today the john wall remains cold / We're going to pee in the
Wiener Wald [restaurant / Vienna Woods]). Substitutes found
for *pinkeln* (to pee) are *pissen* (to piss), *wichsen* (to mastur-
bate), *scheißen* (to shit), or any other appropriate two-syl-
lable verb.

Heh-heh!
Who said,
"Yes sir,
Yurafart"?

Kinky Friedman, irreverent comedian-singer
(and leader of his band, The Texas Jewboys),
probably was the first one to use publicly
"Yessir Yurafart" for Yasser Arafat.

THE SEMANTICS OF ABUSE
IN THE *CHASTUSHKA*
WOMEN'S BAWDY

Victor Raskin

INTRODUCTION

This paper deals with numerous instances of verbal abuse of various kinds expressed by Russian obscene words and expressions in a relatively recent genre of Russian and Soviet folklore, the *chastushka*.

As a genre, the *chastushka* has existed in Russia for about a century (*see*, for instance, Gorelov, 1965, p. 5). Formally, the *chastushka* is a quatrain, i.e. "a stanza of 4 lines, rhymed or unrhymed" (Preminger, 1974, p. 684). While both rhymed and unrhymed *chastushkas* may be encountered, the former heavily prevail and while they do allow for a certain degree of metrical freedom, the *chastushkas* seem to be much more restricted in this respect than other Russian poetical forms. Their even lines may occasionally blur into iamb but most *chastushkas* are typical trochaic four-footers with the even lines often lacking the last unstressed syllable:

> *Dévkĭ v ózĕřě̆ kŭpálĭs',*
> *Xúj rĕzínŏvȳ̆j nāšlí.*
> *Célȳ̆j dén' ŏní ĕbálĭs' —*
> *Dážĕ v škólŭ nĕ pŏšlí.*

(The girls were bathing in the lake and found a rubber prick [dildo]. They fucked [themselves with it] for the whole day so that they even missed school.) As in the example, the rhymed *chastushkas* usually have the A-B-A-B rhyme.

Note: Throughout this article, substitute *evoke* for every *invoke*.

301

Many *chastushkas*, just like their Anglo-Saxon counterpart, the limerick, relate interesting events which take or took place. However, unlike the limericks, such information-bulletin *chastushkas* only very rarely specify the geographic location of the event, assuming that it coincides with the location of the speaker either in the narrow sense (a village or a town) or in the broad sense (Russia). The speaker is always implicitly or explicitly present in the text, which may be explained by the nature of the authorship and of the form of presentation of the *chastushkas*.

Unlike the limericks, again, which are believed to be a part of the men's world and authored by men, the *chastushkas* are usually sung by (drunken) women on family and community events in Russian villages, small towns and working-class suburbs of large cities. The singer dances while delivering the *chastushka* and is accompanied by the same simple tune played on a harmonica, balalaika or a Russian variety of the accordion. Most of the original *chastushkas* are also believed to have been authored by women.

Just as in the case of the limericks, there exists a powerful stream of obscene or bawdy *chastushkas* which constitute a large part of all the recorded units. It is hard to say whether the obscene *chastushka* emerged at the same time as the non-obscene variety or later on, since for a long time only the latter were recorded. Note that even the non-obscene *chastushkas* are usually frivolous, familiar and/or presumptuous.

The obscene *chastushka* came into fashion among the Russian intellectuals about two decades ago and became a form of dissent similar to the political joke (it is never sung in this milieu but rather recited as a poem). Since that time, intellectuals have obviously, though inconspicuously, contributed to the genre, and at the present stage, out of the approximately 800 available *chastushkas* collected by Kabronsky and this author and published in part by the former (Kabronsky, 1978), nearly a half may be suspected to be of a fake-folk origin.

The obscene *chastushkas* constitute a subset of all the existing Russian *chastushkas*. This subset is usually characterized by the presence of one or more obscene words (*see* Raskin, 1978a), very rarely of an obscene situation described without obscene words. *Out of this subset, this paper will be dealing with a much narrower subsubset of those obscene* chastushkas *which contain abusive or offensive obscenities.*

The first part of the paper will present and describe the material selectively exemplified in the Appendix, and those readers who happen to be interested only in the Russian material *per se* may ignore the second part. It is the second part of the paper, however, presenting a semantic theory underlying the obscene abuse in the *chastushkas*, which is believed to constitute the bulk of the paper. To this author's knowledge, it will be the first attempt to propose a formal semantic explanation for a certain specific form of language use and thus to provide an application for a semantic theory. Since no suitable ready-made semantic theory is available, it has to be developed. This paper is an extension of a larger research on semantic mechanisms of humor (*see* Raskin, 1979) and uses the identical or similar techniques, all based on the notion of a script-oriented semantic theory. Elements of that theory and of those techniques are briefly outlined in Part 2 and then applied to the material, already pre-processed in Part 1 (for some discussion of the theory, *see also* Raskin, 1978c, d).

It is contended by this author that the proposed analysis of verbal abuse, or for that matter, of humor, is language-independent and is equally applicable to English limericks, international party jokes, etc. It is, in fact, being applied to multilingual material by Raskin (forthcoming).

A few selected *chastushkas*, illustrative of the types distinguished below, are given in the Appendix, in Russian transliteration (the European variant, with diacritics) and in faithful, though not literal, prosaic translation. (The few poetical renderings, into British English, were accomplished by Dr. Gerry S. Smith of The University of Birmingham, England; if any reader manages to render any of the examples into equally idiomatic American, he/she will deserve the author's and especially his non-Russian-speaking friends' immense gratitude.)

Table 1: Analysis of Corpus

Type No.	Name of Type	Sub-type No.	Lexical Manifestation		Translation	Chastushka No.	Degree of Abuse
			Abuse	Target			
1	Fuck	1	ebut	nas (pizd)	(They) fuck us (cunts)	44	G
			ebut	devok	(They/we) fuck girls	92	IA or G
			ebut	kommunist	(They) fuck and give birth to a communist	211 212	D
			na xuju trepeščetsja	milka	My girl friend is quivering on (somebody else's) prick	64	IA or G
			xuj votknuli	milka	(They) stuck a prick into (raped) my girl friend	125	IA or G
			doebu	milka v grobu	I am going to fuck up my (dead) girl friend in her coffin	127	D
			ne budu/stanu ebat'/ et'	tebja	I will not fuck you (my girl friend)	218 364-367 380 381	DA
		2	ebanaja v rot	Man'ka	Mary fucked in her mouth	25 228	IA or N
			ebanaja v rot	caplja	A heron fucked in its (her) mouth	117	N or IA

(cont'd.)

Type	Name	Sub.	Abuse	Target	Translation	No.	Degree
			otsosala	gensek	Piexa (a popular female singer) gave a blow job to the General Secretary (Brezhnev)	194	D x 2
			pososi u išaka	Gitler	(You) Hitler, suck a donkey's prick	289	D
		3	vyebli	popa	The girls fucked the priest	30 217	D
			v žopu vyebli	popa	(They) fucked the priest in his ass	77	D
			v žopu vstavili / vstavim sveču	Il'ič (Lenin)	(They/we) stuck / will stick a candle into Lenin's ass	37 82	D
			v žopu vstavili / vstavim sveču	Il'ič	The pioneers stuck a candle into Lenin's ass	230	D x 2
			v žopu vstavili / vstavim sveču	Ivan Kuz'mič	(They) stuck a candle into Ivan Kuzmich's ass	69	D
			v žopu ebanyj	narod	(Come out) people fucked in your asses	234	D
2	Cunt	1	pizda	pizda	A cunt tells another cunt...	44	M or IA
			pizda	staruxa	"You, the red-haired cunt," / an old man says to his old woman	45	M or DA
			pizda	ženščina	A cunt came by taxi	89	M or IA
		2	pizda otvisnet	moja milaška	(My girl friend's) cunt would hang out like the peak of a German's cap	35	G or IA
			polnaja pizda karasej	moja milaja	(My (drowned) girl friend's) cunt got packed full with crucians (carps)	129	N or IA

(cont'd.)

Type	Name	Sub.	Abuse	Target	Translation	No.	Degree
		3	(pizda) šire kepočki moej	u nej	She has (a cunt which is) wider than my cap	383	IA
			pizdorvanka	ty	You (a woman) have a torn cunt (are not a virgin)	158 171 188 191	DA
			ne ce	ty	If you are not a virgin...	280	N or DA
		4	bljad'	pop	You a... whore (priest)	30	N or DA
			bljadi	devki	You whores, girls	46	N or DA
			bljadi	devki	The girls are whores	50	DA
			probljaduški xuevy	devčuški	The (little) girls are fucking whores	164	IA
			bljadi, bljadej	bljadi	Why do whores have curly hair?	102	T or IA
			bljad'	kolbasa	The salami, a whore, troubled me	361	G
3	Prick	1	xuj	xuj	A prick came by taxi	89	M or IA
		2	xuiško nebolšoj	na mne	I have a small prick	47 110	G
			xuj korotkovat	(u menja)	(I) have a shortish prick	109	G
		3	xueva	semejka	(Svetlana Allilueva (Stalin's daughter) comes from) a fucking family	95	IA or D
			xueva	železjaka	A fucking piece of iron	257	N
			xueva	raskorjaka	You, a fucking bow-legged (person)	311	N or DA

(cont'd.)

Type	Name	Sub.	Abuse	Target	Translation	No.	Degree
4	Go to (your) fucked mother	1	eb tvoju mat'	—	Fuck your mother (interjection)	7, 8	G
			mat' tvoju eti	—	Fuck your mother (interjection)	79	G
			mat' ego eti	konduktor	Fuck his (the guard's) mother	101	IA or G
			ebena mat'	(Tanja)	(Your) honor (Tanja) is not a football, fuck your mother	195	IA or G
			katis' k ebenoj materi	(predsedatel')	Roll to a fucked mother (you) (chairman)	236	DA or D
			idi k ebenoj materi	predsedatel'	If we see the chairman, we'll tell him, Go to a fucked mother	237	DA or D
			zaebis'	trudoden'	Let the work-day (pay) go to a fucked mother	375	G or IA
5	Incompetence	1	raz''ebaj	kapitan	(How can they) entrust a steamship to such a fucking (incompetent) captain?	229	IA
6	Bad	1	suki	devki	The girls are bitches	53	IA
		2	mandavoxa	kukuruza	The corn, that pubic louse...	103	G
7	Shit / Ass	1	(ebut) v navoze	devki	The girls are fucked in manure	92	N or IA
			ispačkannyj govnom	agronom	The agronomist dirtied with shit	98	N or D or IA
			kupaemsja v govne	strana	Our country swims in shit	98	D
			zasunul v žopu palec (i vytaščil ottuda govna 4 puda)	amerikanec	An American stuck a finger into his ass (and brought out of there 4 tons of shit)	209 210	D or IA
			v žope razorvalas' klizma	milaška (kommunizm)	An enema burst in my girl friend's ass	223	D

PART 1: THE CORPUS

0. General. The analyzed corpus comprises 65 *chastushkas*, each of which contains at least one abusive obscenity. These are all the *chastushkas* which satisfy this condition from the only available publication of obscene *chastushkas* (Kabronsky, 1978). For obvious reasons of the non-availability to the reader, no *chastushkas* from the unpublished part of this author's collection have been used in the paper. The corpus has been analyzed and classified along various relevant dimensions, and the results are shown in Table 1 and explained, along with a few abbreviations used there, in the sections which follow.

1. Lexics of the Abuse. Lexically, three of the listed types (1, 4, 5) use either a form of the verb *ebat'* 'fuck' or a derivative of this verb. Two more types (2, 3) use a form or a derivative of either *xuj* 'prick' or *pizda* 'cunt' and are, therefore, directly related to the first group (*see also* Raskin, 1978a, on these three lexical groups of derivatives). Within Type 2, however, another root, *bljad'* 'whore', related to *pizda* semantically but not lexically, is made use of. Type 6 uses a number of marginal (and much less rude) swearwords and Type 7 is the least obscene of them all. Type 4 is, of course, heavily idiomatic and is, in fact, based on various forms of the same interjection.

2. Degrees of Abuse. The abuse ranges in the corpus from the abasement to the neutral, i.e. to no abuse at all. Abasement, or denigration (D), takes place when an obscene word is applied abusively to a person or value of a higher stature. In the case of direct abuse (DA) it is applied to the hearer (H). Indirect abuse (IA) has a third person, i.e. other than the speaker (S) or the hearer, as the target of scolding. Grievance (G) is either subject-abuse (self-criticism) or zero-object abuse, i.e. the unsatisfactory state of affairs which is commented upon is blamed either on the speaker him-/herself or on nobody in particular. When no abuse is intended, the result is either a neutral (or neutralized) use of the abusive obscenity (N) or the terminological (T) or metonymical (M) variants of neutrality. The necessary and sufficient conditions for each of the 7 types of abuse are tentatively formulated in Part 2, Section 1.

3. Motives of Abuse. The most popular motive of abuse is the participation by the target in a sexual act which happens to be disapproved of by the speaker. The perception of coitus is heavily sexist and asymmetrical: there is always the aggressive participant, usually male, and the passive participant, usually female (*see*, however, Type 1.3, Nos. 30, 217). The passive participants of all kinds of sexual acts or even persons associated with them are the likely targets for abuse. The active participants of oral sexual acts (Type 1.4) may be scolded along with their recipient partners. The participants of all those acts in which the speaker does not take part are universally abused. In relatively few cases in the corpus, people or even objects are scolded for their non-sexual bad or hostile behavior and are then awarded pejorative epithets (Type 2.4, Nos. 50, 361; Type 6.1-2). In a couple of cases the reason for the speaker's displeasure and therefore, his/her use of an abusive obscenity remains somewhat obscure (Type 3.3, Nos. 257, 311). The pejorative interjection of Type 4 is used indiscriminately of persons, objects or states of affairs. Any association with excrements is usually utterly disapproved (Type 7), and so seems to be an individual case of professional incompetence. An attempt to formalize the situations of verbal abuse in the corpus on the basis of a script-oriented semantic theory is undertaken in Part 2, Section 2.

PART 2: SEMANTIC MECHANISMS OF VERBAL ABUSE

0. General. In this part of the paper the data will be analyzed from two different angles. In Section 1, for the purpose of preliminary analysis, the necessary and sufficient conditions for the 7 degrees of abuse will be presented in the format of an extension and modification of Searle's (1969) speech acts. In Section 2, after a very brief introduction into script-oriented semantics, the nature of various types of abuse will be presented as the realization of certain types of scripts.

1. Speech Acts of Abuse. The 7 types of abuse used in the corpus are represented in terms of their necessary and sufficient conditions in Table 2 (cf. the Table in Searle, 1969, Ch. 3.4). Table 2 describes some potential cases of abuse along with the ones actually represented in the corpus, e.g. the neutral type predicated of S.).

Table 2: Speech Acts of Abuse

Type of Abuse / Type of Condition	Abasement/Denigration (D)	Direct Abuse (DA)	Indirect Abuse (IA)	Grievance (G)	Neutral (N)	Terminological (T)	Metonymical (M)
0. Propositional Content	Any proposition predicated of V, where V is a person / phenomenon of high stature	Any proposition predicated of H	Any proposition predicated of X, where X is a third person	Any proposition predicated of S or W, where W is a state of affairs	Any proposition predicated of H, S, X or W	Any proposition predicated of H, S, X or W	Any proposition predicated of H, S, X or W
1. Preparatory	S considers p offensive and may be committed to the appropriateness of its application to V. S may be committed to the literal truth of p	S considers p offensive and is committed to the appropriateness of its application to H. S may not be committed to the literal truth of p	S considers p offensive and is committed to the appropriateness of its application to X. S may not be committed to the literal truth of p	S considers p offensive and is committed to the appropriateness of its application to S/W. S may not be committed to the literal truth of p	S does not consider p offensive and is committed to its literal truth	S does not consider p offensive and is dialectally committed to the appropriateness of its application to H/S/X/W. S is committed to the literal truth of p	S does not consider p offensive and is dialectally committed to the appropriateness of its (metonymical) application to H/S/X/W. S is not committed to the literal truth of p

(cont'd.)

(p = proposition)

Type of Abuse / Type of Condition	Abasement/ Denigration (D)	Direct Abuse (DA)	Indirect Abuse (IA)	Grievance (G)	Neutral (N)	Termino- logical (T)	Metonymical (M)
2. Sincerity	S is dissatis- fied with V	S is dissatis- fied with H	S is dissatis- fied with X	S is dissatis- fied with S/W	S is neither satisfied nor dissatis- fied with H/S/X/W	S is neither satisfied nor dissatis- fied with H/S/X/W	S is neither satisfied nor dissatis- fied with H/S/X/W
3. Essential	Counts as an attempt to lower V's stature	Counts as an expres- sion of S's hard feel- ings about H	Counts as an expres- sion of S's hard feel- ings about X	Counts as an expres- sion of S's hard feel- ings about S/W	Counts as an under- taking that p represents an actual state of af- fairs	Counts as an under- taking that p (dialect- ally) repre- sents an ac- tual state of affairs	Counts as an under- taking that a "metaphor- free" trans- lation of p represents an actual state of affairs

(p = proposition)

2. Semantic Scripts of Abuse. Scripts are understood here as complex notions, represented semantically as graphs with semantic nodes and semantic links between the nodes, which express standard human routines and procedures, such as EAT, SEE, READ, LOVE, GO TO MOVIE, etc., presumably in the form in which they are actually stored in the mind of the native speaker where, together, they constitute the cognitive structures of common sense. In the script-oriented semantic theory which is being developed by this writer (*see* Raskin, 1978c, d and 1979) the emphasis is put very strongly on the linguistic, empirical justification of the postulated script and every effort is being made to avoid the pitfalls of arbitrariness to which recent developments in artificial intelligence—where scripts are also used—have exposed themselves. What follows in this Section is a considerably simplified application of the script-oriented theory.

Any semantic analysis of text involves a lexicon of a kind where each lexical item is provided with an entry. On the script-oriented semantic theory, each constituent of a sentence (word, etc.) contains in the entry a reference to the script(s) it invokes, and the semantic interpretation of the sentence is that script or those scripts which is/are invoked by all the constituents of the sentence.

Most of the cases represented in Table 1 invoke the same script COITION (FUCK) which may be assigned the following format:

COITION (FUCK): **Subject, Object, Condition, Instrument, Target Location**

Subject: [+Human]
Object: [+Human] or [+Animate] [-Human]
Condition: Physical Contact
Instrument: Penis or penis-like object (belongs to Subject)
Target Location: Orifice: Vagina or Anus or Mouth (belongs to Object)

Thus, the lexical items of Types 1 and 4 would contain direct references to the action or indirect references to the target location of the script in their lexical entries. The lexical items of Type 2 would directly or indirectly invoke the script through one of the locations (e.g., indirectly, 'whore'—the owner of an (available) target location). The nature of the abuse seems to be uniform: any association with the object of the script or with the target location as a part of the object is shameful and any reference to such an association may constitute an act of verbal abuse. In more formal terms, *if a lexical item predicated of a person in the* chastushka *invokes the script* FUCK *through its object or target location, the person in question is verbally abused.* The obscene nature of such a lexical item constitutes a conspicuous indicator of verbal abuse, the function of which is to make the abuse more obvious. Obscenity, however, is optional in the sense that the same script may be elaborately invoked and used for verbal abuse in exactly the same way without resorting to obscene words.

Depending on whether the occupant of the object slot of the script is the hearer, a third person, or an inanimate state of affairs, the degree of abuse ranges from direct to indirect to grievance. A person or a value of a high stature in the object slot involves denigration. In some cases, however, and in some dialects of Russian, the abusive and obscene term should not necessarily invoke the script and then no offense may be meant. Thus, the metonymical use of *pizda* in Type 2.1, Nos. 44, 45 involves a polysemy in the lexicon associated with the script-oriented semantic theory. On the one reading of *pizda*, the involved script differs from FUCK but rather coincides with that invoked by a word like *ženščina* 'woman' and is completely neutral to offense. On the other reading, the word means one of the most popular target locations of FUCK and, therefore, invokes our script immediately and falls under the rule of offense formulated in the previous paragraph. The relative weight and distribution of the readings of a polysemous item may, of course, vary from dialect to dialect and depend heavily on the context as is the case with all polysemy or ambiguity. As a result, many ambiguities in the Degree of Abuse column of Table 1 are of this dialectal/contextual character. Thus, if *agronom* 'agronomist' is considered a person of elevated stature, as he may well be in the *chastushka* world, then denigration takes place; if he is not, there is no abuse (Type 7.1, No. 98).

This latter example is associated with another popular script used for abuse in the *chastushkas*, that of SHIT:

EXCREMENT (SHIT): (Result of) Action: Subject, Location, Object

Subject: [+Human] or [+Animate] [-Human]
Location: Place Characteristic
(*Object:* [+Human] or [+Animate] [-Human] or [-Animate], ≠ Subject, = Location, ⩾Time), i.e. another human being, animal or thing who/which happens to be in the same place at the same time or immediately after; the parentheses around the whole line render *Object* optional for the script.

Any close proximity to the excrements produced by another person or creature is reprehensible in the *chastushkas* and any reference to such an association is offensive. Again, if a lexical item is predicated of a person in the *chastushka* and this item invokes SHIT through its object this constitutes an act of verbal abuse. Type 7 is associated with this second script.

Types 5 and 6 are associated with a more trivial and much less specific script of BAD which will be standardly invoked by any lexical item characterized in the lexicon as pejorative:

BAD: (Attribute of) Subject

Subject: [±Animate]

Since the lexical entries for *raz"ebaj*, *suka* and *mandavoxa* are vague as far as the non-literal readings are concerned (*raz"-ebaj* does not even have any literal meaning) they cannot invoke any more detailed script. On this script, obviously, any association with the subject constitutes an act of verbal abuse.

The availability of certain scripts, their justified composition and observable distribution provide interesting data about the mentality of their users. Thus, the subject-object structure of the script FUCK for the world of the Russian *chastushka* excludes any symmetry in the activity or mutual respect of the participants and thus commits the speaker and his/her audience to the heavily chauvinistic, aggressive and largely male-prevailing model of sex (cf., however, Type 1.3, No. 30, 217).

REFERENCES

Al. Gorelov. 1965. "Russkaja častuška v zapisjax sovetskogo vremeni" (The Russian *chastushka* as Recorded in Soviet Times). In Z. I. Vlasova and A. A. Gorelov, *Častuški v zapisjax sovetskogo vremeni* (Leningrad: Nauka), pp. 5-27.

Vladimir Kabronsky (ed). 1978. *Nepodtsenzurnaya russkaya chastushka.* New York: Russica Books.

Alex Preminger *et al.* (eds.). 1974. *Princeton Encyclopedia of Poetry and Poetics.* Enlarged edition. Princeton: Princeton University Press.

Victor Raskin. 1978a. "On Some Peculiarities of the Russian Lexicon." In D. Farkas *et al.* (eds.), *Papers from the Parasession on the Lexicon* (Chicago: Chicago Linguistic Society), pp. 312-25.

— — —. 1978b. "Semantika nepristojnoj častuški" (The Semantics of the Bawdy Chastushka). Preface to Kabronsky, 1978.

— — —. 1978c. "Presuppositional Analysis of Russian, I: Six Essays on Aspects of Presupposition." In V. Raskin and D. Segal (eds.), *Slavica Hierosolymitana* 2 (Jerusalem: Magnes), pp. 51-92.

— — —. 1978d. "Speech Acts and Literal Meaning," *Theoretical Linguistics* 4/3 (1977), pp. 208-25.

— — —. 1979. "Semantic Mechanisms of Humor." In C. Chiarello *et al.* (eds.), *Proceedings of the Fifth Annual Meeting of the Berkeley Linguistic Society* (Berkeley: University of California Press), 325-35.

— — —. *Semantic Mechanisms of Humor.* Forthcoming.

John R. Searle. 1969. *Speech Acts.* Cambridge University Press.

APPENDIX
EXAMPLES OF CHASTUSHKAS

No. 25 (Type 1.2, IA or N)

Vnizu rečka protekaet,	*Down the hill there is a garden,*
A za rečkoj ogorod.	*By the garden there is a stream.*
Tam za rečkoj proživaet	*By the stream down there lives Manka,*
Man'ka, ebanaja v rot.	*She gets (a) cock between her teeth.*

No. 44 (Type 1.1 and 2.1, G or M)

Govorit pizda pizde:	*A cunt tells another cunt,*
"Xuj li nas ebut vezde?	*"Why the hell do they fuck us everywhere?*
I v ovrage, i v lesu,	*Down the ravine, and in the forest,*
Čerez žopu, na vesu. . ."	*And in the ass, and in balance. . ."*

No. 92 (Type 1.1 and 7.1, IA or G or N)

Kak u našem u kolxoze	*In our kolkhoz*
Ebut devok u navoze.	*They fuck girls in manure.*
Ix ebut — oni perdjat,	*They fuck them, they (girls) fart,*
Bryzgi v storonu letjat.	*And shit flies all over.*

No. 110 (Type 3.2, G)

Menja devki zvali v gosti,	*The girls invited me to visit*
A ja v gosti ne pošel:	*But I did not go (to visit):*
Pidžačiško na mne rvanyj,	*My jacket is torn*
I xuiško nebolšoj.	*And my prick is small.*

No. 171 (Type 2.3, DA)

Na gore stoit točilo,	*There is a whetstone on the hill,*
Na točile — banka.	*And on the whetstone there is a jar.*
Ja sovetskij čelovek,	*I am a Soviet man,*
A ty — pizdorvanka.	*And you have a torn (deflowered) cunt.*

No. 230 (Type 1.3, D)

Pionery Il'iču	*The pioneers stuck a candle*
V žopu vstavili sveču,	*Into Ilyich's (Lenin's) ass,*
Čtob gorela ta sveča	*So that the candle should burn*
V krasnoj žope Il'iča.	*In Ilyich's red ass.*

No. 236 (Type 4.1, DA or D)

Po derevne my idem,	*Down the village street we ramble,*
Ni k komu ne pristaem.	*We don't want no bother.*
Vse my predsedateli,	*Each of us (is) a kolkhoz chairman,*
Katis' k ebenoj materi.	*So go and fuck your mother.*

No. 25

Внизу речка протекает,
А за речкой — огород.
Там за речкой проживает
Манька, ебаная в рот.

No. 44

Говорит пизда пизде:
Хуй ли нас ебут везде?
И в овраге, и в лесу,
Через жопу, на весу.

No. 92

Как у нашем у колхозе
Ебут девок у навозе.
Их ебут, они пердят,
Брызги в сторону летят.

No. 110

Меня девки звали в гости,
А я в гости не пошел.
Пиджачишко на мне рваный,
И хуишко небольшой.

No. 171

На горе стоит точило,
На точиле — банка.
Я — советский человек,
А ты — пиздорванка.

No. 230

Пионеры Ильичу
В жопу вставили свечу.
Чтоб горела та свеча
В красной жопе Ильича.

No. 236

По деревне мы идем,
Ни к кому не пристаем.
Все мы председатели,
Катись к ебеной матери.

The Russian originals
are used by permission
of Mr. Kabronsky. *Ed.*

RXRXRXRXRXRXRXRXRXRXRXRXR
X   X
R   R
X   **THREE OUT OF FOUR**   X
R   **DOCTORS RECOMMEND**   R
X   *MALEDICTA*   X
R   (The fourth one is a hopeless nerd)   R
X   X
R   R
X   X
RXRXRXRXRXRXRXRXRXRXRXRXR

MERRY XXX-MAS

'Twas the night before Christmas, and all through the house,
    The whole goddamn family was drunk as a louse;
      Grandma and Grandpa were singing a song,
    And the kids were in bed a-flogging their dongs.

Ma, home from the cat-house, and me out of jail,
    Had just crawled into bed for a nice piece of tail;
    When out on the lawn there arose such a clatter,
    I jumped out of bed to see what was the matter.

    Away to the window I flew like a flash,
    Threw open the shutters and fell on my ass.
    The moon on the crest of the new fallen snow,
Gave a whorehouse-like luster to the objects below.

When what to my bloodshot eyes should appear,
    But a rusty old sleigh and two mangy reindeers,
      With a little old driver a-pounding his dick,
    I knew in a moment it must be St. Nick.

    Slower than snails his reindeers they came,
He bitched and he swore, and he called them by name:
    "Now Dancer, now Prancer, up over the walls,
Quick now, goddamn it, or I'll cut out your balls."

    And up to the roof he stumbled and fell,
And came down the chimney like a bat out of hell.
    He staggered and stomped and went to the door,
    Tripped on his peter, and fell to the floor.

    I heard him exclaim as he rode out of sight,
    "Piss on you all, this is a hell of a night!"

(Robert Th., Nevada)

FEEDBACK

3.6 RIDICULING PLACE NAMES

Attleboro, Mass.: *Cattleboro.* Used for 20 years by a visitor from Philadelphia who says, "We treat hogs better."

Champaign-Urbana, Ill.: *Chambana, Shambana* (said to be endearing rather than derogatory). *Shambanana* (because of its rural isolation). *Shampoo-Banana* (since at least 1973)

Chicago, Ill.: *Cago* (from Spanish, "I shit"). *Shitcago.* Also, *chie* sounds like a French verb form, from *chier* "to shit."

Fort Dodge, Iowa: *Fart-and-Dodge-It*

Fort Lauderdale, Fla.: *Fart Lauderdale*

Glens Falls, N.Y.: *Glans Falls*

Houston, Texas: *Whorestown*

Ignasio, Cal.: *Ignausea*

Indianapolis, Ind.: *Indianóplace* (because of its blandness)

Louisville, Ky.: *Louseville, Lousyville, Louisvile*

Muncie, Ind.: *Munchie*

Naperville, Ill.: *Raperville* (perhaps because this once peaceful town is now raped by a construction boom)

Newark, N.J.: *New Arse*

Norfolk, Va.: *Shit City* (common term by Navy personnel)

Pittsburgh, Pa.: *Pitstop*

Pocahontas, Iowa: *Poke-a-hog-in-de-ass* (many hog farmers)

Reston, Va.: *Restive, Vagina*

Terra Linda, Cal.: *Sterile Linda*

Texas City, Texas: *Texas Shitty* (when downwind from the high-sulfur crude refineries)

Toronto, Ontario: *Hogtown.* Also, formerly, *Toronto the Good* (because of Blue Laws, and boring after sundown). Before its renaissance, Toronto "had the largest hotels, the tallest building, and the dullest Sundays in Canada."

Urbana, Ill.: *Urpain* (generally not known; several claimed coining it. A linguist coined it from the German *Ur-* meaning "source, origin")

Wyckoff, N.J.: *Whack-off.*

Contributed by: Fred Chambers, C. Cohn, Tom Cravens, Robert Davis, Harry Ellis, Robert Fritz, Dan Lewis, S. Moe, Frank Nuessel, David Perlman, Joe Salemi, Cliff Scheiner, Frank Shults, Roy West, Leah White, *and* Editor.

4.13 DEROGATORY NEWSPAPER NAMES

Austin American-Statesman (Austin, Texas): Austin American Snakeman

Bayonne Journal (Bayonne, N.J.): Bayonne Urinal

Daily News (Ball State University, Muncie, Ind.): Daily Snooze

Daily Texan (University of Texas, Austin, Tex.): Deadly Toxin (used for the annual lampoon issue)

Deseret News (Salt Lake City, Utah): The Deserted News

East Village Other (New York City): East Village Offal (trashy)

Halifax Chronicle Herald (Halifax, Nova Scotia): Halifax Comical Herald

Herald Banner (Greenville, Texas): Herald Banana, Horrid Banana

Independent Journal (Marin County, Cal.): Independent Urinal

Indiana Daily Student (Indiana University, Bloomington, Ind.): Daily Stupid, Indiana Stupid, Stupid

Louisville Courier Journal (Louisville, Ky.): Louisville Curious Jumble

Milwaukee Journal (Milwaukee, Wis.): Milwaukee Urinal

New York Times (N.Y.): New York Izvestia

News of the World (London): News of the Screws (sex)

News & Observer (Raleigh, N.C.): Nuisance & Disturber

Ottawa Citizen (Ottawa, Ontario): Ottawa Shitizen

Ottawa Journal (Ottawa, Ontario): Ottawa Urinal

Red and Black (University of Georgia, Athens, Ga.): Retch and Barf

Reporter Dispatch (White Plains, N.Y.): Distorter Rehash

San Francisco Examiner (Cal.): The Brand-Ex-Paper (used by the *S. F. Chronicle*). Also known as *That Other Paper* and *That Paper That Dares Not Speak Its Name*

Scarsdale Inquirer (Scarsdale, N.Y.): The Inkwaster

Soho News (New York City): So-So News (rather dull)

Toronto Globe and Mail (Toronto, Ontario): Glib and Blob, Mop and Pail, Slop and Pail

Village Voice (New York City): Village Vice (from the large number of sexually-oriented personal ads)

Washington Post (Washington, D.C.): Washington Pus, Washington Pustule

Il Resto del Carlino (Bologna, Italy): Il Resto del Cretino

Turun Sanomat ["News of Turku"] (Turku, Finland): Surun Sanomat ["News of Sorrow"].

Contributed by: Joachim A., Tom Cravens, Harry Ellis, Robert Fritz,

John Keirstead, Richard Lederer, Dan Lewis, Richard Maas, Douglas McKay, Frank Nuessel, M. Ruhlen, Chris S., Joe Salemi, Maija Salo, John Spragens, Larry Thompson, *and* Jenny Wade.

MISCELLANEOUS NICKNAMES

I. Academic Institutions. Fairleigh Dickinson University: *Fairly Ridiculous.* — City University of New York (CUNY): *Cunny, C.U.N.T.* — Iowa State University: *Moo U.* (famous for its College of Agriculture). — New York University (NYU): *N.Y. Jew* (because of high percentage of Jewish students). — Northwest Missouri State College (NWMSC): *Not Worth Much Serious Consideration.* — Sam Houston Institute of Technology: *S.H.I.T.* — University of Wisconsin-Milwaukee: *Asshole U., Dungheap U.* — Washington University (St. Louis): *Washout U.* —Yale: *Jail.*

II. Country. U.S.A.: *Untidy States, Jewnited States.* German: Vereinigte Staaten, "United States": *Verunreinigte Staaten*, "Polluted States."

III. State. Missouri: *The State of Misery*

IV. County. Marin County, Calif.: *Murine County* (full of allergy-triggering pollen; Murine = trade name of medicated eye drops, to combat red, itching eyes caused by pollen).

V. Streets. Gratiot (Detroit, Mich.): *Gray-shit.* — Livernois (Detroit, Mich.): *Liver-noise.*

VI. Park. Hancock Park, Los Angeles: *Handcock Park* (reportedly frequented by many homosexuals).

VII. Buildings. The transmission tower of the Canadian Broadcasting Corp., located on Jarvis Street, in Toronto's red-light district: *The Biggest Erection* (Colombo's *222 Canadian Jokes*, p. 14). — The new Catholic Church in Liverpool, England, shaped like a funnel or tent: *The Mersey Funnel, Paddy's Wigwam* (Lane's *The ABZ of Scouse*, p. 66-67). — Congress Hall (Kongresshalle), Berlin: *Schwangere Auster*, "Pregnant Oyster" (because of its shape). — A building complex put up in the eastern part of Montréal, Québec by its former mayor: *Drapeau's Last Erection.* — Well-endowed nude male statue by Jacob Epstein in the center of Liverpool, England: *Moby Dick* (*The ABZ of Scouse*, p. 69). — UNO-City in Vienna, Austria, officially known as Internationales Zentrum Wien: *Die Uncity* (huge building complex erected at extreme cost to the taxpayers; thus also called *das Grabmal des unbekannten österreichischen Steuerzahlers*, "the tomb of the unknown Austrian taxpayer" (*Die Zeit*, Nr. 36, 1979).

VIII. Company Names. Allegheny Airlines (now USAir): *Agony Airlines.* — Chatto & Windus (London, publishing house. Its director, D.J. Enright, snidely rewiewed *Maledicta* in the *TLS* (*see* MAL II:238): *Chatter & Windy, Shitty & Windy.* — Ford Motor Co.: *Fix Or Repair Daily.* — Pitney Bowes (Postal Meters): *Pitstop Bowels.* — U.S. Post Office/Postal Services: *U.S. Post Orifice, U.S. Putz Office, Pestal Services.*

IX. Television Stations. WHAS (Louisville, Ky.): *Who Has Any Sense?* — WIXT (Syracuse, N.Y.): sounds like German *wichst* "you jack off?" — WKRP (Cincinnati, Ohio, TV Series): *Who Keeps Reputable Prostitutes? W-KRAP.* — WPTF (Raleigh, N.C.): *We Pester The Family.*

X. ETC. Federal Trade Commission: *Federal Tirade Commission* (John Lewis, president of Free Enterprise, in *The Wall Street Journal*, 11 June 1981, 2:1). — German business abbreviation, *GmbH* = Gesellschaft mit beschränkter Haftung (= Ltd.): *Gerhard mit beschissener Hose,* "Gerhard with shat-in pants." — Italian Postal and License Plate abbreviation, *PG* (Perugia): *Povera Gente,* "poor people, paupers, beggars." — An Assistant Attorney General (Wisconsin): *Attorney Genital.*

Contributed by: Len Ashley, John Colombo, Tom Cravens, Harry Ellis, Robert Fritz, Ken Grabowski, Susan Isović, Dan Lewis, Anne McConnell, Alexandra Merrill, Frank Nuessel, Cliff Scheiner, Larry Thompson, Roy West, *and* Editor.

SUBMIT NEATLY

When submitting material for Feedback, Reactions, News, Miscellany, Publications, etc., please ALWAYS use SEPARATE cards or sheets of paper (3 x 5" or larger) for EACH *SEPARATE* item. Two different newspaper nicknames are two separate items. For example, do NOT scribble five different items on your Order Blank (margins & back), like some fink from Indiana, because I have to copy that information on five SEPARATE cards (to organize for later alphabetization), and I may make mistakes copying your scribbles. The same holds true for letters: please separate *personal matters* from *material for publication*; if your letter contains 20 different bits of information, I have to copy the stuff onto 20 different cards, each with your name and ZIP code. The neater and more considerate your submissions, the earlier they get published.

You be neat now, heah!?

ELITE MALEDICTA

- Bonnie Prince Charles is not a Prince Charming, according to 88% of the American women asked in *People* magazine's 1981 "Readers' Poll": They advised Lady Di not to marry Charles, considering him **"spoiled, stuffy, a little kinky, goony-looking, a nerd, a stuffed shirt,"** and having **"the personality of a bowl of cold oatmeal." "Our children would look like horses,"** said one. Men were also quite catty, saying that he is **"arrogant, a drip, looks like a jerk and is uppity."** (*People*, 18 May 1981, p. 31 — M. Helfrich & Ed.)

- Chicago columnist Mike Royko is as bored with Charles and Di as he was with his great-uncle, the Duke of Windsor, **"that weak-faced wimp** who gave up the throne of England 'for the woman he loved,' **a nasty, thin-lipped woman who led him around by his nose."** (*Waukesha Freeman,* 29 July 1981, p. 6)

- Israeli Prime Minister Menachem Begin was upset by German Chancellor Helmut Schmidt's trip to Saudi Arabia and his comments on the Palestinians. In May 1981, Begin called Schmidt **"greedy"** and **"arrogant,"** said he had **"no principles, no heart and no memory,"** and insinuated that the Chancellor had backed Nazi persecution of Jews and had remained faithful to Hitler until the last moment. Schmidt responded by saying that Begin was **"a threat to world peace"** and remarked off the record that the Jews had taken 2,000 years to found a state, "and then 30 years later, along comes **a lunatic like Begin** and puts everything at risk." In October 1981, at the funeral of Egypt's Anwar Sadat, both politicians shook hands and exchanged polite words." (*Time* Magazine, 18 May 1981, p. 37, and *Milwaukee Journal*, 18 Oct. 1981, A-10)

- Austria's Jewish Chancellor, Bruno Kreisky, does not care for Begin: **"He is a political grocer, a little Polish lawyer from Warsaw or whatever he was."** Begin, being an "eastern Jew," "is so alienated" and **"thinks in such warped ways."** Kreisky also called Nazi-Hunter Simon Wiesenthal **"a Jewish Fascist."** (*The Jewish Almanac*, 1980, p. 204)

• Israel's Begin called Irak's head, Saddam Hussein, "**the bloodthirsty arch-enemy of the Jewish State,**" and called him and Libya's Khadafy **meshuggene** ("crazies"). (*Süddeutsche Zeitung*, Munich, 11 June 1981, p. 2)

• Egyptian President Anwar Sadat dubbed Libya's head, Moammar Khadafy, "**an infantile nitwit.**" (*Daily News*, N.Y., 20 August 1981, p. 2 — Joe Salemi)

• Libyan radio commented on Sadat's death: "**He lived like a Jew and died like a Jew.** He was buried on Saturday (sabbath)." (*Milwaukee Journal*, 11 Oct. 1981, p. 1)

• The nation's youngest congressman, Rep. John LeBoutillier (R-NY), said in Niagara Falls, N.Y. about House Speaker Thomas O'Neill (D-Mass.), who opposed President Reagan's budget proposals, that O'Neill was "**big, fat and out of control - just like the federal government.**" O'Neill also "**personifies everything about politics that the public hates today.**" And: "**You don't walk by him** (O'Neill), **you walk around him. And it's a long trip.**" Asked about LeBoutillier, O'Neill said to reporters that he "**wouldn't know him from a cord of wood.**" — Later, LeBoutillier called Sen. George McGovern "**scum**" and accused the Kennedy family of "**snobby, elitist, condescending politics.**" (AP, *Milwaukee Journal*, 12 July 1981, p. 3)

• New York's mayor, Edward Koch (rhymes with 'crotch'), whether he fibs: "It's not my habit to employ duplicity.... But I'm not Billy Budd. **Billy Budd was a schmuck.**" Also, Koch, refusing to pose with a live tiger: "No, the mayor is not a coward and **the mayor is also not a schmuck.**" (*Time* Magazine, 15 June 1981, p. 27)

• At the Duke University Law School, former President Richard Nixon was known as "**Iron Butt**" and "**Gloomy Gus.**" (Lucaire, *Celebrity Trivia*, 1980)

• Milwaukee's mayor, Henry Maier, upset by the newspaper's repeated and detailed reports on the garbage collection system's waste of money, told the reporters "**Go to hell!**" and "**Stick it right up your butts!**" (*Milwaukee Journal*, 6-12-81:10)

• During her visit to the Royal Wedding, *The Guardian* called Mrs. Reagan "**a onetime starlet of B-films.**" (AP, 7-26-81)

COLORFUL SPEECH

★ **Let's have a drink. My mouth tastes like the inside of a Greek wrestler's jockstrap.** (Martha Cornog, Penna. Found in G. Legman's *No Laughing Matter*, p. 477)

★ **You're playing hockey with a warped puck.** ("Crazy." "Carol Burnett Show")

★ **The kid was so obnoxious that his parents had to tie a pork chop to his ear so that the dog would play with him.** (Don Krabbe, Illinois, in letter to Ed.)

★ A Czech insult: **Než ti vodřízli pupeční šňůru tak si s tebou hráli jak s jójem.** "Before cutting your umbilical cord, they played with you yo-yo." (Petr Skrabanek, M.D., Ireland)

★ **May all you ecological bastards freeze to death in the dark.** (Howard Shooshan, Mass., in letter to Ed.)

★ **My dick is so hard a cat couldn't scratch it.** (Common remark while shaving, U.S. Army. Stephen Gregory, Mich.)

★ **May a diarrhetic dromedary defecate in your décolletage.** (To an obnoxious woman. Paul Runey, Va. 1981)

★ **Thanks for.... It was almost as exciting as nestling with a nymph in a nightie.** (Michael Fandal, NY., in letter to Ed.)

★ **Some minimal life form which sucks farts at a diaper service absconded with my *Maledicta*.** (Tom Frillman, Cal., in letter to Ed.)

★ **You're as slick as snot on a marble.** (S. Moe, Cal., an admiring, witty geriatric cat, in letter to Ed.)

★ **Her mother is as busy as the dildo in a fag sultan's harem.** (Merritt Clifton, Québec, in letter to Ed.)

★ **Thanks for sending *Maledicta*. I had so much fun I felt like a whore in a navy yard.** (Bruce Jones, Missouri, to Ed.)

★ **He was happier than a baby in a barrel of tits.** (A comic on the "Tonight Show," 22 Jan. 1981)

★ **He ain't worth shit in a handbag.** *And:* **I don't know whether to shit or wind my watch.** (George Carlin, on a record)

★ **She's a girl who can suck the chrome off a trailer hitch.** (R. Redford's friend about a young woman, in the movie *The Electric Horseman*, 1979)

★ **Colder than the Devil's Prick.** (Feminist reprise to the common "Colder than a Witch's Tit." Jessica Sheridan, Illinois)

★ Heard from a male grade school teacher discussing a sexually active fellow-teacher: **She'll drop her drawers for a mop-handle if you leave it at a forty-five-degree angle.** (Joe Salemi, New York)

★ **It smells like a sack full of sour dick heads.** (Jacquard Guenon, Mich., in letter to Ed.)

★ **Some of my best friends are genitals.** (L. Fischer, Mass.)

★ **May you be like Chicago—chronically plagued by winds.** (Editor, to an annoying "Is it out yet?" inquirer)

★ **Just so that you shouldn't have a loss, may one of your eyes drop in and the other drop out.** (Yiddish curse. Abraham Eiss, NY., in letter to Ed.)

★ **May the smell of their pudenda attract large and horny German shepherds.** (Dave A., Penna., complaining about his slovenly fellow-editors. 1980)

★ **He's so ugly he could open up a branch face.** (Heard from two blacks on the bus. Robert S., Washington, D.C., 1981)

★ **She's so dumb she couldn't add up to 2 without taking off her blouse.** ("Benny Hill Show")

★ **Helloran's bibliographical entry was shorter than the shriveled-up penis of a Hungarian hermaphrodite.** (Editor, referring to some cacademic asshole he once knew)

★ **He's so dumb he thinks manual labor is a Mexican immigrant.** (Editor, read somewhere)

★ **The river is frozen harder than the shady side of a banker's heart.** (Ed McCarthy, Penna., 70, quoted in *Time* magazine, 26 Jan. 1981, p. 37)

★ **You should have been a hemorrhoid because you're such a pain in the ass.** (Novelty card, NY., 1981)

★ Marine to paratrooper: **Only two things fall out of the sky: bird shit and idiots.** (Don Krabbe, Illinois, in letter to Ed.)

★ German insult: **Wenn du so lang wärst wie du dumm bist, dann müßtest du in einer Kegelbahn übernachten.** "If you were as tall as you are stupid, you would have to sleep in a bowling alley." (Editor)

MISCELLANY

♦ Ambrose Bierce's *Enlarged Devil's Dictionary*, ed. by Ernest Hopkins (1967), describes the common housefly as **musca maledicta**, "damned, cursèd fly." (Robert Smith)

♦ **"My sharp Cheddar Balls are back...."** (Advertisement in *The Adventurous Cheeselover: International Cheese Newsletter*, N.Y., March 1981, p. 4. — Thanks for telling us, Gerard)

♦ Found in "Dr. Wing Tip Shoo's X-Rated Fortune Cookies" (N.Y.): **Woman who cooks carrots and peas in same pot, unsanitary. — Stenographer not permanent fixture until screwed on desk. — Girl who sleep with judge get honorable discharge.** (Page Bernstein)

♦ *Q:* What's the difference between a vitamin and a hormone? *A:* You can make a vitamin. ("Benny Hill Show")

♦ John Lahr published the biography of Joe Orton (1978) called **Prick Up Your Ears.** (Rather messy, and painful.)

♦ Does your female sexual partner treat you like your banker? **"Substantial penalties for early withdrawal."**

♦ **Happiness is a Good Screw.** (Advertising on matchbox cover, Tyco Fastening Products, N.Y. — Keith Denning)

♦ *Poetic Justice:* When your brother-in-law who neither smokes, drinks nor swears catches VD. (Roy West)

♦ **Garden Bouquet** Beauty Soap: New brand name for the former **Gay Bouquet** soap. (Henry Madden)

♦ Would you say that a seven-year-old homosexual is a kid who turned prematurely gay?

♦ The headquarters of **Women USA** (Bella Abzug, president) is located in N.Y. City, **76 Beaver St.** (Denison Hatch)

♦ Baltimore Police Commissioner Donald Pomerleau, testifying in a sex discrimination lawsuit: "All women are little balls of fluff in the eyes of the creator." (*Debris* 8, June 1981, p. 2. — John Boston). The Creator must have been blind in the case of Abzug, Friedan & Co.: nothing fluffy about them!

♦ After Tennis Star Billie Jean King's lesbian affair became known, jokes started to fly: *Q:* Who will be B.J.K.'s new sponsor? *A:* Snap-on Tools. — *Q:* How did Billie become champion? *A:* She licked her opponents. — *Q:* Why won't they let Billie play at the World Championship in Holland? *A:* Because she wants to stick her finger in every dike. (Dennis D., Gordon W.)

biBLioGRApby

Afanas'ev, Aleksandr. **Erotic Tales of Old Russia.** Russian & English, transl. by Yuri Perkov. Oakland: Scythian, 1980. Paper, 177 pp., $6.95.

Arora, Shirley L. **Proverbial Comparisons and Related Expressions in Spanish.** Berkeley: Univ. of California Press, 1977. Paper, 521 pp., $16.

Beaumatin, Eric. **Recherches sur la censure verbale: L'euphémisme dans le catalan parlé de Barcelone.** Paris: Université de Paris—Sorbonne, 1980. Thesis. Paper, 137 pp., $18.

Berman, Sanford. **The Joy of Cataloging: Essays, Letters, Reviews, and other Explosions.** Phoenix: Oryx, 1981. Paper, 249 pp., $16.50.

Borneman, Ernest. **Lexikon der Liebe: Materialien zur Sexualwissenschaft.** 4 vols. Frankfurt: Ullstein, 1978. Paper, 1,542 pp., $?

Bourke, John G. **Les Rites scatologiques.** Transl. & annot. by Dominique Laporte and Hélène Boisseau-Riou. Paris: Presses Universitaires de France, 1981. Paper, 317 pp., $? (French transl. of Bourke's *Scatalogic* [sic] *Rites of All Nations,* 1891).

Carothers, Gibson and James Lacey. **Slanguage: America's Second Language.** New York: Sterling Publ. Co., 1979. Cloth, 88 pp., $4.95.

Colombo, John Robert. **Colombo's Names & Nicknames.** Toronto: NC Press, 1978. Cloth, 211 pp., $11.95.

Constantin, Theodor (comp.). **Berliner Schimpfwörterbuch.** Berlin: Haude & Spener, 1981. Paper, 93 pp., DM 9,80.

Cornulier, Benoît de. **Meaning Detachment** (Pragmatics & Beyond, vol. 7). Amsterdam: John Benjamins, 1980. Paper, 124 pp., $14.

Dance, Daryl Cumber. **Shuckin' and Jivin': Folklore from Contemporary Black Americans.** Bloomington: Indiana University Press, 1978. Cloth, 390 pp., $15.

duGran, Claurène [Pseud.]. **Wordsmanship: A Dictionary.** Essex, CT: Verbatim, 1981. Cloth, 95 pp., $9.95.

Dunkling, Leslie. **The Guinnes Book of Names.** Enfield, Middlesex: Guinnes Superlatives Ltd., 1974. Cloth, 256 pp., £3·20 (Excellent).

Enckell, Pierre. **Matériaux pour l'histoire du vocabulaire français: Datations et documents lexicographiques.** Paris: Klincksieck, 1981. Paper, 257 pp., $? (16th - 19th centuries).

Enevig, Anders. **Lokumsdigte og Retiradenvers: Graffiti—når det er værst.** Odense: Privately printed, 1980. Paper, 60 pp., 48.00 D.Kr. or $6.00 ppd. (101 Danish graffiti, verses & scatology. Order from author, A. E., Skovløkkevej 13, Seden, DK-5240 Odense NØ, Denmark).

Flanagan, Cathleen C. and John T. Flanagan. **American Folklore: A Bibliography, 1950-1974.** Metuchen & London: Scarecrow Press, 1977. Cloth, 406 pp., $16.

Flexner, Stuart Berg. **I Hear America Talking: An Illustrated Treasury of American Words and Phrases.** New York: Van Nostrand Reinhold, 1976. Cloth, 505 pp., $18.95. Paper, $7.95.

Forrest, David V. **Selected American Expressions for the Foreign-Born Psychiatrist and Other Professionals, with Street Slang Supplement.** New York: Educational Research, 1976. Paper, spiralbd., 71 pp., $10.

Gaignebet, Claude. **Le Folklore obscène des enfants.** Paris: Maison-neuve & Larose, 1980. Second ed. Paper, 355 pp., ca. $18.

Haan, Marina and Richard B. Hammerstrom. **Graffiti in the Big Ten.** Madison, Wis.: Brown House Galleries, 1980. Paper, 161 pp., $3.95. (Typescript forerunner of next item).

Haan, Marina N. and Richard B. Hammerstrom (comps.) **Graffiti in the Big Ten / Graffiti in the Southwest Conference / Graffiti in the PAC 10 / Graffiti in the Ivy League.** New York: Warner Books, 1981. Paper, ea. ca. 146 pp., each $4.50.

Haight, Anne Lyon. **Banned Books: 387 B.C. to 1978 A.D.** Updated and enlarged by Chandler B. Grannis. New York: R. R. Bowker, 1978. Cloth, 196 pp., $13.95.

Hook, J. N. **The Grand Panjandrum & 1,999 Other Rare, Useful, and Delightful Words and Expressions.** New York: Macmillan, 1980. Cloth, 392 pp., $13.95.

Kálmán, Béla. **The World of Names: A Study in Hungarian Onomatology.** Translated by Zsolt Virágos. Budapest: Akadémiai Kiadó, 1978. Cloth, 199 pp., $12.50.

Kaufman, Gloria and Mary Kay Blakely. **Pulling Our Own String: Feminist Humor & Satire.** Bloomington: Indiana University Press, 1980. Paper, 192 pp., $7.95. Cloth, $20. (Contains repulsive crap, too).

Kennedy, X. J. (ed.). **Tygers of Wrath: Poems of Hate, Anger, and Invective.** Athens: University of Georgia Press, 1981. 268 pp., $?

Koch, Hans-Jörg. **Wenn Schambes Schennt. Ein Rheinhessisch-Mainzer Schimpf-Lexikon.** Fourth, enlarged ed. Alzey: Rheinhessische Druck-werkstätte, 1978. Cloth, 239 pp., DM 19,80.

Kunitskaya-Peterson, Christina. **International Dictionary of Obscenities.** Oakland: Scythian Books, 1981. Paper, 93 pp., $4.95. (Liberal borrowings from *Maledicta* and Drummond & Perkins, without credit).

Lakoff, George and Mark Johnson. **Metaphors We Live By.** Chicago: University of Chicago Press, 1980. Cloth, 242 pp., $13.95.

Lane, Linacre. **Lern Yerself Scouse; Or, the ABZ of Scouse.** Edited and annotated by Fritz Spiegl. Liverpool: Scouse Press, 1966. Paper, 121 pp., 60p. (The dialect of Merseyside).

Markert, Ludwig. **Struktur und Bezeichnung des Scheltworts: Eine gattungskritische Studie anhand des Amosbuches.** Berlin: de Gruyter, 1977. Cloth, 330 pp., DM 112. (Very scholarly. Biblical).

Matisoff, James A. **Variational Semantics in Tibeto-Burman.** Philadelphia: ISHI, 1978. Cloth, 331 pp., $21.95.

Maurer, David W. **Language and the Underworld.** Collected & ed. by Allan Futrell and Charles Wordell. Lexington, Ky.: University Press of Kentucky, 1981. Cloth, 417 pp., $30.

McCosh, Sandra. **Children's Humour: A Joke for Every Occasion.** With an Introduction by G. Legman. London: Granada Publishing, 1979. Paper, 336 pp., £1·50.

McDowell, John Holmes. **Children's Riddling.** Bloomington: Indiana University Press, 1979. Cloth, 272 pp., $17.50.

McPhee, Nancy. **The Book of Insults Ancient & Modern.** New York: Penguin Books (1978), 1980. Paper, 160 pp., $2.95.

Michaels, Leonard, and Christopher Ricks (eds.). **The State of Language.** Berkeley: Univ. of California Press, 1981. Paper, 609 pp., $8.95.

Morris, Desmond, Peter Collett, Peter Marsh, and Marie O'Shaughnessy. **Gestures: Their Origins and Distribution.** New York: Stein & Day, 1979. Paper, 296 pp., $7.95. Cloth, $12.95. (Excellent).

Naiman, Arthur. **Every Goy's Guide to Common Jewish Expressions.** Boston: Houghton Mifflin, 1981. Paper, 172 pp., $4.95.

Pearl, Anita. **The Jonathan David Dictionary of Popular Slang.** Middle Village, N.Y.: Jonathan David, 1980. Cloth, 191 pp., $9.95.

Peñalosa, Fernando. **Introduction to the Sociology of Language.** Rowley: Newbury House, 1981. Paper, 242 pp., $13.95.

Promblés, E. Slove [Pseud.]. **Fee! Fie! Foe! Fum! A Dictionary of Fartology.** Brockport, N.Y.: Melodious Publications, 1981. Paper, 113 pp., $5.95. (Order from M.P., P.O. Box 343-A, B., NY 14420).

Pursch, Günter. **Parlamentarisches Schimpfbuch.** Frankfurt: Ullstein, 1980. Paper, 204 pp., DM 6,80.

Pütz, Robert (ed.) and Alfred Limbach (comp.). **Der Furz.** Köln: Argos Press, 1980. Cloth, ca. 150 pp., ca. DM 30. (On farts & farting).

Radtke, Edgar. **Sonderwortschatz und Sprachschichtung: Materialien zur sprachlichen Verarbeitung des Sexuellen in der Romania.** Tübingen: Gunter Narr, 1981. Paper, 83 pp., DM 32,00. (Sex + MAL Bibliography).

Rawson, Hugh. **A Dictionary of Euphemisms & Other Doubletalk.** New York: Crown Publishers, 1981. Cloth, 312 pp., $14.95.

Reyna, José R. **Raza Humor: Chicano Joke Tradition in Texas.** San

Antonio: Penca Books, 1980. Paper, 147 pp., $6.95. (Engl. Intro., 206 Jokes in Spanish only).

Rodale, J. I. **The Synonym Finder.** Completely revised by Laurence Urdang and Nancy LaRoche. Emmaus: Rodale Press, 1978. Cloth, 1,361 pp., $17.95.

Rosenbaum, Samuel. **A Yiddish Word Book for English-Speaking People.** New York: Van Nostrand Reinhold, 1978. Cloth, 180 pp., $9.95.

Rössler, Gerda. **Konnotationen: Untersuchungen zum Problem der Mit- und Nebenbedeutung.** Wiesbaden: Franz Steiner, 1979. Paper, 177 pages, DM 38,00.

Saitz, Robert L. and Edward J. Cervenka. **Handbook of Gestures: Colombia and the United States.** The Hague: Mouton, 1972. (Now distributed by Walter de Gruyter, Berlin & N.Y.). Cloth, 164 pp., DM 72.

Santamaría, Francisco J. **Diccionario de Mejicanismos.** Third Ed. México: Porrua, 1978. Cloth, 1,207 pp., ca. $55. (Distr. by Valcour & Krueger, San Diego).

Schur, Norman W. **English-English: A Descriptive Dictionary.** Essex, Conn.: Verbatim, 1980. Cloth, 332 pp., $24.95. (An expanded, improved version of his earlier *British Self-Taught*).

Sharp, Donald B. **Commentaries on Obscenity.** Metuchen: Scarecrow Press, 1970. Cloth, 333 pp., $4.98. (Legal matters).

Souto Maior, Mário. **Dicionário Folclórico da Cachaça.** Second ed. Recife: Massangana, 1980. Paper, 149 pp., $?

———. **Folclorerotismo.** Second ed. Recife: Ed. Pirata, 1981. 50 pp.

———. **Galalaus & Batorés.** Recife: Ed. Universitária, 1981. Paper, 73 pages, $? (Terms for tall and short people).

———. **Nordeste: A Inventiva Popular.** Rio de Janeiro: Cátedra, 1978. Paper, 139 pp., Cr$ 40.00.

Spears, Richard A. **Slang and Euphemism: A Dictionary of Oaths, Curses, Insults, Sexual Slang and Metaphor, Racial Slurs, Drug Talk, Homosexual Lingo, and Related Matters.** Middle Village, N.Y.: Jonathan David, 1981. Cloth, 448 pp., $24.95. Paperbound at $12.95=good buy.

Sperling, Susan Kelz. **Poplollies and Bellibones: A Celebration of Lost Words.** New York: Clarkson Potter, 1977. Cloth, 114 pp., $7.95.

Syatt, Dick. **Country Talk.** Secaucus, N.J.: Citadel Press, 1980. Cloth, 218 pp., $7.95.

Sykes, J. B. (ed.). **The Concise Oxford Dictionary of Current English.** Sixth ed. Oxford: Clarendon Press / Oxford University Press, 1976. Cloth, 1,368 pp., $16.95. Thumb-indexed, $19.95. Excellent.

Tarpley, Fred. **From Blinky to Blue-John: A Word Atlas of Northeast Texas.** Wolfe City: University Press, 1970. Cloth, 338 pp., $10.95.

Thiel, Alex and Jürgen Beyer. **Graffiti in Kassel: Ein Bilder-Buch.** Kassel: Privately printed, 1981. Paper, 115 pp., DM 25. (Spray-can art).

Twain, Mark. **The Diaries of Adam & Eve.** Lawrence, KS: Coronado Press (1962), 1980. Cloth, 91 pp., $6.50.

Urdang, Laurence (ed.). **Twentieth Century American Nicknames.** Comp. by Walter Kidney and George Kohn. New York: H. W. Wilson, 1979. Cloth, 398 pp., $18.00.

Waugh, Daniel Clarke. **The Great Turkes Defiance: On the History of the Apocryphal Correspondence of the Ottoman Sultan in its Muscovite and Russian Variants.** Columbus: Slavica Publishers, 1978. Cloth, 354 pages, $18.95. (Scholarly. Facsimiles).

Wehr, Hans. **A Dictionary of Modern Written Arabic.** Fourth ed. Ed. by J Milton Cowan. Wiesbaden: Harrassowitz, 1979. Cloth, 1,301 pp., DM 198 (ca. $100). (Contains 13,000 new entries. Excellent).

Wehr, Hans. **Arabic-English Dictionary.** Ed. by J M. Cowan. Ithaca, N.Y.: Spoken Language Services, 1976. Paper, 1,100 pp., $8.50. (Low-priced version of the preceding item, earlier ed. Excellent).

———

PUBLICATIONS BY OUR MEMBERS

Yoël Arbeitman and Allan Bomhard edited *Bono Homini Donum: Essays in Historical Linguistics, in Memory of J. Alexander Kerns* (John Benjamins, Amsterdam & Philadelphia, 1981), a two-volume, 1,100-pp. collection of scholarly essays. ● **Osmond Beckwith** published *Vernon: An Anecdotal Novel.* Wood engravings by Michael McCurdy. New York, Breaking Point, 1981. Cloth, 195 pp., $10.00. (Order from Breaking Point, P.O. Box 328, Wharton, NJ 07885). Set in the 1920s, an account of rural and small-town life. "A splendid evocation of a country childhood," wrote G. Legman. ● **Ernest Borneman** recently published *Sexuelle Reifungsphasen des Kindes* (or *Reifungsphasen der Kindheit: Sexuelle Entwicklungspsychologie* — the publishers list different titles). Vienna & Munich: Jugend und Volk, 1981. ● **Jan Harold Brunvand** published *The Vanishing Hitchhiker: American Urban Legends and Their Meanings* (N.Y.: Norton, 1981). ● **Elizabeth Claire's** *Dangerous English* (MAL 4/2) was recently published in a Japanese translation. ● **Virginia Clark** (with Paul Eschholz and **Alfred Rosa**) edited *Language: Introductory Readings,* second ed., 1977 (St. Martin's Press). ● **John Robert Colombo** published *222 Canadian Jokes* (Highway Book Shop, Cobalt, Ont. P0J 1C0), 93 pp., $5.70 ppd. — He also published *Trans-*

lations from the English: Found Poems (Toronto, Peter Martin Assoc., 1974) and translated, from the Bulgarian, with Nikola Roussanoff, *Remember Me Well: Poems* (Toronto, Hounslow Press, 1978). ● **Tom Dunn** puts out the illustrated *Pipe Smoker's Ephemeris*, crammed full with information on pipes, tobacco, smoking. Pipophiles write to T. D. at 20-37 120th St., College Point, NY 11356. ● Paul Eschholz and our **Alfred Rosa** and **Virginia Clark's** *Language Awareness* was published in its second edition in 1978 (St. Martin's Press). ● Rabbi **Alexander Feinsilver's** *The Talmud for Today* was also published by St. Martin's Press, 1980. This work contains much on proper behavior. Translated from the original sources (cloth, 307 pp., $14.95). ● **Francis L. and Roberta B. Fugate** published *Secrets of the World's Best-Selling Writer: The Storytelling Techniques of Erle Stanley Gardner* (New York: William Morrow, 1980. $12.95). It details how Gardner learned to write and reveals for the first time his mystery formulae. ● **Walter Glanze** (Man. Ed.) and **Roger Steiner** (Assoc. Ed.) labored on the 1,078-pp. *Scribner-Bantam English Dictionary* (1979, paper, $1.95). ● **Denison Hatch's** novel, *The Stork*, was published by Jove (New York, 1978). This 269-pp. paperback costs $1.95. ● **Einar Haugen** compiled the best available *Norwegian-English Dictionary / Norsk Engelsk Ordbok*. Published in Oslo (Universitetsforlaget) and Madison (University of Wisconsin Press, 1974), this tightly-packed large paperbound dictionary (504 pp., $13.75) contains an important introduction to this language, and the new Additions now list seven naughty words formerly overlooked. ● **Hermann Hochegger** (Bandundu, Zaïre) just finished his *Le Langage de gestes rituels*, a 1,200-pp., three-volume opus printed by Steyler, St. Augustin, Germany. ● **Nancy Huston's** French-language romance, *Les Variations Goldberg*, was published in Paris (Éd. du Seuil, 1981). 190 pp., 54 F. ● **Vladimir Kabronsky's** booklet of Russian "limericks" (MAL 4/2) is sold out, but an enlarged new edition is planned for Dec. 1981: *Novaia nepodtsenzurnaia chastushka* (in Cyrillics). This 300-pp. edition, $12.50, can be ordered from Valery Kuharets, Russica Book & Art Shop, 799 Broadway, New York, NY 10003. ● **J. Peter Maher** edited *Papers From the Third International Conference on Historical Linguistics* (Hamburg, 1977), ca. 350 pp., soon available from John Benjamins (Amsterdam & Philadelphia). ● **James Matisoff** who, like other friends, did not like my honest comments about his book's avoidable shortcomings (cursèd gray print), has informed me that his *Blessings, Curses, Hopes, and Fears: Psycho-Ostensive Expressions in Yiddish* (MAL 4/1) has been reprinted nice & **black**. ● **Richard de Mille** edited and wrote the greater part of *The Don Juan Papers: Further Castaneda Controversies*, the uproarious, definitive study of Uclanthropus Piltdunides Castanedæ, one of the great intellectual hoaxes. Published in 1980 by Ross-Erikson Publishers (629 State St., Santa Barbara, CA 93101). Cloth, 528 pp., $17.95; softbound, $9.95. In 1981, the same publisher re-issued de Mille's *Put Your Mother on the Ceiling: Children's Imagination Games*, an oft-quoted book of didactic fantasies for children, parents and teachers. Cloth, 176 pp., $9.95 (also a Penguin paperback). ● **Elias Petropoulos** kept the printers hopping with *The Graves of Greece* (Paris: Private Bibliophile's Edition, 1979. An album, 909 numbered copies, cloth, 135 pp.), *Ironwork in Greece/Ellinikes Sidheries* (Athens: Nefeli, 1980.— A photo album, cloth, 223 pp.), *Mikrá keímena, 1949-1979* (Athens: Grámmata, 1980.—Paper, 167 pp.), and *Old Salonica* (Athens: Kedros, 1980.—A photo album, cloth, 235 pages). ● **Marion Pharnos** (pseud.) published Harriman Spoon's *Scatastrophes*, a 200-copy edition of the recently-discovered Chillons-sur-Thoussat manuscript. Fourteen scatological poems, in French only, with an Introduction & Notes by M. P. Softbound, hand-sewn, 37 pp., $8.75. (Order from Limited Ed. Ltd., 8 Plympton St., Suite 26, Cambridge, MA 02138). ● **Gert Raeithel** published *"Go West": Ein Psychohistorischer Versuch über die Amerikaner* (Frankfurt: Syndikat, 1981.—Paper, 124 pp., DM 20). ● **Laurence Seits** edited *Papers of the North Central Names Institute 1980* (Sugar Grove, Ill.: Waubonsee Community College, 1980). Paper, 116 pp., under $10. ● **A. Reynolds Morse** published, with introductions, bibliographies, updates *The Works of M. P. Shiel*, a most unusual writer, in a most unusual edition: in three ring binders ($110) and conventional cloth ($125). This four-volumes-in-three edition runs to some 1,150 pp. Published in 900 copies, 1979-80. Available from J.D.S. Books, Dayton, Ohio, or Jon Wynne-Tyson, Arundel, West Sussex, England. ● **Karen Dalziel Tallman** did it with Bruce A. Shuman: their article "Sex Magazines: Problems of Acquisition, Retention, Display, and Defense in Public and Academic Libraries" appeared in *Sex Magazines in the Library Collection* (New York: Haworth Press, 1981), pp. 27-46. ● **D. Eugene Valentine** and Ellen Vidalakis Furgis in 1979 published their *Greek Cooking at Its American Best*. The spiralbound, 118-pp. cookbook is available from Almond Tree Publications (1850 East Fremont Dr., Tempe, AZ 85282) for $8.00. ● **John Vriend** published with Wayne Dyer *Counseling Techniques That Work: A No-Nonsense Approach to Individual and Group Counseling* (Funk & Wagnalls, 1977).

INTER-CURSE

BENEDICTA
DEAR & DAMN EDITOR
ANNOUNCEMENTS

BENEDICTA
VERY PERSONAL COMMENTS
FROM THE EDITOR

It's two o'clock in the morning, November 19, and I have to whip out another *Benedicta* — the last two pages before sending this volume to the printers. The late hour and the pressure to finally finish this volume are responsible for more *male* than *bene* in these *dicta*. If my all-too-personal comments annoy you, skip these two pages; but if you wonder what makes me tick and gets me ticked off, read on.

I don't like having to tell you what follows. It sounds tear-jerking and morbid. But it's simply *reality*. Last year I had to fly to Europe, just a few days before the Winter issue of *Maledicta* was to be sent to the printers in Michigan. But instead of meeting old and new friends there, I had to bury my father, took care of my mother, worked at night on *Maledicta*, and always worried about the next issue which was late, again. Earlier, on trips to New York, Los Angeles, and Toronto, several friends asked me to stay a few days and unwind. No. I had to take the first plane back to Milwaukee, to keep working on the next issue which was late, again. This frantic pace has been going on for too many years. Instead of living, I am driving myself into an early grave.

However, with our annual publication schedule, all will be more bearable. Instead of two 160-page issues, our journal will now appear as a combined 320-page double-issue, every December. The main reasons for this painful change are my health and those funny "Acts of God." Working many years like a demented beaver has taken its toll: I'm almost burned out, have severe chest pains, stomach cramps, headaches you wouldn't believe, and similar shite. A real *mal vivant.*

Then there are illnesses and deaths in my family in Europe (two more to go) which interrupt my tightly scheduled work for two months. Arranging funerals in Europe while worrying about the delay of the next issue is more than I can hack.

For the past five years I've felt like a pederast — always behind! Always behind! With an annual publication, the present twice-yearly pressure is cut in half. Now, if I have to go to a hospital or funeral, there will be enough leeway to make up for time lost. If no Acts of God happen, I'll be able to catch up and even work ahead for a change. Now I can plan on our meetings, work on our books, finish my own four book manuscripts, learn how to use a computer for more efficient research, and maybe even stop and smell the bloody roses before my olfactory sense is shot.

This whole Maledicta thing has grown too big. It's out of hand. If a man's thing grows too big to handle it decently (you should have my problems), it's time to reassess it. I can't get myself to handle this thing with mechanical contraptions or to have others help me handle it. The most common well-meant advice I receive is, "Get help!" Sure. That's like saying, "Get laid!" I do want help—but who would do it for love? Those helpers whom I would have to hire need a salary and fringe malefits, which I can't pay. They necessitate a dozen tax and other government forms, which I refuse to waste my time on. They would need training but would still make endless mistakes, which I can't afford.

Rather than training a helper and having to correct a zillion mistakes, I might as well do it all myself, alone. Then it's done *right.* No typist, no packer, no *nobody.* This way, production proceeds slowly but accurately and with a minimum of aggravations.

I'll be able to live longer this way, I guess. And you'll be able to enjoy more years of *Maledicta.* Amen.

DEAR & DAMN EDITOR

The reaction to the necessary change of publishing MAL only once a year, for the time being, was very good, and I do appreciate very much your understanding. — Here are a few comments from our readers:

¶ Only an anal-compulsive crypto-sadist and wetback via the Danube could dream up the fiendish scheme of making us wait until Christmas for our *Maledicta*.... In the meantime, stay well and thanks for putting out a beautifully designed magazine that helps make living in the Big (Horse) Apple a little more tolerable. (Fred S., New York)

¶ Sorry to hear that MAL is going to yearly. I'll settle for that, though, just as long as it comes. (Henry B., Colo.)

¶ I'm afraid I'm not going to be happy with your one-volume MAL. I spent many pleasant hours reading MAL twice a year. Now you tell me I've got to wait until Christmas. Tsk. But I suppose once a year is better than nothing. (T. S., Mich.) *Become a quarterly-freak: read ¼ of* MAL *every 3 months.* Ed.

¶ Please keep well and in good spirits so that you can carry out your invaluable and oh-so-much-needed labors. This is the first fan letter I have ever written. (Anthony G., Nev.)

¶ Thanks for your announcement which helps me remain calm while waiting for the treat of the next issue. Let me assure you that *nothing* could be more important than a living and healthy Uncle Mal who has done so much to keep me out of a padded cell. (Sharon M., Michigan)

¶ Disappointed but...you are better READ than DEAD! (Ed J., Illinois) ———————————

¶ I keep showing MAL to people when they visit. They are at first frightened, then embarrassed, and then burst into roars and guffaws. (Norman S., New Zealand)

¶ Sorry to advise you that we are getting a divorce. She gets the kid, house, car, TV, and cats. But I got custody of MALEDICTA. (Joseph M., Michigan)

¶ Help! I'm in need of a MALEDICTA fix! When will I get my next copy? Soon?? (Fred T., Calif.) — *Why don't you read earlier issues? All volumes have been reprinted. This journal is not "dated" and thus the first issue from 1977 is as timely as next year's. If you are truly MAL-addicted, order 1977 through 1979, which you don't have.* Ed.

¶ I'm now catching up on my correspondence and have reached the bottom of the barrel. I started, naturally, with the nice people who had sent me cards and gifts while I was holding hands with Jesus [during a heart operation. *Ed.*]. I went from there to the feckless assholes who write to editors because no one else, including their pets, will listen to them. And then I came to you. (Henry G., Newspaper Editor, Wash.)

¶ Gexdex shex, you fexing bexard, for thinking of DASVAR first! The worst part is that I've taught school for 19 years with only "Rats!" as a public expletive. The latest issue (4/1) came just in time to prepare me to cope with the little bexards and the big exholes. (Judith W., Calif.)

¶ My pollack, pig-sucking, baseborn, sniveling, slavish wife has taken to calling me a 'dago, guinea, pimp, cocksucking whoremonger.' Is she being redundant? (Matt C., New Jersey) — *Not much. But then I haven't met you yet.* Ed.

¶ I honestly don't see where you got the guts to launch MAL in the first place. My colleagues who hear of it are even more impressed that you run, edit, print it yourself than they are by the fact that there is a scholarly publication, or even a non-pornographic publication, that prints "dirty words." It seems to give them a *frisson*: imagine being Out There in the hard, cold world instead of in a cozy tenured position, a job they complain about constantly but are damn glad to have to *isolate* them from Reality and other bogeymen. It is a thrill to them to see that someone with academic training in linguistics can make a living outside Academia other than by driving a cab. I suspect it encourages them that they just *might* be able to make a living if their tenured position gets eliminated. (Prof. Len A., New York)

¶ How do you spell "relief"? M-A-L-E-D-I-C-T-A. (Nancy C., New Jersey)

¶ Your magazine cheers me up. I'm in my seventies, suffering from arthritis, and living in a retirement home you can call a geriatric ghetto. Thanks for your Bad Words. (Elspeth R., Illinois)

¶ Hear and understand: It is not what goes into the mouth that defiles a man, but what comes out of it (Matt. 15). Out of your heart and mouth comes evil thoughts, murder, adultery, fornication, theft, false witness, slander. As you can see, I'm very Christian. I really feel very sorry for you, for someday you are going to have to meet your Creator — with *all* the *filth* you have in your heart. *Repent* and clean up your job, or you shall be lost in eternal Damnation. Let it be known to God and *You* that you have been warned! (Paige, Montana) — *You're right about Fornication, Paige. Like Jimmy Carter, I have lust in my heart. As for the rest — why don't you put something into Anal Roberts and then listen to what's coming out of his mouth?* Ed.

¶ MAL hasn't got a touch of sleeziness: its outrightness is its chief asset. (Dr. Edward G., S.J., Pennsylvania)

¶ You and your work should be declared a National Treasure, so that you and it would always be protected and supported. Given the current campaign by such mental midgets as the so-called Moral Majority, you should consider printing MAL on fireproof paper. May all the daughters of all MM members be *shtupped* by an uncircumcized warthog. (Dr. Lynn C. Connecticut)

¶ MAL must be the only entertaining scholarly journal in the world. You are a brave man and a national treasure. (Prof. X. K., Massachusetts)

¶ I cease not to marvel at your patience, dexterity, versatility and design sense in composing all of MAL yourself. But most importantly, you seem to have the rare combination of the right kind of humor, the scholarly qualifications and the moral courage necessary to handle the field. (...) You would rather starve at what you're doing than be rolling in dough as a phony academic. Success will come. So starve a little — you are having a ball! (Prof. M. C., New York)

ANNOUNCEMENTS

● **1982 SUBSCRIPTION**: *Maledicta* 6 (1982), a 320-page double-issue, will be published in December, 1982. List price: $23.50. If you subscribe **before 1 July 1982**, pay only U.S. $17.50 (plus $1.00 postage ONLY if your mailing address is *outside* the USA, as foreign postage cost me at least $1.38). Those who have not renewed by July 1982 will receive a Renewal Reminder in the fall and will have to pay $20.00 (plus foreign postage). This year, I will *not* accept ancient order forms and $16.00 or $17.50 checks mailed in October and November, way after the deadline (*blush*, niggards!), because double and triple renewal notices cost much time and money; and it's just *not frigging fair* to pay the same low price as our conscientious members who pay early.

● **MAL 5 IMPROVEMENTS**: As you can see, this double-issue is nothing to sneeze at: expanded to a fat 352 pages, quality sewn, extra strong covers, and mailed in a nifty, air-tight shipping bag (with a new address label). Unlike the big, greedy publishers who make everything smaller & cheaper to save a penny per book, I keep on improving the physical appearance and durability of our baby. Also, like the good wine that won't be sold "before its time," MAL won't be published before its time: every line has to be perfect before the volume goes to the printers in Ann Arbor. For example, it took me two days driving all over Waukesha and Milwaukee Counties until I found the Japanese ideograms *umi-umi* (in this issue) exactly as I wanted them. I can't get myself to whip out a sloppy quickie — either I do it right, or not at all. This is the reason why it takes me *one full year* to prepare one volume. A businessman I am not.

● **DO IT**: I received stacks of excellent **Do Its** (*see* 4/2, p. 174). Thus, during 1982, I will put out a separate **DO IT** booklet and send it to you, around August, *at no charge if I receive your 1982 renewal check by June.* This booklet will also be made available to the masses, for about $3.50, but our

342 - MALEDICTA V

members pay nothing — even the cheapskate niggards who paid only $16.00 during October and November. Those who renew MAL 6 *after 1 July 1982* can order DO IT for $2.80.

● **REACTIONS, NEWS, QUERIES**: As this volume is already 32 pages over our customary 320-page-per-year limit, there was no space for these three Departments. Our next volume will carry many Reaction and Feedback items, to start catching up on the huge backlog.

● **WHY I READ MAL**: In MAL 4/2, Query 4.14, I asked for the reasons why you read MAL. I received 14 replies. Let's have a few more, so that I can report on this matter. Don't be apathetic.

● **WHO READS MAL?** On our advertising flier, we list many professions, to show the broad appeal of MAL. Some readers whose professions were not listed were unhappy, including Aerospace Engineers, Archivists, Insurance Agents, Social Workers, Teamsters, and Travel Agents. I listed those of which I knew *at least ten* readers of the same profession or specialty. For example, Millionaires also were not listed because I know of only 8 readers who are millionaires (that's in dollars, not lire or yen). At any rate, don't feel slighted if your profession is not included.

● **THANKS FOR ADDRESSES**: Many readers sent addresses of friends, acquaintances or colleagues who might be interested in MAL. In most cases, I did not tell them your name (bad business practice, again) to prevent embarrassment for you if your pal turned out to be a latent prude. If you want to spread the Good Word, it will be better if you wrote to prospective victims and told them about MAL, urging them to write to us for more information.

● **NO INDEX FOR MAL 1-5**: Until I have a computer, I can't put out an Index of names, words, languages, subjects treated, etc. I am buying a computer during 1982, Fate willing, and if I can get my shifty wifey to help me type that information onto the disks, we will be able to whip out all sorts of goodies, including indexes, address labels and a bibliography.

● **NO MORE BOOKSELLING**: Selling books for other

publishers was a mistake. While trying to be Dr. Benefactor, I wasted a lot of time on this service, for a gross profit of 75 cents per book. Plus all the grief: publishers sent us the wrong books, too few, too many, badly bound and printed copies, and several copies were stolen/lost in transit. I will send you a list of available titles next time I'm masochistically inclined.

● FOREIGN CHECKS: If you pay by check from outside the USA, *please* make the check out to "Reinhold Aman," *not* to a bank. Those S.O.B.s deduct a $5.00 to $7.50 "collection" or "handling" fee, which does not leave me much. Also, all checks must bear the magnetic bank code number at the bottom of the check, otherwise the local banks sock me with another $7.50 fee. — We now have a bank account in Europe, to make it cheaper for you to transfer money.

● MEDIA PROBES: This 8-part Public Television special featuring Uncle Mal is now scheduled for airing in April, 1982. Consult your *TV Guide. See also* MAL 4/1, p. 154 for details.

● MEETING: *The Third International Conference on Humor* will be held in Washington, D.C., August 27-30, 1982. I am scheduled to speak on "Pshitt, Fockink & Dunk: How Not to Name Your Product." For information about this conference write to Prof. Lawrence Mintz, American Studies Program, University of Maryland, College Park, MD 20742. — If this conference again charges an admission fee of $60 or more, out of reach for most people, we may have an additional informal MAL meeting in the D.C. area. Members residing in the vicinity of Washington will receive an invitation, if we meet.

● HOW TO STUFF BIG THINGS: Most people don't know how to fold our order blanks, and therefore do terrible things to a piece of paper to get it into our allegedly too small envelopes. As a public service, here's how to fold a normal 8½ x 11" sheet of paper: if the envelope is a "No. 10" business size, fold sheet into thirds; if the envelope is a small "No. 6¾" (like our reply envelopes most of you throw away), fold paper in half, to the size of this page, and then fold twice, into thirds. Now the bleeding thing fits perfectly. No more complaints about our "too small" envelopes! Now you can stuff at will.

BOOK SELLERS

ARCANE BOOKS: Unusual Books on History; The History of Medicine, Science and Religion; Classics; Folklore; Politics; Ancient Greece; Physicians; European Literature, etc. Write for free catalog to **Coronado Press,** P.O. Box 3232, Lawrence, KS 66044.

EROTICA & CURIOSA: Write for catalog to **C. Scheiner,** 275 Linden Blvd., D1-14, Brooklyn, NY 11226.

FOLKLORE, U.S. & EUROPEAN: Write to **Elliot Klein,** 19 West 44th St., New York, NY 10036.

GAMBLING: Huge collection of books on gambling, *Casino* and *Systems* magazines, *Overlay Newsletter*: write to John Luckman, **Gambler's Book Club,** P.O. Box 4115, Las Vegas, NV 89106.

SCIENTIFIC JOURNALS: Large stock of current and hard-to-get back issues of technical and scientific journals (U.S. & foreign), and publications of learnèd societies. Write to **Zeitlin Periodicals Co.,** 817 S. La Brea, Los Angeles, CA 90036.

SLAVICA: Books on Russian Reading Rules, Phonology, Word Structure, Syntax, Verbs, etc., as well as Polish, Lithuanian, and Politics. Free catalog: **Slavica Publishers,** P.O. Box 14388, Columbus, OH 43214.

SPANISH DICTIONARIES: Eugene Valcour specializes in scientific, technical and general dictionaries, bilingual and esp. Spanish. Also works on Anthropology, Archaeology, Mythology, History, Miscellaneous. As the owner will retire soon, write for catalog now: **E. Valcour,** 3003 First Ave., Suite 1, San Diego, CA 92103.

UNCOMMON LANGUAGES: Textbooks, tapes, readers in some 45 common & exotic languages. Catalog from: **Spoken Language Services,** P.O. Box 783, Ithaca, NY 14850.

UNUSUAL FOLKLORE: Recent catalogs of books on Vampires, Catastrophes, Death, Witches, Homosexuality, Scatology. Write **Rainer Feucht,** Antiquariat, Am Rain 23, D-7936 Allmendingen, W. Germany.

JOURNALS & NEWSLETTERS

Ethnic and Racial Studies. Vol. I, No. 1 (1978). London: Routledge and Kegan Paul. Scholarly.

DEBRIS: A Journal of the Bizarre, Ridiculous, Morbid & Merely Contemptible. Bi-monthly. Inexpensive or free: John Boston, Ed., 225 Baltic St., Brooklyn, NY 11201.

INTERFACES: Linguistic and Psychoanalysis Newsletter. Two issues per year. Inexpensive or free. Write to Dr. Robert Di Pietro, Department of Languages, University of Delaware, Newark, DE 19711.

Jewish Folklore and Ethnology Newsletter. Quarterly. $7.50/yr. Barbara Kirshenblatt-Gimblett, Ed. New York: YIVO Institute for Jewish Research, 1048 Fifth Ave., New York, NY 10028.

Lettres from Limerick: Vol. I, No. 1 will make its debut in November, 1981. Quarterly. 16-20 pp. per issue. Subscription of $15 (U.S.A.) or $20 (elsewhere) includes membership in The Limerick League. Specializes in limericks new and old, contests, bibliography, articles. "J. Beauregard Pepys" is the chairman-editor. Write: The Limerick League, 1212 Ellsworth St., Philadelphia, PA 19147.

Logophile: The Cambridge Journal of Words and Language. Quarterly. $25 (individuals) or $50 (institutions)/yr. Jeremy Geelan, Ed. Logophile Press, 47-49 Caledonia Rd., London N1 9BU, England. (A popular language journal with a British twist. Presumably still published).

The Washington CRAP Report, ed. by William Leavell, is a monthly political newsletter "dedicated to exposing the Washington standards of greed, corruption, self-indulgence," etc. Interesting news about waste, politicians, newest lingo, nicknames. 12 issues/year, $12.00. Write to W.C.R., P.O. Box 10309, St. Petersburg, FL 33733.

WORD WAYS: The Journal of Recreational Linguistics. Quarterly, $10. Specializes in palindromes, puzzles, letter symmetry, transposability, word counts, mathematical aspects of words, etc. A. Ross Eckler, Ed. Spring Valley Rd. Morristown, NJ 07960.

Ye Olde Bastards Journal. Published bi-monthly. Dues & annual subscription (4 pp./issue) $5.00; higher outside the U.S.A. Popular quickies and one-liners. Published by the International Order of Old Bastards, with 1 million members and chapters worldwide. Archbastard and Editor James Carroll, P.O. Box 23730, Fort Lauderdale, FL 33307.

Zeitschrift für Semiotik. Vol. I, No. 1 (1979). Wiesbaden: Akademischer Verlag Athenaion. Scholarly.

T T T T T T

CLEVER T-SHIRTS: Softwear Unlimited (Star Route Box 38, Winthrop, WA 98862) offers high-quality Hanes brand "50-50" T-shirts, sweatshirts, and ladies' French cut, in all sizes and several color combinations. Write to the above address for an illustrated six-page catalog. These T-shirts are far above the usual garbage one sees printed on such garments; most of the imprints are science-oriented (mathematics, geology, physics, meteorology), but a few deal with language. Samples: **Reunite Gondwanaland — Life is like a Computer: what you put into it is what you get out of it — Friction is a Drag — I have the Hardware if You have the Software — Time flies like an Arrow, Fruit flies like a Banana.** If you are a T-shirt freak, you'll be in T-shirt heaven. Recommended.

NOTES ON CONTRIBUTORS

IRVING ALLEN (Ph.D. University of Iowa) is Associate Professor of Sociology at the University of Connecticut, Storrs. He specializes in urban and community studies, especially in the cultures of city life. Professor Allen is the author of more than thirty publications, mostly articles in professional journals. He is also editor of *New Towns and the Suburban Dream: Ideology and Utopia in Planning and Development*, Kennikat Press, 1977. Dr. Allen says that he long has had an interest in the reflections of society and of the times in American slang. This interest soon carried him into studies of the interplay of words, language, and social ideology. He has just completed a study of the language of ethnic conflict, which reviews the historical vocabulary of slang produced by intergroup contact, especially in diverse city life.

REINHOLD AMAN (Ph.D., University of Texas, 1968, in Medieval Literature and Germanic Philology) singlehandedly edits, typesets, publishes and distributes *Maledicta*. He is a prime candidate for a heart attack, working 16 hours a day, seven days a week on *Maledicta*, including packing and *schlepping* his publications to the †&%*&@! post office for shipment to 57 countries. Dr. Aman was recently lauded for MAL-Practice: his research and publishing have been honored by his inclusion in the 1982 *Who's Who in America*. (More information in earlier issues.)

JAY AMES, born over 70 years ago in Banff, Alberta, enjoys wordsmithing, learning languages, and the study of names. He is a member of the American Name Society, English Name Society, and the Canadian Society for the Study of Names. Mr. Ames saw most of the world in the Armed Forces and working as a *robotnik* and steward on ships. He now lives in Toronto and writes verses for children's magazines.

LORRAYNE Y. BAIRD, previously known as "the Appalachian Kid," now is Distinguished Professor of English at Youngstown State University, where she has taught since 1968. She has studied at Appalachian State University, the University of Kentucky (Ph.D., 1969), Duke University and Princeton (NEH grant, 1973), and has done research in libraries and museums of Rome and England. Her current work includes studies in medieval medicine and a monograph, *Gallus-Deus: The Origins and Traditions of a Literary Grotesque* (to appear in Studies in Iconography). In addition to several articles, such as on Urine and Uroscopy in Medieval Medicine and Literature, and the Fabliau Form, Dr. Baird published the *Chaucer Bibliography 1964-73* (G. K. Hall, 1977). Professor Baird's honors include listings in *The World's Who's Who of Women* and *Outstanding Educators of America.*

SCOTT BEACH is an eclectic. As an actor, with a command of some sixty accents, dialects and character voices, he was a member of "The Committee," a satiric improvisation review in San Francisco. His films include *American Graffiti, THX1138, Star Wars, Bullitt, One Is A Lonely Number,* and *Chu-Chu And The Philly Flash.* As a broadcaster, Mr. Beach has worked in radio and television since 1954, as disk jockey, newsman, writer, producer, and director. As a writer, he has a regular column in the San Francisco *Paper* and contributes articles to various magazines. His book, *Musicdotes*, was published in 1976 by Ten Speed Press. He makes regular appearances as narrator, singer, or conductor with the San Francisco Opera and symphony orchestras. He took his B.A. at Lewis & Clark College, Portland, Oregon, in 1953, and received a Fulbright scholarship for postgraduate study in Paris, taking advanced degrees at the Sorbonne and the Conservatoire National de Musique. Mr. Scott also studied anatomy and speech pathology at the University of Oregon School of Medicine. He lives in San Francisco.

*****DONALD CHARLES** is an anonymous New York writer, loosely associated with a satirical magazine.

MARTHA CORNOG is a free-lance consultant, technical writer and editor. Previously, on the staff of a Philadelphia consulting firm, she was involved in designing information systems and retrieving and organizing technical information for a variety of government clients. Earlier, she worked as a public librarian, a university library assistant and a computer programmer. Since 1972, she has reviewed books for *Library Journal* in the areas of popular psychology, male/female relationships and human sexuality. She holds an M.A. in Linguistics from Brown University and an M.L.S. in Library Science from Drexel University.

CLIFFORD MORTIMER CRIST, a retired university professor and limericks specialist, lives in Texas. Despite his advanced age, he produces copious outpourings of pun-filled letters to the Editor. (More information in earlier issues.)

*****JOHN DAVENANT** was born in Liverpool, in 1947. He studied Classics at Emmanuel College, Cambridge, and the University of London. Mr. Davenant published a critical survey of the English translations of Homer's *Iliad*, and now is working on a bibliography of erotic magazines and the first good translation of Pierre Louÿs's *Songs of Bilitis*. He works at a university and lives near Cambridge with his disobedient wife, disobedient daughters and his obedient son.

GAVIN EWART lives in London, England.

ALEXANDER FEINSILVER is rabbi emeritus of a Reform congregation in Easton, Pennsylvania. He formerly directed Hillel foundations at Purdue University and the University of Connecticut. He is author of many articles and three books, the latest being *The Talmud for Today* (St. Martin's Press, 1980).

HARRY FELDMAN is currently a Lecturer at the School of Australian Linguistics (Batchelor, NT 5791) and a Research Scholar in the Department of Linguistics at the Australian National University. He received his M.A. in Linguistics from the State University of New York in 1978. He taught English and Linguistics at 'Atenisi Institute in Nuku'alofa, Tonga from 1977 to 1979 and has done fieldwork on Nahuatl dialects in the States of Oaxaca, Puebla, and Vera Cruz, Mexico in 1976-77. Mr. Feldman has recently returned from fifteen months of field research on the Awtuw language spoken near Lumi in the West Sepik Province of Papua New Guinea and is now preparing a Ph.D. thesis entitled "A Grammar of Awtuw." His research interests include language universals and typology, language planning, grammatical theory, and the cross-cultural investigation of juridical reasoning and argumentation. He is active in the human rights and indigenous peoples' rights movements.

GARY ALAN FINE is Associate Professor of Sociology at the University of Minnesota. He received his Ph.D. from Harvard University in 1976 in Social Psychology. His interests span the area from folklore (children's folklore, humor, and urban legends) to small-group research, focusing particularly on the way in which small groups create, use, and diffuse culture. Dr. Fine is the co-author (with Ralph Rosnow) of *Rumor and Gossip: The Social Psychology of Hearsay.*

FRANK HEYNICK, when awake, can be heard to curse with impressive fluency in English, Dutch and French (and on occasion in German and Spanish), but feels most competent in this regard in his native Brooklynese. He did his undergraduate work at the City University of New York and the University of Reims (France), and has graduate degrees in Linguistics and Psycholinguistics from Columbia University and Nijmegen (Netherlands). While serving as a lecturer at the University of Groningen, he wrote on linguistic and Einsteinian relativity, but became ever more fascinated with verbal and cognitive processes in sleep, and now devotes up to ten hours a day to obtain first-hand information. In between he works as a lecturer at the Department of Applied Linguistics of the Eindhoven University of Technology and is writing his doctoral dissertation in Medicine (University of Groningen) entitled "Theoretical and Empirical Investigation into Linguistic Aspects of the Freudian Model of Dream Generation."

SHU-MIN HUANG is Assistant Professor of Anthropology at Iowa State University. Born in China in 1945, he received his training in Anthropology from Michigan State University, and the Ph.D. in 1977. His main interests include agricultural production and rural developments in Taiwan, Hong Kong, and China. In addition to Mandarin, Dr. Huang also speaks a number of Chinese languages, such as Cantonese, Min-nan, and Wu (Shanghai dialect).

JOHN HUGHES is a writer and lives in Illinois.

NANCY HUSTON is a Canadian who has been living in Paris since 1973. Her book *Dire & interdire* (*see* MAL IV/2:312-13) has won a prize from the Académie Française, and she just published her first novel, *Les Variations Goldberg*. (More information in MAL II.)

CHARLES J. JAMES is Assistant Professor of German at the University of Illinois at Chicago Circle. Before that he spent six years as a *Wissenschaftlicher Assistent* in Applied Linguistics at the Friedrich-Alexander Universität Erlangen-Nürnberg in Erlangen, Germany. While in Germany, Dr. James acquired an appreciation of the vitality of the culture of Northern Bavaria, and not only in terms of its maledictions, which are considerable. He holds an M.A. in German from Indiana University and a Ph.D. in Foreign Language Education from the University of Minnesota.

GERSHON LEGMAN, born in 1917 in Scranton, Pennsylvania, is the world's leading authority on erotic folklore and literature. He is the author of many tomes, including *Rationale of the Dirty Joke* and *The Limerick*. He lives in Valbonne, France. (More information in MAL I/2.)

PETER MAHER (1933–) grew up in an ethnically rich milieu and studied ancient and modern languages. He is an etymologist and culture historian, which has led him to take a disrespectful stance towards recent gurus in linguistics. Dr. Maher once changed a flat tire for Prince Nikolaj Trubetskoj's ex-son-in-law. He was Professor of Linguistics and Philology at the University of Hamburg, Germany where he dozed through Marxist speeches. Professor Maher now teaches at a State University in Chicago. He has no academic affiliation.

HUGH MORGAN, born in 1936 in Cleveland, Ohio. He received his B.A. degree in journalism in 1958, and his M.A. in journalism in 1967, University of Oklahoma. He completed his comprehensive exams for a doctorate in history from Southern Illinois University and is working on his dissertation "The Image of Mexican President Lazaro Cardenas in the American Press during the 1930s." Mr. Morgan was a journalist for 16 years, nearly half of them for the Associated Press (Detroit; Jackson, Miss.; New Orleans, and Lansing, Mich.). He became an Assistant Professor of English at Miami University in August,1980.

DON L. F. NILSEN received his B.A. in French from Brigham Young University in 1958, his M.A. in Applied Linguistics from American University in 1961, and his Ph.D. in Theoretical Linguistics from the University of Michigan in 1971. He is presently Director of Linguistics and TESL at Arizona State University, Tempe. Before coming to ASU, he was director of Linguistics and TEFL at the University of Northern Iowa, and before that he taught at Kabul University in Afghanistan. With his wife, Alleen Pace Nilsen, he has written *Language Play* (Newbury House, 1977), *Semantic Theory* (Newbury House, 1975), and *Pronunciation Contrasts in English* (Regents, 1971). He has also published *Toward a Semantic Specification of Deep Case* (1972), *Syntactic and Semantic Tests for the Instrumental Case in English* (1973), and *English Adverbials* (1972), all by Mouton. Professor Nilsen was co-editor with Francine Hardaway of the *Public Doublespeak Newsletter* from 1978 until 1980, edited *Rocky Mountain Review of Language and Literature* from 1977 until 1980, and is presently on the MLA executive committee on General Linguistics. Dr. Nilsen's current work includes a book on language diversity, and coordinating the first national conference of the Western Humor and Irony Membership (WHIM), April 1-3, 1982.

SORAYA NOLAND is an Assistant Professor in the Sociology/Anthropology Department at Iowa State University, Ames. She is a native of Iran and received her Ph.D. in Cultural Anthropology from SUNY at Buffalo in 1976. Professor Noland did fieldwork in Iranian villages during 1974-75 and 1977-1979. She taught at the University of Teheran and the University of Farabi from 1976 to 1979. Dr. Noland's research concentrates on technological and social change in the Middle East.

*****SHIRL PIPERGLOW** is a middle-aged professor of Slavic languages and literatures at a Midwestern university. Dr. Piperglow's interest in scatology in general, and the subject of her consummate article in particular, dates at least back to the time in her undergraduate school days when she was balled by a scroungy-looking, runty Frenchman whose only possible claim to her attention and indulgence was his avowal that he was a direct descendant of the Marquis de Sade.

CATHY LYNN PRESTON is a Teaching Associate in the English Department at the University of Colorado at Boulder. Her academic interests include folklore and medieval and nineteenth-century English literature. She is a co-author of *Urban Folklore from Colorado: Typescript Broadsides* and *Urban Folklore from Colorado: Photocopy Cartoons.* Her "Folk Comparisons from Colorado" appeared in *Western Folklore* (1976). She is now working on a concordance to the Child ballads.

MICHAEL J. PRESTON is an Associate Professor of English and the Director of the Center for Computer Research in the Humanities at the University of Colorado. He received his Ph.D. in Renaissance English literature in 1975. The recipient of a research grant from the American Council of Learned Societies (1974) and a National Endowment in the Humanities Younger Humanist Fellowship (1974), he has published more than thirty articles in such journals as *Comparative Drama*, *The Bibliotheck*, and *The Journal of American Folklore.* He is the editor of several computer-generated concordances, among them *A Concordance to the Middle English Shorter Poem* (1975) and *A Complete Concordance to the Non-Dramatic Poetry of Ben Jonson* (1975). Present work includes concording all Middle English drama and the standard collections of limericks while working on an extended study of the British folk plays.

VICTOR RASKIN was born Виктор Виталиевич Раскин in Irbit, the U.S.S.R., on April 17, 1944. He used his patronymic to obtain the Russian equivalent of Ph.D. in Linguistics from Moscow State University (not the one in Idaho) in 1970. From 1966 to 1973, Dr. Raskin taught Structural and Computational Linguistics at MSU (not the one in Michigan). However, an uncle (a famous humorist) had taught him to see things exactly as they are, and so, in 1973, Dr. Raskin emigrated, cheerfully but statelessly, to Israel. For five years he taught linguistics at the Hebrew National University of Jerusalem and at Tel-Aviv University. After a term at the University of Michigan, Professor Raskin went to Purdue University, where he now is Professor of English and Chairman of the Interdepartmental Program in Linguistics. He has authored several books and dozens of articles on linguistics. His wife of 16 years, Marina Bergelson-Raskin, a poet, does not appreciate his sense of humor.

JOSEPH S. SALEMI teaches English at Pace University and Marymount Manhattan College in New York City. (More information in earlier issues.)

*SIR MAURICE SEDLEY, *Baronet*, lives in Nevada and recently received the Doctor of Education degree from UCLA. Even though he is employed as a school administrator, he is a very decent and learnèd man. (More information in MAL I/1.)

JOHN TAYLOR was born in Des Moines, Iowa, in 1952. He studied Mathematics at the University of Idaho, and Philosophy and Literature at the University of Hamburg, Germany. He has written a volume of poetry entitled *The Voyage to Tenderness.* Mr. Taylor translated Elias Petropoulos's *The Good Thief's Manual, Ironwork in Greece, The Graves of Greece, Old Salonica,* and a selection of 150 Rebetic Songs, *Rebetika.* He lives in Paris, France.

MARIO E. TERUGGI, born in Argentina in 1919, is a Senior Professor and Head of Division in the School of Natural Sciences and Museum of La Plata University. As a scientist he does research work on geology, petrology and sedimentology. A mineral, *teruggite,* was named in his honor. Dr. Teruggi is also a linguist, literary critic and novelist. He has published *Panorama del lunfardo* (2nd edition, 1978; *see* MAL IV:152), short stories, *nouvelles* and a novel, *La tunica caida* (1977). He is now working on a critical study of James Joyce's *Finnegans Wake* and has published various articles on this subject.

LAURENCE URDANG is a lexicographer and the editor and publisher of *Verbatim: The Language Quarterly.* He lives in Essex, Connecticut. (More information in MAL III/2.)

BENJAMIN URRUTIA lives in Guayaquil, Ecuador.

DENNIS MICHAEL WARREN is a Professor of Anthropology at Iowa State University, Ames. (More information in earlier issues.)

DANIEL N. WEITZNER, B.S. in Communication, Fitchburg State College, is a retired Army clinical laboratory officer. He was a Prisoner of War in Japan and survived the Bataan Death March in the Philippines. He now teaches student nurses how to reproduce (photos) and audiovisual instruction in Anatomy and Physiology. Mr. Weitzner lives in Leominster, Massachusetts.

WAYNE WILSON is Professor of Psychology at Stephen F. Austin State University in Nacogdoches, Texas. His research interests include relating male and female behavior to the use of dirty words, to humor, and to the psychology of rape. These interests aside, his obsession-compulsion centers on writing a book for students which explores the psychology of sexuality and murder, played out in reality and projected through movies and television.

· FINIS ·
DEO GRATIAS